RECALLING

Chögyam
Trungpa

RECALLING
Chögyam Trungpa

COMPILED AND EDITED BY

FABRICE MIDAL

SHAMBHALA
Boston & London
2005

Shambhala Publications, Inc.
Horticultural Hall
300 Massachusetts Avenue
Boston, Massachusetts 02115
www.shambhala.com

9 8 7 6 5 4 3 2 1

First Edition

Printed in the United States of America

♾ This edition is printed on acid-free paper that meets the
American National Standards Institute z39.48 Standard.

Distributed in the United States by Random House, Inc.,
and in Canada by Random House of Canada Ltd

Designed by Jeff Baker

Library of Congress Cataloging-in-Publication Data

Recalling Chögyam Trungpa / compiled and edited by Fabrice Midal.
    p. cm.
Includes bibliographical references.
ISBN 1-59030-207-9 (pbk.: alk. paper)
1. Trungpa, Chögyam, 1939– I. Midal, Fabrice, 1967–
BQ990.R867R43 2005
294.3'923'092—DC22

2005009368

Contents

CONTENTS

With the Vajradhatu Board of Directors, waiting to welcome the Dalai Lama outside the New York Dharmadhatu, November 1979. (*Left to right*) Vajra Regent Ösel Tendzin, Derek Kolleeny, Chögyam Trungpa, Peter Volz, Karl Springer, Brad Upton, Jeremy Hayward, Ken Green, John Roper, Chuck Lief, Samuel Bercholz. (*Back*) David Rome, Loppon Lodro Dorje. Photograph © 2004 by Mary Lang. Used with permission.

A Message from His Holiness
the Fourteenth Dalai Lama

FOLLOWING THE CHINESE takeover of Tibet in 1959 and the flight of many Tibetans into exile, Tibetan Lamas began to be invited to visit other parts of the world. Chögyam Trungpa Rinpoche was among the first. Even though a young man and destined to be the abbot of his monastery in Kham, Eastern Tibet, he had already undertaken the intensive training of a recognized reincarnate Lama. While studying at Oxford University, he was able to develop a sharp understanding of the modern world that he was able to put to good effect when he began to be invited to teach about his own tradition.

When he began to teach in America in the 1970s, Trungpa Rinpoche seems to have caught the public imagination. His books such as *Cutting Through Spiritual Materialism* were among the first and very successful books about Tibetan Buddhism. Earlier works had been either rather dry academic studies of traditional texts or ill-informed travelers' accounts filled with exotic tales of magic and mystery.

His was an influential attempt to share some of the insights and bene-fits of the teachings of Tibetan Buddhism with a modern audience in terms that they could easily understand and put into effect. Exceptional as one of the first Tibetan lamas to become fully assimilated into Western culture, he made a powerful contribution to revealing the Tibetan approach to inner peace in the West.

March 18, 2004

Foreword

DIANA J. MUKPO

CHÖGYAM TRUNGPA RINPOCHE, my late husband, understood very clearly that the buddhadharma, the teachings of the Buddha, needed to be presented in a way that would allow dharma to be assimilated into Western culture. Over many centuries, Buddhism had successfully traveled from one society to another in Asia, and it always adapted itself to the particular culture into which it entered. Basically, this was possible without weakening the foundation of the teachings because dharma is fundamentally about mind. The truth of dharma is the truth of mind; therefore it should be applicable in every place and time. Whatever particular cultural scenarios there may be, the basic makeup of the human mind is the same; this cuts across all cultural boundaries. Trungpa Rinpoche understood this at the most basic and profound level.

Rinpoche also understood that Western society is fundamentally a secular society and that the transmission of dharma would have to take place in a secular context. In the West, we will never have a monastic culture like the one in Tibet. The Buddhist teachings, he felt, should relate to our everyday lives in the West, so that we can have a living religion, a living spirituality. The teachings must apply to ordinary life: what we do when we get up in the morning, what we do at work, how we relate to our families, even what we do in our spare time.

Rinpoche had studied the ancient teachings of Shambhala in Tibet, and he had received very profound teachings from the Shambhala tradition, which he shared with his students in the West. In addition to these terma teachings, he presented the path of the Shambhala warrior as a means to promote wakefulness, bravery and gentleness in one's life. He realized that these teachings on the nature of warriorship and enlightened society would be the very teachings that would be most effective in bringing Buddhism to the West.

Chögyam Trungpa Rinpoche applied the basic wakefulness and compassion of Buddhism and the Shambhala teachings in many realms of human life. This was part of his uniqueness and his genius. From ikebana to poetry, from theatre to psychology, from the administration of Naropa Institute to the discipline of dressage, he was able to transmit the sanity of the buddhadharma in an absolutely fresh and up-to-date way. From my own perspective, in my study of the riding discipline of dressage, I was amazed at how Rinpoche was able to tune in, and how accurate and to the point his instruction was. He had ridden horses in Tibet, but he didn't have any formal training in dressage. Nevertheless, when he came out to watch me ride, he often gave me excellent instruction. He would point out the things I was doing that were good and those that needed attention. Even though he didn't know the technicalities, he had tremendous feeling for dressage, and he was always right! I believe this is because he had a fundamental overview; he was constantly in touch with the basic thread of mind, which is the same no matter what one is doing. Because of this, his influence permeated many disciplines and his teaching applied to many aspects of our secular society.

What Trungpa Rinpoche gave to the West, the Buddhist world that he created here, was actually beyond his own heritage and what he had learned in Tibet. Such a thing has never existed before in the history of Buddhism. He established a stream of teachings that is totally new, fresh and up-to date. At the same time, he was completely true to his heritage and transmitted the most profound truths of his lineage.

I am profoundly grateful to Fabrice Midal for compiling this anthology, *Recalling Chögyam Trungpa*. My husband did not just teach for one generation. I know that it was very important to him that his work be understood and transmitted beyond his own lifetime. Fabrice has made a very important contribution. He has been a binding factor, collecting and transmitting the wisdom and understanding of so many different people. This is truly a noteworthy accomplishment.

I am also grateful to all of the teachers and students who contributed to this book. By sharing their understanding, they are helping many more people to appreciate the work of Trungpa Rinpoche. Indeed, I hope that many readers will benefit from this book, and that it will help people to understand the brilliance of Rinpoche's work and its applicability to our present situation and to the future as well.

With the blessings of the Mukpos,

Diana J. Mukpo
Providence, October 2004

Preface

FABRICE MIDAL

THIS PROJECT ORIGINATED from the proposal of Éditions de l'Herne to devote a volume in its prestigious *Cahier* series to Chögyam Trungpa—prestigious, since principal figures of world thought are the subject of each volume: Heidegger, Pound, Rimbaud, Guénon, Thoreau, Joyce. . . . Each volume brings together numerous selections, many of them published for the first time, as well as photographs.

Shambhala Publications welcomed the idea of publishing an anthology in commemoration of Chögyam Trungpa. However, it was not possible to replicate the work done in France for a specialized readership, which would have been an unusually long work. Shambhala has, in effect, produced a different project.

A selection of texts was made, excluding, not without difficulty and regret, a number of entries that will appear in the French edition. Extracts from texts or interviews were chosen for a chapter titled "Testimony and Reminiscence" in order to allow a few more authors to participate in this homage.

An effort was made to represent French thought—which is particularly active in examining the work of Chögyam Trungpa—and four texts, translated here, are the result.

The authors presented here are diverse, representing the wide range of Chögyam Trungpa's readers today. Sometimes they were friends, companions on the journey, or students of Chögyam Trungpa, but sometimes, as in my case, they never even met him. There are Buddhists involved in various traditions, whether Theravada, Zen, or Tibetan Buddhism, including teachers responsible for transmitting the dharma; there are also those who are not especially concerned with this tradition. Their presence is indicative of how Trungpa Rinpoche's work as an artist or a visionary thinker has influenced fields beyond Buddhism.

I would like to thank all the authors and photographers, whether included or not in this American edition, for having accepted the invitation to participate in this adventure with such enthusiasm and grace.

I would especially like to thank His Holiness the Dalai Lama for his encouragement toward this project and the alacrity with which he responded to the invitation to contribute the opening message.

Such a book could not be possible without the constant efforts of Carolyn Rose Gimian, who has continuously accompanied me in this enterprise. Beyond even the personal debt that I owe her, it is important to emphasize what any study of the work of Trungpa owes to her. As the head of the archives that she founded and for a long time directed, she preserved a considerable collection of documents, without which no serious study could be imagined. Her edition of *The Collected Works of Chögyam Trungpa* is a historic event and an incomparable reference.

Also crucial was the involvement of Kendra Crossen Burroughs, an editor at Shambhala Publications, whose work in giving this volume its own coherence was done with an exemplary discipline and seriousness. Her attention to the work of Chögyam Trungpa, whose books have been placed in her editorial care at Shambhala Publications for a number of years, is extremely precious and of the highest level of refinement, and I could rely on it with confidence.

I am well aware that the greatness of the work of Chögyam Trungpa, the richness of interpretation that it can sustain, makes this undertaking quite limited. A number of important authors could not be invited to participate here because of the lack of space, and many aspects of the work of Chögyam Trungpa could not be approached. May many other projects be successfully undertaken in order to allow the depth of this work to be plumbed, this work that inspires a new way of thinking about the "spiritual"—a way of thinking that speaks to the destiny of our times.

I would also like to thank the following people for their help and their loyalty, without which I could not have been involved in this adventure, which has taken over three years: Françoise Dufayet, Lucie Clair, Douglas Penick, Martha Bonzi, Steve Brooks, Fabien Ouaki, and Greg Seton.

On his horse, Drala, 1980. Photograph by Marvin Moore. Used with permission.

Introduction

Fabrice Midal

O F THOSE WHO introduced Buddhism to the West, Chögyam
Trungpa had a genius for understanding how to cross those cultural,
historical, and ideological barriers that make the transmission of any genuine spiritual tradition so difficult today. His efforts to find a living language that would be faithful to the origins of the Buddhist tradition led
him to an unusually piercing analysis of the "modern world"—that world
which has, for better or worse, become the only horizon open to us. In this
world, language has become insignificant and deprived of its own resonance[1] for various reasons, primarily the triumph of advertising.

A number of spiritual masters illuminated the twentieth century, but
few departed from the religious context in which they were raised.
Although this in no way prevents us from drawing on their wisdom and
compassion, their language does not enrich our culture. It no longer communicates with us. It may move or inspire us, but without initiating or
helping to provoke the collapse of those long-standing barriers that keep
our world stagnant.

One point should be made at the outset, to avoid any misunderstanding: the true focus of this volume is not primarily Chögyam Trungpa's advanced spiritual accomplishment, but his effort to find a form of language

that would correspond to that experience and thus reveal (in the words of René Char) *"l'espoir du grand lointain informulé (le vivant inespéré)"*—"the hope of the great unformulated beyond (unhoped-for being)."[2] His language is audacious, striking a blow at all our conceptions, especially those born of sentimentality and naiveté, or cynicism and artifice, or else words adopted for the moment that do not actually apply to anything in particular, that don't address anyone and leave no return address, that succeed in blunting or even terminating the salutary adventure that they should be revealing to us.

Religious discourse is particularly in crisis. It has lost its tongue. When it speaks, the words it utters are worn out and often stillborn.

The modern art introduced by Cézanne or Rimbaud provides one path that can be followed, because it confronts this crisis: it faces up to the death of the Academy by trying to invent a more complete relationship to tradition, by looking afresh with fertile attentiveness at each aspect of our experience. These artists are the great witnesses of our time, and Chögyam Trungpa walked in their footsteps. He presents us with the utterly individual face of a spiritual master who became an artist and thinker or, better, a human being in dialogue with art and thought.

Living Language

Chögyam Trungpa's immense work ranges over the most varied fields. His teachings have led to the publication of a large number of books—nearly a hundred in English—and a great many transcripts remain to be edited and published. His work covers art, contemplative psychology, cinema, various aspects of the Buddhist path, a presentation of the path of chivalry (or, as he called it, warriorship), a detailed exposition on meditation and its meaning for the West, and many other topics. Chögyam Trungpa also wrote plays and an impressive body of lyric poetry, in Tibetan and English. He translated a vast array of liturgies and traditional Tibetan texts. He was a painter, calligrapher and photographer, and sought to revitalize the meaning of art exhibitions through the installations that he organized at various museums. A body of texts he wrote in Tibet, totaling nearly a thousand pages, which was believed lost, has also recently been rediscovered.

As vast and disparate as this work is, it is not an encyclopedic attempt to grasp the whole of reality, nor is it the production of an unusually talented dilettante. Chögyam Trungpa's ambition was entirely different. His approach is an adventure that firmly takes the initiative, going to the heart of the unexpected and unimagined—the space where all transformation takes place—leaving nothing unscathed. In a crisis, when language is no longer naturally alive but instead becomes the vehicle for arbitrary concepts and for the habits of mechanical and moribund thought, the salutary importance of such a challenge is clear.

The meaning of this book will not be immediately clear to anyone who has not observed the wretched banality of current spiritual discourse, or who has not been overwhelmed by the mass of volumes published every year which are full of either nice sentiments or pointlessly erudite discussions.

But some of us struggle under the yoke of such empty words that no longer say anything, that spin in empty space and whose discourse is meaningless and fails to engage us; and such people cannot fail to be dazzled by what Chögyam Trungpa attempted. In being so insightfully demanding, he was the brother of Martin Heidegger, William Carlos Williams, Marcel Proust, James Joyce, Paul Celan, or William Faulkner, each of whom, in his way, sought to discover a new and living language that would enable us to grow, develop, and elevate our condition.

Seen in this way, the work of Chögyam Trungpa does not belong to the world of conformity that has been set before us, as created by Hollywood, fast food, instant communication, and the drive for profit. His was one of the great acts of open resistance to our era. Furthermore, at a time when sociologists are describing the reception of Buddhism, and the way it is being experienced, as one of the best examples of a new postmodern orthodoxy, aimed at well-being and calling for a vague, comfortable humanism, the work of Chögyam Trungpa is a matchless resource, even an antidote.

For him, Buddhism is neither a fixed body of work to be recited by heart, nor a promise of happiness, nor an appeal to a natural moral order, but an *adventure* that leads to a way of thinking far from any well-trodden path. In this sense, his work is truly hermeneutical; in other words, it displays an understanding of how the perception of an object's mode of existence also depends on the way this understanding is received.

This approach is unquestionably what makes his work so staggering. Chögyam Trungpa detached himself from everything he had learned. He took a step backward in order to obtain an overview of his spiritual heritage and assess its relevance, as well as the various forms it had assumed over the course of the centuries. It is especially difficult to take this kind of step since our heritage—the place where we live, our mother tongue—is so close to us that generally we cannot see it. It is what constitutes us. But Chögyam Trungpa passed through such a trial, renewing the history of Buddhism and the experience that we can have of it.

When we look at the heroic but tragic life of Chögyam Trungpa we see that, in a sense, he sacrificed everything to his task—comfort, health, honors—and we comprehend how he was able to make such a leap beyond the familiar. One does not become truly free without paying a heavy price.

His upbringing in Tibet provided him with an exceptional traditional education, which is practically impossible to receive today, for obvious reasons. From a very young age, he was surrounded by extremely demanding tutors who left him not a moment's respite. He did not give himself up wholeheartedly to the discipline that was imposed on him until he met his true teacher, the great Jamgön Kongtrül of Shechen, and was finally able to recognize the greatness of the path. He was then faithful to it, even to the point of rising above all the conventions that were destroying Tibet from within.

At the age of nineteen, already recognized as a peerless master, he escaped to India and quickly became known as one of the great hopes for the future of a Tibet that was now in mortal danger.

Several years later he became a brilliant student at Oxford, displaying an astonishing curiosity about the society he encountered there. He studied philosophy and comparative religion with an ardor and an open-mindedness that very few Buddhist masters could achieve. Contrary to the popular opinion that sees him as an American author, he always considered himself to be English and remained a British citizen all his life, proud of his Oxford education.

In the United States, he came into contact with the mainstream intellectual currents of the time, which allowed him to enter into an extraordinary dialogue with America—a dialogue whose depth remains misunderstood, because its full scope has not yet been studied.

No study of the composition of his work, its different stages, and the coherence of its vision has yet been made. I should also emphasize here that in all of the four phases of his life, he displayed a unique genius without ever accepting the slightest compromise of the sort that transforms a human being into a cowardly, soulless pen-pusher. He paid the price for it. But the spiritual truth declared by the Buddha remained a recourse for him which nothing could take away; to his mind, it meant being ready to destroy any convention that would stifle the possibility of a direct, nonhierarchical view of the world we in which we live.

The subtle paradox of Chögyam Trungpa's thought is that his rejection of any authority that has become arbitrary was never unilateral. He denounced institutions while endlessly creating new ones himself. He sought to go beyond the strict framework of Buddhism in order to better celebrate human existence in its universality, even as he offered an introduction to a tradition of unequaled profundity. He was a master in the "crazy wisdom" school who nevertheless devoted himself to anchoring the strictest form of the monastic tradition in the West. He was truly free.

The absence of any sort of naiveté was particularly characteristic of him, giving his work that singular power of resistance that was a source of constant irritation to those who remain mired in self-satisfaction. It allowed him to stay as far from the cynicism of "political realism" as from the euphoria of a pseudo-revolution with its inexorable descent into criminal insanity.

An Author's Purgatory

Following his death in April 1987, Chögyam Trungpa went through a kind of purgatory that now seems to be nearing its end, as the publication of works such as this one attests. By "purgatory" I mean a period in which, after the death of an author, his work passes into obscurity, while for various reasons, sometimes even contradictory ones, his life moves into the foreground, creating a veritable obstacle, a screen that actually blocks access to the work.

This is a twofold phenomenon. First of all, a legend composed of a host of clichés prevents readers from seeing for themselves. The brainwashing concerning first Nietzsche's madness, and then secondly his responsibility for the rise of Nazism, carried on for some time. The mechanism works like this: in defiance of any real analysis, indeed countering any possibility of serious investigation, a catch phrase is repeated often enough to become deafening. It works like a rumor. No one tests the validity of the accusation any longer; it is simply parroted. After all, "there must be something in it." And so people end up believing it. In a similar way, Charles-Ferdinand Ramuz was turned into a Swiss regionalist author, even though he was one of the greatest writers of the twentieth century. Very few people grasped the importance of his work; but Céline thought him the greatest stylist of the French language of his time, after Proust. The attempt to turn Chögyam Trungpa into an eccentric master whose behavior was bizarre—he consumed huge quantities of alcohol and acted in a highly unorthodox manner—is part of the same phenomenon. When presented in this way, his personal characteristics are trees that hide the forest. One cannot understand his significance without making an effort to enter into the meaning of his work. So long as you stare through the wrong end of the telescope, you cannot see anything.

Otherwise—and this is the second phenomenon—an author can enter literary purgatory because his work depended so much on his actual presence as a living person. Chögyam Trungpa's aura so impressed his contemporaries that it immediately opened a channel of attention. So in the end, the writings didn't matter much; it seemed to be enough just to see such a being. When he was there before you, the strength that emanated from him was such that the importance of his ideas was immediately clear, while the inevitable misinterpretations they would create were of little consequence. No misunderstandings could possibly appear on the Richter scale next to the seismic ripples set off by his speech, his look, his gestures.

The death of Chögyam Trungpa poses a decisive question: without his presence, can his work sustain itself and maintain its capacity to provide a fresh look at reality? This does not seem at all inevitable, especially in the eyes of many people who knew him. For them, it is difficult to get past the conviction that nothing can replace the experience of being close to a man who was so charismatic, so capable of conquering the unconquerable.

For those who did not know him, it is easy to regret this absence or, on the contrary, to feel horrified at the idea of a man who was so radically immoderate.

In this sense, what I have termed purgatory is the inevitable period of mourning. One aspect of Chögyam Trungpa is dead. Is there something of him that remains alive?

The only way to find the answer is to go back to his work and attempt a rigorous investigation of the content that keeps it in motion. This is of course the sort of approach and effort that did not really need to be undertaken while he was alive. The ambition of the present book is to step onto this path.

In extending this invitation to analyze and study Chögyam Trungpa's work, the aim is to avoid taking the dead-end street of superficial admiration: in other words, not religiously repeating the work itself. Great authors who try to open up a new relationship with the real, which is freed from the dross of habits, are often cast in stone after death and their work becomes a pretext for a new dogmatism. To appreciate the risk involved, one only has to see how the provocative works of Arthur Rimbaud or René Char are now quoted and emptied of their meaning in the most conservative contexts, or to consider how the teachings of Friedrich Nietzsche or Jacques Lacan are so often caricatured and reduced to abstruse jargon.

It is not necessary to turn Chögyam Trungpa into a mummy or a piously celebrated icon in the history of Buddhism. There could be no worse insult to his memory. Analysis of his work from a critical perspective is undoubtedly the only way to avoid this risk. Or, to put it another way, it is time to stop speaking *about* Chögyam Trungpa and to be true to him by taking him as a starting point, and thus undertake a true effort of thought.

It must be recognized that such a stance is not generally encouraged, because the conventions of spirituality do not invite questioning of this sort; rather, everyone is invited to cultivate the virtues of trust and blind faith which, particularly in our time, lead to plain ignorance and folly.

The state of purgatory in which Chögyam Trungpa's work finds itself can be related to the place spirituality has in the public sphere. The only discussion that now seems to be accepted is one that toes a party line and eliminates the possibility of reflection and intelligence. A large number of books appear every day full of well-chosen personal examples, practical advice, calls for transcending the material world, and a preoccupation with the details of experience, which is merely a way to become utterly devoid of character. They seek to satisfy our need to reassure ourselves and forget the difficulties and pain in an epoch that prescribes submission to the consolation of authority. They try to deny, to cover up, even to erase, the experience of anguish or fear, but only the endurance of such experiences allows greatness to come to light. The distress that darkens our world, social destitution, the exhaustion that pervades everything, seem to leave such a discussion inert. In this context, Buddhism is reduced to an appeal for personal happiness, a friendly call for soft-heartedness, which is basically a naive and even somewhat narcissistic posture. Meanwhile, scholars dissect the objects of their study and lose themselves in the irrelevant quarrels of the specialist.

Chögyam Trungpa exposed these deceptions while he was alive, and his mere presence created awareness and comprehension of another way, which would allow us to come closer to the unknown, to a vaster world. But how can we rediscover this path of heart and mind today? The influence that Chögyam Trungpa exerted brought him readers and listeners, and he did not have to fit into the categories of our networks of information. His work was neither religious, political, nor artistic, and yet belonged in part to all three of these fields, renewing and illuminating them, while turning each one into a setting for genuine encounters. To relegate Chögyam Trungpa to the department of spirituality—though he never tired of exposing the narrowness, not to say imposture, of that realm of study—is to refuse him a truly resonant space; but perhaps such a petition can no longer be understood today.

Anyone who begins to work seriously on Chögyam Trungpa's writings can easily be daunted by the impression of what is still a virgin territory: there is so much left to do!

The preservation of his teaching remains in delicate balance, and the editing of his work is far from complete. Several dozen volumes still await publication, and hundreds of hours of teachings have to be transcribed, all of which will open new perspectives, because Chögyam Trungpa never repeated himself, and each of his talks provided a unique experience.

Above all, a labor of thought, which would allow his work to find a new resonance and to refresh our understanding of the problems that confront our world, remains to be undertaken. But the enthusiasm that the present anthology has aroused in those authors whose contributions have been included demonstrates that there are still people who, in the depths of their hearts, long to connect with the mystery of their own being.

Notes

1. As Martin Heidegger remarked: "Since everything today is valid or invalid only as determined by the dictatorship of 'publicness,' which is a function of technology, it may be impossible for centuries to come for what is essential and original simply to allow itself to unfold." Letter of March 21, 1948, to Elisabeth Blochmann, in Martin Heidegger and Elisabeth Blochmann, *Briefwechsel, 1918–1989*, ed. Joachim W. Storck (Marbach: Deutsche Schillergesellschaft, 1989).

2. René Char, "Feuillets d'hypnos no. 174," *Fureur et mystère* (Paris: Édition Gallimard, 1967), p. 132.

Near Boulder. Photograph by Hudson Shotwell.
Used with permission.

Genuine Water

The Legacy of Chögyam Trungpa

THE DZOGCHEN PONLOP RINPOCHE

IN 1980, I TRAVELED with His Holiness the sixteenth Karmapa to the United States. During this visit, I had the great fortune to meet Chögyam Trungpa Rinpoche and experience his sharp presence and kind and gentle heart. I was fortunate to also hear him translate some of His Holiness Karmapa's short teachings.

It was a great opportunity for me to witness Trungpa Rinpoche's impeccable devotion to the lineage and to His Holiness Karmapa, which in itself is a valuable teaching for vajrayana students. I saw him attempt to prostrate to His Holiness Karmapa every time they met, although His Holiness used to tell Rinpoche not to put himself through such a struggle, as he was physically unwell. However, he would not listen to this and each time did his three prostrations, while looking at Karmapa's face with such great delight and devotion. This taught me the meaning of devotion, which became the basis of my vajrayana journey. So I am happy and feel honored to have this opportunity to write a short tribute to Chögyam Trungpa Rinpoche, with whom I share the lineage and gurus.

Based on "The Legacy of Chögyam Trungpa: A Review of *The Collected Works of Chögyam Trungpa*" by The Dzogchen Ponlop Rinpoche, originally published in *Buddhadharma: The Practitioner's Quarterly* (summer 2004), www.thebuddhadharma.com.

Buddhism in the West

The light of buddhadharma started to dawn in the Western Hemisphere approximately one hundred and fifty years ago, when in 1852 the *Lotus Sutra* was translated into German, and in 1853 a Mahayana temple was established in San Francisco. Subsequently, many masters traveled from the East to Europe and North America, bringing with them particular streams of dharma and establishing places for study and practice, such as the Buddhist Society of Great Britain, founded in 1907. These events presaged the beginning of the establishment of Buddhism in the West. However, the real sun of dharma began to shine on Western soil with the arrival of one master in 1963—the Very Venerable Chögyam Trungpa Rinpoche.

Now, because of the timely ripening of his aspiration and dedication, as well as the openness, confidence, and genuine interest of many Western students, buddhadharma in the West is beginning to see the possibility of enjoying the fruition of the complete inheritance of the Buddhist wisdom tradition.

Chögyam Trungpa Rinpoche was a master genuinely confident of his mission and realization. He demonstrated a sharpness of intellect that cut through all delusion and doubt, a calmness of mind unmoved by neurotic chaos, and a total fearlessness of all threat of egocentricity. Meeting such a master makes your dualistic head spin and go beyond time and space— you may not know where, or with whom, you actually are—perhaps you are in the company of an ancient Indian Buddhist saint, or a modern, avant-garde Japanese-type saint, or just a completely crazy Tibetan man!

Genuine Water

The essence of Buddhism is like pure water; it is wisdom that is transparent and fluid. Like pure water, it is without any inherent shape or color of its own. Yet at the same time it is capable of adopting any shape and reflecting all the colors of the container into which it is poured. It is a science of mind and a philosophy of life that addresses the emotions as well as the intellect and offers a basis for understanding the meaning of life and the nature of the world.

Historically, as Buddhism traveled from its homeland of India to other lands—to Tibet, China, Sri Lanka, Japan, and so on—this pure water, the genuine wisdom of Buddha, took on the shape of its different containers and reflected the languages and social forms of each country.

This is the water Chögyam Trungpa Rinpoche began pouring from his Tibetan container into the vessel of Western culture, to quench the thirst of beings overwhelmed by poverty mentality and spiritual materialism. Thus, Chögyam Trungpa Rinpoche played a very important role in bringing the complete buddhadharma to the West.

When the great wisdom of the East met with this completely open-minded vessel of the West, both found a new home, a new heart, and a fresh meaning to life. Trungpa Rinpoche leaped right into this meeting place to explore and deepen his connection to the West and Western students, as well as to ponder the right vessel for the wisdom that benefits all beings. As he wrote in *Born in Tibet*, "there remained some hesitation as to how to throw myself completely into proclaiming the dharma to the Western world, uprooting spiritual materialism, and developing further compassion and affection." With great courage and love, he engaged fully in Western culture, language, and tradition, and dedicated the rest of his life to transplanting "on the spot" the lineage teachings of Buddhism.

Dharma without Borders

Chögyam Trungpa Rinpoche was a pioneer in bringing the Buddhist teachings to the West and one of the most dynamic masters of Tibetan Buddhism in the twentieth century. He was a great scholar, meditation master, artist, and poet. He became renowned for his unique ability to present the essence of the highest Buddhist teachings using forms that made them accessible to his Western students.

There are many stories telling of his skillful means in transmitting the essence of dharma to his students. In order to meet the minds and hearts of his Western students, he sometimes stepped beyond the bounds of conventional propriety and into the realm of the outrageous. Whenever someone does not abide by the mundane rules of the social hierarchy, that person becomes the subject of controversy and rumor. Like many masters in the past, he became a controversial, almost mythical, teacher, with many versions of his activity still perpetuated today.

Looking back, we can see and appreciate the depth of his contemplations as he faced the task of establishing a genuine Western sangha—

students who shared his commitment and could follow his insightful and sometimes daring approach to introducing the buddhadharma to the Western world. He made it possible for many Western students to understand dharma by teaching in English, relating to Western psychology, and using examples of everyday Western culture.

His approach to planting dharma in the Western soil was a traditional as well as a radical and creative one. It was traditional in the sense that he always returned to the roots of Buddhism, to the original Indian Buddhism of Shakyamuni Buddha and the lineage of the Tibetan masters. It was radical in the sense that he experimented broadly with form, dropping altogether many of the Eastern cultural forms or mixing Tibetan forms with Japanese, British, and American elements. It also was creative in the sense of not allowing itself to be determined by the immediate past of the Eastern traditions and cultures.

At the same time, he introduced many Tibetan cultural practices through the Shambhala teachings, such as the lhasang (purification ceremony), along with practices associated with drala and werma (deities). He saw the task for Western Buddhists to be the creation of a new Buddhist culture—one with its own forms that, while being genuinely Buddhist, would speak the language of Western culture. This underscores the importance of the container—the cultural expressions of language, custom, and symbol through which people make use of and benefit from the water that is contained within it.

Trungpa Rinpoche introduced many important Buddhist concepts into the English language and psyche in a fresh and unique way. He was one of the first Buddhist masters to introduce the notion of "spiritual materialism," the tendency of ego to enhance itself through appropriating the spiritual path and creating a more subtle "spiritual ego" as the basis for one's clinging and rationalization for remaining in a state of self-deception. In his groundbreaking book, *Cutting Through Spiritual Materialism*, he spoke directly of the potential dangers and distortions that could occur when walking the spiritual path, as well as the means of transforming these experiences by cutting through our confusion, spiritual pride, and concepts, and uncovering the awakened state. The timely appearance of *Cutting Through Spiritual Materialism* benefited not only the new Tibetan Buddhists in the West, but also the practitioners of many other Buddhist traditions.

Chögyam Trungpa Rinpoche later introduced the Shambhala teachings, which were his mind terma, and the culture of the Great Eastern Sun. This cycle of teachings, presented from a more secular perspective, proclaims the message of human dignity and basic goodness. It offers a vision of enlightened society based on unwavering gentleness and an appreciation of oneself and the natural sacredness of the world. From this perspective, the bravest warrior is the one who is most open to others and most sensitive to the tenderness and sadness of his or her own heart. The wisdom of the Great Eastern Sun, which illuminates every aspect of our human experience, says, "Cheer up, sweetheart," as Chögyam Trungpa Rinpoche often expressed it.

Some of his students have described to me how they began to assimilate the message of this "new" transmission, based on the principles of warriorship found in many ancient cultures. More than anything, they understood the qualities of dignity, gentleness, and fearlessness by simply observing Trungpa Rinpoche. "His very being," one said to me, "was a full-blown manifestation of celebration and confidence." This kind of confidence and bravery transforms situations; it is an antidote to aggression and depression. It makes our world and our minds workable.

Who Was Chögyam Trungpa?

Chökyi Gyamtso—"Chögyam" in its shortened form—Trungpa Rinpoche (1939–1987) was recognized by the sixteenth Gyalwa Karmapa as the eleventh descendent in the line of Trungpa incarnations, an important teacher of the Kagyü lineage, one of the four main schools of Buddhism of Tibet. In addition to being a key master within the Kagyü lineage, Chögyam Trungpa also received training and transmissions of the Nyingma school, the oldest of the four schools, and was an adherent of the Ri-me (nonsectarian) ecumenical movement within Tibetan Buddhism. From this we can see that the penetrating wisdom inherited by Trungpa Rinpoche came from the Kagyü and Nyingma lineages of Tibetan Buddhism. He studied with many great masters of these two lineages, and his principal teachers were Shechen Kongtrül and Khenpo Gangshar Rinpoche.

The origin of the special lineage of Trungpa Rinpoche traces back to the most renowned Indian mahasiddha, Tilopa. A great Kagyü yogi in fourteenth-century Tibet named Trung Ma-se, or Ma-se Tokden, held the ear-whispered lineage of the Nine Cycles of the Formless Dakinis, a cycle of teachings that came directly from Tilopa. Trung Ma-se received these secret teachings from the fifth Karmapa, Deshin Shekpa, and he passed this lineage down to Kunga Gyaltsen, later to be known as the first Trungpa Tülku.

As prophesied by the fifth Karmapa, Ma-se established the first monastery, which came to be known as the Surmang Namgyal Tse, and later his student Trungpa established the Surmang Dütsi Tel Monastery. The ear-whispered lineage of the dakinis is to be passed to only one student at a time, and this lineage continues until this day. It is now known as the ear-whispered lineage of the Surmang.

Successive incarnations of the Trungpa Tülkus continued to be remarkable masters of the Kagyü lineage, and through continuing this wisdom tradition, they benefited many people in this world. The tenth Trungpa, Chökyi Nyinche, became one of the principal disciples of Jamgön Kongtrul the Great, who was the cofounder of the nonsectarian movement in Tibet. Through this and other sources, Trungpa Rinpoche became the holder of various other traditions, especially the Dzogchen lineage of the Nyingma school.

As taught in the Buddhist scriptures, there are nine qualities of a perfect master of buddhadharma. The eleventh Chögyam Trungpa Rinpoche possessed all nine of these. He first went through the rigorous trainings of studying the dharma, contemplating its meanings, and finally engaging in meditation to attain the complete realization of what the Buddha taught as the true nature of the world. He also accomplished the three inner qualities of tantric discipline, was well versed in Buddhist scholarship, and possessed the tender heart of compassion. For the benefit of others, he was fully equipped with the ocean of wisdom to teach and show the genuine path, to cut through wrong views and doubts with great skill, and to compose many treatises.

Contemporary Activities

The eleventh Trungpa Tülku, Chögyam Trungpa Rinpoche, was forced into exile by the communist Chinese invasion of Tibet in 1959, and he made the perilous journey over the Himalayas to India on horseback and on foot. In the early 1960s, Trungpa Rinpoche served as the spiritual adviser for the Young Lamas Home School in Dalhousie, India, as appointed by His Holiness the Dalai Lama.

It was with the encouragement of His Holiness Karmapa that Trungpa Rinpoche began his travels in the West. In 1963, he moved to England to study comparative religion, philosophy, and fine arts under a Spaulding Fellowship at Oxford University. During this time, he founded meditation groups in England and established in Scotland one of the first Tibetan Buddhist meditation centers in the West. He became the first Tibetan teacher to lecture in English.

Shortly after his move to England, a deeper contemplation on how to truly plant the dharma in the modern-day world and benefit the greatest number of students led Chögyam Trungpa Rinpoche to the decision to give up his monastic robes and serve as a lay teacher. In 1970, he married Diana Pybus. This moment of decision is clearly expressed by Trungpa Rinpoche himself in *Born in Tibet:* "With a sense of further involving myself with the sangha, I determined to give up my monastic vows. More than ever I felt given over to serving the cause of Buddhism."

He moved to the United States, through Canada, and founded his first North American meditation center, Tail of the Tiger (now known as Karmê Chöling) in Barnet, Vermont. The ancient Buddhist wisdom and practical instructions that Trungpa Rinpoche brought with him found an enthusiastic audience in the America of the 1970s. During this period, he traveled and taught throughout North America. These early seminars, which introduced students to his extraordinarily clear, precise and to-the-point naked wisdom teachings, were later compiled into books, such as *Cutting Through Spiritual Materialism* and *The Myth of Freedom and the Way of Meditation.* Throughout his life, Chögyam Trungpa Rinpoche sought to bring the teachings he had received from the most renowned masters of the East to the largest possible audience in the world. His teachings became one the largest bodies of published works by a single author on Buddhism in English.

In a period of less than two decades, Chögyam Trungpa Rinpoche made great strides toward accomplishing his goal of establishing a genuine Buddhist tradition in the West. In 1973, he founded Vajradhatu, the umbrella organization for many meditation centers throughout the world; soon after, in 1974, he founded Naropa Institute (now Naropa University), which became the first fully accredited Buddhist-inspired university in North America. He taught thirteen three-month Vajradhatu Seminaries, at which he presented a vast body of three-yana teachings within an intensive meditation practice atmosphere. He also invited great Tibetan Buddhist masters, such as His Holiness the sixteenth Gyalwang Karmapa, to come to the West and offer teachings.

Chögyam Trungpa Rinpoche passed away in 1987 in Nova Scotia, Canada, and his sacred body was cremated at Karmê-Chöling. However, his legacy of teachings and his lineage continue. Ösel Tendzin (formerly Thomas Rich, 1943–1990), became heir to his Buddhist lineage, having been appointed Vajra Regent in 1976. He was the first Westerner to be acknowledged as a holder of the Kagyü lineage. Sawang Ösel Rangdrol Mukpo (now known as Sakyong Mipham Rinpoche), his eldest son, became heir to the Shambhala teachings. In addition to the training received from his father, Sakyong Mipham Rinpoche received training from many other Kagyü and Nyingma masters. He is currently head of Shambhala International and leads his students and centers with wisdom and compassion.

The present incarnation of the Trungpa lineage, Chökyi Sengay (Lion of Dharma), lives at Surmang Dütsi Tel Monastery in eastern Tibet. He is currently receiving the traditional training in Buddhist studies and meditation practices. He has yet to visit the West.

Holding the Banner of the Dharma

Celebrating Chögyam Trungpa

JACK KORNFIELD

THE TIBETAN LAMA and dharma teacher Chögyam Trungpa Rinpoche was a beloved friend of mine, a benefactor, and a deeply respected person in my life. When he died in April, 1987, he was the leader of one of the largest Buddhist communities in America. In July 1974, he had founded Naropa Institute along with many of us who taught there. He had thousands of students connected with the main meditation centers he founded in Colorado, Nova Scotia, and rural Vermont. He established centers in almost one hundred cities and small towns across North America, as well as throughout Europe. When he died at the age of forty-eight, he not only had a large following but had also brought the dharma to life in the West in a remarkable new way.

The Life of a Bodhisattva

Chögyam Trungpa's life reminds me of a beautiful sutra in the mahayana teachings of Buddhism, called the *Vimalakirti Nirdesa Sutra*. Vimalakirti, the subject of the sutra, was a great bodhisattva and teacher who, rather

---

Based on a talk given in April 1987.

than appearing as a monk or a priest, decided to incarnate as a layman and to go among the peoples of the world to teach in a language or a way that could be understood by every person he met. In this sutra, Vimalakirti appears in different guises. At one point, he's married and he has a whole flock of children. In this way he could show the merit of family life and the possibilities it offers for surrender, awakening, and practice. Later in the sutra, he works in a wine shop and teaches the dharma to those who come for drinks, enlightening them in the process. In another part of the sutra, Vimalakirti makes himself sick to give the healers and others around him an opportunity to serve him, so that they can learn caring and compassion in ways that are appropriate to their situation. He goes through all of these different guises, entering into the very thick of life with a tremendous sense of joy and ease, demonstrating that each situation in life is workable as a part of one's practice.

In some ways, Chögyam Trungpa Rinpoche was closer to Vimalakirti than anyone I've ever met on my travels in the dharma. He escaped from Tibet in 1959, around the same time that the Dalai Lama and many other great teachers also escaped. In *Born in Tibet,* a very harrowing and compelling account of his early life and departure, Trungpa Rinpoche describes the whole process of escape over the Himalayan mountains. He went first to India and in 1963 to England, where he studied at Oxford University. In 1967 he founded Samye-Ling in Scotland, one of the first major Tibetan centers in the West.

Chögyam Trungpa has been a tremendous supporter of the vipassana community in America. Trungpa Rinpoche got Joseph Goldstein, Sharon Salzberg, me, and a number of others to join together to teach in the first year of Naropa Institute in 1974, and after collaborating there we all began to teach vipassana in large retreats across the country. My first personal talk with Rinpoche was in 1973 at a cocktail party in Cambridge, Massachusetts, when he was thinking about starting Naropa. It was a group from Harvard University, with professors and dharma practitioners. We were drinking cocktails and chatting, and he was interested in the training that I'd had as a monk and about my experiences in monasteries in Asia. Rinpoche asked a lot of interesting questions about my training. Then he said, "I think you should join us and teach at this Buddhist university we're going to establish, Naropa Institute." I was reluctant. I had had some training in teaching while I was in Asia, and I had done a bit of teaching on a very small scale while I was in graduate school. "I don't know if I'm ready to teach at that level," I told him. He was quite pleased with that, actually. He said, "Then it's clear you should be teaching. Come on, I'll sign you up, and you'll be our teacher of Theravada Buddhism." So I went. I had met Joseph Goldstein briefly before that, but it was that summer at Naropa that he and Sharon Salzberg and I really struck up a deep friendship and began to teach together, and we have led our community since then.

Besides being a supporter in those early days, over many years Chögyam Trungpa was a great supporter of the vipassana practice. When the great Burmese master Mahasi Sayadaw came to teach at our American centers in 1979, Rinpoche was in Europe, but he telephoned and tried to arrange a flight to come back just to pay his respects to Mahasi Sayadaw.

Trungpa was a follower of the path of the bodhisattva, the path of opening one's heart and one's life to all circumstances and all beings. His way combined discipline and openness in a remarkable fashion. I hope that describing some of the qualities that I've learned from him will help to inform and inspire the practice of dharma for all of us.

The Quality of Brightness

The first of the key elements in his teachings that I want to honor is the tremendous quality of brightness. Over many years, at Naropa and elsewhere, I must have heard almost one hundred dharma talks by Rinpoche. Although he might arrive late for a lecture and was sometimes in a somewhat inebriated state, there was still an amazing quality of brightness and clarity to his mind. Lama Govinda once spoke to me about Trungpa Rinpoche. While Lama Govinda was living in Almora in the Himalayas of India in the 1950s and early 1960s, many people escaping from Tibet came through his household, and many of the lamas would stay with him. He said that of all the young tülkus, the young incarnate lamas, to leave Tibet, there was none so bright as Trungpa Rinpoche. He meant bright in the sense of the field of his being and his energy. Lama Govinda told me this at a point when he wasn't very happy with the way Trungpa Rinpoche was behaving. He said, "I still have to admit that there was no one who walked across the Himalayas and came out of Tibet who had that light more than Trungpa."

This quality of brightness in his teachings relates to what Rinpoche called the Lion's Roar. In the Pali texts, there is a very famous discourse of the Buddha, called the *Lion's Roar Sutra*, where someone asks, "How do you know about all the things that you claim to know about? Have you really practiced? Have you really done it yourself?" In his reply, the Buddha says, "If there is any ascetic practice that has ever been done on the continent of India in all of the thousands of eons of world systems, I have tried it. I've fasted; I lay on beds of nails; I went down to eating one grain of rice, one sesame seed, a day. When I put my hand on my belly, I touched my backbone." He said, "I sat up with my eyes open to the moon. I sat with my eyes open to the sun." He said, "Whatever practice you could name, I did. And finally, after all of those austerities and all of those practices, I discovered that self-torture wasn't the point. The point wasn't to torture the body, nor was it to indulge it. But I discovered that the secret of the middle path, of the way of being free in the midst of every experience with clarity and simplicity, is that which brings one to liberation." It's a very powerful sutra. You get a tremendous sense of the strength of the Buddha just in reading it. Trungpa Rinpoche also spoke of the teachings as the Lion's Roar. He said:

> The Lion's Roar is the fearless proclamation that any state of mind, any circumstance, any part of ourselves, including the most difficult emotions, is a workable situation, a reminder in the practice of meditation. We can realize that the chaotic situations must not be rejected, nor must we regard them as regressive, as a return to our confusion. We must sit and respect whatever happens to our state of mind. Even chaos should be regarded as extremely good news. . . . We can learn to accept our states as part of the patterns of mind, without question, without reference back to the scriptures, without help from credentials, directly acknowledging that they are so, and that these things are here and are true. . . . That is the lion's roar, that whatever occurs in the samsaric mind (the mind of cycles) is regarded itself as the path: everything is workable.[1]

This openness is an amazing quality to bring to one's practice. In 1977, while I was still teaching at the summer session of Naropa Institute, my book *Living Buddhist Masters* was published. I exchanged books with

Trungpa Rinpoche. I gave him a copy of my book, and he gave me an autographed copy of *Cutting Through Spiritual Materialism*. As an inscription, he wrote, "Dear Jack, Welcome back," which I took to mean something like "Welcome back to the West." Then the inscription continued, "Can you hold the banner of the dharma? Let us celebrate!" This inscription was written in great big letters. To me, it's been a very meaningful inscription. Can I, can all of us, hold the banner of the dharma, and can we proclaim the lion's roar?

Trungpa Rinpoche not only taught Buddhism, but he also started a secular system to present the practice of meditation, called Shambhala Training, which taught people meditation without all of the Tibetan and Buddhist framework around it. When Shambhala Training is presented, the hall where people practice is hung with beautiful banners, depicting some of the symbols of what he called the state of mind of the rising sun, the Great Eastern Sun. He said that you can look at the sun and see it as either rising or setting. You see it as setting when you're depressed and feeling sad, because everything changes and it's all impermanent; there's nothing to hold on to, and it's such a shame. Or you can see everything that arises as an opportunity. The whole spirit of Shambhala is to see what arises as an opportunity in practice.

Trungpa Rinpoche had a very droll sense of humor. He could be very, very funny, but his jokes were usually short one-liners rather than long stories. I remember one evening when he was talking about how the practice of meditation was to not remove oneself, not to shield or armor oneself, from experience, not to hide in a box or a cave or inside our fancy car or whatever. He used all kinds of metaphors for hiding from our experience, such as being inside our house and turning up the heat or the air conditioning and closing the curtains to try to make ourselves feel safe. He said the way of the warrior, or the bodhisattva, was to have no distance between ourselves and our experience. After he finished speaking, someone raised his hand and said, "No distance? No distance?" Then the questioner asked, "Well, what if there are circumstances where things are fearful or difficult or dangerous?" The questioner went on for a long time. And Trungpa looked back and said, very simply, "No distance." Then he picked up his glass and raised it to the questioner, and he said, "Good luck, sir." And everyone laughed. That was an ending line he often used: "Good luck, madam." "Good luck, sir." So the quality of brilliance in Rinpoche's teaching was this quality of radiating freedom like the rising sun, which illuminates a path for us. In his teachings, there was this encouragement to proceed—not out of self-confirmation, not to make ourselves into some bigger, stronger ego, but rather to be willing to stay with our experience as it presents itself, to see whatever arises as practice, and to move forward.

Showing the Way of Openness

This leads into the second quality that Chögyam Trungpa manifested in his life, which is available to all of us, as much as when he was alive. This is the quality of openness, or showing the open way, a quality of fearlessness in practice. In the 1970s, Rinpoche wrote about "dharmas without blame," dharmas not meaning only the law or the teachings, but also as a term for all the elements of body and mind that make up experience. He says that all the dharmas or the elements that arise

are without blame because there was no manufacturer of dharmas. Dharmas are simply what is. Blame comes from an attitude of security, identifying with certain reservations as to how things are. Having this attitude, if a spiritual teaching does not supply us with enough patches we are in trouble. The Buddhist teaching not only does not supply us with any patches, it destroys them.

As ego's patches are destroyed, there comes a point where relating to the teaching means the continual death of ego. . . . Therefore the teaching of dharmas without blame should be regarded as good news. It seems that it is good news, utterly good news, because there is no choice. When you see it clearly, there is no choice whatsoever. Even praise and blame, fear and difficulty, are the conditioned experiences of a beautiful patchwork.[2]

Then, in the same spirit, he goes on to talk about "buddhadharma without credentials," not getting a Ph.D., not making oneself into a professional meditator, not turning spiritual practice into a thing that distances us from the world. His image for this is of the child:

The child's world has no beginning or end.
To him, colors are neither beautiful nor ugly.

The child's nature has no preconceived notion of birth and death.
The golden mountain is solid and unchanging.
The ruby sun is all-pervading.
The crystal moon watches over millions of stars.
The child exists without preconceptions.3

Rinpoche taught this quality of openness, of finding within your own mind, within your own experience, a willingness to relate to whatever presents itself. The curriculum at Naropa Institute included psychology philosophy, music and art, poetry and dance. Especially in the early years, Naropa was really an expression of the breadth of his vision of dharma. It was very colorful. The banners were colorful; the way the people dressed was colorful. Gradually, they went from madras and paisley to three-piece suits with a cocktail in one hand and a cigarette in the other. There was a real sense of theater and play with everything Rinpoche did. With anything he did, he was willing to engage in life and to play with it as a part of practice. It was anything but dull.

Out of his early talks at Naropa, Rinpoche wrote a wonderful book about the practice of Tibetan tantra called *Journey without Goal: The Tantric Wisdom of the Buddha*. Although he mentioned various tantric exercises and visualizations and so forth, the main message of his book was to encourage a willingness to touch the raw feelings of our life. The highest goal or stage of tantra is working directly with passions, fears, greed, and aggression—the emotions that fuel our action, the feelings themselves. He taught a willingness to open to all of these things. From one perspective in Buddhism, difficult emotions can be seen as hindrances and defilements, things that we get caught up in and wish to free ourselves from. However, from the point of view of the teachings of the bodhisattva, these are all qualities that have promise in them. According to how Trungpa Rinpoche taught the dharma, the way of practice wasn't to see that the things that make up our personality are a problem, but rather to see that they're part of the fabric and pattern of being, and that they become workable and in fact usable as we become wiser. Part of the playfulness of Trungpa Rinpoche was that he saw not only the difficulties but also the potential in all of the aspects of practice.

So in addition to the brightness to his teaching, there was this openness, a willingness to engage with life and play with its elements. The path of the bodhisattva in the dharma is to not withdraw from life, but to go inward and discover that which is timeless, compassionate, and free, and to bring that into manifestation in every realm of the world.

The Power of Devotion

The next quality that Rinpoche represented was devotion. When his teachers Dilgo Khyentse Rinpoche and the sixteenth Gyalwa Karmapa came to America, it was beautiful to see how respectfully and kindly he served them. In a text called *The Sadhana of Mahamudra*, which he wrote in a cave in Bhutan in the 1960s, he talks about the dark ages of the dharma and how the winds of sectarian bitterness blow between the different countries and the sects of the buddhadharma. He says that, even though the dharma has been proclaimed by the Buddha and carried on by many great teachers and lamas over centuries, people get lost in the philosophy, in the psychology, in the sects, in the territoriality of it, and the true essence is often lost. Then he goes on to pray, or ask, that those who receive the teachings of dharma in this age of difficulty will take them and use them to the very best of their abilities. It is a deeply devotional text that calls for wisdom in a heartfelt way. Its spirit is carried in a poem that Rinpoche and his students translated from the Tibetan, which is called, "Intensifying Devotion in One's Heart: The Supplication 'Crying to the Gurus from Afar.'" The poem says in part:

> Death is certain to come, but I am unable to take this to heart.
> The dharma truly benefits, but I am unable to practice it properly.
> Karma and its result are certainly true, but I do not properly discriminate what to accept and reject.
> Mindfulness and awareness are certainly necessary, but not stabilizing them, I am swept away by distractions.
> Guru, think of me; look upon me quickly with compassion.
> Grant your blessings so that I maintain undistracted mindfulness. . . .
> Grant your blessings so that genuine devotion arises in me.
> Grant your blessings so that I glimpse the natural state.
> Grant your blessings so that insight is awakened in my heart.
> Grant your blessings so that I uproot confusion.
> Grant your blessings so that I attain buddhahood in one lifetime.[4]

This is a wonderful text that was originally composed by Jamgön Kongtrül Lodrö Thaye, who was an earlier incarnation of Trungpa Rinpoche's root guru, or main teacher. In embodying one's practice, these kinds of supplications are recited over and over again, evoking a great sense of devotion by crying to the gurus from afar.

Rinpoche talks about the quality of devotion in another way in *Shambhala: The Sacred Path of the Warrior*. He talks about devotion, without calling it that, as the path of practice leading to the birth of a tender heart of sadness. The opening and the devotion that arise out of practice is a devotion to the dharma, to the truth, to one's teachers, to one's self, one's own being, and then through that to all the world. Rinpoche says that the practice of a warrior gives birth to a tender heart of sadness, which he likens to a reindeer who is just beginning to sprout horns. They are fuzzy and raw, and they kind of hurt. At first, the reindeer can't quite figure out what these little things on his head are for. Yet, as they grow harder and more magnificent, the reindeer discovers that he should have horns. In the same way, the warrior opens his or her heart and begins to realize that, in fact, one's heart *should* be able to touch all things in the world.

In another place in that book, he talks about how opening the heart leaves it exposed, like a piece of raw meat. You become so sensitive that you are touched by even a mosquito landing on the heart. The quality of opening oneself in this way is not particularly dramatic. You're not going to weep; it's not like hearing Beethoven's Ninth Symphony. It's much more ordinary and much more human, and in that way, even more special.

Trungpa Rinpoche was a genuinely warm and charming person. He had a very big sangha, and at times it was difficult to get to see him because he was so busy. However, when one could be with him, there was a tremendous sense of warmth and of caring and of ease and charm. During the first summer of Naropa, I remember going to his office to be with him. I expected to see pictures of the Karmapa and of Jamgön Kongtrül and of all the lamas of his lineage, but I didn't notice any at all. There was only one picture on the wall in his office, and it was of Shunryu Suzuki Roshi, the founder of the San Francisco Zen Center. Rinpoche met him when he first arrived in America, and they became great friends for a short time, until Roshi died. I asked Trungpa Rinpoche about that picture, and he said that it was an amazing thing that he should come to America to meet his father. He said this in the most loving and respectful way. It wasn't like working something out with your father, but just that here was somebody who really loved and accepted him as he was, and saw his greatness, even in the very earliest years that he was here. I was very impressed by Rinpoche's expression of devotion for Suzuki Roshi.

Rinpoche had this tremendous sense of a great heart. The power of his devotion inspired other people to participate or to join in.

Uncompromising Discipline

Another quality Trungpa Rinpoche expressed was an uncompromising discipline. When he was first teaching at Tail of the Tiger in Vermont in 1970, he would just hang out with people. If they were taking acid, he sometimes would take a little acid. If they were talking about transcendental consciousness, he would join in the discussion. Whatever people were doing, in those early hippie days, he would just get down and hang out and be willing to participate. In addition to the rural scene at Tail of the Tiger, there grew a center in Boulder, Colorado. A lot of people came because they were intrigued by the stories of this interesting Tibetan lama who would hang out with you and speak about things in this dharma language. There was very little real practice taking place. After a short period of time, maybe a year or two, he called his students together, especially the ones who were key in running his community, and he said, "Now we will all sit two hours a day." Many of them thought he was joking. This was radically different from what they'd come to expect. In the first years, he attracted a collection of poets and artists and many other people who would never have gone to study with any other regulation Buddhist teacher. These were people who wouldn't be caught within miles of an official religion. Yet somehow, through his art and his calligraphy and his visionary works and his poems and his willingness to just get down and play with everybody, he attracted this remarkable group of people. There were theater people and interested scientists and artists, and they were all there thinking that the dharma was some kind of groovy picnic out in the country where you talked about meditation in action, or something like that. And then Rinpoche said, "You will now sit two hours a day." They couldn't believe it.

In the years that followed he strongly encouraged everyone who wished to stay in the community to do a one-week group or solitary retreat two or three times a year, and he suggested that anyone who didn't have a family should do a one-month retreat every year. His students were so shocked. But they did it.

When Chögyam Trungpa first came to North America, he gave instruction in basic sitting practice. For three or four years, people were working with the breath and basic sitting practices that are very similar to vipassana practice. In 1973, the year before he started Naropa Institute and a year before the head of his lineage, Gyalwa Karmapa, made his first visit to America, Rinpoche accepted one hundred students for a three-month Seminary in which he introduced the formal practice of tantra, or vajrayana, for the first time in America. He always insisted that his students continue to regard sitting as the basic, fundamental practice, but he also introduced them to what the Tibetans call the preliminaries of practice, the warmups, which are one hundred thousand prostrations from standing to lying out and back again standing, one hundred thousand repetitions of a purification mantra, one hundred thousand visualizations of a mandala offering, and one million seed or devotional mantras. This is the initial practice for anyone undertaking the Tibetan vajrayana path of training. At that point, he said to all these people, "You will now do your ngondro, the entire set of preliminaries," which for most people takes one to five years—sometimes longer. Amazingly, there were more than three thousand people in his community who went from sitting around and talking about the dharma and having a good old time to not only learning meditation practice and doing a lot of retreats, but to undertaking the full training of the Tibetan path of practice. When they finished their one hundred thousand prostrations and all the other preliminaries, they went on to dedicated practice of various Tibetan sadhanas. I marvel at Rinpoche's skillful means of attracting people and then gradually seducing them, convincing them to willingly do more and more genuine practice.

He was quite uncompromising. In his foreword to my first book, *Living Buddhist Masters*, Rinpoche said that meditation begins by slowing the speed of our culture and neurotic mind. He spoke of meditation as an especially important discipline for the twentieth century. He wrote that "the age of technology would like also to produce a spiritual gadgetry—a new, improved spirituality guaranteed to bring quick results. Charlatans manufacture their version of the Dharma, advertising miraculous, easy ways, rather than the steady and demanding personal journey which has always been essential to genuine spiritual practice."5 He truly knew that, and over the years he inculcated that understanding in the members of his community.

At one large talk in Berkeley, when many people came to listen to him, he was as usual very late in arriving. He told us, "If you want your money back, it's all right. Just go to the door and ask for it back. It's quite fine. In fact, if you haven't started the spiritual path, best not to begin! It's difficult, it's terrible, and you have to face all kinds of things that you won't like. As far as the ego is concerned, it is one insult after another." And so he said, quite seriously, "If you don't even start, you'll probably be better off. Best not to begin. But if you do start, best to finish!" Unfortunately we have all started. What else are we going to do? Go back and cultivate greed, hatred, and delusion? He had this great sense of earthiness and discipline and humor about it all.

When we were in the very first summer session of Naropa Institute, there were two big evening classes that alternated. Monday and Wednesday were Ram Dass; and Tuesday and Thursday, or something like that, were Trungpa Rinpoche. Two thousand people would gather in the main hall. Ram Dass would come and teach about love and surrender, and we would sing to his guru and chant kirtan and get high on bhakti, opening the heart. It was great. That was Monday night. Then Tuesday night we'd come back. Trungpa would be a little late, and when he arrived, he would just sit there very quietly for a long time. Then he would give a simple talk about how practice really meant being where you are, coming down to earth, not getting lost in all the hoopla of Eastern mysticism. He was sort of making fun of all the things that Ram Dass was doing. And then on Wednesday night, Ram Dass would come back and talk about his guru and the yogas of the *Bhagavad Gita*, and we would all sing together and get high and dance with devotion and so forth. And then Thursday night Trungpa would come back again and say, "Impermanence. The fact of death. Remember that there's also suffering in life." This went on week after week. It was driving a lot of people crazy. Finally, one night, someone raised his hand after Trungpa gave his lecture and said, "Ram Dass has been talking to us about what great power there is in the grace of the guru, and that to surrender to a guru allows you to open to the spirit of grace, the grace of God, allowing the grace of God to come and illuminate us. Is there anything in Buddhism that corresponds to this sense of God's grace?" Chögyam Trungpa sat there quietly for a minute, and then he looked up and he said, "Yes." This surprised everyone. Then he smiled. "Patience." That was all he said.

Trungpa was unswerving in his teaching of the dharma. He just put it out directly. He taught people to practice with a great deal of discipline, year after year. He taught them to make practice a part of daily life. He taught that practice can include group and solitary retreats, long periods of practice, short periods of practice, and studying the dharma as well. He taught that we should be willing to investigate all the possible avenues of practice, and find the power and the strength of the dharma throughout our practice and our life and bring it alive in our being. I believe, as he did, that the genuine practice of vipassana and the buddhadharma, listening with the inner ear and the heart and the mind, can bring us to realize the deepest truths of the Buddha's enlightenment. We can discover the meaning of the Buddha's awakening very directly, if we're willing stay meticulously present even for one day. In sitting and walking and eating with attention, we can see that the five processes, the five skandhas, are empty of the self, that they are ungraspable, that our whole being is a process that's ungraspable and not at all separate from what is around us. This is visible to any person who practices deeply. All of us can participate in this timeless and liberating understanding. This is our buddha nature. Trungpa Rinpoche communicated an uncompromising belief in this, in our own awake nature, in the capacity to touch what the Buddha and every other great sage has discovered.

A Mysterious Genius

The final quality that I think of as expressed by Chögyam Trungpa is the quality of mystery. He was one of the most enigmatic people I have ever met. He was clearly a genius. He was a beautiful calligrapher; he wrote plays; he wrote some wonderful poetry. He was interested in photography; he was interested in science. He started a university. He started an enormous church. He wrote a brilliant best-selling book, *Cutting Through Spiritual Materialism*, based on his teachings in America. He looked around and saw that people in this country were misusing spiritual practice, which was intended to lead to freedom from self and freedom from self-involvement and self-delusion. Instead they were using spiritual practice as an imitation, to create the persona of a spiritual person, using practice as a new kind of mask or identity. He recognized this as soon as he arrived here, and he wrote this book, *Cutting Through Spiritual Materialism*, that goes to the very heart of spiritual practice. In the first year he was here, he taught how to use practice, not to make a new improved version of our personality, but to cut through clinging and awaken to the very essence of our being.

He also was peculiar. He drank; he was a womanizer. He was very open about these things. He wasn't one of those gurus that you read about in the paper that was supposed to be celibate and then you discovered later it wasn't true. As far as I know, there was nothing hidden about him. That was part of what was so mysterious. In the later years, he also organized his community as a kind of feudal kingdom. It was as if he were the ruler of a small country. His home was transformed into a court, and there were ministers and guards and princes and princesses and things like that. I actually enjoyed visiting it. I thought it was quite terrific theater. All of this was quite mysterious.

I feel that he gave himself as fully to the West as any Buddhist teacher that I know. And he did so in a most remarkable way. He absorbed our culture and our language and our customs. He took who we are into himself and then said, "All right, let's play. Let's take the seed of the dharma and make it sparkle and alive in the West." He did this more than any Buddhist teacher who's come to the West so far. And he did it with his heart and his body. He gave so much that you might say it killed him. Certainly, he died at a very young age. I think his drinking was a big part of that as well, but he gave himself in a remarkable way. There was something completely mysterious about all that: how this person who grew up as the ruler or the prince of some monastery in a remote corner of Tibet could come to America and enter into our culture so completely.

Once, a student of Rinpoche's was ill in the hospital, and the doctors thought she was dying. She later recovered. But as she felt herself fading away, she thought of the meditation practice that she had done, and she didn't know what to do at the impending moment of her death. She was thinking of Trungpa Rinpoche and wondering how one should work with the *Tibetan Book of the Dead* or how to approach dying. As she got very close to losing consciousness—she was very, very ill—all of a sudden, the form of Trungpa Rinpoche appeared cross-legged, seated on her chest, and began to give her instructions and practice in dying. Now, you can take that for what it's worth, but that was her mysterious experience. I believe in that level of things, and it has been part of my own experience, with my own teachers and even with my own students. In any case, there is a mystery around Chögyam Trungpa Rinpoche, things that I don't understand at all, many quite remarkable things. He was such a combination of qualities.

A Great Inspiration

Trungpa Rinpoche's books are like a treasure trove. Opening one of his books is like going into the basement of some wealthy museum. Every few pages there is some beautiful new explanation of some aspect of the dharma. What his books do and what his teaching did was invite each of us directly to become inheritors of this majestic spiritual heritage or lineage. Some of the banners he designed had a drawing on them called the knot of eternity. It's a linking of loops that go round and round and round and reconnect with one another. The knot of eternity is the eternal and timeless dharma, the dharma of liberation, the dharma of the liberation of the heart. In the same way, with the practice that you undertake, you are invited to take this practice and make it your own and to carry the banner of the dharma for yourself in this world.

Trungpa Rinpoche touched a lot of hearts and a lot of people. I loved him very much. I will miss his being here. I'd love to go talk to him. He's one of the few people I feel I could sit down with and say, "This is what I'm doing and teaching and the kind of community we're trying to create, and what do you think?" and he would really understand. But somehow I feel his spirit to be here, perhaps as much as or more than anyone I've ever known who's died. Someone asked him once whether he would come back as the twelfth Trungpa Tulku in his next reincarnation. I believe his answer was that he wasn't certain whether he was going to bother to come back in that form or not, but perhaps he would come back in Japan as a businessman or a scientist or something else more interesting.

He was a wonderful person, a remarkable teacher, and a great inspiration. I hope that what I've shared here gives you a sense of the empowerment that he gave to me and to many people around him: to take the dharma and bring it into our own lives and our own hearts and our own minds and to make it true for ourselves.

NOTES

1. *The Myth of Freedom and the Way of Meditation*, pp. 69–72.

2. "Dharmas without Blame," in *The Collected Works of Chögyam Trungpa*, vol. 2, p. 494.

3. *Garuda III: Dharmas without Blame* (Berkeley: Vajradhatu in Association with Shambhala Publications, 1973), p. 35. See also "The Nameless Child," *The Collected Works of Chögyam Trungpa*, vol. 7, pp. 333–334. Used by permission of Diana J. Mukpo.

4. "Intensifying Devotion in One's Heart: The Supplication 'Crying to the Gurus from Afar'" by Jamgön Kongtrül Lodrö Thaye, translated by the Nālandā Translation Committee, in *Journey without Goal: The Tantric Wisdom of the Buddha* (Boston: Shambhala Publications, 2000), p. 15. Used by permission of the Nālandā Translation Committee.

5. Jack Kornfield, *Living Buddhist Masters* (Boulder: Shambhala Publications, 1977), p. ix. Reissued as *Living Dharma: Teachings of Twelve Buddhist Masters* (Boston: Shambhala Publications, 1995), where the quote appears on p. vii.

Tantric Alchemy and the Transmission of Dharma

At the Heart of the Western Mandala

FRANÇOISE BONARDEL

To SAY TODAY THAT Chögyam Trungpa was a "pioneer" in terms of the transmission of dharma to the West would be to not fully account for what such an event would mean in the United States in the seventies,[1] nor the current cultural resonances aroused by the use of this term, laden with connotations in the Western mind: a pioneer clears and seeds uncultivated land, even if in so doing he must show himself as conquering. Immediately struck by the "rough, savage ways" of American culture,[2] Trungpa came to compare his mission in the West to that of Padmasambhava bringing the light of dharma to the Tibetans, no less savage, in the eighth century. Indeed, until then, what was Buddhism for most Westerners—Europe and America misunderstanding it in a similar way—if not one of those attractive but vague words that could indiscriminately encompass nostalgia for a mythic Orient and right-thinking disapproval toward the "cult of nothingness"? Thus the welcome reserved by Westerners for what they thought was Buddhism reflected, culturally, a curious mental wavering between a desire for eternity that remained unsatisfied from contact with monotheistic religions, and an ambivalent attraction for

Translated from the French by John Sell.

"emptiness," supposedly inherent in this, at the very least, disconcerting exotic wisdom. Despite appearances, circumstances in this regard were thus highly favorable for the transmission of the dharma, since it was when confronted with a comparable spiritual wavering between choices (asceticism or hedonism?) coupled with a metaphysical alternative (eternalism or nihilism?) that the Buddha Shakyamuni one day made the resolution to "show the way of deliverance to the world of creatures in the grip of the feverish sleep of life."[3]

For, if the name "pioneer" indeed adequately conveys the verve of the intrepid explorer that Trungpa undoubtedly was, constrained by exile to discover this terra incognita that the West was for him, it presupposes also that one could not at the same time open the way and complete the exploration during one's lifetime. It would fall to others, who came later, to pursue the task and to gather the fruits of a first planting. Such would be the hidden "holiness" of the authentic pioneer, rarely enjoying what he bequeaths during his lifetime, not even knowing what will become of his message and who will be his true heirs. Assuring his succession in the person of his eldest son, the spiritual heir of his lineage, was Trungpa able, for all that, to judge beforehand how the dharma and Western culture would integrate after he was gone? All pioneering work is indeed recorded in historic time, from a Western point of view, and this work has also espoused the progressivist movement characterizing European humanism since modern times. Forgetting sacred history, on this basis the moderns relegate to the second rank these other pioneers who before them also "founded" the West: martyrs, theologians, and Christian mystics, obeying in this the only Master of truth who exists in their eyes—Christ—and recording their action in another, eschatalogical time. Despite a rapid entry into the Western world, the immense work of Chögyam Trungpa—his various teachings and educational institutions—is not in this regard the Buddhist equivalent of the *Foundations* of Teresa of Ávila; nor does it carry traces of the conquering heroism of the first European immigrants to the New World any longer. The art of the warrior rehabilitated by the Vidyadhara (holder of crazy wisdom) in the context of the Shambhala teachings would be something else altogether! The bravery that characterizes the activity of the bodhisattva in Mahayana Buddhism would be something else altogether! "A very humble pilgrim who works in the soil of samsara to dig out the jewel embedded in it," as Trungpa described him.[4] To make such a difference disappear in the name of the pioneer ideology presumed common to the great founders or transmitters of religion runs the risk of cultivating the confusion between the spontaneous influence of an authentic spiritual message and the orchestrated dissemination of a consensual, planetary ecumenism, of which Trungpa was justly suspicious: "The standard approach to ecumenism is to try to pretend that theism and nontheism are not different. But this is another theistic attempt to conceal the discomfort or the energy that comes from experiencing duality. We should be aware that differences exist. Then true ecumenism, or continuity, can come about *because* of the differences."[5] To concede nothing to the mixture, indeed to heighten the distances until it would let a certain irreducible gap appear, would become the preparatory course Chögyam Trungpa required of his students.

Always more or less implicit in the Western mind, this twofold conception—humanist or religious—of the adventure in the act of founding runs aground in at least two ways when one relates it to Trungpa, who could only begin to open this gap in the West because he embodied the Buddhist path: a path with no other perspective, with no other horizon than the total and definitive obliteration of karmic traces, since then recognized as enlightenment: "It seems there is something to begin with and there is nothing to end with, so I suppose in between, there is the dissipation of something into nothing, which is called 'the path.'"[6] In this regard, in terms of the global expansion of Buddhism, Trungpa never taught anything but the most extreme vigilance with regard to higher bids, through which one "puts dharma on the market" in detached pieces, the way we would cut up a side of beef: "That is, it is necessary to preserve the wholesomeness of the whole path";[7] nothing left to hope for from each of his students but to rediscover the strength to "make a relationship with our suffering, frustrations, and neuroses"[8] and to thus arrive at square one, individually, indeed the pioneering work of all bodhisattvas, renouncing enlightenment as long as the last living being has not been delivered from samsara. A curious stance, that of the Buddhist "pioneer," who, transfixed by compassion for suffering humanity, certainly opens the "Way of Enlightenment"—in Shantideva's phrase—while at the same time ensuring that the rear guard does not leave behind a single latecomer! Trungpa probably would not have been able to assume this "pioneer" vocation of the bodhisattva in such an intrepid way, at the opportune moment, for the good of all beings, if he had not known to make evident the exceptional coincidence between his personal situation of being a refugee, an exile, and the traditional act of "taking refuge," which his students were invited to do: "Becoming a refugee is acknowledging that we are homeless and groundless, and it is acknowledging that there is really no need for home, or ground. Taking refuge is an expression of freedom, because as refugees we are no longer bounded by the need for security. We are suspended in a no-man's-land in which the only thing to do is to relate with the teachings and ourselves."9 That Trungpa was easily in this sense a "pioneer" showing by example to future or new "refugees" the necessity of abandoning everything and reinventing everything also invites us, to better understand and accept, with respect to Buddhism and the Western mentality, all that can distinguish the act of founding, building, transmitting to its heirs.

In *The Temptation of the West*, a small, prophetic book written in 1926, André Malraux had already drawn the attention of Westerners to the immensity of the mental space that separates the "careful avoidance of nurturing the 'I'" of the Buddhist countries from the frenzy for building of the humanist, Christian West. Malraux's short novel focuses on the exchange of letters between two young intellectuals, one Asian and one Western, at the beginning of the revolution in China. "These notions of a world that you are unable to find in yourselves, you replace with a rational construct," as the Asian petrified of such an "avoidance of nurturing" wrote to his Western correspondent.10 It is not enough to speak of planting—of Buddhism in the West—to fill the gap—that well and truly exists between two ways of "planting." So, beyond the modern separation between atheist humanism and Christianity, the West is entirely built thanks to the analogy making the Kingdom of Heaven—which is certainly not "of this world"—the archetype of all the civil and religious constructions of any importance that exist in this world. The Buddhist monuments—in particular Borobodur—were built on a reversed analogy, lending themselves to a glimpse in stone of the erosion of karmic ties, and according an importance, paradoxically connected to "founding," to the eradication of reasons to suffer, correlative of the reasons to exist: "You have been seen, maker of the house; you will not rebuild again. Your framing is all broken, your ridgepole destroyed. The mind set on detachment from created things has attained extinction of craving" (Dhammapada).11 Also, the benevolent challenge to the Western mentality issued by the first masters arriving from Buddhist countries was to institute this deconstruction of the ego at the heart of their work of building, vowing to rest midway between nihilist temptations (what good is it to build anything?) and eternalist ones: "The whole samsaric structure, samsara and its seductions, is based on making something eternal out of something impermanent and transitory," Trungpa reminds us,[12] attentive to protecting from that illusory alchemy, the transmission, which remains authentic from its renunciation of the attempt to "achieve spirituality."[13] Indeed, what temptation could be stronger than that of canceling out the erosion to which one knows everything is condemned through constructions—architectural or mental?

This event, the establishment of a vajra master in the United States, was unprecedented in Western and Tibetan history, and the surprise effect has blurred with time. Despite everything, however, it remains fresh for us, as much because of the unalterable and timeless power of the transcribed and published teachings as because of an effect of *putting things in perspective*, an effect created, precisely, by the distance of this unexpected event in time. Thirty-five years is very little, but it is nonetheless considerable, of course in regard to the preservation of the heritage itself, which the rich biography of Chögyam Trungpa written by Fabrice Midal[14] perfectly accounts for; and greater still is the perceivable distance here and now between contemporary neo-Buddhism, which has become more accommodating of Western weaknesses, and the abrasive message of the Vidyadhara. This established fact, of the distance between neo-Buddhism and Chögyam Trungpa's teaching, would call for teachings from other eminent masters as well. It seems to us now to have been a fortunate era, in any case, when American materialism was at once so massive and so naive that it offered matter that was easier to transmute than the more subtle "spiritual materialism," which has infiltrated the current spreading of dharma in the West at every turn, in the most ostentatious cultural forms that it has taken for its own, at the very least. Our retroactive sense of surprise is indeed great when we notice that Trungpa almost never speaks of Buddhism in terms of the science of mind, of an atheistic, rational religion, of the art of happiness, and even less of a palliative therapy. Would he have not taught the true, the pure, the authentic dharma? The comparison deserves to be made even more between the teachings of yesterday and certain discourses today, since it is in the texts alone that we can find the presence and power of a vajra master. If he in any way distorted the transmission, we must now look in his texts for traces of possible omissions, and not in the atypical, extravagant, or aberrant behavior that could have been his throughout his life. One will then be more free to ask oneself if the progressive readability acquired by a "Westernized" Buddhism in the European culture, if the troubling flexibility of certain of its canonical positions, and the current volatility of its humanitarian discourse, do not harbor at least a few of these root distortions pointed out by Trungpa, already thirty-five years ago, under the name of spiritual materialism.

Finding the Gap

The formula still has something shocking about it, even today: don't the two terms—*finding* and *gap*—seem to set themselves in opposition to each other to the point of being mutually exclusive? More than a paradox inviting an overinvestment of logical activity, it is rather a cleansing oxymoron, the verbal equivalent of a diamond cutter (*vajracchedika*) coming near the better to cut, cutting the better to transmute. In this type of materialism—unknown, it goes without saying, among Western philosophers—Trungpa claims to recognize a "rationalization of the spiritual path."[15] It is therefore not rationalism that is in itself the target, to the degree to which it operates without contaminating the spiritual path. But Trungpa very quickly took into account that this theoretical independence from "orders," to speak as Pascal did, was in the West a conceptual view. In practice, rationalism wants to rationalize everything, including, and above all, the spiritual path; and spiritualism—"the golden chain of spirituality" that Trungpa often makes fun of—from its point of view seeks to spiritualize everything in order to make the world into that blessed land of gods from which suffering and death would disappear. One could therefore logically anticipate the time when, after centuries of conflict and rivalry—materialism or spiritualism?—these two major components of the Western mind, tired of competing without direct benefit for their respective ambitions, end by producing this perverse hybrid, "spiritual materialism," in which Trungpa claims to expose the "distorted, ego-centered version of spirituality."[16] There was only one step left to make, consisting of showing that, if rationalism could avail itself of a non-egocentric transparency—that of an "I" that had become transcendental—the process of rationalization, which is always at advantage in the game of ego, is able to "convert everything to its own use, even spirituality."[17]

To transmit the dharma to Westerners already contaminated by "spiritual materialism," infinitely more harmful than ordinary materialism, one would understand that one should not start off by picking the wrong target, as does Western so-called "spirituality," compared by Trungpa both to the realm of gods (devas) in Tibetan Buddhism and to a Hollywood western, "where the 'baddies' are going to get smashed."[18] Such discernment with respect to the nature of the real situation that he had to confront and transform is evidence of the pedagogical genius of Trungpa, whose spiritual authority was strong enough to impose on Americans a form of logic and of tantric therapy based on an alchemical inspiration, which had long been forgotten by Westerners: "It is necessary to use the existing material, what is already there," he indeed advocated, adding: "The general pattern of American karma as well as of the American approach to spirituality is another element that causes us to emphasize our confusion rather than purely making promises. Making promises tends to encourage spiritual materialism, which is an involvement with wanting to be saved rather than an understanding of what there is to be saved from."[19] Humorously naming such confusion the "lubrication of samsara," Trungpa equally displayed his rhetorical dexterity, making up neologisms for his students, false reasoning capable of drawing their neuroses out of hiding, all while immersing them from the beginning in the "current" of the teachings, reinvigorated by these verbal finds, which are without equivalent in traditional Tibetan culture, more conventional in this regard than the Zen tradition.

There is indeed no point in intellectually exposing ego's intrigues. Better to catch it in the act, red-handed, so to speak, causing one to visualize—more than understand rationally—its crudest maneuvers, its grandiloquent pantomimes, its ridiculous or pathetic subterfuges, all aimed at legitimizing and comforting its illusory "lordship": whether that of form (the neurotic quest for security and comfort), speech (the use of intellect in relating to our world), or mind (affirmation of the awareness of self). Totally innovative with regard to the Western and even Buddhist philosophical traditions, the pages Trungpa devoted to these three Lords of Materialism in Cutting Through Spiritual Materialism (1971) are reinforced and illustrated in most of his other teachings by comic sequences that make Westerners see—as if outside, on a giant screen—what comic or catastrophic inflation (promoted as culture!) the game of ego is capable of, whether on the individual or collective level. In more than one way, the teaching of Trungpa sometimes seems to borrow from commedia dell'-arte or the satiric and comic American cinema of the fifties, showing the misadventures of a lost hero—one of the Marx Brothers, for example—in a supermarket where he would only find poisoned food, magnificently wrapped; because this certainly concerns "supermarket mentality," although in this case applied to spirituality. Certainly Trungpa was an adept instructor in the material, although one cannot really speak of "method," as one inevitably does in the West, except in the proper sense of the word—that which shows, which opens the way. With Trungpa, the "me-thodic" demystification can never be dissociated from the preparation and ingestion of the antidote: to show humans in general, and particularly Westerners, the tragicomic spectacle of their confusion until, disheart-ened, they find the strength not to create a new sun but to clear away their own clouds. Trungpa had certainly made a subtle and explosive cocktail in this regard, between the "skillful means" (upaya) of the Tibetan Buddhist tradition and the sense of theatrical artifice with which the West some-times managed, in the best cases, to cut through the tragicomic illusion. In this respect there is often Shakespeare in Chögyam Trungpa.

If the first virtue of the teachings of Buddha is to be "refreshing" inso-far as they extinguish the fire of the passions, then Trungpa's teachings could well be freshness itself: "Thus the tantric approach to the world means refreshing our contact, reopening ourselves constantly so that we are able to perceive our cosmos properly and throughly."[20] It is a freshness nevertheless inhabited by a fire that burns even more brightly than that of the passions, since it is capable of transmuting any state of confusion into the purest gold: "Everything is workable," he notes laconically.[21] Why not, therefore, the extraordinary Western confusion, a veritable gold mine for a vajra master of the spiritual stature of Trungpa? When faced with Westerners so fundamentally frivolous or naive in spite of or because of their intellectual orientation, when they are not frankly cynical, it was in-deed useful to restore a lost sense of *dignity*—"the basic elegance of en-lightenment, as the Buddha exemplified"[22]—and to do this by means that, in order to be effective, no longer conceded anything to the general solemnity that Western devotees associated with religious fervor. Under-standing that in the West, more than before, transmission is also a matter of "style"—existential, rhetorical, and pedagogical—Trungpa worked to find his, adapted to the exceptional circumstances in which it was given to him to teach: "a mix of humor, intimidation, and a sharp precision that seeks to transmit the nature of space and egolessness,"[23] notes Fabrice Midal. Fully aware of the virtuosity with which Westerners intellectualize their experiences, Trungpa nevertheless put less emphasis on the discovery of the "nature of mind" through meditation, as masters today often do, than on *giving space*, making the meditator the non-egocentric center of an ever-changing mandala. To intellectualize that space—the "texture" of which is shunyata—is truly to risk falling into a hell that Vimalakirti and Nagarjuna were already on guard against.

Would the West be so rapidly improved—thanks to the Buddhist teachings?—that one would hardly recognize, in the panorama erected today by most masters, the infinitely more highly contrasted picture painted not even forty years ago by Trungpa? Would some of them be so well acclimated, acculturated, so to speak, to a situation of which Trungpa—like an extraterrestrial freshly landed on this planet—discovered the burlesque, often exasperating, usually suicidal character? This picture gains both freshness and flavor if, renouncing the discovery, in each brushstroke, of the harshness of a verdict ("the Buddhist position suspends judgment"), one recognizes the glance, necessarily incredulous and abrasive, of a compassionate bodhisattva. For an authentic transmission to take place, it was not enough to drive the egotistic games of spiritual materialism out of hiding without looking to dissolve, through finer strokes, the multiple facets of a process of solidification that blocked any transformation. These are the first glimpses of Western failings that Trungpa worked to bring to light; but they are faults so profoundly anchored in the modern mentality that they are not susceptible to any amendment, any correction that does not also sooner or later involve a real "turning on the crucial point," as the Zen masters say of satori. The Vidyadhara never stopped repeating to his audience: "Disappointment is the best chariot to use on the path of dharma."[24]

And the extraordinary technology that Westerners are so proud of? Trungpa sees it as accompanied by an "enormous arrogance" and denies it the power of being a "saving grace," thus demystifying the dreams he had as a young Tibetan monk: "With such wisdom in the gadgetry world, I thought that the makers of the gadgets must have a similar personal discipline."[25] The young barbarian coming from his faraway country wasted no time in discovering that the technological sophistication is a vast "warning system," feeding fear instead of eradicating it. There was no set language for saying out loud that, of all these gadgets, the invention of television "is one of the worst crimes ever committed," in that watching it all the time deflects from apprehending things "as they are." What would he have thought of the increasingly patent conjuring of the real with the dizzying thrust of the virtual? For technology does not content itself with diverting the real, which it pretends to master, indirectly favoring avoidance through dreams. From this fact, technology induces behaviors marked by the seal of dilettantism, a baroque mixture of artistic or intellectual pretension and of superficiality with respect to the essential: "Spiritual materialism develops because we are willing to take a chance on all kinds of trips, like holding a grain of sand in our hand and meditating on that for three months, or fasting for ten months. We fall for all sorts of promises."[26] One person collects metaphysical experiences, or those that seem to be so, another abhishekas (initiations) like so many spiritual provisions "out of a need for security."[27] How would Trungpa view the Buddhist high masses where initiations are generously distributed to an unprepared public, he who already considered this possible accumulation "a serious problem," indirectly holding the master responsible for these "nouveaux-riches" of spirituality? In the case of an initiation for which one is insufficiently prepared, no doubt one can receive it as a simple blessing, always beneficial when it is given by an authentic master. But can these same masters, speaking hereafter to thousands of the faithful in a culture where Buddhism is not ancestrally rooted, dissuade them from "capitalizing" on the supposed benefits of their devotion? Without being able to speculate on what Trungpa would have done if he were to teach at the beginning of the twenty-first century—in Europe, where spiritual materialism has taken forms even more sophisticated than in America in the seventies—one can at least affirm that, in his time, he only remodeled the forms of transmission because he never compromised it at root: "The approach presented here is a classical Buddhist one—not in a formal sense, but in the sense of presenting the heart of the Buddhist approach to spirituality . . . dharma is applicable to every age."[28] Dharma is applicable to the age and to the context, which is to say to the karmic situation and to the mentality of those who prepare to receive the teachings.

A Mirror Held Up to the West

An optimal situation in this sense, that American karma, sufficiently sunk in materialism, ordinary and spiritual, sufficiently changed to confusion and paranoia so that an explosion was being prepared there, served up as a prelude to a possible transmutation: "Something is trying to come out of American karma. It's dying to burst, dying to blast." [29] Trungpa therefore also gave his American students a glimpse—as the Western alchemists had done earlier—of the extremely close proximity of poison and remedy, for the remedy could only be effectively prepared from the poison specific to each person: "Buddhism wouldn't be here on this continent if there wasn't enough pain. Your pain has brought fantastic energy. That's why I'm here. That's why Buddhism, buddhadharma, is here. That's why tantra is here." [30] For the master, then, everything is a question of discernment and judgment since he must first become the mirror in which the Western world will become aware of its fake and adulterated character; then he must know how to dissipate these reflections at the right time so that they do not become the comforting trap of Westerners in their quest for an identity as polymorphous as their activities, as one sees for example in the protagonist of Hermann Hesse's *Steppenwolf*, emblematic figure of an aborted depersonalization. Aware that polemic and consensus are the two extreme attitudes that Westerners constantly oscillate between, Trungpa chose to show without demonstrating or judging, to further excavate the gap between extreme views, and to dissolve deceptive proximities, until *contact* with the neurotic situation itself became possible again: "We have to use the existing material, which is ego's hangups and credentials and deceptions, as a starting point." [31] Pragmatic but inspired, this pedagogic and initiatory realism consists at first of "finding a stepping-stone," as Trungpa said many times. In the mirror held up by the master, Westerners will therefore discover their right-thinking militancy: that of the opponents of the Vietnam War, for example, capable of reacting against that scourge but not of "transforming all mishaps into the path of bodhi"; [32] their pointed sense of legalism, soon ridiculed by the master: "Hiring a lawyer to attain enlightenment is not done. It is not possible. Buddha did not have a lawyer himself"; [33] their "exhibitionistic impartiality" and their frantic rights-of-man-ism behind which the "bureaucracy of ego" reserves for itself the privilege of exercising its rights more than anybody else; their taste for machinations and dramatics, their prohibiting entry on equal footing in the dance of life, and, to crown everything, their visceral intellectualism feeding the water-wheel of spiritual materialism through its propensity to abstract and conceptualize: "Openness could be appropriated as a philosophical concept as well, but the philosophy need not necessarily be fixed."[34]

Trungpa's attitude toward Western philosophy, which he studied with great interest while at Oxford, was complex—"The reading of Plato and other Western philosophers became fascinating"[35]—although one does not know whether he owed, at least through this study, a different relationship to the language from what had been taught him in Tibet, where monks sometimes used rhetoric and dialectic during their famous debates, but within very well defined logical and metaphysical contexts. As practiced in the West, especially under the Anglo-Saxon and "analytic" form, philosophy certainly represents the danger that the Buddhist teachings lead one to guard against: "The point is not to philosophize," Trungpa repeats a number of times, inciting his students to drop all "logical games."[36] But does whatever can be recommended in the name of a fundamental letting go authorize one to challenge the operational validity of the logical processes of thought? Does one run the risk of confining oneself to a dualism incompatible with the middle way of Buddhism? As much from personal temperament as from the philosophical education he received in the West—which he recognized as having its own dignity—Trungpa seemed to have looked there too for *a way of transformation* and not one of rejection or compromise, even if it was unclear what kind of dialogue between East and West there could be from this point of view: "The thing that we have is that our philosophers and yogis are at war. . . . So what we are trying to do is establish some link between the two, so that the approaches of both philosophers and yogis could both be regarded as valid."[37] Valid from which point of view? That of Buddhist tolerance, refusing to exclude anything? Or that of inseparability, already subtler, in whose name the relative and the ultimate state the same reality, on different levels? The relative truth of philosophical reasoning and the ultimate truth of yogic practice would in this case be called to respect each other, without Trungpa's specifying which common language would allow them to have a dialogue. To call a ceasefire is one thing, but to provide a linguistic foundation for peace is something else! If it is clear that Trungpa challenges in philosophical conceptualization the very mechanism of imputation (subjects/predicates and subjects/objects) according to which Western logic indeed functions, reinforcing in this egoic appropriation; if, faithful in this to the teachings of the Buddha, he had every reason to distrust sterile metaphysical speculations that at best lead to irreducible antinomies, without therapeutic effect, then the margin of maneuver therefore would remain narrow, and one would be led to conclude this fictitious dialogue between yogis and philosophers from a lack of evidence, except that Trungpa had in his teachings related the possible coexistence, traditional in Buddhism, between intellectual method and intuitive method; and except that this "back and forth between being wise and being knowledgeable"[38] had proved that the alchemical practice of *solve et coagula* at the heart of speech makes this dance between the relative and the ultimate spiritually operative.

If the teachings of the vajrayana undertake to dissolve egoic solidifications and recoagulate the material thus purified in an adamantine "body," one does not see why language could not also be the laboratory where such a practice is done, in its meditative essence, thanks to which "thought processes also become, in some sense, real, because at this point there is no longer any reason to condemn thoughts or try to mold them into a different pattern. It is just a spontaneous thinking of thoughts."[39] Thus giving verbal transmission a new impulse, Trungpa also showed indirectly that the real obstacle for Westerners lies less in the rhetorical diversity of their discourse than in imputing these modalities to an ego-centered "subject," and in the attachment of ego to its own statements or to those it happens to appropriate in the name of culture. Therefore, the concern here is not only the adaptation of these teachings for a Western public, even if such adjustment plays an integral part in traditional transmission and its ethics. The open way of Trungpa is at once both much more ambitious and more rigorous in its own logic—that of tantric vajrayana—in that it refuses to exclude language from a global process of transformation and an energetic constellation figured by the "mandala principle": "That's a question of how much you are willing to give in as opposed to wanting to learn something out of this. When you want to learn something out of it, that is very fishy. You have an ulterior motive of wanting to do something with your learning that automatically puts the whole thing off balance. If you are willing to just give in without learning, if you are willing to become rather than learn, that clears the air entirely."[40] So it is not an accident if this meditation on the need to restore a reciprocal respect between yogins and philosophers takes place in the teachings devoted to the mandala; nor is it the considerable progress achieved in a matter of decades with respect to translating the original texts; nor the uncontested authority of the great masters in the order of the traditional transmission, and less still the proliferation of current discourse on the "acculturation" of Buddhism in the West, all from this more or less hybrid point of view, which look as though they would take over the innovative impulse—but in spirit entirely traditional—given in this regard by Trungpa.

Speaking of spiritual materialism as excessive rationalization and "powerful subverter" of spirituality, Trungpa did not therefore condemn all forms of rationality as such, which, through its detail-oriented and operating efficiency, can contribute on the relative level to total intelligence and the outcome of a situation. On the other hand, one would search his teachings in vain for either favorable or unfavorable positions on contemporary scientific disciplines and one would search there with no more success for the premises of current discourse concerning the "bridges" between dharma and sciences, cognitive sciences in particular.[41] Would he have failed in his vocation of pioneer in this context, neglecting to become interested in what would become a "must" in subsequent Western discourse? It is true that recognizing the direct experience of "reality" as having priority over abstract theorizing, as the Buddha proposed, is already in itself a response that seems to allow the Buddhist tradition and the "scientific" modern approach to come together and have a dialogue, each animated by a comparable concern for experimentation rather than speculation. But experiment with what, and to what end and in what way? The question is worth posing all the more since clarity of the vajra vision, dignity before situations "as they are," and acknowledging the sacredness of the phenomenal world tend to meet in the tantric teachings of Trungpa. Is this to say that the West, set on the scientific but having forgotten its esoteric traditions—in particular alchemy—is to rediscover through the vajrayana an art of transmutation held in suspicion if not in contempt since the Enlightenment?

Such a rediscovery, if it were accepted, would give some difficulty to the proponents of "rational religion" and the "science of mind" of which one commonly speaks these days as being the true nature of a Buddhism resolutely, presciently positivist and atheist. Is it because he sensed the dangers of such a formulation that Trungpa did not emphasize the "transcultural" character of the practice of meditation, as is now commonly done? The indeed spontaneous decompartmentalization brought about by letting go in meditation could leave always-busy Westerners to expect Buddhism to equally spontaneously reconcile cultures, social milieus, individuals . . . whereas taking into account these possible tensions and differences constitutes the "prima materia" from which tantric alchemy gets its workability.

The Texture of the Real

It is true that Trungpa speaks very rarely about Buddhism in terms of "religion," generally reserving that name for theism, whose degeneration he thinks he can see, affirming the superiority of vajra clarity over "any other approach to spirituality, even within the Buddhist tradition."[42] Could he consequently not clearly distinguish between theism and nontheism, earlier brought together by others in the name of a supposedly transcendental unity of religions or out of a genuine ecumenism? And if certain of his statements around theism and God ("old man with a beard") are sometimes caricatures, one will come away, most importantly, with the following formula, worthy of Meister Eckhart: "The truth is free of God,"[43] a truth the discovery of which rebuilds neither faith, in the theistic sense of the word, nor the scientific character of meditation practice, as one frequently hears these days: "The truth only comes from the experience of reality, the absence of God, from personal experience, how we relate with reality."[44] Far from subordinating the real to the true—as philosophy in the West does—Trungpa sees in what he calls "truth" the nonintellectual result of this rediscovered contact with reality: "I am using 'scientific knowledge' in the sense of the most accurate knowledge on how to react to situations. . . . This is continuously scientific in the sense that it is continuously in accordance with the nature of the elements."[45] However continuous it might be—since it is inseparable from daily life and involvement on the path—this approach does not therefore have much to do with putting in place an experimental protocol, controlled by an objective observer looking for results.

In such conditions, to experiment—which is another way of saying "have the experience of life as it is"—cannot take on the meaning accorded to it by modern experimental sciences, for which only that which is observable is "real" and only that which has been confirmed by logical reasoning is "true." When Trungpa then is amazed that American astronauts "can really communicate with this type of space"—cosmic, he means—it is to emphasize that such an acclimatization, sometimes followed for them by a real spiritual transformation, reveals the existence of a potential, human more than religious; of a native affinity of buddha nature, present in each human being, with a type of space introduced by the practice of meditation.[46] The vastness of such a quality of space, beyond geometry, and a rediscovered contact with reality are then in this respect the two "scientific" components of the meditative experience according to Trungpa, insisting in this statement on the phenomenological and cosmic dimension of mahamudra (the "great symbol"): "The whole world is symbol—not symbol in the sense of a sign representing something other than itself, but symbol in the sense of the highlights of the vivid qualities of things as they are."[47] Thus the notion of "texture" often used by the Vidyadhara allows one to posit the existence in each situation of one such impalpable "fabric," of an informal weave, whose nonsubstantial density makes manifest the experience of nonduality and emptiness, in the form of luminosity.

Recurring expressions in these teachings that are clear at first glance—such as "enter into contact with situations" or "work with life situations"—can, on closer inspection, suggest a proximity of the Buddhist approach to the "return to things themselves" advocated by the phenomenology of Husserl and then Heidegger. It is indeed a relevant comparison, to the degree in which Western phenomenology has taken up the task of breaking with a "representative" knowledge so as to better grasp the spontaneous mode of manifestation of phenomena, for which the possible essence no longer depends on a substratum, a substantial background, as was the case in classical metaphysics. Reverting spontaneously to such apparently simplistic formulations, Trungpa could even seem to be "beating a dead horse," as is commonly said, or "breaking down an open door," as the French expression would have it, if this popular expression did not indeed point in the direction of the "situation" par excellence of which the master favors the denouement, close to the famous "gateless gate"[48] of the Zen tradition: open, the gate is indeed very big, then and always, even if someone continues to try to break it down by uselessly bumping against his mental projections, obstructing the access to "reality," which is understood as the absence of the existence as such of phenomena and, at the same time, a potential mandala with which to work. The contribution of Trungpa was here again to break the ideal image that Westerners had of mandala—a kind of celestial Asiatic Jerusalem!—in order to reconstitute the formidable potential of an "orderly chaos."

That which he called, when necessary, a strictly scientific approach,[49] worthy of being followed, does not have very much to do with an experimental objectification of the real, since the "letting be" accorded phenomena and situations through a free and penetrating vision (shamatha-vipashyana) allows one to enter into "friendship" with the world and with oneself, and coincides with the discovery of a certain brilliance specific to the sacred: "Obviousness becomes sacred from the point of view of vajrayana. It is not that things are sacred because they are beyond our imagination, but because they are so obvious."[50] Anyone who rereads the teachings of Trungpa today can only be struck by his insistence on the decisive importance of this rediscovered contact, of this connection to reality, indefinitely postponed by mental twitchings and projections, always eager to make new links, to assure itself of getting a new hold on the world. So this entering into relationship is not an ordinary relationship, a link, since it unbinds. Incomprehensible from the point of view of dualistic logic—that of Logos, which by nature binds—such a relationship of unbinding, therefore liberating, nevertheless only allows one to glimpse the permanent play of relative and absolute in each situation: "If confusion exists, then enlightenment exists." Nevertheless there is no causal link between one and the other, nor is there a purely logical deduction, but rather there is a tantric vision of the Buddhist dependent co-origination (pratityasamutpada), a vision that from all wood makes fire, and from all fire lucidity and vajra clarity: "The tantric tradition speaks of being here. It speaks of transmutation and the analogy of alchemistic practice is used a great deal. For example, the existence of lead is not rejected but lead is transmuted into gold."[51]

How many Westerners today are ready to replace alchemy among the sciences—because that is what this is about!—and accept that Buddhism could be in this regard a "science of mind"? One imagines that it would be more comforting to place some electrodes on the body of meditators, and to record harmonious graphs attesting to which of the modifications of consciousness, little by little freed from "mental states," has become the field of inquiry. Whether or not Western science could prove the efficacy of meditation techniques, and then, indirectly, could guarantee the validity of the dharma, does not seem to have greatly interested Trungpa, who was also quite definite about the possible psychologizing of Buddhism: "Meditation is not therapeutic practice at all. We seem to have a problem in this country, with the sense that meditation is included with psychotherapy or physiotherapy or whatever. A lot of Buddhists feel proud because meditation is accepted as part of the therapeutic system, a landmark of the Western world. But I think that pride is simple-minded pride. Buddhism should transcend the therapeutic practice of meditation. Relating with gurus is quite different from going to your psychiatrist."[52] "Ceremonies of unmasking 'me'" was the way Trungpa characterized all the supposedly therapeutic practices by which Westerners, thinking that they are coming to the end of their existential suffering, believe that they are excused from "taking refuge" in the Buddhist sense of the term.

Trungpa never stopped pointing out the fundamentally neurotic character of the ego-centered attitude and the confused quagmire in which most human beings flounder: "The realization of the confusion is the teaching."[53] Trungpa possesses the secret of this elliptical formula, pointing out the latent process of transmutation while at the same time masking it: What actually happens to cause meditation, supported by the relationship to the teacher, to indeed serve a "therapeutic" function, in the sense in which Buddha taught? And what happens to incline the "rotting manure of neurosis"[54] to free the dharmakaya of stains that had hidden the uncreated luminosity? Nothing, actually, since the temporal unfolding of such an operation—undeniable on the relative level—collapses like a house of cards from contact with the ultimate; moreover, buddha nature is not acquired progressively, since it has always been there. To take into account a possible transmutation of neurotic lead into the purest gold of buddhahood therefore points to the most skillful of means, the final mirage necessary for encouraging the practitioner to enter where he would not go if he felt trapped forever in time—but this particular skillful means has no more basis, however, than ego, which has been emptied little by little of all substantiality through meditation. Doubtless it carries the risk—assumed by the holder of crazy wisdom—of revealing to practitioners that "the intensity of the confusion itself demands its own destruction."[55] Nevertheless, such is the path of tantric self-healing; a homeopathy-inspired path (destroy confusion with confusion!), finding in alchemy its most accurate reference, even if the notion of transmutation only clothes with dignity the process—in this sense "therapeutic"—of confusion's self-correction, involving the spontaneous dissolution of coagulations or dissolutions that are neurotic because they are ego-based: "Transmutation takes place with the understanding of shunyata and then the sudden discovery of energy."[56]

To want to use Buddhist practice to cure a particular neurosis generally tied to childhood conflicts therefore not only risks being unworkable on a relative level, but also risks accumulating an additional mental opacity that obscures the clear vision of the ultimate. Insisting on the necessity of "healing our personal, elementary connection with the phenomenal world,"[57] Trungpa did not give carte blanche to a palliative psychotherapy derived from Buddhism. Instead, he invited his students to dare to experience a staggering compassionate openness to which, he said, no "purely logical, professional, or scientific reasoning" can lead one;[58] demonstrating the path of a new kind of sacredness—because it was neither religious nor profane—that Westerners must protect from assimilating into a vague mysticism developed to compensate for their lack in religious matters: "The tantric approach is not mystical experience alone, but it is concerned with how we can perceive reality in a simple and direct way."[59] To learn to recognize in all circumstances, and in the "dry and brilliant weave of the phenomenal world," the spark of prajna (transcendental wisdom) thus coincides with the discovery of a sacredness that is disconcerting at first glance. Aren't Westerners accustomed to treating the sacred and the profane as opposites, and to infer the sacredness of being or things from their subordination to a creator principle or deity?

The art of happiness presented as a new spiritual idea, whether supported or not by scientific knowledge, but directly assimilated into the "great bliss" (mahasukha) of enlightenment, was not really Chögyam Trungpa's cup of tea. He warned his students that such research could even constitute a powerful obstacle on the path: "Any pursuit of this life's happiness, joy, fame, or wisdom, or the hope of attaining some state of glorious liberation in the life hereafter, could be regarded as a problem."[60] Thus unmasking in advance all the processes of subtle "capitalization" by which ego pursues a feigned wisdom, Trungpa remained faithful to the Buddhist tradition and already pointed a finger at this new avatar of spiritual materialism that Buddhism "for the West" could become, filling in the gaps that are too cruel, euphemizing the necessary sudden awareness of a radical hopelessness, and planning the mental and cultural space in such a way that ego and non-ego can clandestinely cohabit, each simply relieved of their most exorbitant pretensions. In the era of products relieved of their undigested surplus, it is true that one could expect that Buddhism too could have been rendered assimilable by those Westerners who would reject its demands, at least as unyielding as those of the monotheistic traditions: "So the nontheistic tradition is much harsher than the theistic tradition. It is very skeptical, unyielding, and somewhat outrageous."[61]

As well, the regret that Trungpa sometimes expressed over having prematurely transmitted the teachings of crazy wisdom to immature Americans would perhaps have been doubled by another observation, undoubtedly not for a Tibetan teacher to make: that the recurrent drama of the West may not reside in its possible immaturity, which can always be educated, but in a certain spiritual frivolity sufficiently anchored in the minds, the hearts, and the mores to lead it to rapidly intellectualizing, aestheticizing, or gadgetizing the essential: thus changing its potential gold into lead, as the poet René Daumal had already observed at the beginning of the twentieth century.[62] As for the essential, it is certainly tantric vajrayana—Trungpa was not mistaken on this point—that is susceptible to becoming one day the most appropriate "remedy" for the cultural and karmic situation of the West, thus, by way of a detour to the Buddhist East, indirectly renewing its own operative tradition. Already maintaining its exceptional impact in the West from its "pioneer" position, the adamantine work of Chögyam Trungpa could very well be called upon soon to play a role as ultimate recourse in the face of certain tendencies of contemporary neo-Buddhism.

NOTES

1. On this subject, see the testimony of his wife, Diana J. Mukpo, "Here Comes Chögyam," *Shambhala Sun*, November 2003, pp. 56–94.

2. *Crazy Wisdom*.

3. Heinrich Zimmer, "Buddha," *Mesures*, no. 2 (April 1935), p. 140.

4. *The Myth of Freedom*, in *The Collected Works of Chögyam Trungpa*, vol. 3, p. 256.

5. *Journey without Goal*, p. 43.

6. *Orderly Chaos*, p. 161.

7. *Journey without Goal*, p. 135.

8. Ibid., p. 47

9. *The Heart of the Buddha*, in *Collected Works*, vol. 3, p. 377.

10. André Malraux, *The Temptation of the West*, trans. Robert Hollander (New York: Vintage, 1961), p. 59.

11. *Dhammapada*, chap. 11, "Old Age," verse 9, trans. Thomas Cleary, in *Classics of Buddhism and Zen: The Collected Translations of Thomas Cleary*, vol. 5 (Boston: Shambhala Publications, 2002), p. 37.

12. *Orderly Chaos*, p. 40.

13. *Cutting Through Spiritual Materialism*, in *Collected Works*, vol. 3, p. 56.

14. Fabrice Midal, *Trungpa* (Paris: Seuil, 2002). English edition: *Chögyam Trungpa: His Life and Vision* (Boston: Shambhala Publications, 2004).

15. *Cutting Through Spiritual Materialism*, in *Collected Works*, vol. 3, p. 15.

16. Ibid., p. 7.

17. Ibid., p. 10.

18. Ibid., p. 86.

19. *Orderly Chaos*, p. 47.

20. *The Heart of the Buddha*, in *Collected Works*, vol. 3, p. 369.

21. *The Myth of Freedom*, in *Collected Works*, vol. 3, p. 234.

22. *Great Eastern Sun*, p. 131.

23. Midal, *Chögyam Trungpa: His Life and Vision*, p. 269.

24. *Cutting Through Spiritual Materialism*, in *Collected Works*, vol. 3, p. 24.

25. *Great Eastern Sun*, p. 73.

26. *Orderly Chaos*, pp. 28–29.

27. *Journey without Goal*, p. 89.

28. *Cutting Through Spiritual Materialism*, in *Collected Works*, vol. 3, pp. 7, 18.

29. *Illusion's Game*, p. 51.

30. *The Lion's Roar*, in *Collected Works*, vol. 4, p. 213.

31. *The Myth of Freedom*, in *Collected Works*, vol. 3, p. 215.

32. *Training the Mind and Cultivating Loving-Kindness*, p. 72.

33. Ibid., pp. 91–92.

34. *The Myth of Freedom*, in *Collected Works*, vol. 3, p. 248.

35. *Born in Tibet*, in *Collected Works*, vol. 1, p. 262.

36. *Orderly Chaos*, pp. 20, 81.

37. Ibid., p. 13.

38. *The Heart of the Buddha*, in *Collected Works*, vol. 3, p. 322.

39. *The Dawn of Tantra*, in *Collected Works*, vol. 4, p. 367.

40. *Orderly Chaos*, pp. 36–37.

41. See, for example, B. Alan Wallace, *Buddhism and Science* (New York: Columbia University Press, 2003), and Jeremy Hayward and Francisco Varela, *Gentle Bridges: Conversations with the Dalai Lama on the Sciences of Mind* (Boston: Shambhala Publications, 2001).

42. *Journey without Goal*, p. 29.

43. *Crazy Wisdom*, p. 84.

44. *Glimpses of Space*, p. 58.

45. *Crazy Wisdom*, p. 46.

46. *Glimpses of Space*, p. 44.

47. *The Myth of Freedom*, in *Collected Works*, vol. 3, p. 289.

48. *The Gateless Barrier: The Wu-Men Kuan*, trans. Robert Aitken (San Francisco: North Point Press, 1991).

49. *Orderly Chaos*, p. 4: "We have to approach this scientifically."

50. *Illusion's Game*, p. 133.

51. *Cutting Through Spiritual Materialism*, in *Collected Works*, vol. 3, pp. 162–163.

52. *Glimpses of Shunyata*, p. 157.

53. *Crazy Wisdom*, p. 69.

54. *The Myth of Freedom*, in *Collected Works*, vol. 3, p. 273.

55. *Crazy Wisdom*, p. 24.

56. *Cutting Through Spiritual Materialism*, in *Collected Works*, vol. 3, p. 173.

57. *Shambhala: The Sacred Path of the Warrior*, p. 132.

58. *Training the Mind*, p. 18.

59. *Journey without Goal*, p. 101.

60. *Training the Mind*, p. 177.

61. *Journey without Goal*, p. 43.

62. René Daumal, *L'évidence absurde* (Paris: Gallimard, 1972), p. 175: "Les mains occidentales changent l'or en plomb" (Western hands change gold into lead).

Exposing Ego's Game

Spiritual Materialism

Sherab Chödzin Kohn

IN HIS EARLY TEACHING in the United States, Chögyam Trungpa Rinpoche introduced the notion of spiritual materialism, "a distorted, ego-centered version of spirituality" that is a major obstacle to spiritual practice. He told us, "We can deceive ourselves into thinking we are developing spiritually, when instead we are strengthening our egocentricity through spiritual techniques."[1] Spiritual materialism became one of the main themes in his talks and his interactions with students. He made it clear that this phenomenon was very widespread, nearly all-pervasive, and that it had to be rooted out for genuine spirituality to proceed.

Spiritual materialism can be defined intellectually. We could simply say that it means relating to spiritual teachings and teachers in a goal-oriented fashion. It is also possible, as Trungpa Rinpoche did, to point to many examples of it. However, spiritual materialism is such a deep-seated attitude that it is very difficult for practitioners to truly see and understand it in themselves, even after it has been explained and pointed out to them repeatedly and they have glimpsed it many times. It is so much a part of people's overall approach to life, so widely taken for granted, that it remains an unperceived but constant accompaniment to their spiritual practice.

Spiritual materialism is a wriggling shape-shifter. Unmask it in one form and it quickly takes another. Many practitioners familiar with Trungpa Rinpoche's teachings on this subject may associate it with the rampant spiritual supermarket of the 1970s, which provided Rinpoche with many colorful examples. Thus they may think of it as outdated subject matter, belonging to a bygone day. Unfortunately, spiritual materialism is as insidiously pervasive today as it has ever been—among Westerners, Easterners, even Tibetans. Thus Trungpa Rinpoche's teachings on spiritual materialism, which have rarely been understood in their profundity, remain precious and timely.

In order to understand the inner workings of spiritual materialism, it is necessary to have a sense of the basic dualistic split, the projection of self and other on which the illusion of ego is based. One must also have an inkling of emptiness (shunyata). These are central teachings of the buddhadharma.

Ego exists only as the precarious smoke-and-mirrors game of the basic split: it takes the form of an internal watcher captivated by something that is supposed to be happening. If watcher loses interest in this game, ego dies—which happens all the time. This reality resembles that of a soap opera on TV. The drama might be juicy and intriguing, but suppose the broadcast should momentarily fail. The screen goes blank. The show is gone. The emptiness behind the program has shone through. For a moment, you have fallen into space, which is terrifying from ego's point of view. Ego cannot manipulate this basic truth of emptiness. Any gap in its program is an absolute gap, so ego has to keep the program going in your head constantly in order to keep a gap from happening. The little ego puppet(s) is in a constant state of panic. It tries anything to keep control of the watcher. It shouts, it cries, it fights, it pleads, or merely tries to parade the sad and pathetic quality of its predicament. When the show wears thin, ego's illusion collapses.

Ego is like a fish flopping on dry land. There may be no water anywhere nearby, but from ego's point of view this does not really matter. All that matters is the flopping, which continues to fascinate the watcher. In the flopping, the watcher sees heroism, contemptible inadequacy, grounds for hope, despair, sin, redemption, and so forth.

So when presented with the spiritual path, ego exploits the spiritual landscape to thicken its illusion. It projects unattainable goals and ideals, separate from itself so it can keep up the pretense for flopping. What a superb context for the ego show—marvelous, miraculous teachers somehow beyond us and spiritual realizations tantalizingly and deliciously out of reach. This is a framework in which one can constantly construe oneself as a hero on the path or as a woefully inadequate failure (delicious guilt, a drama that ego can milk forever!). The spiritual journey should be a great challenge to ego; but by adding the basic twist of goal-orientation, ego turns it into a glorious discovery! What material for solidifying of our personal story!

The goals with which people usually approach spirituality are familiar: power, energy, certainty, invulnerability; transcending the troubles of this life, becoming one with a higher power, bliss, ecstasy; enhanced abilities, greater flexibility and skill; peace, relaxation, relief from mental pain and fear; long life, health, vitality. In many ways, striving for these things seems so natural that it is difficult to see what is wrong with this approach to spirituality, or even to conceive of another approach. Trungpa Rinpoche helps us here. He talks about

> two possible approaches to spirituality: spiritual materialism and transcending spiritual materialism. Padmasambhava's [the genuine] way is that of transcending spiritual materialism, or developing basic sanity. Developing basic sanity is a process of working on ourselves in which the path itself rather than the attainment of a goal becomes the working basis. The path itself is what constantly inspires us rather than . . . promises about certain achievements that lie ahead of us. In other words . . . the difference between spiritual materialism and transcending spiritual materialism is that in spiritual materialism, promises are used like a carrot held up in front of a donkey, luring him into all kinds of journeys; in transcending spiritual materialism, there is no goal. The goal exists in every moment of our life situation, in every moment of our spiritual journey.[2]

The carrot held out before the donkey is a graphic form of the basic split of duality. Spiritual materialism takes too many forms to catalog, but all of them have this shape and feel. Keep your eyes on something miraculous that is beyond you or some expectation for the future, and you will be able to play deaf and dumb to the messy qualities of your present situation. You will be able to use a juicy spiritual project to distract you from the raw and rugged embarrassment (from ego's point of view) of what is. Or else: Keep your focus on how you keep screwing up, how you keep failing to live up to your spiritual project; this storyline will be just as successful at making it unnecessary to face how you really are. Also, make sure you keep your teacher on a pedestal; that way you will be sealed off from the awkwardness and threat to your ego of direct, plain, ordinary exposure to him or her, which might actually destroy your whole spiritual-materialism construct.

The basic taste of spiritual materialism has everything to do with self-preservation, with saving your little selfie. In that way it is closely bound up with all the self-improvement trips that pop culture has propagated over the last few decades: health-food trips, purity trips, longevity trips, bodybuilding trips, and so on. In his early days in America, Rinpoche never tired of exposing this materialistic approach in its endless forms. He emphasized continually that unless spiritual materialism were rooted out, real dharma was impossible. One of the main targets of his lopping sword was fascination with the exotica of Eastern religious forms. In the case of Tibetanism, for example, there was enthrallment with marvelous-seeming sand mandalas, ritual objects, far-out chanting styles, theistic belief in the power of "high lamas," and the collecting of initiations from them. This flagrant fascination with holy men, mantras, and the potpourri of spiritual paraphernalia that was on offer was perfect spiritual materialism, which he endlessly popped, spitted, cleaved, and crushed.

As soon as I met him in 1970, Rinpoche sent me into a four-month solitary retreat in the woods. There were as yet no retreat huts on his land at Tail of the Tiger Meditation Center in Vermont, so I had to build one. Getting the materials up the mountain and constructing the tiny building took me a month. The day before I went into retreat, Rinpoche made a state visit to see the hut. The farmer we'd bought the land from brought Rinpoche up the hill and through the woods in a cart hitched to his tractor. A special seat had been rigged for him. As he came into sight, he looked stately and lighthearted in a tweed sport coat with his scarf blowing in the wind.

The first thing he did was look at the hut. It was covered with black building paper, so it looked flimsy. He made some deprecatory remark about its insubstantiality. I assured him it was sturdy. Then he sat down sidesaddle on one of the foundation beams that protruded at the front of the hut. I sat facing him. He offered me one of his English cigarettes, a Piccadilly. I protested I had just quit smoking and was about to go into retreat, where no more would be available. "Oh, go ahead, have one," he cajoled insidiously, his voice still quite high pitched as a result of the crippling car accident he'd had only months before. There was no refusing him, and the cigarette was good.

We made small talk. I could think of nothing important to say, and that seemed fine with him. Then he was ready to go. He said a word or two of encouragement, then stood up and started to walk away. As if by afterthought, he turned back and asked if I wanted another cigarette. I was trying to say, "No, no, that's all right, forget it." But he preempted that and leaned up into my face with his amazing smile and said in a voice dripping with insinuation, "Go ahead, take the pack." He gave me his pack of Piccadillys with four or five cigarettes left in it. Then he limped to the rear corner of the retreat hut and banged on it with his good right hand as if half expecting it to fall down. I assured him it really would not fall down. He laughed a bit and assented but did not quite seem to believe me. Then he was helped into the cart and driven away down the hill.

After the first few days of retreat and the rest of the Piccadillys, I had a renewed and urgent cigarette habit, which gave me no peace.

Rinpoche was not particularly trying to keep me a smoker. The message I got is that the desire for survival is an obstruction to surrendering to things as they are, which is the essence of meditation, of compassion, of dharma. This attitude is at the heart of the bodhisattva's way, which is putting other's welfare before one's own. In one of the Jataka tales, the Buddha feeds himself to a wild animal to save another would-be victim's life. Trungpa Rinpoche was such a bodhisattva who continually and freely sacrificed his own health, privacy, and well-being for the sake of transmitting real dharma. He had no barriers to that at all. His example told us that in genuine spirituality, one surrenders all personal safeguards as well as preconceived goals. As he taught us, the path itself becomes the goal. This is the precise opposite of spiritual materialism, where the goal is the prize, and whatever is not the goal or the process of urgently striving toward it is second class, beneath consideration. When the practitioner's preconditions, preconceptions, and requirements are surrendered, even for a moment, as we have said, that is the discovery of emptiness, shunyata. With that discovery, vajra mind—indestructible awareness itself—begins to shine through every aspect of one's experience.

So spiritual materialism is all full of prerequisites: I and my goals. An approach that to many seemed blameless and good, Rinpoche revealed at every juncture as the essence of cowardice, an inability to face one's life without a saving grace, a safety net, a salvation proviso. Trungpa Rinpoche liked the idea of "straight, no chaser."

But spiritual materialism was just one flagrant, endemic form of ego trip that Rinpoche showed us. He used spiritual materialism as a prime example of all ego trips. He let us know in a thousand direct and personal ways that, short of enlightenment, life is one ego trip after another, attempt upon attempt of a panicked, fundamentally bogus identity to substantiate itself. For months and years every gesture and word of his, every smile and every sneer, told us about those ego trips in ourselves. It was a continual exposé. Just as twenty years previous in Tibet the very presence of his root guru Jamgön Kongtrül of Shechen had corroded every inauthenticity in the young tulku, burning through to the natural and spontaneous nature beyond, so Rinpoche's presence continually (as he himself put it) "pulled the rug out" from under us. How often one found oneself suddenly in an inhospitable psychological no-man's-land, the rug having been pulled out completely sometimes by a gesture of Rinpoche's as minimal as merely having averted his eyes.

"I want to use meditation to further my ideal vision of myself. I'm going to meditate, eat pure food, give up smoking, exercise, relax, live longer. In every way I'm going to enhance and expand and maintain my personal territory. At the same time, to ward off attack, I'm going to play safe in every way. I'm going to be moral and kind, make friends, and charm the world. Or, if that isn't working, I'll maintain a flow of complaints, find endless slights in the way other's treat me—I'll maintain a vivid, undeniable ego presence that way. Or perhaps my specialty will be: I don't need the world. I pound my hairy chest and say fuck you—that will juicily perpetuate ego's preoccupation. And in addition, as a backup, I will maintain many forms of guilt and tricks of self-deprecation and humiliation." These were the kinds of ego strategies we students realized we were all hanging on to. Rinpoche revealed ego's menagerie as endless, all-pervasive; and owing to the way he pointed his awareness during that phase of his teaching, suddenly the whole zoo was on naked display.

What revealed ego for what it was, was vajra mind—awakened, pure perception. And astonishingly, that too was (mostly indirectly) revealed. Every exposed ego trip was limned by "awake"; every quake and quaver of doubt manifested it. There was the continual thrill of Rinpoche's illumined communication when one felt open, but how often a sense of menace crushed one down! Sometimes the aggrieved, cringing mind of ego turned Rinpoche into a sinister devil. We loved, feared, and resented him simultaneously. But despite our thickest projections, with Rinpoche there, the sense of unconditioned mind, awakened mind, indestructible awareness, always lurked behind the acted-out gestures on the stage of situations. It was there, insinuating, cutting, piercing, shining through. No prerequisites or preconceptions, no trips, no self-deception of any kind, could withstand its corrosion. Vajra mind was there in your life no matter what you did, demolishing nihilism and eternalism, the extreme tricks of ego.

Once it has been discovered, vajra mind becomes like a pebble of radioactive plutonium in the pot of your existence. It will contaminate and destroy everything you try to hold on to, and the fully irradiated rubble will become the vajra world.

A genuine teacher is the spokesman of the vajra world. A genuine teacher has the compassion and fearlessness to abandon the snug safety of his own achievement and insight in order to provide a path for his students. He is willing to get down with his students fully and completely into the dirt of ego and samsara so that they can build a bridge together beyond spiritual materialism and enter the dance of the vajra world. For the student, the act of building that bridge is called surrender.

In Rinpoche's own words, which are best:

"Surrender" means opening oneself completely, trying to get beyond fascination and expectation.

Surrender also means acknowledging the raw, rugged, clumsy and shocking qualities of one's ego, acknowledging them and surrendering them as well. Generally, we find it very difficult to give out and surrender our raw and rugged qualities of ego. Although we may hate ourselves, at the same time we find our self-hatred a kind of occupation. In spite of the fact that we may dislike what we are and find that self-condemnation painful, still we cannot give it up completely. If we begin to give up our self-criticism, then we may feel that we are losing our occupation, as though someone were taking away our job. We would have no further occupation if we were to surrender everything; there would be nothing to hold on to. Self-evaluation and self-criticism are, basically, neurotic tendencies which derive from our not having enough confidence in ourselves, "confidence" in the sense of seeing what we are, knowing what we are, knowing we can afford to open. We can afford to surrender that raw and rugged neurotic quality of self and step out of fascination, step out of preconceived ideas.[3]

We may be surprised at how Rinpoche tells us to do this. The same passage continues:

We must surrender our hopes and expectations, as well as our fears, and march directly into disappointment, work with disappointment, go into it and make it our way of life, which is a very hard thing to do. Disappointment is a good sign of basic intelligence. It cannot be compared to anything else: it is so sharp, precise, obvious and direct. If we can open, then we suddenly begin to see that our expectations are irrelevant compared with the reality of the situations we are facing. This automatically brings a feeling of disappointment. Disappointment is the best chariot to use on the path of the dharma. It does not confirm the existence of our ego and its dreams. However, if we are involved with spiritual materialism, if we regard spirituality as a part of our accumulation of learning and virtue, if spirituality becomes a way of building ourselves up, then of course the whole process of surrendering is completely distorted.[4]

Perhaps we might resent this seemingly negative approach to spirituality, which we thought was supposed to be beautiful. If you have trouble grasping the meaning of this approach, think for a moment of the famous guru-disciple stories. Think of Naropa, of Milarepa. Think of the endless cruel trials imposed on their disciples by Zen and even martial arts masters. Cutting through spiritual materialism is an essential part of the path of dharma. Exposing and cutting through ego's game is the only way to clear the ground. It is only when, mortally exhausted with disappointment, the fish of ego begins to spill its guts upon the beach that the way of genuine compassion and devotion may begin to open its glorious doors.

Notes

1. *Cutting Through Spiritual Materialism* (1973), p. 3.
2. *Crazy Wisdom*, p. 15.
3. *Cutting Through Spiritual Materialism*, pp. 24–25.
4. Ibid., p. 25.

Heart to Heart

Interreligious Dialogue

JUDITH SIMMER-BROWN

O N A VISIT to Asia in 1968, Chögyam Trungpa met the American Trappist monk Father Thomas Merton, shortly before Merton's sudden death. Rinpoche was deeply affected by the encounter, for they spoke intimately on topics that were important to them both. Years later, Rinpoche often referred to these conversations when he inaugurated the Christian-Buddhist dialogues at Naropa Institute that spanned the 1980s.

Yesterday, quite by chance, I met Chögyam Trungpa Rinpoche and his secretary, a nice young Englishman whose Tibetan name is Kunga. Today I had lunch with them and talked about going to Bhutan. But the important thing is that we are people who have been waiting to meet for a long time. Chögyam Trungpa is a completely marvelous person. Young, natural, without front or artifice, deep, awake, wise. I am sure we will be seeing a lot more of each other, whether around northern India and Sikkim or in Scotland, where I am now determined to go to see his Tibetan monastery if I can.

—Fr. Thomas Merton, Calcutta, October 20, 1968[1]

Father Merton's visit to Southeast Asia took place when I was in Calcutta. He was invited by a group that had a philosophy of spiritual shopping, and he was the only person who felt that it was full of confusion. He felt there was a sense of ignorance there, but nonetheless he joined them. We had dinner together, and we talked about spiritual materialism a lot. We drank many gin and tonics. I had the feeling that I was meeting an old friend, a genuine friend. In fact, we planned to work on a book containing selections from the sacred writings of Christianity and Buddhism. We planned to meet either in Great Britain or in North America. He was the first genuine person I met from the West.

—Chögyam Trungpa Rinpoche, Boulder, Colorado, August, 1983[2]

These meetings were never to materialize. For less than two months after their joyous meeting in Calcutta, Father Merton was accidentally electrocuted in his Bangkok hotel bathroom while stepping from the shower. That morning he had delivered his talk to a Bangkok conference of the Benedictine order, recalling among other topics his conversations with Trungpa Rinpoche, and commenting on his discovery of a common core between Buddhist and Christian contemplative traditions. As he said in his address, these two great traditions share the view "that if you once penetrate by detachment and purity of heart to the inner secret of the ground of your ordinary experience, you attain to a liberty that nobody can touch, that nobody can affect, that no political change of circumstances can do anything to. . . . [Behind these two traditions is] the belief that this kind of freedom and transcendence is somehow attainable."[3]

Trungpa Rinpoche's meeting of the minds with Thomas Merton reflected his unique approach to interreligious dialogue, which was characterized by interest in the contemplative journey of prayer or meditation; appreciation of lineage and tradition; and authentic communication between traditions for the purpose of mutual awakening, nurture, and respect. All this was far from the norm in North America at that time.

When Rinpoche first came to the West in the 1960s, interreligious dialogue was limited in scope. Dialogues were confined to two primary spheres. The first was theological dialogue with a missionary agenda. The World's Parliament of Religions, held in Chicago in 1893, was organized to prove, once and for all, the superiority of Christianity. Instead, what occurred was an encounter with noble saints and teachers of non-Christian religions, who astonished the four thousand participants with their eloquence, humanity, and deep spirituality.[4] By the middle of the twentieth century, Christian dialogue theologians began to recognize the importance of respecting the wisdom traditions of those to be converted. Nevertheless, they retained a strongly inclusivist agenda—that is, they worked from the assumption that the Christian tradition is so profound that it can include aspects of other traditions, even while holding them as lesser views.[5] The ultimate goal in inclusivist dialogue is to demonstrate the superiority of one's own tradition, so that people of other traditions might be converted. This, of course, created a dialogue atmosphere in which listening was less valued than proclaiming. The legacy of this kind of agenda still pervades many European and North American theological dialogue settings.

The second kind of interreligious dialogue attempted in late-twentieth-century Europe and North America was political dialogue. These are not so much dialogues as they are well-intentioned meetings of religious leaders who wish to allay tensions between their religious communities. Such dialogues often do not involve much actual conversation. Their purpose is to symbolically ameliorate strife and to lay the groundwork for future reconciliation and theological dialogue. An example of the best kind of political dialogue occurred in 1965 when Vatican II's Pope Paul VI acknowledged the possibility of salvation being known in traditions other than Christianity, and created a Secretariat for Non-Christian Religions.[6] This political act of leadership sent waves throughout the Catholic and the broader Christian world, impacting dialogue encounters for all the decades to come. However, most of these dialogues continue to carry an inclusivist agenda.

By the 1970s, a venturesome new spirit had begun to emerge in the world of interreligious dialogue; this was especially evident in the respectful exploration of non-Christian wisdom traditions by Christian theologians. Theologians such as Hans Küng, John Hick, Raimundo Panikkar, and Paul Knitter began to critically examine the limits of Christian inclusivism, suggesting that it may be time to interact with non-Christians without the expectation that they convert.[7] John Cobb, through his dialogues with Japanese Buddhism, began to suspect that the ultimate benefit of dialogue was that a mutual transformation could occur, and he suggested that it was time to go "beyond dialogue."[8] Thomas Merton was the most famous contemplative advocating such an approach, eagerly seeking out his counterparts from other traditions during his only journey to Asia, in 1968.

The Ri-me Nonsectarian Movement in Tibet

Trungpa Rinpoche did not come to the conversation with Merton without his own training and perspective. Rinpoche's spiritual teachers in Tibet came from the famous nonsectarian Ri-me (literally, "without bias") movement in Tibet, which grew in strength and popularity in the nineteenth century. Ri-me was not, strictly speaking, a school in the sense of its rival Tibetan tradition, the Gelukpas. It did not constitute an organized monastic order with its own temples (gompas) or lineages. Rather, it was an association of masters of several mainstream Tibetan Buddhist schools and lineages who shared an orientation toward meditation, realization, and the preservation of teachings and lineages of teaching. While the movement was concentrated in monastic settings, many lay yogis and yoginis of Tibet also were counted among their numbers. This movement has shaped the training of many teachers and incarnate teachers (tülkus, usually given the title Rinpoche, or "precious jewel") who have come to the West. Trungpa Rinpoche has been recognized as being in the vanguard, creatively applying Ri-me principles in his teaching and activities in the West.[9]

The Ri-me movement developed in response to an environment of intense sectarian rivalry, parochial propagation of texts and transmissions, economic corruption, and an increasing scholasticism with regard to doctrinal distinctions. The movement can be traced to Jigme Lingpa, an eighteenth-century master of the dzogchen (great perfection) meditation lineage.[10] Dzogchen emphasizes the innate, natural state of mind, an open, expansive experience of reality unfettered by discursive thought. Ri-me developed on these yogic foundations, emphasizing the openness and purity of realization, the centrality of meditation, and the importance of scholastic study in service of practice rather than the other way around.

Jigme Lingpa stated, "To become attached to intellectual models of the experience or meditational states encountered in the course of trying to achieve it is to mistake the path for the goal, whereas the real aim is to turn the goal into the path."[11]

Jigme Lingpa's spiritual successors[12] became the founders and leaders of Ri-me in nineteenth-century Tibet, the most important for Trungpa Rinpoche's lineage being Jamgön Kongtrül Lodrö Thaye (1813–1900).[13] During this period, Ri-me exhibited four specific characteristics that are relevant to interreligious dialogue today. First, Ri-me's abiding interest was in meditation and contemplative practice as the ground of spiritual life. This meant that Ri-me focused on fostering communities of practice, encouraging extensive solitary meditation retreats, preserving the texts and oral traditions of authentic practice lineages, and respecting the uniqueness of each lineage. Ri-me masters refrained from syncretism, the mixing of all kinds of spiritual paths and techniques in the name of ecumenism.[14] While it is not clear what exactly constituted "authenticity" of lineage in a Tibetan setting, the concerns of the Ri-me masters were an unbroken lineage of oral transmission, corresponding texts (both ritual and meditation) preserved within the lineage, accompanying preserved oral instructions on the conduct of the practice, and living teachers who can serve as spiritual guides. Ri-me lamas are primarily tantrikas who experience visions, discover hidden treasure texts (termas), and place emphasis upon intensive meditation practice in retreat. Their sainthood can sometimes take unorthodox forms, especially in settings of excessive institutionalization and scholasticism.

Second, the Ri-me advocated that all traditions of meditation practice be appreciated and valued, regardless of the lineages or schools from which they have come. While many of the Ri-me proponents were from the Nyingma ("ancient") school, leaders of the movement hailed as well from the Kagyü, Sakya, and Jonang schools. Gelukpas were also occasionally included. A contemporary Ri-me teacher commented in a talk in North America: "To adopt the Ri-me approach means to follow your own chosen path with dedication, while maintaining respect and tolerance for all other valid choices."[15]

Third, meditation is not to be regarded with naive passivity; on the contrary, the Ri-me viewed intelligent investigation and inquiry as crucial concomitants of a mature meditation practice. In an atmosphere of sectarian rivalry, the Ri-me movement cultivated a new kind of philosophic view that refrained from obscure points of contention. Instead, the nonsectarian movement focused on the Indian traditions from which much of Tibetan scholasticism derived. Ri-me monastic colleges (*shedras*) focused on a small number of classical scriptures from Indian Buddhism, with simple commentaries in Tibetan translation. The emphasis of such study was comprehension that would "eliminate many controversies that arose through variant expositions of the same texts by different Tibetan exegetes."[16] As a further move away from sectarian traps, Ri-me scholars refused to accept the labels of their opponents in debate. (In traditional Tibetan debate, derogatory nicknames were sometimes coined to caricature the opponent, such as "half-eggists" or "false aspectarians.")

Fourth, Ri-me was intent upon preservation of a contemplative tradition seen to be in peril of being lost or overly codified in the atmosphere of sectarianism and scholasticism of nineteenth-century Tibet. The movement is based on the view that the Buddha gave eighty-four thousand different kinds of teachings based on the propensities and uniqueness of individual practitioners. From this view, it was important that all these teachings and practices be preserved so that the full resources of the dharma be available for future generations.[17] Great Ri-me masters such as Jamgön Kongtrül Lodrö Thaye devoted their lives to collecting, editing, and preserving the texts of Tibet's various practice lineages, and receiving the corresponding empowerments and oral instructions associated with those texts. This led to the powerful collections of "treasuries" (*dzo*) of the various genres of practice texts of the nineteenth century that are now being transmitted by Tibet's leading rinpoches.[18]

Trungpa Rinpoche was a prominent heir of the Ri-me tradition, having trained with its leading exponents, most notably His Holiness Dilgo Khyentse and Jamgön Kongtrül of Shechen. His Ri-me training included yogic training with Khenpo Gangshar;[19] and, like Ri-me students who were his contemporaries, he went to lamas from the Nyingma and Sakya orders, in addition to his hereditary Kagyü gurus, for meditation and associated scholastic training. Throughout his teaching career in the West, he exhibited characteristic Ri-me creativity and originality in his adaptations of the Tibetan tradition to a brand-new cultural setting.[20]

Rinpoche Enters Dialogue

After escaping from Tibet in 1959, Chögyam Trungpa Rinpoche arrived tattered and penniless in India with a small party of lay students and monks. A young tülku still in robes, he had his first encounters with Christians in Kalimpong in 1960. A missionary organization gave Tibetan refugees cartons of milk powder and Spam along with a Bible and missionary literature translated into Tibetan. Rinpoche later humorously observed that the literature reported that "Tibetan Buddhists practice by themselves and try to attain enlightenment in their own way, while the Christians, on the other hand, go out and produce milk powder and Spam and try to save others."[21]

A few years later, when Rinpoche attended Oxford University as a Spalding Visiting Fellow in Comparative Religion, he was assigned a Belgian Jesuit priest as a tutor. Father DeGives, who had spent seven years in Sri Lanka, guided Rinpoche's study in Bible and Western religion for two and one-half years. Rinpoche especially enjoyed studying Christian contemplative practices, but was surprised to discover that "when people receive blessing, or when they receive the presence of Christ—or Jehovah, for that matter—no preparation has been made, at all. There is no shinjang [taming of the mind], there is no mindfulness, there is no awareness. The only possibility of shinjang at all is that people are terrorized: they believe that if they don't do things properly, they will be punished."[22]

Through Father DeGives's connections, Rinpoche was regularly invited to interreligious conferences in Britain, where he presented in broken English the fundamentals of his tradition. Though he encountered a pervasive Christian chauvinism, he enjoyed his contacts with the many priests, rabbis, imams, and pandits he met in those years. He was especially attracted to the Franciscans he met at an old monastery in Midlands. He fondly remembered the abbot, whom he called "extremely saintly, reminding me of one of my Tibetan teachers, but speaking in a broad Irish accent. He was a wonderful person, with neat but dirty robes, with a real monastic flavor about him."[23]

During his Oxford days, Rinpoche was also attracted to the Eastern Orthodox tradition, "because its followers understand the notion of meditation, and they understand that meditation is not just doing nothing but also involves radiating one's openness. The contemplative traditions within both Judaism and Christianity, particularly the Jewish Hasidic tradition—and also the Orthodox Christian Prayer of the heart, which I've studied a little bit—seem to be the ground for Eastern and Western philosophy to join together. It is not so much a question of dogma, but it is a question of heart; that is where the common ground lies. One of these days I am going to take my students to Mount Athos to see how the Orthodox monks conduct themselves."[24] His dialogues with Metropolitan Anthony Bloom, the London patriarch of the Russian Orthodox Church, left a lasting impression on him.

Adaptations of Nonsectarian Perspectives

In 1968 Rinpoche returned to Asia to do an extended retreat in Bhutan, at a Guru Rinpoche cave called Tagtsang. In Calcutta, he auspiciously met Thomas Merton, and they joyously shared gin and tonics over lunch, then roared off in a Jeep to shop the markets for Divali (festival of lights) treats. "Rinpoche bought a firecracker from a small, very black, bright-eyed crouching little boy," wrote Merton in his journal entry that evening. Rinpoche later commented, "Father Merton himself was an open, unguarded, and deep person. During these few days, we spent much time together and grew to like one another immensely."[25] The two men shared their poetry, their dreams for dialogue, their spiritual aspirations, and even plans for collaborative publishing projects. Most significantly, they shared their mutual concerns about the increasing materialism that affected monastic life, and the "progressive" monks who give up contemplation to become more productive and academic.[26] Recalling this conversation, Rinpoche simply said that they had discussed "spiritual materialism."[27]

During his time in the West, Rinpoche had become increasingly depressed by the prevalence of a culture of acquisitiveness and the pursuit of wealth for its own sake, which deepened rather than alleviating suffering. What was particularly of concern to him was the use of spiritual practice in an acquisitive way. Rinpoche coined the term "spiritual materialism"[28] in English to refer to the use of spiritual disciplines as an expression of one's ambition and self-cherishing, as the maintenance of control and personal agenda rather than the surrender and openness valued in authentic spiritual practice. He expressed concern that this appropriation of spiritual practice by the ego would manipulate and constrain the inner spiritual frontier of openness and nonconceptuality. He reflected that spiritual materialism had also been an issue in Tibet, where monastic corruption, mere ceremonialism, and sectarian rivalry had become epidemic. In Tibet, the Ri-me movement had arisen to address these issues. In his conversations with Merton, Rinpoche reflected how spiritual materialism could be reversed in a Western setting as well. During his three-week retreat at Tagtsang just prior to meeting Merton, Rinpoche had entered a visionary state and composed a short and powerful ritual text (sadhana), *The Sadhana of Mahamudra Which Quells the Mighty Warring of the Three Lords of Materialism and Brings Realization of the Ocean of Siddhas of the Practice Lineage*.[29] In this treasure text, he expressed traditional Ri-me concerns, such as joining together the essential teachings of the Kagyü and Nyingma, and the themes of renunciation and devotion. The central theme of the text is that only by practicing meditation in an authentic and heartfelt way, recognizing the obstacles of materialism, can genuine spirituality be revitalized. The text opens with these lines:

> This is the darkest hour of the dark ages. Disease, famine, and warfare are raging like the fierce north wind. The Buddha's teaching has waned in strength. The various schools of the sangha are fighting amongst themselves with sectarian bitterness; and although the Buddha's teaching was perfectly expounded and there have been many reliable teachings since then from other great gurus, yet they pursue intellectual speculations. . . . The yogis of tantra are losing the insight of meditation. They spend their whole time going through villages and performing little ceremonies for material gain. On the whole, no one acts according to the highest code of discipline, meditation and wisdom. The jewel-like teaching of insight is fading day by day. The Buddha's teaching is used merely for political purposes and to draw people together socially. As a result the blessings of spiritual energy are being lost. Even those with great devotion are beginning to lose heart.[30]

Rinpoche and Merton each lamented the decline of genuine spirituality in the West, because of the prevalence of greed and materialism and the loss of authentic contemplative practices and lineages. Merton was going through struggles of his own, including the administrative and authoritarian demands of his home monastery, pressure from his publishers, and his yearning for more retreat and instruction in meditation from Asian masters. As Rinpoche reflected on Merton's impending conference in Bangkok, he later commented that Father Merton "was in Calcutta attending some kind of collective religious conference, and he was appalled at the cheapness of the spiritual values that various of the conference participants were advocating."[31] Rinpoche presented Merton a copy of the newly composed sadhana,[32] and though Merton did not mention this in the published version of his Journals, it is clear that the content of their conversations set the tone for Merton's Indian pilgrimage.[33] Years later, at Naropa University, Rinpoche created a series of dialogues in Merton's memory that sought to revitalize contemplative practice and life in North America and Europe.

Naropa University Conferences

Shortly after Naropa University's founding in 1974, Rinpoche began speaking of his dream for a unique center for contemplative practice and interreligious dialogue. Rather than the theological or political dialogues that he encountered in Britain and Europe, his real interest was in bringing together authentic contemplatives from a variety of traditions for exchange, practice, and conversation. He used the moniker "yogi school" for this project and periodically asked his close students whether they had begun to plan it.[34]

In 1980, with Rinpoche's guidance, Naropa professor Reginald Ray drafted a plan for "A School of Meditative and Contemplative Studies," and sought foundation funding.[35] It was decided that the first dialogues sponsored by the school would be between Christian and Buddhist contemplatives, eventually broadening to include contemplatives from a range of religious traditions. This proposal formed the ground for a series of annual conferences on Buddhist and Christian meditation, sponsored by Naropa University, from 1981 to 1988.

The inaugural conference, held in 1981 in Boulder, Colorado, was called "a major breakthrough in the Christian-Buddhist dialogues" by Sister Pascaline Coff, a Benedictine nun and a founding member of Monastic Interreligious Dialogue.[36] The innovation was in the conference's focus on contemplative practice and meditation in Buddhism and Christianity. In addition to Trungpa Rinpoche, the major presenters included His Holiness the Dalai Lama, Eido Shimano Roshi, Brother David Steindl-Rast, Mother Tessa Bielecki, and Father Thomas Keating. Periods of meditation were punctuated by presentations and dialogue conversations, all with a contemplative emphasis. The response was electric as two hundred signed on for the inaugural conference. Participation soared the next year, with four hundred people from all over the United States attending the second conference; comparable numbers came in the years to follow. Over the seven years of annual conferences, most of the core group of faculty presenters returned each year. A number of these conferences included preconference faculty retreats that promoted deep conversation, shared practice, and a growing collegiality of contemplative life. The attendees also became a loyal following, returning again and again to participate in the dialogues.

What was so riveting about these conferences? Each contemplative spoke directly, without compromise, from the heart of his or her tradition. These presentations were gems of contemplative realization, full of authenticity, depth, and humanity. Between presentations were public conversations among the faculty, and these conversations were extraordinary. The atmosphere was one of discovery of an ancient friendship, rather than of conversion, disputation, or debate. In a comment that echoed the sentiments of Father Merton, his spiritual mentor, the Christian lay contemplative James Finley wrote:

> Here we are concerned . . . with the unity of the contemplative way. Where is this unity to be found? It is in the compassion of those who walk it. It is in their humility, their integrity, and in their nonimpositional conviction. It is a unity that in no way denies the order of sameness and difference. Rather, it acknowledges and reveres all sameness and all differences as such, because it speaks with the wisdom of knowing that that order is not the ultimate order.[37]

This new kind of dialogue, which could be called "contemplative dialogue" or a "dialogue of practice," was to generate a widespread appreciation for the contemplative life, both monastic and lay. Eventually, a book containing transcripts of the conference presentations and conversations was published, and has been recently reissued.[38]

The topics covered in these conferences were classic Ri-me concerns: meditation practice and the spiritual quest, the dynamics of the spiritual path, the spiritual mentor, tradition and innovation. The atmosphere of these conferences was one of respect for each contemplative tradition; teachers met as peers in an environment of inquiry and disclosure. Each presentation was rich with scriptural references and theological sophistication, revealing the depth of training of each contemplative. The faculty did not attempt any kind of syncretism; instead, they discovered deep resonance with the common themes between traditions while respecting the unique qualities of each. On a personal level, this shared commitment to fostering sympathy and appreciation for the contemplative life served as a bond, forging abiding friendships that were to last for the following decades. Ri-me sensibilities of mutual appreciation, commitment to contemplative practice, and respect for differences had been translated to a new and very different cultural setting.

Rinpoche's guidance in the conference design was focused and subtle. He never overtly talked about his Ri-me orientation, but it was reflected in his choice of faculty presenters, his preferences for conference topics, and his abiding curiosity in the proceedings and conversations. He saw himself as the host of the dialogue, but never dominated the conversations. At one conference opening, he commented, "The only way to join the Christian tradition and the Buddhist tradition together would be by bringing together Christian contemplative practice with Buddhist contemplative practice."[39] He gave presentations at many of the conferences, and participated in public dialogue with the other faculty. For later conferences, other responsibilities removed him from the events; but he always followed the proceedings from afar.

Rinpoche's students had been raised in Christian or Jewish environments, and regarded these conferences with ambivalence. Many were frankly puzzled by, or even hostile to, the events. As Reginald Ray commented, "typical of new converts, we shared a resistance and lack of curiosity toward other religions, and especially toward those with which we had grown up."[40] Accustomed to the old world of dialogue, his students often expected Rinpoche to trump his guests, asserting the superiority of

Buddhism in general and Tibetan Buddhism in particular. But this never happened. In his final conference, the year before his untimely death, Rinpoche said in his presentation:

> As far as I can see, there is no difference between theism and non-theism, basically speaking. . . . Whether you worship someone else or you worship yourself, it is the same thing. Both theism and non-theism can be problematic if you are not involving yourself personally and fully. You may think you are becoming spiritual, but instead you could just be trying to camouflage yourself behind a religious framework and still you will be more visible than you think. . . . We are not trying here to sort out which tradition, or which particular type of merchandise is better. We are talking in terms of needing to develop a personal connection with one's body and one's mind. That is why the contemplative traditions of both East and West are very important.[41]

Rinpoche's Ri-me training and concerns remained at the forefront. His students were to follow their own contemplative path with dedication while appreciating and respecting all other authentic spiritual lineages and practices.

Rinpoche's dream was that Naropa University would become a place where the authentic contemplative traditions of North America would be nurtured, studied, and practiced in an environment of nonsectarian appreciation and conversation. What was necessary for such a project to be successful, however, was that its participants have a dedicated individual practice and a genuine connection with the teaching lineage that has given rise to their practice. He warmly invited into the Naropa community practitioners of all traditions who were willing to make this kind of commitment, and he fostered dialogue and joint practice, whether from a variety of Buddhist traditions, or from Hindu, Christian, Jewish, Muslim, or indigenous traditions like the Native American. In this way, perhaps an invigorated American Ri-me movement could help preserve contemplative lineages in a way that combats the depressing forces of materialism, especially spiritual materialism.

Notes

1. Thomas Merton, *The Asian Journal of Thomas Merton*, ed. Naomi Burton et al. (New York: New Directions, 1975), pp. 30–31.

2. Chögyam Trungpa, "Manifesting Enlightenment," in *The Heart of the Buddha*, p. 213.

3. Thomas Merton, *The Asian Journal of Thomas Merton*, p. 342.

4. Richard Hughes Seager, *The Dawn of Religious Pluralism: Voices from the World's Parliament of Religions, 1893* (Lasalle, Ill.: Open Court, 1993).

5. Inclusivism is contrasted with exclusivism and pluralism in a dialogue context. See Diana Eck, *Encountering God: A Spiritual Journey from Bozeman to Benares* (Boston: Beacon Press, 1994), pp. 190–195.

6. Pope Paul VI, *Nostra Aetate: Declaration on the Relations of the Church to Non-Christian Religions*, 1965.

7. Paul Knitter, *No Other Name? A Critical Survey of Christian Attitudes toward the World Religions* (Maryknoll, N.Y.: Orbis Books, 1985).

8. John B. Cobb, Jr., *Beyond Dialogue: Toward a Mutual Transformation of Christianity and Buddhism* (New York: Fortress Press, 1982), pp. 47–53.

9. Geoffrey Samuel, *Civilized Shamans: Buddhism in Tibetan Societies* (Washington: Smithsonian Institution Press, 1993), pp. 345–349.

10. Ibid., p. 534.

11. Ibid., p. 535.

12. These successors included Do Khyentse Yeshe Dorje (1800–1866), Paltrül Rinpoche (1808–1887), and Jamyang Khyentse Wangpo (1820–1892).

13. Richard Barron, *The Autobiography of Jamgon Kongtrul: A Gem of Many Colors* (Ithaca, N.Y.: Snow Lion, 2003).

14. Ibid., xvii.

15. Jamgön Kongtrül of Shechen, in a talk in Victoria, British Columbia, Canada, in the mid-1980s. Quoted in Richard Barron, *The Autobiography of Jamgon Kongtrul: A Gem of Many Colors*, p. xviii.

16. E. Gene Smith, "Jam mgon Kong sprul and the Nonsectarian Movement," in *Among Tibetan Texts* (Boston: Wisdom Publications, 2001), p. 246.

17. Comments of Ringu Tulku Rinpoche, cited in Reginald A. Ray, *Indestructible Truth: The Living Spirituality of Tibetan Buddhism* (Boston: Shambhala Publications, 2001), pp. 207–208.

18. For a comprehensive listing of the treasuries collected by Jamgön Kongtrül the Great, see Richard Barron, *The Autobiography of Jamgon Kongtrul*, pp. 515–549.

19. Samuel, *Civilized Shamans*, p. 307.

20. Ibid., p. 349.

21. Chögyam Trungpa, *1979 Hinayana-Mahayana Seminary Transcripts* (Boulder: Vajradhatu Publications, n.d.), pp. 20–21.

22. Chögyam Trungpa, 1980 *Vajrayana Seminary Transcripts* (Boulder: Vajradhatu Publications, 1981), p. 31.

23. Ibid., p.28.

24. *The Heart of the Buddha*, p. 214.

25. *Born in Tibet*, in *The Collected Works of Chögyam Trungpa*, vol. 1, p. 263.

26. Thomas Merton, *The Asian Journal of Thomas Merton.*

27. *The Heart of the Buddha*, p. 212.

28. "Materialism" is a gloss of *kla-klo*, which means "barbarian," especially a human being from an uncivilized area unreceptive to the compassionate and wise teachings of the Buddha.

29. Selections of this sadhana are published in *The Collected Works of Chögyam Trungpa*, vol. 5, pp. 303–309.

30. *Collected Works*, vol. 5, p. 303.

31. *Born in Tibet*, in *Collected Works*, vol. 1, p. 263.

32. Richard Arthure, personal communication, 2004. Also in Carolyn Rose Gimian's introduction to *Collected Works*, vol. 5, pp. xxii–xxiii.

33. For more details on this, see Judith Simmer-Brown, "Liberty That Nobody Can Touch: Thomas Merton Meets Tibetan Buddhism," in Bonnie Thurston, *Thomas Merton and Buddhism* (Louisville, Ky.: Fons Vitae, forthcoming).

34. Reginald A. Ray, "Background: Contemplative Dialogue at Naropa Institute," in Susan Walker, ed., *Speaking of Silence: Christians and Buddhists on the Contemplative Way* (New York: Paulist Press, 1987), pp. 11–18.

35. Reginald A. Ray, "Proposal for a School of Meditative and Contemplative Studies," unpublished grant application, 1980.

36. Monastic Interreligious Dialogue, founded in 1977, is a Benedictine-Cistercian initiative to foster contemplative dialogue of the sort described here. This quote is taken from the *NABEWD Newsletter*, September 1981. See also her description of this conference in Donald Mitchell and James Wiseman, eds., *The Gethsemani Encounter: A Dialogue on the Spiritual Life by Buddhist and Christian Monastics* (New York: Continuum, 1997), p. 6.

37. James Finley, in Susan Szpakowski, *Speaking of Silence*, p. 2.

38. Susan Szpakowski, ed., *Speaking of Silence: Christians and Buddhists in Dialogue* (Halifax: Vajradhatu Publications, 2005).

39. Chögyam Trungpa, "Manifesting Enlightenment," talk given at the Third Naropa Conference on Buddhist and Christian Meditation, August 1983, in *The Heart of the Buddha*, p. 213.

40. Reginald A. Ray, "Proposal," p. 11.

41. Chögyam Trungpa, "Theism and Nontheism," in Szpakowski, *Speaking of Silence*, p. 154.

A rare photo of Chögyam Trungpa at the second Vajrayogini Abhisheka, at the
Dorje Dzong building, Boulder, 1978. Photograph by Paul C. Kloppenburg.
Used with permission.

A Spiritual Master in the Age of Democracy

FABRICE MIDAL

A REVOLUTION IS A shock from top to bottom, in consequence of which, in the words of the poet Friedrich Hölderlin, *then* no longer rhymes with *now*. This is the sense of Chögyam Trungpa's work. Without doing anything to alter the spirit of Tradition[1]—which protects and transmits a state of being beyond all conditioning—it revolutionizes our understanding of it. Chögyam Trungpa was one of the most committed champions of this revolutionary change that marks our age, which I will, perhaps provisionally, call democratic. I use the term not in its technical sense, as the political regime defined by a typology canonical since Aristotle,[2] but as a *poetic* undertaking—"poetic" because it was originally the work of poets who conceived of an unprecedented way of being "democratic," dependent above all not on a specific organization of power but on a renewed regard for human existence. The "democratic" vision is one whereby *each person* is actually destined for excellence.[3] Whereas a classical painting is constructed around a vanishing point, a central axis around which everything is organized, a painting by Cézanne is constructed so that each place in the painting becomes its own center. To put it another

---

Translated from the French by John Sell.

83

way: according to a democratic poetics, henceforth *each* person is fully placed in the center—a center that is therefore everywhere.

This situation gives rise to two steps. First, we do not allow ourselves to become lost in the misty metaphysical hinterlands that Nietzsche exposed,[4] but instead firmly subscribe to the indivisibility of "the physical world and conceptual space,"[5] of outside and inside. The second step consists in recognizing every individual as a being responsible for the state of the nation, something that is no longer the special concern of an intellectual elite, as Voltaire saw it, but the concern of every individual, however ordinary he or she may be. These two steps take place in the context of a renewed thinking about "everydayness" and the meaning of authentic existence.[6] The thinking that results is a way of giving each person the conditions of his or her freedom. In America, Emerson, Thoreau, and Whitman were the poets of such a vision, which Chögyam Trungpa brought to fulfillment in the spiritual realm.

An Ordinary Man

The facts of how Chögyam Trungpa was led to this "revolution" are known. He spoke about it on several occasions. Nevertheless, it remains difficult, in light of the few documents available to us, to fully appreciate the circumstances of this chain of events.[7] Arriving in England in 1963, Chögyam Trungpa was struck by the difficulty of transmitting the Buddhist heritage that he had received. If Buddhism is fully part of our cultural environment today, for better or for worse, such was not the case in the 1960s, when preconceptions surrounded the tradition.[8] Chögyam Trungpa found himself extremely isolated. To be Tibetan was then the height of exoticism. Buddhism was at best reduced to a mysticism that made T. Lobsang Rampa's fortune and for which Theosophy had earlier laid the ground.[9] Chögyam Trungpa sensed the deception that would be involved in responding to the expectations of people he spoke with. Removed from its Traditional context, the mystical aspect of the Tibetan tradition is meaningless, mere entertainment.

Those who took Chögyam Trungpa seriously in Britain were few, and his seeming confusion, his ambition, and his fervor were absolutely misunderstood. People tend to want a spiritual master who embodies a certain kind of holiness, someone they can even revere—the better to keep him at a distance and thus not have to follow him. At this point, uncertain about what he should do, he had a very serious automobile accident that left his left arm and leg paralyzed. In a way that was characteristic for him, this crisis was the occasion of a sudden gap, in which he saw the need for a decisive commitment involving the sacrifice of all reference points. He renounced his monastic vows, his robes, and the status of a monk, and married a young Englishwoman, Diana Judith Pybus, with whom he left for the United States shortly thereafter. He thus reclaimed an ordinary mode of being in order to manifest himself more freely, free from the social conventions that so deeply mark Tibetan culture.

Behind the simple facts of this event, one must recognize its historical dimension.[10] Chögyam Trungpa abandoned the Tibetan way of life in which he had grown up, as he did every form of social hierarchy. He renounced his privileged status, something he never ceased to emphasize, as in the following quote from 1972: "The speaker doesn't regard himself as superior to the audience except that he is sitting on a platform, which does not mean anything very much."[11] It is important to get beyond the legendary picture of Chögyam Trungpa dressed as a Westerner, drinking alcohol and smoking cigarettes, to look at the deeper meaning of this attitude. In response to a letter in which someone expressed surprise at this state of affairs, which seemed so unworthy of a monk, Chögyam Trungpa replied: "With regard to your inquiry about my lifestyle, you must understand that I regard myself as an ordinary person. I am a householder who makes mortgage payments. I have a wife and three children whom I support. At the same time my relationship with the teachings is inseparable from my whole being. I do not try to rise above the world. My vocation is working with the world."[12] As a common man,[13] Chögyam Trungpa no longer highlighted his status as "lama" or "rinpoche." His teaching commanded attention not because he was a holder of the Kagyü and Nyingma lineages of Tibetan Buddhism, nor because he was a "guru," but because of the truth that emerges in his texts and that has such direct bearing on every individual's existence.[14] It is a teaching that depends not on an external authority but on the direct experience that concerns us in the most intimate way possible, and which we can decide to follow or not. Chögyam Trungpa, refusing to take shelter behind any dogmatic form of erudition, relied on his own experience of Tradition. In so doing he abandoned Tibetan scholasticism, which had lost its stature centuries earlier and exhausted itself, in order to uphold another teaching.

This kind of commitment is never self-evident, and the Tibetans living with him at that time in England refused to follow him. Chögyam Trungpa no longer wanted to employ any form of coercion that would, under the guise of religiosity, serve to manipulate people. With great courage, he broke with a set of political and religious customs operating everywhere in Tibet that had been imported to the West, without legitimacy, from his point of view. They seemed to him to be foreign to Buddhism, even contrary to its spirit.

Let us examine the consequences of the revolution that led Chögyam Trungpa to present himself as an ordinary being.

From this perspective, separating the sacred and the profane becomes impossible; it is essential to perceive their more fundamental unity, even if it is not apparent. Such a demand cuts duality at its root, and, faithful to Buddhist teaching, recognizes the awakened nature of each being, and of each phenomenon—enlightenment, which we mistakenly think of as a separate state to be attained; or even as an unattainable state of awareness, the privilege of the happy few, to whom we must submit.

Chögyam Trungpa would no longer rely on a theoretical and dogmatic teaching—the mode of transmission of a hierarchical society in which one owes respect and obedience to the holder of knowledge and power. That social framework, when alive, is more worthy of respect than we of the twenty-first century are inclined to think; but it is no longer operative. Chögyam Trungpa took note of this without the least nostalgia, but he sought to understand the potential concealed in such a situation. We might call this phenomenon "existential," not in the sense of existentialist philosophy, but as the most characteristic quality of our time: that is to say, the necessity for all thought to aim at the very heart of human existence.[15]

When the social structure can no longer reflect a sacred order, one must retreat into oneself and have a direct and personal relationship with the essential. This is our current situation precisely: on the one hand, the highest teachings are now being presented publicly, and on the other hand there is no longer a social ground to preserve them, to provide them with a hospitable terrain in which to grow. But distress harbors within it the seeds of salvation. Henceforth each individual has the duty of assuming responsibility as a human being, a circumstance that Heidegger, following Kierkegaard,[16] described as marked by the seal of anxiety:[17] an anxiety conceived of not negatively but rather as an element in the process of unveiling our freedom, the impossible responsibility that one can never completely avoid. Such a trial has nothing psychological about it; rather, it brings each of us back to the duty to be the center of our own life—not a center fixed once and for all, in relationship to which everything must be oriented, but the expanding center that each of us has to be, something "centrifugal," fundamentally open and "empty."[18]

Friendship and the Spiritual Encounter

Our age is characterized by the fact that every human being is brought back one-pointedly to his or her own liberty. The revolution that Chögyam Trungpa implemented was to imagine a mode of transmission that would address this need. However, one of the crucial problems of Buddhism in our time is the superficiality to which it is reduced—to being the latest therapeutic trend, a way of attaining happiness cheaply, a handy wisdom. And the fact that some Tibetan teachers come to teach in the West only in order to collect the funds they need for their monasteries in Nepal or India condemns them to a quick tour of their various centers and doesn't allow them to establish personal relationships with those who come to hear them. The teaching remains confined to a strict hierarchical context in imitation of Tibetan usage and creates profound confusion between elements peculiar to this culture and the authentic meaning of Buddhism. Even when this hierarchy is not reduced to something arbitrary and political, which tends to be the case, it maintains an abstract distance between Tradition and the personal experience of the individual; it is imposed with an authority that prevents any real questions from being raised.

Guided by the poetic revolution I have described above and the need for another way of thinking about Tradition, Chögyam Trungpa took up a completely different direction. He invited each person to develop his or her own intelligence and entered into a relationship with each of those he encountered in the most direct fashion possible—refusing, for example, to let his students prostrate themselves in his presence in accordance with Tibetan custom.[19] To prevent a terrible misunderstanding, however, I must stress that his decision in this regard had nothing to do with the libertarian mentality of our times, which in fact he vigorously decried. It was not a modernization of Tradition, but a decisive rethinking of it.

Aspiring to a direct understanding with each person and fully entering into his time, becoming an ordinary man, Chögyam Trungpa established a relationship of friendship with his students. In a public talk given in 1973, he explained: "We relate to each other as friends rather than student and master as such."[20] Even in the late seventies, when he had several hundred disciples, Chögyam Trungpa maintained direct contact with each one of them. When I examined his private correspondence, I was struck by the intimacy revealed there. A number of his letters ended with expressions such as "Your friend in the vajra dharma," "Regards to you, with profoundest love," "My love to you"; and sometimes he even enclosed poems he had written to celebrate the qualities of his friends. Such a rapport is not only the mark of Buddhist compassion, but is found on a truly intimate, personal horizon.

Chögyam Trungpa abandoned once and for all the type of relationship founded on the model of obeying orders, as this remark from a teaching given in 1972 attests: "I'm talking tonight to the members of the community whom I have made friends with, related with, expressed a true expression of love and hate towards. Community members have become my own lovers and haters."[21]

It seems to me necessary to go a step further in order to think more decisively about the meaning of this kind of friendship. It was not merely an affective mode but the very space in which Chögyam Trungpa could henceforth display a relationship to the truth. To put it another way, it was not a subjective choice on his part but the very dimension of the unconditional openness of dharmakaya—like the experience of no-thought that is enlightenment—in which each person can share.[22]

As Aristotle emphasized in book 8 of the *Nichomachean Ethics*, friendship is only possible between equals—among whom, indeed, it is the political virtue par excellence. Chögyam Trungpa established a world in which each person is recognized for what he is in his own right. That is why the success of his teachings in the West comes not from his understanding of Western psychology—insofar as such a thing exists—but rather from his extraordinary capacity, in accordance with the very meaning of friendship, to see the best in each person. In this sense, Vajradhatu was created not by a guru but through the radiation released by his friendship, the work of a community of men and women.[23]

Political Engagement

In the course of creating a space for friendship, Chögyam Trungpa rejected anything that could lead to the infantilization of people by putting their intelligence to sleep. He took particular care never to deign to respond to the expectation of interlocutors who wanted to lock him into the role of a sage with all the answers, as the following exchange attests: "What, for example, is buddhahood? What is enlightenment? Are they just nothing, or are they something? Well, I am afraid I am really no authority to answer this. I am merely one of the travelers, like everyone else here."[24]

In rejecting an authoritarian pose, Chögyam Trungpa added his voice to many other critiques of religion, which, by turning into a "system of doctrines and promises,"[25] makes it possible to dominate the masses. It is important not to believe anything: "Your doubts," he explained, "are very useful, for yourselves and us and our kingdom altogether. If you had no doubt, you would all become jellyfish. You would be like flocks of pigeon or sheep. They only follow their leader, therefore they run into trouble. They have no social conscience and no political vision. Lenin was right in this one little occasion."[26] He encouraged his students to develop a lucid, critical attitude, which at one point he even called "cynical," in order to question all spiritual pretense. Any form of submission or domination undertaken in the name of spirituality seemed to him dangerous. He never stopped exposing these forms of pretense, with various spiritual teachers who came to the West as well as with his students.

Certainly, Trungpa continues one of the basic principles of the Buddha's teaching here, preserved particularly within the Zen tradition, inviting us to believe nothing that we have not examined ourselves. But in practice, Buddhism remains today as it was in the past, strongly marked by a certain dogmatism.[27]

Exposing all these manipulations and compromises that uselessly distort who we are, Chögyam Trungpa could not just set aside the political situation he encountered: "There has been a problem of corruption. The world has been seduced by physical materialism as well as by psychological materialism, let alone spiritual materialism! The world is beginning to turn sour."[28]

Before any analysis of what this engagement might mean, let me begin by noting this fact: the political situation mattered to him. Chögyam Trungpa broke free from the stance of the spiritual teacher who lives beyond the contingencies of reality.

For him this did not mean exposing the various injustices that mark our era—in what has become, for us, the moral stance of the witness, whether intellectual or religious. In another way altogether, Chögyam Trungpa applied himself to meditation on the meaning of human community in the present age of its destruction, when the atomization of the individual is strangely linked to the world's globalization. He explained it as follows: "People involved with a spiritual discipline have a tendency to want nothing to do with their ordinary life; they regard politics as something secular and undesirable."[29]

This attitude takes up one of the great political challenges of our time, something that Hannah Arendt was able to analyze with a rare acuity. Western thought has been marked since antiquity by a concept of freedom—having nothing to do with action or politics—that only manifests itself fully for someone who withdraws from the world into himself.[30] Hannah Arendt calls for a reconsideration of action—as the possibility of a pure beginning, a free spontaneity—which we find in many of Chögyam Trungpa's analyses, particularly in the Shambhala teachings, which aim at restoring a path of chivalry, or what he termed warriorship.

Chögyam Trungpa never stopped considering what would allow a group of human beings to live in an authentic community. The only true society, he remarked, is one in which its members are continually guided by a common vision. Indeed, as Georges Bernanos writes, "there is something more precious than unity, and that is the principles in whose name one unites."[31] Chögyam Trungpa exposed the way in which our world is now *managed* technically—that which signals the end of politics, which can in no way limit itself to being "a social means."[32] Management belongs to the economic order,[33] something the ancients knew to distinguish strictly from politics—which *alone* is the art of living together.

A common vision is not a project we have to accomplish. Any utopia that one wants to attain—a contradiction in terms, since *u-topia* literally means "no place"—tends inevitably toward barbarism, as demonstrated by the Nazi and Stalinist regimes, which started off with a rejection of reality (a rejection that precisely denies everydayness); reality was required to bend itself to their will. Chögyam Trungpa pointed to a sane dimension that already virtually exists—in this sense he was not a man with a doctrine in the usual sense, but rather a man whose work is a continual transmission. He reveals in this way an unconditional dimension of being, a presence that does not depend on any condition and that nevertheless constitutes the background of all existence—a background that is indestructible because it has no need for a foundation and that actually opens up the possibility of a renewed political engagement that would no longer separate the realm of private life from that of the social world.[34]

In this context, Chögyam Trungpa developed the notion of "enlightened society" as the enlightened quality inherent in any society, which should be recognized and cultivated. Inasmuch as each person inherits a vision that does not belong to any individual as such, this vision corresponds completely to a "democratic poetics." Whether this vision is brought to life depends on each person. The seed syllable of the enlightened society reveals itself in the degree to which each person can reflect it.

Chögyam Trungpa's Critique of Democracy

This democratic revolution permeates the entire work of Chögyam Trungpa, which could be studied entirely from this perspective. For him, such a revolution, which demands that we rethink the very meaning of transmission, is focused on an analysis basically driven by the nontheistic approach characteristic of the Buddhist tradition: "The Buddhist approach . . . does not have a concept of uniformity, particularly—just basic unity. And because of this, there is no hierarchy, like a belief in God. Therefore, since everything is self-reliance, purely self-reliance, that does encourage people to think more for themselves. In time that would have a great effect."[35] The idea of nontheism is eminently tied to that of a democratic poetics; both bring each person back to his or her infinite freedom. Both rest on a requirement that is far more existential than theoretical concerning what it is to be human: the actual space itself where the truth takes place. To put it another way, the reversal described here aims above all at our relationship to the truth, which is no longer connected with a revelation or authority, but rather with an experience. Such a perspective transforms the usual notion of what the spiritual path is: it does not promote the need to believe in something external to ourselves, but presents a discipline allowing us to open to what is.

If this is indeed the project of a democratic poetics—inviting each person to full and complete responsibility—our "democratic" political regime is a thousand miles away from realizing such a plan; it even tends to make it impossible.

Theoreticians of this regime have often been aware of this pitfall, and each one has attempted a critique—in the true sense of "sifting" or discerning—of the matter at hand. Rousseau, for example, stipulated the conditions necessary for establishing a democracy in a way so specific that none of our democracies would meet with his approval. All authentically democratic thought contains its own critique within itself. The current absence of clear thinking about this concept, which is now as empty and overused as "the rights of man," is a very disquieting sign. Although we cannot go into all the analyses developed with respect to the nature of democracy, it is important to take into account the way in which Chögyam Trungpa made his mark in this story.

Aristotle was the first to distinguish the *polity*, wherein each person uses his or her sovereignty for the benefit of all, from *democracy*, a regime in which everyone asserts the establishment of his or her individual rights with an eye toward the immediate satisfaction of desires. Without concern for the highest good, there cannot be society in the strict sense of the word.

The examination of democracy to which Chögyam Trungpa devoted himself, particularly in relation to what he witnessed in America, continues this critique. The democratic ideology specific to our times involves a naive and dangerous conception of liberty as following what we desire—in Buddhist terms, the *kleshas*. But above all, this ideology leads people to think of themselves as "subject-kings" who can decide for themselves what is real. [36]

Here is the crux of the matter. If it is up to the individual to answer to the necessity of making an enlightened society manifest itself, the current misperceptions of that imperative as an invitation to impose one's will everywhere and at any time is the source of "the crisis of the modern world" declared by René Guénon and called by Heidegger the age of "conceptions of the world," whereby the world is conceived solely in relation to the self, which then becomes the province where all worth is evaluated.[37] Chögyam Trungpa called this phenomenon, which he equated with democratic ideology, the triumph of the "territoriality of ego."[38] It leads to a point where people no longer pay allegiance to Aristotle's "common good," or what Chögyam Trungpa calls the primordial health of an enlightened society, which is, he emphasizes, a dimension properly existential, "a deeply rooted and very real human desire."[39]

The Opposition of Mass Society to All Hierarchy

The democratic universe reduces humanity to a mass. But "the masses do not exist, they represent an abstract entity directed against the individuals of whom they are composed."[40] This reduction of human beings into a quantified mass implies a condemnation of all hierarchy: the only thing that counts is the autonomous individual, that "postmodern illusion of the transparent, liberated individual," in Pierre Legendre's analysis.[41] Not only is such an individual in no sense free,[42] but the institutional basis of the individual's humanity is endangered under a mechanical and biological administration.

Mass democracy regards any hierarchy as a threat to the general leveling effect that it produces, and to every person's right to a content-free equality. Such a view reflects the extreme confusion of our times. In reality, the authentic meaning of hierarchy is not at all the repressive idea of the ancien régime; it is an invitation extended to each one of us to achieve our fullest blossoming, like flowers in a garden, where none is superior to the others and each one has its place. The good gardener is concerned not about whether one flower grows higher than the others, but only that each should display itself in its own way.

Authentic hierarchy is no more possible within our culture than it is within that of the former Tibet or in the France of the ancien régime.[43] It is not a question of establishing a hierarchy that resembles "a ladder or a vertical power structure, with power concentrated at the top. If you are on the bottom rungs of the ladder, then you feel oppressed by what is above you and you try to abolish it, or you try to climb higher on the ladder."[44] Stimulated by a thirst for greater justice and by a deep respect for the teaching of the Buddha, Chögyam Trungpa denounced both the corruption of Tibetan society that he knew and the violence specific to our time.[45]

In reality, the authentic meaning of hierarchy—which perhaps should be called the "sacred order"—is the truth of a democratic poetics. It is an order based on a respectful approach to the uniqueness of each person. The cognitive scientist Francisco Varela coined the term *enaction* for the way that such organization emerges naturally from itself rather than being imposed and constructed by someone from the outside.[46] To envision this harmony, Chögyam Trungpa used the image of the sky and the earth, which a society must be able to join together: "When people have lofty ideas that they aspire to, they do not fall into the depressions of practicality alone. At the same time, to avoid purely having lofty idealism, you need the working basis of earth."[47] In a surprising way, this social and poetic conception is, in essence, truly philosophical, reflecting fully upon what is real. The exercise of power cannot be reduced to mere administration, relegating "democracy" to the status of management, which views people as "a crowd of individuals, a lump of volatile groups, precarious and manipulable networks in a universal business empire that has as its motto: 'Survive who can.'"[48]

The sacred order, it is crucial to recognize, is not based on any inter-est in domination. Writing on Traditional Indian government, Ananda Coomaraswamy identified its basis as the idea that each action, each role played in life, is like an altar upon which occurs the liberating sacrifice of individuality, indispensable to the unveiling, in each person, of the "Inner Man."[49] In Buddhist terms, a true action is one performed without ego. This renunciation of possessing anything liberates a living space.

Chögyam Trungpa specifies this: "Too often, people think that solving the world's problems is based on conquering the earth, rather than on touching the earth, touching ground."[50] Having one's feet on the ground and looking toward the sky is a balance that is denied us today. Indeed, Chögyam Trungpa explains that the Industrial Revolution saw itself as a proclamation of the earth opposing the sky—and thus contributed to a real disequilibrium, of which we are now the victims.

Democratic Nobility

The liberal ideology of a mass culture aims at the destruction of what is truly poetic: "The rising tide of democracy," writes Baudelaire, "which invades and levels everything, is daily overwhelming these last representatives of human pride and pouring floods of oblivion on these stupendous warriors."[51] In a way that is certainly paradoxical—but how else would he make himself understood?—Chögyam Trungpa brings up a surprising thought about royalty, for from now on it is each human being who is a monarch, who must recover his or her own dignity.

He had a radical way of cutting across all perverse and reductive conceptions of democracy, as well as a concern to fulfill completely the poetic vision that calls upon each human being to become the living center: "You could be king or queen—every one of you. That's the switcheroo, the great switcheroo."[52]

A democratic poetics does not in any way aim to destroy greatness or to reduce everything to the mediocrity of the lowest common denominator; it aspires to offer each person the possibility of experiencing his or her own excellence. Chögyam Trungpa revealed this possibility to everyone he met, though it was often hidden from their own eyes.

The nobility he spoke of no longer depends on one's birth but is a quality inherent in everyone. This is a democratic revolution in the most moving and ambitious sense, one that relates to the sense of Rimbaud's formula: "Poetry will be made not by one but by all." Democracy in its true sense should not mean, as is the case for us, abandoning poetry in the name of all, but rather recognizing the poetic call in each person, as the dimension of the authentic life, the life that is ceaselessly reinvented. Chögyam Trungpa's insistence, especially in the Shambhala teachings, on this royal quality particular to each person addresses the alienation of the modern world, which plunges humanity into an unparalleled rootlessness[53] whereby each person is deprived of his or her dignity. Indeed, this is what Nietzsche was able to identify as "the most universal sign of modern times: man has incredibly lost dignity in his own eyes."[54]

This concern that each person be given the opportunity to find a suitable place—without any privilege—is what Chögyam Trungpa called "ultimate democracy," explaining: "Everybody has a chance. Small plants can grow into gigantic plants."[55] Current Buddhist teaching is often a mass teaching. We reduce the teaching to the lowest common denominator without thinking about what harm we might be doing to the Buddhist tradition. Chögyam Trungpa's genius lay in his absolute rejection of this stance. Embracing the West, establishing a friendship with each of his students, he rejected this "mass democracy" transmission, this way of seeming to make oneself available to everyone, and of presenting Buddhism as some kind of easy wisdom, a method of self-improvement and personal development, or an experimental science of happiness that would allow one to identify the reasons for one's emotions and sufferings, in order to master them in the wish to get rid of them.

Within the Tibetan tradition, a distinction is made between the teaching given to all and everyone, and that given to tülkus, holders of the spiritual heritage. Chögyam Trungpa abandoned this distinction. He decided to present the teaching without keeping anything for himself, as if, he explained, each of his students were a tülku.

At the death of a teacher, when he is in samadhi, only very close disciples are authorized to stay in his presence. Chögyam Trungpa explained that each of his students was a close disciple, and without a doubt for the first time in the Tibetan tradition hundreds of people were able to take their turn in sharing this moment with the one who was the first spiritual teacher to understand the opportunity inherent in the age of democracy.

No doubt it was because he was a poet himself, in the highest sense of the term—he who names the sacred, seeing far higher than the man of religion—that Chögyam Trungpa could be the poet of this ultimate democracy, the opportunity secretly concealed in our age.

But it seems to me that one cannot understand this extraordinary commitment better if one neglects to consider the extreme fervor that led Chögyam Trungpa to interest himself completely in each person he met. If there is a secret to Chögyam Trungpa, perhaps it is this incandescent love that led him to cherish each human being so profoundly and personally. Thinking was for him a work of celebration. Even before he was a spiritual teacher preoccupied with any particular task, he was a spectacularly authentic human being. How remarkable that such a love could be the sacred word that supports the true meaning of true democracy—and that a master from the East would be the one to teach it to us, show it to us!

NOTES

1. In this specific sense, authentic Tradition—which I indicate by using the capital T—has nothing to do with the current usage of the term *tradition*, which refers merely to the concern for preserving that which is past because it is past, sealing it up like a museum piece; this sort of conservation stifles the truly Traditional mind. In the current usage, it would be more accurate to speak of fixed, unexamined habits.

2. Aristotle distinguishes the just regime from the corrupt regime, and then considers the number of those wielding sovereign power. If power is held by one, the just regime is royalty and the corrupt one tyranny; if it is held by the many, the just regime is aristocracy and the corrupt regime, oligarchy; if it is held by all, the just regime is a polity, and the corrupt regime, democracy.

3. The question of knowing whether "our" democratic regime accomplishes this initial aspiration is obviously highly problematic. To speak here of a "poetic undertaking" is to try to distinguish between an aspiration that has led so many men to an indisputable excellence and our current political situation.

4. Friedrich Nietzsche, *The Joyful Science*, trans. Thomas Common (New York: Russell & Russell, 1964).

5. Dominique Fourcade, "Rêver à trois aubergines . . . ," *Critique* (Paris), no. 324 (May 1974), p. 484. Fourcade, who in this study of Matisse takes as a starting point the painter's masterpiece *Intérieur aux aubergines*, Musée de Grenoble, explains: "*Intérieur aux aubergines* does not lead us, as painting has customarily done, from the periphery toward the center. It does the opposite: it reveals to us a universe that is not centripetal, but centrifugal, expanding. And no point of this universe is pictorially privileged in relation to the rest, since the center is everywhere."

6. The concept of everydayness allows Heidegger (*Being and Time*, p. 122) to elucidate an atheoretic intentionality, that is to say, Being-in-the-world. Cf. F.-W. von Herrmann, *Hermeneutik und Reflexion* (Frankfurt: Klostermann, 2000), p. 72. For my reading of Heidegger here, I am indebted to the remarkable text of Hadrien France-Lanord, *L'être ensemble chez Martin Heidegger*, which clears up a number of misunderstandings with respect to the latter's work. He concludes his essay with this remark: "The analysis of Being-with has enabled us to extract the true meaning of everydayness, not, therefore, an improper sphere of existence, but rather the immediate, and nontheoretic, dimension in which Dasein is always at first sight, and which the initial theoretical position of every metaphysics has already overtaken."

7. See the epilogue of his first book, *Born in Tibet*, and his journal, which has not yet been published. For the moment, research on Trungpa is only in its infancy, and although we possess a number of documents on his seventeen years in the United States, we are seriously lacking specifics regarding his seven years in England.

8. These preconceptions arise as much from an esotericism that today seems very hazy and turns Tibet into a land of myth as they do with an error that identifies Buddhism with a terrifying sort of nihilism. See Roger-Pol Droit, *The Cult of Nothingness: The Philosophers and the Buddha* (Chapel Hill: University of North Carolina Press, 2003).

9. See "The Eye," in Donald S. Lopez, Jr., *Prisoners of Shangri-La: Tibetan Buddhism and the West* (Chicago: University of Chicago Press, 1998).

10. Heidegger makes a distinction between the historic conception—the recording of facts in the most scientific manner possible—and a "historial" (*geschichtlich*) account of destiny that plays out in and comes from our actual way of life.

11. Chögyam Trungpa, "Work, Sex, and Money," seminar given in Burlington, Vermont, April 1972, p. 2. Buddhist masters are often said to come to the West to tame the barbarians, which is also seen as one of the accomplishments of Chögyam

Trungpa. Nothing could be more mistaken. Far from considering the West a barbarian world, Chögyam Trungpa knew how to recognize its greatness as well as the collapse that threatens it. On this path, he saw through the corruption of the contemporary Tibetan world, and he was one of the first to expose its idealization. Taking the position of an ordinary man is a simple and direct response to the stereotyped fascination that Tibet has elicited since the success of James Hilton's *Lost Horizons*, and is thus part of the effort to safeguard its true resources.

12. Unpublished, unedited letter, May 10, 1973, Shambhala Archives. Reprinted by permission of Diana J. Mukpo.

13. See the title of Jean Dubuffet's *L'homme du commun à l'ouvrage* (The Common Man at Work) (Paris: Éditions Gallimard, 1973).

14. Chögyam Trungpa was reunited with the spiritual and initiatory authority of the Kagyü and Nyingma lineages and their holders the sixteenth Karmapa and Dilgo Khyentse, who, for their part, never stopped emphasizing the unequaled importance of his activity in the West in presenting the dharma. But to understand the meaning of this spiritual authority, we need to be a little clearer than usual about the notion of authority. Hannah Arendt emphasizes that this concept has entirely disappeared from our modern world—it is no longer understood except as something that forces people to obey. Either one is well disposed toward authority in order to deal with the problems of a mass society or one is opposed to it, thinking that society should govern itself. But the real meaning of authority excludes the use of external means of coercion. The obedience that authority demands can only be based on freedom. (See Hannah Arendt, "What Is Authority?" in *Between Past and Future: Six Exercises in Political Thought* [New York: Penguin Books, 1977]). One understands that it has become impossible to rely on such a notion, which has become impossible to hear. The use of the word can signify what one understands either in its original sense, "that which increases and authorizes," or in its current sense, "the coercion that takes away my freedom and my capacity to determine for myself."

15. Martin Heidegger has brought this to light in a radical fashion in this celebrated proposition from *Sein und Zeit:* "The 'essence' of Dasein lies in its existence." *Being and Time*, p. 42.

16. Søren Kierkegaard, *The Concept of Anxiety*, trans. Reidar Thomte in collaboration with Albert B. Anderson (Princeton, N.J.: Princeton University Press, 1980).

17. Cf. M. Heidegger, *Sein und Zeit*, p. 184: In anxiety, Dasein gets "brought before itself [*vor es selbst gebracht*] by its own Being." Here the entire theme of authentic existence is at stake and is revealed through an open relationship with our own finiteness.

18. Such a concept is highly paradoxical for Western thinking, since the notion of an empty center seems to be an oxymoron. Chögyam Trungpa: "One should always remain in the center and not react to the situation. . . . So it often occurs that one is not being at the center of the potter's wheel, as it were, and if one accidentally throws clay on the edge of a potter's wheel, it flies off. There is nothing wrong with the clay and nothing wrong with the wheel; you simply threw the clay in the wrong spot. And if you throw the clay in the center, then it makes beautiful pots. So the whole point is that you have to be in the center all the time and not expect some external person or situation to act for you" (*Meditation in Action*, p. 48).

19. It was obviously a completely different matter when, as a lineage holder, in the context of initiation, he gave a spiritual transmission.

20. Chögyam Trungpa, "Work, Sex, and Money," Burlington, Vermont, April 1972. This is not an isolated formula but a leitmotif found for example in numerous talks from meetings organized by his students. See, e.g., the group of texts in *Selected Community Talks* (Boulder: Vajradhatu Publications, 1978).

21. Chögyam Trungpa, "Phase Two," *Selected Community Talks*, p. 19.

22. It is important to understand friendship here from the Buddhist perspective of non-ego, whereby it cannot be understood as the meeting between two egos. It is the fact of being open to oneself through another, however little one can understand this distinction between ego—the vain fiction of a centralized point of view—and one's true self. Cf. François Chenique, Introduction, *Ratnagotravibhaga Mahayanottaratantrasastra: Le message du future Buddha* (Paris: Éditions Derby, 2001), p. 32

23. Few spiritual organizations would place such emphasis on individual responsibility; Chögyam Trungpa invited many individuals to teach, give meditation instruction, organize seminars, etc.

24. *Meditation in Action*, pp. 13–14.

25. Sigmund Freud, *Civilization and Its Discontents*, trans. James Strachey (New York: Norton, 1961), p. 21.

26. Chögyam Trungpa, *1978 Kalapa Assembly Transcripts* (Boulder: Vajradhatu Publications), talk 2.

27. Since the relationship with the teacher is a bond based on affinity, free not only in how it is formed but also in how it is used, it preserves and develops the student's freedom from the beginning until the end. Nothing in it, particularly from the point of view Chögyam Trungpa developed concerning tantra, relates to clergy.

28. *Great Eastern Sun*, p. 27.

29. "A Buddhist Approach to Politics: An Interview with Chögyam Trungpa, Rinpoche" (1976), in *The Collected Works of Chögyam Trungpa*, vol. 8, p. 420. In this sense, his entire work is, from a widened perspective, political.

30. Hannah Arendt, "La politique a-t-elle encore un sens?" trans. Patrick Levy, in Hannah Arendt, *Ontologie et politique*.

31. G. Bernanos, *La France contre les robots* (Paris: Robert Laffont, 1947), p. 19).

32. Hannah Arendt, "La politique a-t-elle encore un sens?"

33. Economy should be understood, according to etymology (*oikos* + *nomos*), as the law or rule of the house, the habitat, the home. "Inspiring people has become problematic. It wasn't problematic in the time of the Buddha or Christ, or even much later, in the time of Mohammed or the Emperor Ashoka or Alexander the Great. There were never any problems in those days because the vision was not based purely on payment or on merchandising a product." Chögyam Trungpa, *1979 Kalapa Assembly Transcripts* (Boulder: Vajradhatu Publications), p. 2.

34. Whereas economics tends to reduce the political space to domestic management, Chögyam Trungpa continuously showed that domestic life is already profoundly political.

35. "A Buddhist Approach to Politics," in *Collected Works*, vol. 8, pp. 423–424.

36. Pierre Legendre *La 901ᵉ conclusion* (Paris: Éditions Fayard, 1998), p. 29.

37. A person becomes the "center of reference of being as such." Martin Heidegger, "L'époque des conceptions du monde" (The Era of "Conceptions of the World)," in *Chemins qui ne mènent nulle part*, trans. Brokmeier (Paris: Éditions Gallimard), p. 115.

38. Chögyam Trungpa, *1978 Seminary Transcripts: Vajrayana* (Boulder: Vajradhatu Publications), p. 69.

39. *Shambhala: The Sacred Path of the Warrior*, p. 25.

40. Gérard Conio, *L'art contre les masses* (Lausanne: Éditions L'Âge d'Homme, 2003).

41. Pierre Legendre, *Sur la question dogmatique* (Paris: Éditions Fayard, 1999), p. 10.

42. A major work published by Chögyam Trungpa in the United States, after his criticism of spiritual materialism, attacked the "myth of freedom."

43. If one relies, for example, on Dumézil's three-function theory, it becomes clear that the submission of the clergy to a temporal power definitively ruins such an order. The order of the ancien régime is not, in this sense, traditional and legitimate.

44. *Shambhala*, p. 128.

45. Chögyam Trungpa, *Sadhana of Mahamudra Sourcebook* (Boulder: Vajradhatu Publications, 1979), p. 9: "We definitely had a lot of spiritual problems in my country. People just conducted their little spiritual business affairs. . . . There was no real practice going on; it was a big racket."

46. Francisco Varela, Evan Thompson, and Eleanor Rosch, *The Embodied Mind: Cognitive Science and Human Experience* (Cambridge: MIT Press, 1991).

47. *Great Eastern Sun*, p. 98.

48. Pierre Legendre, *Miroir d'une nation* (Paris: Mille et une Nuits, 1999), p. 13.

49. See Ananda K. Coomaraswamy, *Autorité spirituelle et pouvoir temporel* (Spiritual Authority and Temporal Power): *Dans la perspective indienne du gouvernement* (Paris: Éditions Arché, 1985).

50. *Shambhala*, p. 97.

51. Charles Baudelaire, "The Dandy," in: *The Painter of Modern Life*, trans. John Mayne (London: Phaidon Press, 1964), p. 29.

52. *Great Eastern Sun*, p. 100. He elaborates: "Royalty in the Shambhala world is not based on creating a Shambhala elite or class system. In that case, I wouldn't share the Shambhala vision with everybody. I wouldn't be telling you about this at all. I would probably have selected about ten or twenty people to hear about the universal monarch who joins heaven and earth rather than discuss this openly."

53. See the analyses of Simone Weil, *The Need for Roots*, trans. Arthur Wills (London: Routledge, 2001).

54. Friedrich Nietzsche, *Fragments posthumes*, in *Oeuvres complètes*, vol. 12 (Paris: Éditions Gallimard, 1978), p. 253.

55. Chögyam Trungpa, "Lids and Flowers," *Selected Community Talks*, p. 128.

A Buddhist Military

James Gimian and Kidder Smith

Aggression is very deep rooted. Anger is like the heart of the earth: it has brewed for years and years and years, thousands of years. And when it is just about to give a little peep out on the surface of the earth, that is aggression. Don't try to make it go away, and don't try to invite it—that is what's called the path.

—Chögyam Trungpa, *Dharma Art*[1]

WHEN CHÖGYAM TRUNGPA arrived in North America in the early 1970s, the United States was involved in an unpopular war in Southeast Asia. Seeking an antidote to the aggression they felt all around them, many young Americans adopted Asian spiritual practices that promoted peace, love, and bliss. But Trungpa Rinpoche—rather than encouraging his students to sidestep, ignore, or cool out their aggression—had them work directly with it. In particular, he created a practice of meditation in action that took the form of a Buddhist military. Their motto: "Victory Over War." In this way Trungpa Rinpoche brought his students into the heart of aggression, showing them how to turn that fierce energy into a means of liberation. His military teachings are applicable everywhere conflict arises—internationally, interpersonally, and within our own being.

This Buddhist military began with the visit of His Holiness the sixteenth Karmapa to North America in the fall of 1974. The Karmapa is the head of the Kagyü lineage, one of the four orders of Tibetan Buddhism; his visit to the West was the first for someone of his rank. At this time Trungpa Rinpoche was becoming widely known, and his provocative style and emphasis on cutting through spiritual materialism challenged expectations of what a spiritual teacher should be. Some people made threats to his safety and that of the community. In view of the profile created by His Holiness's well-publicized national tour, Rinpoche enlisted a few of his students to accompany the Karmapa as he carried on his activities and another small group to attend to his own personal safety.

After His Holiness departed North America, more men and women in the community became involved in the practice of "guarding." Wearing blue blazers and gray slacks or skirts as their uniform, they performed duties such as driving visiting Tibetan monks to the airport, escorting teachers to talks, and acting as security guards at public events. Their presence provided a certain crispness and dignity to situations that were otherwise a bit sloppy.

The challenge was to create a practice based on Buddhist principles of nonaggression—that is, to act in ways that were at once precise and gentle. The basis of the discipline was sitting meditation. But being a guard always brought one into engagement with the world. Thus it was from the beginning a practice of meditation in action.

Dorje Kasung, or Vajra Guard, is the formal name for the military organization that Trungpa Rinpoche created. *Dorje* is Tibetan for adamantine, diamondlike, or indestructible (Skt. *vajra*). *Ka* is the first letter in the Tibetan alphabet and implies "sacred word." *Sung* means "protector." Thus the basic meaning of *Dorje Kasung* is "indestructible protector of dharma teachings."

The official birth of the Dorje Kasung occurred in January 1976. In establishing it, Trungpa Rinpoche wrote:

> You can be a great help. In order to save my life, I could become a charlatan. I could become soft and ingratiating, encouraging people's ego trips. But by doing so, I would be contributing to the pollution of the world and would be desecrating the tradition of the Practicing Lineage. If that were the only alternative, I still would

If you wish to receive a copy of the latest Shambhala Publications catalogue of books and to be placed on our mailing list, please send us this card, or e-mail us at: info@shambhala.com

PLEASE PRINT

Book in which this card was found
_____

NAME
_____

ADDRESS
_____

CITY & STATE
_____

ZIP OR POSTAL CODE   COUNTRY
_____
                                      (if outside U.S.A.)

E-MAIL ADDRESS
_____

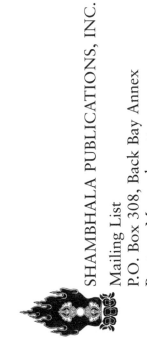

SHAMBHALA PUBLICATIONS, INC.

Mailing List
P.O. Box 308, Back Bay Annex
Boston, Massachusetts
02117

have no choice. I have been developing the security guard group in order to intelligently work with this situation, and share my confidence with you. As practitioners as well as guards you have the proper vision to deal with any obstacles. It is not just a matter of ceremony. It is an expression of dedication rather than confirmation. We must be aware of what we're doing and do it properly.[2]

Here Trungpa Rinpoche established the ground of Dorje Kasung–ship as life and death: not simply the physical threats that might occur but the very life of the teachings and the death that spiritual materialism brings. With full confidence, he gave us no choice but to rely on the intelligence arising within our own practice. To provoke that intelligence further, he also at this time bestowed eight slogans on the Kasung, including "Be a warrior without anger" and "Not afraid to be a fool." These slogans—simple-seeming yet always slightly elusive—functioned as reminders rather than as rigid protocol.

Three years later, in 1979, Trungpa Rinpoche introduced the "container principle," which became widely used to describe the overall function of the Dorje Kasung. A container holds something safe—a substance, activity, or state of mind. It simultaneously constitutes the boundary and offers structure, organizing the ground of a situation while allowing the content to manifest in various ways. A static example is the walls of a house, which mark the edge between domestic and public, and also provide a secure living environment. More dynamically, imagine the difference in the flow of a river, first as it dashes through a narrow gorge, then later as it meanders across a plain. Like the earth of this example, the container is the ground for all that takes place within it.

A common misunderstanding arises when only the boundary function is emphasized and when those boundaries are invoked solely to exclude undesired forces such as confusion or chaos. But a genuine container, by regulating the energy flow between inside and outside, creates an environment where such confusion can be either excluded or accommodated and exposed, and thus clarify itself.

Over time more practice forms were developed. The most intensive of these was an annual encampment, when thirty to three hundred Dorje Kasung would gather in the mountains for a week or two of meditation, marching practice, and teachings. Here's how a practitioner remembers the first encampment, in which he experienced directly the way the container principle could be applied.

Spring in the Rockies. About thirty of us, wearing makeshift military uniforms that ranged from thrift-store khaki to elegant British wool, camped at seven thousand feet, marching unsteadily in formation, learning how to be Buddhist soldiers. It was cold, rainy, and we had no idea what this encampment was supposed to be.

Rinpoche warned that the outrageousness of our activities—proclaiming the dharma in military uniform—could lead to an aggressive response from other members of our community who were genuinely disturbed by what we were doing. They might even invade us, he said—not exactly to wreak havoc, but as a disruptive prank at once playful and serious. We debated the right response and determined to create an impenetrable barrier of human bodies around the perimeter of camp. This would physically ward off invaders. But there weren't enough of us to make the barrier impenetrable, so we spent the night in shifts, running back and forth to fill the gaps, making noise and waving our flashlights to keep the enemy out, anxious to track down each hint of an incursion.

Rinpoche allowed us to carry on with our strategy. But after a day of scrutiny, he moved us within the camp's perimeter and had us lie down silently, resting at ease in the grass, so that an invader would pass right over us. That night we were "attacked." (Later, of course, we learned that Rinpoche had encouraged some of his other students to invade.) After the enemy had passed us and reached the center of camp, we stood up and captured them. We treated them as prisoners of war and showed them the nature of our encampment practice. Thus we created a ground for our mutual respect.

The basic teachings of a Buddhist military are contained here. First Trungpa Rinpoche put us into an environment where we could discover how our habitual responses to fear—warding it off, separating ourselves from it, and thus multiplying it—were ineffective, exhausting, and destructive. To show us that, he then heightened our paranoia by warning of a grave danger. Our immediate reaction was to amplify our own aggression to meet the aggression we feared outside ourselves. In response to this activity, he offered us a different way to work with our minds and bodies, a practice employing what he called "the greatest weapon we have, gentleness." We lay on the earth, allowing the enemy's attack to spend itself without causing harm. Then we captured our enemies and included them in our encampment life. In this way Trungpa Rinpoche took old forms, combined them with his own insight, invited us to participate in their continual development, and created a teaching vehicle uniquely suited to our contemporary world.

This is how Trungpa Rinpoche describes his own experience within the mandala of a military container:

> In certain other places where I've visited, where there is a good, strong military situation, I can contain myself in it thoroughly and teach properly. That is not because everybody runs around being a busybody, driving me around and providing lots of valets and cooks and all the rest of it. It's simply that the particular presence of your militariness helps me to teach a lot, to teach further. Otherwise, the whole teaching situation becomes like a giant wick with its flame burning, but there's no lamp to hold the oil, and I find myself stupid, wasted.[3]

So, too, Trungpa Rinpoche acted as container for the Dorje Kasung, creating a military that is a form of basic Buddhist training. As in a monastery, there is uniform dress, regimented activity, and a strong discipline of awareness. As a form of meditation in action, this sets us out into the world, continuously on the spot. As a practice of compassion, it affords multiple opportunities for putting others' welfare before our own and taming our own minds.

And as a manifestation of enlightenment, the discipline is never accomplished by the rote following of orders, but only by being awake at every moment, which manifests as an individual's intelligence and good human heart. Thus a foundational slogan Trungpa Rinpoche bestowed at one of the earliest encampments: "If you can maintain your sense of humor and a distrust of the rules laid down around you, there will be success." A Kasung recalls a moment of inspection: "On one occasion

Trungpa Rinpoche reviewed the troops, each of us standing stiffly at attention beside our pup tent as he walked round the camp perimeter. Gathering us together just after, he remarked, 'It makes me sad that none of you soldiers was brave enough to smile when I walked past.'"[4]

All military forces stress bravery. The bravery of the Buddhist military lies in identifying our enemy as aggression, whether found outside or within ourselves. Aggression is the heavy hand of ego, which tries to impose its order on the world like an abusive sergeant major. Thus humor plays a vital role in and about the Dorje Kasung, expressing our appreciation for primordial unpredictability.

Although Trungpa Rinpoche used the Dorje Kasung as a form of mind training in the specific context of a Buddhist community, his military teachings have wide-ranging implications for the conduct of war, politics, and society on the national and international levels. In order to extend his teaching to those realms, he made particular use of the Sun Tzu *Art of War*, a strategy text from ancient China.

Several of us had been reading that book in the early 1970s. Though the translations available then were often opaque, we found that its broad strategic thrust resonated in unanticipated ways with what we were learning from Trungpa Rinpoche. At the same time, we were looking for a way to make Kasung practice available to more people than could be trained by working directly with him. When we asked Rinpoche how this might be done, we were surprised to hear, "Study the *Art of War*."

The *Art of War* came together about twenty-three hundred years ago in what is now northern China, when a lineage of generals put their collective wisdom into written form for the first time. For two millennia their text has shaped the military thinking of all East Asia, and over the last fifty years it has deeply penetrated the strategic culture of the West. Because it begins by recognizing that conflict is an integral part of human life, its teachings have sometimes been invoked simply as a ruthless means of conquest. But when read more attentively, the book shows how to conquer without aggression, whether our conflict is large or small, personal or national. One of its most famous couplets states:

One hundred victories in one hundred battles is not the most skillful.
Subduing the other's military without battle is the most skillful.
(Chapter 3)

This is less a strategy than a profound understanding of our relatedness to the world. Its perspective can be represented by what the *Art of War* calls "taking whole." Taking whole means conquering the enemy in a way that keeps as much intact as possible—both our own resources and those of our opponent. It does not preclude the use of force, but in using force it seeks to preserve the possibilities and take into consideration the welfare of the other.

Such a victory leaves something available on which to build, both for us and for our former foe. By contrast, destruction leaves only devastation, not just for those defeated—their dwellings and their ground—but also for conquerors attempting to enforce their "peace" long after battle has passed. True victory is victory over aggression, a victory that respects the enemy's humanity and thus renders further conflict unnecessary. Each of us already possesses elements of that wisdom. It is neither Chinese nor Tibetan, nor does it come from any single source outside us.

Dorje Kasung training is a potent means to draw that wisdom into our life stream. It begins with sitting on a meditation cushion. But quickly it takes us out into the world of action, a world of kindness mixed with conflict and aggression. Thus it tempers our meditation practice in ways that sitting alone cannot. It also shows us patterns of effective behavior. The most prominent of these is "taking whole," which is not only the core principle and practice of the *Art of War* but also the basis of Dorje Kasung training and activity.

As we come to see the ineffectiveness of wielding aggression to curb aggression, these teachings of the Dorje Kasung take on heightened significance for the well-being of the container that is our shared world. Taking whole is skillful means for individual practitioners working with agression in and around themselves. It is also a model strategic response to the conflicts exploding all around the globe.

A group of Kasung worked throughout the 1990s to translate the *Art of War* into an English that would make this view and training accessible. By staying unusually close to the Chinese, we were able to prevent the paraphrase and dilution that usually accompany the translation of Chinese into English. We also wrote accompanying essays and commentary, whose insight arose from the Dorje Kasung disciplines. The result of this work was the publication of *The Art of War: The Denma Translation*.

Back to encampment. It is the summer of 1979. Threats of invasion rise again. Kidder Smith reports:

> Our entire water supply rested in a large, wheeled tanker, hauled up creaking from the valley below. I was standing sentry duty late one sagebrush-scented night, when a shout rattled through the camp: someone had cut the tanker's hose, and four days' water had flowed away. Had anyone spotted a lurker? Was a saboteur concealed among us? The whole camp was roused, soldiers fell out in varied forms of nightwear or uniform and stood at attention, while busy officers sought intelligence from the groggy night. Orders came from somewhere for marching practice. Then we were before Trungpa Rinpoche, presenting ourselves one by one for interrogation. As I approached him, flashlights playing in my face, I was given a splosh of Tabasco in my palm to lick as a kind of truth-oath serum. Then in his Oxford-accented tenor he asked me, "Kidder, did you cut the hose?" "No, sir!" I replied, and gave him a wet kiss on the cheek. And eventually we were all back to bed.
>
> At some point in that goofy midnight exercise it had occurred to me that only one person would have enjoyed cutting the hose: Chögyam Trungpa Rinpoche. It perfectly disrupted our normal sense of things, giving him and us the occasion for a joyful confusion, as soldiers sought earnestly for external enemies—a terrorist? pranksters? militant pacifists?—only to find nothing there but the habits of our own mind. Still more, we met him eye to eye for a brief meditation interview snatched out of our normal time for sleep. No perpetrator was ever identified, nothing explained. It was left to each to figure out what had happened or hear it from a friend, like the secret punch line of an intensely practical joke.[5]

Because it is a manifestation of enlightened mind, Dorje Kasung practice depends on the leadership of someone like Trungpa Rinpoche. Then its forms of meditation in action are both confining and liberating, precise and empty, and there is vast space in them to realize nonaggression, the truth of non-ego. If we fail to recognize the playfulness of that space, we may fall prey to the exercise of hollow forms alone. Or, swept away by the strong energies the practices evoke, we may forget how to transform aggression into gentleness.

Engaging with a teacher such as Trungpa Rinpoche, we discover our own innate bravery, our capacity to work directly with the heart of aggression. Then we are not afraid to be a fool, or a soldier, or an ordinary human being who places the welfare of others before our own.

NOTES

This article draws extensively from two sources, *True Command*, vol. 1, *The Town Talks*, and *The Art of War: The Denma Translation*, by Sun Tzu (Boston: Shambhala Publications, 2001). In particular, we adapt materials from James Gimian's introduction to *True Command*.

1. *Dharma Art*, p. 21.

2. "Letter to the Vajra Guards," in *True Command*, p. 2.

3. "This Is Your Duty," in *True Command*, pp. 64–65.

4. Kidder Smith, "Transmuting Blood and Guts," *Tricycle: The Buddhist Review* 10, no. 4 (2001): 76

5. Adapted from Smith, "Transmuting Blood and Guts."

Maitri Space Awareness

The Need for Place

PIERRE JACERME

For Françoise, in memory of Phyang (July 1998)

I N THE PREFACE to a collection of her essays written between 1954 and
1967, Hannah Arendt speaks of the "gap between past and future," and
she quotes an aphorism coined by the poet René Char, nearly at midcen-
tury (1944), to summarize his four years in the French Resistance: "Our inheritance was left to us by no testament" (Notre héritage n'est précédé
d'aucun testament).[1] Nonetheless, the "gap" has not always been such a
dramatic break.

The gap, as Arendt explains, always exists insofar as human beings
think, and are therefore "ageless"—since, for her, to think can only mean
making a fresh start, and must constantly renew this act of beginning.[*]

This gap, therefore, only is "coeval with man on earth"; it is "this small
track of non-time which the activity of thought beats within the time-
space of mortal men."

Nonetheless, *this* gap, in its freshness, its insistence, its edge, was hidden from us as such, through what we, like the Romans, have called *tradition.* Over thousands of years, we have relied on it. But there is a time in
which—and here we return to the twentieth century, to the very moment

Translated from the French by John Sell.

when Arendt entrusts this thought to us—as the modern age progressed, the "thread of tradition" finally broke, and the gap, ceasing to be a condition of thought alone, became a "tangible reality and perplexity for all." With this occurred a change in the activity, the work, and the *position* of human beings.

When authority, or foundation, ceases to exist, transmission itself is affected, and with it, the condition of possibility of culture.

Appearing in the public space, the gap becomes a political phenomenon. It is henceforth that which concerns us—in the sense that it questions us, passes through us, is the object of our interest, of our care.

This thought of Hannah Arendt's, arising out of this rupture, is therefore itself a *new* thought that emerges from that new modality of gap. Henceforth, thought will not be able to mask or bridge the gap, which, however, will not stop attracting it. It will no longer be a question of *what* to think, but of *how* to think in such a space.

The gap now becomes the *motif* of thinking; the motivating force that sets it in motion, that gives it its raison d'être, and before which it settles itself, like Cézanne contemplating Mont Saint-Victoire.

The new thought is an "experiment"; it explores a tangible gap—a void in which "reality" has a particular size. "The concern is solely with how to move in this gap," Arendt concludes. What is the particular *topology* of this movement?

At around the same time that Arendt wrote this preface, the young Chögyam Trungpa, that other exile, who had had to leave Tibet, and who, as well, would work in the United States (beginning in 1970), asked himself how to survive on earth during times of distress and how to explore the gap, whose ravaging effects he perceived as soon as he set foot in North America.

He began by devoting a number of seminars to identifying the gap, which he named, in reinterpreting the Tibetan Buddhist tradition, the *bardo*, specifying that one need not limit the meaning of this term to the bardo of death but could give it a broader significance. "*Bar* means 'in-between' or 'gap' or 'the middle,' and *do* means 'island,' so altogether *bardo* means 'that which exists between two situations.'"[2]

Trungpa thus moves things toward existence, and "the immediate experience of nowness—where you are, where you're at."[3]

As if it were necessary to bring humans back to earth. What was there behind the American "anxiety" that has become a global disease?

After the transformation of wars into "wars of materiel" (which is how the German author Ernst Jünger interprets the First World War in his book *The Storm of Steel*), after the "annihilation" of man by man (the camps), after the "uprooting of all beings"[4] as a unique global perspective (Hiroshima), man can no longer be defined as a "rational animal" but is at minimum torn between his reason and his madness, and constrained to ceaselessly question where they come from. This "inheritance without testament" is nonetheless what he must assume, even if he can barely still be taken for the lord of being, destined to have "dominion" over the earth, as the Book of Genesis declares. Something has indeed shattered for him.

Henceforth man is condemned to create and endlessly reinforce pseudo-certainties to reassure his "I," or ego, central agent of the assumed dominion. Or else he must skirt the gap and get involved in the space between, which means exploring its borders, to live in one or the other extreme, to transform the "space between" into a true, *continuous* thread (but what is such a continuity?); in this way he learns to *inhabit* a space that he doesn't know, or fails to recognize, but which could shelter him, if a sympathy can be perceived there. Or he flees the situation—every situation, which is to say being-in-a-situation itself—and distances himself from human essence, indeed turns against it. This implies that he leaves that which constitutes *world* for him.

Not only does this last possibility exist, but it is what people hurry toward at first; from this arises an anguish that Trungpa felt strongly when he arrived in the New World, a little after man had walked on the moon in 1969.

· That explains his emphasis on the bardo, space, and the six realms, from 1971. It touches on the condition of humans on earth after the explosion at Hiroshima, this point of encounter/non-encounter between West and East, this "burn scar on the skin of the world and all of humanity."[5]

As Maurice Blanchot saw, in dominating atomic energy, man has become a star: "That which until now only stars could do, man does."[6] The year 1945 marked the beginning of this astral evolution, but also of an escape, a *Space Odyssey* (Stanley Kubrick, 1968).

The possibility of ultimate destruction worried people to the point that they began taking the first steps toward leaving the planet. The development of the "conquest of space" is, in fact, closely tied (and not only in time) to that of nuclear research.

Because what is at stake in this expansion, in the final analysis, will always be the relationship between space and human possibility, as a remarkable form of being-in-the-world, what would work best would be not so much to "conquer" space (a delusion of the ego) as to "make friends" with it—in the sense that one makes friends with someone one *loves*.

Curiously, the first person in this era to feel this human need for an enormous space, and above all a friendly space, and to state it strongly, was someone who did not yet know Trungpa but who would meet him later, would work with him (Trungpa would even become his guru), and would later come to teach at Naropa Institute: the poet Allen Ginsberg.

From 1963, Ginsberg explained that, since we have "all failed" (he testifies about the H-bomb: "It's like a big booby trap of massed hatred and anxiety that cuts out all soft feelings in the body and ultimately results in a mass illusion of fear manifested in an H-bomb"), we must "find a friendly human universe where we can all completely exist at once."[7]

In this friendly universe, one would want to "completely exist," that is, with one's body: if each person is treated with the same care (Trungpa would later speak of "dignity"), then "everybody will be reborn back to their bodies which they've been almost driven out of by atomic fear," says Ginsberg.[8] To fight against this fear, there is a need, as he would say in 1965, for "the enormous spaces that open up in Cézanne's landscapes,"[9] where the rocks of the Garonne "seem to be floating in space like clouds";[10] and just as Cézanne created space not through perspective but through the "juxtaposition of one color against another color," in the same way, in juxtaposing one word with another in a "nonperspective" line of verse, Ginsberg imagined that one could create "a gap between the two words which the mind would fill in with the sensation of existence."

He gives an example: "When Shakespeare says, 'In the dread vast and middle of the night,' something happens between 'dread vast' and 'middle.' That creates like a whole space of, spaciness of black night."[11]

The texture of black night gives movement to an ineffable emptiness. Of course, this quality of space is not perceptible unless we give it a chance with "the entire depths of our minds" (which is rarely the case). In allowing this depth to work on us, to unfold, Ginsberg adds, one can "see through [Cézanne's] canvas to God."[12] On the condition of dropping "our shackled perspective," as another poet, Henri Michaux, stressed in 1945, "the space will return to what it was, an immense meeting place of a hundred spaces, which bathe in each other and in which objects and beings bathe with us."[13]

In this way, the emptiness of pure destruction can turn into an animated emptiness, rich and colorful, insofar as the mind, coming back to it, is a living, natural mirror that reflects everything and that *translates* its depth into innumerable places and the spaces in between.

The arts depend on this power of translation, provided that the eye "listens" to let all the harmony of "correspondences" resonate.

The Maitri project, which was first developed between 1972 and 1973, and ended in 1974 with the construction of the Maitri rooms, is like a poet's response, full of humor, to the disquiet that hides behind the boastful arrogance of the conquest of space. It is a poet's response because it seeks to *transmute* all the neurosis of the world. Baudelaire, confronting "spleen," was already speaking of "reversibility" in the previous century.

But first this project is offered as an experimental plan of action, enabling one to perceive the neurosis in its own *quality*, starting at its root.

What message is sent in this neurotic fashion, in some way confiscated by ego (to borrow from the language of psychology)? What from one point of view is "neurosis," from another is a display of energy. But humans are between the two; this is the source of our malaise, our uncertainty.

Fleeing the earth, but not yet completely inhabiting the sky, humans are in a situation of bardo. How can we be "anywhere"?

The conquest of space can only happen because modern science is an "astrophysics" that handles nature from one point of the universe outside earth, and man.[14] Deprived of land, of ground, man is deprived of place; in its stead is a zone of uncertainty, a place that is not a place, a no-place. In an astonishing way, Chögyam Trungpa intreprets the bardo as an undefined zone, a no-man's-land.[15]

Man is in a no-man's-land.

In a sense, this moment is favorable for experiencing, again, the importance of "nonself," of "nonexistence"—for reinventing Buddhism by giving it a greater scope.

The experience of no-place brings the question of primordial space, of an accommodating spaciousness, to the fore.

How can man touch the earth and rise up—gestures that could concisely define a buddha—at the same time?

How can one find the equivalent of earth when there is no ground for support? Or the equivalent of heaven, when man believes in "conquering" space and this heaven is merely the colony of a self deprived of place? And how to live in a nonplace?

In 1967, at age twenty-seven, Chögyam Trungpa wrote in his journal: "*I have no home. Home, I have none,* I have no home. While growing up, since I was little up to now, I have never had a family. Having no family seems very sad, but when I think how I have no home, it is very strange. . . . Therefore, since I have no ultimate heart friend other than myself alone, I think that it is definite that no one can create an ultimate home or family for me. Still, strangely, this home of being homeless is my home wherever I go. Everything is my home, the great home of being homeless."[16]

This text provides several fundamental pieces of information: one can inhabit the gap, the space between, by joining, if not to place, at least to the *need* for place, which arises out of having no "heart friend" but oneself alone, which arises from the emptiness of no-place. This opening of the heart inspires a resolve, a firm resolution that provides the occasion from within "no-place." This allows one to inhabit it: quite suddenly, through an instantaneous transmutation ("strangely," says Trungpa), the no-place becomes "the great home of being homeless."

Enduring the no-place can open up a friendship toward oneself, since the emptiness of the heart and the radiation from this space generates "the great home of being homeless," the community of those who have no community (later identified by Trungpa with the legendary Kingdom of Shambhala). The key point is to show this friendship toward oneself, which Trungpa then makes the very center of enlightenment: "Enlightenment is, as we said, an honest relationship with ourselves."[17]

In a century sick with ego, beyond individualism and collectivism, the rediscovery of oneself is essential. The Maitri experience displays the space of this attempt at opening the heart.

Why this return to Maitri?

Classically, maitri (Tib. *byams pa*) is one of the "four immeasurables" (Skt. *apramana;* Tib. *tshad med*), along with karuna (compassion), mudita (joy), and upeksha (equanimity). It has to do with frames of mind peculiar to one who renounces and prepares to meditate. Customarily, *maitri* is translated in English as "loving-kindness" or "love," in the sense of concern for the well-being of another.

For Trungpa, what is most important here is the dual reference to the *inner* experience—"You have to work from within"[18]—and feminine energy (maitri brings an element of warmth). It concerns turning toward the true self, toward the child that one always is, who, although barely born, already possesses complete maturity, as shown in the legend of the birth of Padmasambhava, which Trungpa identified with.

Wisdom is already there, here and now. Enlightenment is here, to be met—on the condition that one open to one's self, in its entirety.

For someone dominated by ego, this implies a change in direction: from ego toward oneself.

For Trungpa, the thought of "enlightenment" does not require being guided beforehand by compassion but is already displayed in the maitri space, which is a space of complete acceptance of self, including one's own chaos, and from that, accommodation of the other.

Maitri can be further elucidated through an anecdote about Atisha's master, who was not named Maitri-yogi for nothing: "One day while he was giving teachings to his disciples, they heard a dog cry out, and then it suddenly stopped crying. *At that very moment*, Maitri-yogi gave a cry of pain, shrinking almost to the point of fainting. . . . He revealed a large bruise on his back. Then he explained that someone had thrown a rock at the dog, whose suffering he had taken on himself in order to spare the dog. His realization of bodhicitta was such that he had the capacity to literally take upon himself the suffering of others."[19]

"At that very moment": it is worth contemplating this instantaneousness of perception. Every sentient being—a dog, for example—and a human are "the same." Maitri is this sensitivity to the same, when one has seen the situation "as it is"—and understood, here, with this invisible phenomenon that flies through the air and that one sees in the form of a bruise: the rock thrown at the dog, which produced the pain. The important thing is this space of "same," this more open space, where, in a flash, one perceives what *is*. To take another example from Trungpa, when "you are uncertain whether you are bound by passion or whether you are about to awake into compassion," you must become "able to perceive the situation as it is, then neither compassion nor passion exists. It is free, open space."[20]

This space, not easy to see, is in fact the nearest, the most ordinary, the most banal space.

Insofar as the state of the world is a bardo situation, in the sense of being a state of uncertainty, one has the experience of confusion and enlightenment *at the same time* but does not "communicate with those experiences."[21]

The reason for this is that one freezes the opposites, and one's "neurosis" consists of this dualistic *fixation*, which produces a separation between the "I" and the self, between "I" and other, between the "I" and the world.

Trungpa's idea is to reestablish communication in going toward open, free space, which is this space of maitri. Since it is ego that is responsible for fixation, it becomes essential, in order to fight against this tendency, to make friends with *one's self* (understanding that this is a collection much vaster than simply "I"), in appreciating oneself, in accepting oneself, in loving oneself. Thus the importance of maitri.

Beyond that, since the malaise is worldwide, since it cannot be denied by anyone, since no region escapes it, one must try to effect a transmutation that is somehow instantaneous, for example from confusion into enlightenment; otherwise, the situation will not be able to change. This would involve transmitting *all* the teachings to the West—dzogchen, as well as vajrayana, which is itself inseparable from hinayana and mahayana—and combining them.

To have an effect in the world at the level of *reality*, it is necessary, Trungpa believes, to deepen tantra, since it "puts the world back on its feet" (with the triumph of spiritual materialism, through an annoying inversion, the world was appropriated as part of ego, and subjected to ego's frame of reference, whereas it is the other way around—ego is in the world). But what is a world put back on its feet by tantra, this "spiritual atom bomb" (if it is not practiced after having first gone through the hinayana and mahayana)? The question of discipline becomes central, just as it does for all the teachings. How can one propagate these teachings if America is sick? It is reassuring that Trungpa identifies energy and activity behind the anxiety. How can one not try to transmit the teachings, when the state of uncertainty is worldwide? And what practice could one invent that would be sufficiently simple to be undertaken by those most affected?

It would be necessary to create a mechanism that encourages the internal experience of accessing *oneself* and, at the same time, prepares the transmutation of a neurotic situation, which one would properly experience fully before moving in another direction. Out of this necessity comes the progression implemented by Chögyam Trungpa: he begins by interpreting bardo as "gap" in 1971; then, in 1972, he shows the decisive role of "crazy wisdom," the perspective developed by Padmasambhava; and in 1973–1974, he combines the two in the Maitri project, which is, at the beginning, an experimental project of "space therapy" in a community setting, then from 1976, a component of an educational program at Naropa Institute, and, finally, more broadly, a practice for producing a "good citizen," a future member of an enlightened community (Shambhala).

Often presented as growing out of a meeting with Shunryu Suzuki Roshi at San Francisco Zen Center in 1971, this project is in fact the result of a much earlier situation. The groundwork for the idea that arose that day, echoing their conversation—an idea Trungpa was later to characterize as "audacious"—was laid by a spiritual adventure that one can piece together through three texts:

- the discourse recounted in *Born in Tibet* (1966), given in Tibet in 1958 by a teacher and close friend of Trungpa's, Khenpo Gangshar;
- the retreat Trungpa undertook in 1968 in Bhutan, in Padmasambhava's cave, which culminated in a mystical experience and the composition of *The Sadhana of Mahamudra* (September 6, 1968), which he commented on in September and December 1975;[22] and
- finally, the 1976 text on the problem of "planting the dharma in the West," written as an epilogue for the 1977 edition of *Born in Tibet*.

What links these texts is the question of the gap in the transmission, following the Chinese invasion of Tibet—or, rather, made obvious and even more serious by that dramatic event. For, according to Trungpa, things had begun to decay in Tibet considerably earlier: in the name of the sacred, all the teachings had been corrupted.

Returning to *The Sadhana of Mahamudra* in December 1975, he describes things this way: "There was tremendous corruption, confusion, lack of faith and lack of practice in Tibet . . . performing rituals became people's main occupation. Even if they were doing practice, they thought constantly about protocol. It was like one of us thinking, 'Which clothes should I wear today? What shirt should I wear today? What kind of makeup should I wear today? Which tie should I wear today?' Tibetans would think, 'What kind of ceremony can I perform today? What would be appropriate?' They never thought about what was actually needed in a given situation. . . . Tibetan Buddhism was turning out to be a dying culture, a dying discipline, a dying wisdom."[23]

With the dharma in such a weakened state, the pressure from the Chinese communists who invaded the monasteries and imprisoned many people constituted such a menace that it was necessary to think about reforming the entire practice. This decision was part of a difficult time, as recounted in *Born in Tibet* (1966).

Trungpa described how the Chinese spied on his monastery at Surmang in 1957, when he was seventeen years old. At the beginning of 1958, he went on retreat in a cave where Padmasambhava had meditated centuries ago. He went with Khenpo Gangshar, who had been taught by Trungpa's guru, Jamgön Kongtrül of Shechen—a distinguished spiritual connection. The situation seemed to them to be consonant with an ancient prediction: in the golden age, snow was a diamond; in the next age, an onyx. "In the third age, however, it was to become like iron; everything would be dark and our time in Tibet would be over. . . . The legend of the three ages seemed to indicate to [Khenpo Gangshar] how urgent it was to prepare for the dark period before us."[24]

Chögyam Trungpa records the remarkable discourse in which Khenpo Gangshar, seeing what was happening, made the decision to change the form of transmission itself. In these pages, there is also the first mention of Maitri.

First, Khenpo Gangshar explained, since now (in Trungpa's words) "the more immediate need was to teach all the people," lessons would no longer only be given to monks; because "we might no longer be allowed to perform our rituals," "we must build our temples in ourselves," abandoning the divisions between the different schools, and develop the four "divine stations" (i.e., the four immeasurables): universal love (maitri), spiritual joy, compassion, and equanimity. He recommended that they follow the system of the Kadampas, who specialized in the means for developing maitri. And he added that the doctrine of maitri should be combined with those of mahamudra and atiyana, the meditation methods of the ultimate teaching of the Buddha.[25]

Such are the essential points that Chögyam Trungpa in turn advocated throughout his teaching in the West.

The advice to follow the Kadampas in order to develop maitri brings us back to *The Seven Points of Mind Training* that Atisha received from Dharmakirti, and that was transmitted to the Kadam lineage founded by Dromtönpa and extended into the Kagyü lineage (in which Trungpa is a lineage holder) by Gampopa.[26]

When the existence of a mode of initiation by an external master is threatened, the focus turns entirely toward the individual: "We must continue our efforts to follow the promptings of the guru within ourselves," said Trungpa shortly afterward, when he decided to leave Tibet, in his words of farewell to his companions at the monastery that he led.[27]

He was twenty when, for him, the gap became "tangible reality."

There would be a cruel march toward India, and then training in the West, in England and Scotland. And there, Chögyam Trungpa was to understand that the crisis was not limited to Tibet, that materialism infected "the spiritual disciplines in our modern world." In these conditions, how could one spread the dharma in the West? This question obsessed him.

In 1968, he left for Bhutan and decided to do a retreat in the cave of Tagtsang, where Padmasambhava had meditated before bringing Buddhism to Tibet. It was a return upstream to the source of the practice lineage, to begin at the beginning again, but in a different way. Trungpa needed to make a very close connection mystically to Guru Rinpoche in order to find the energy to launch a new form of transmission that would at the same time save spirituality and extend Buddhism to the West.

For "this is the darkest hour of the dark ages. Disease, famine and warfare are raging like the fierce north wind. The Buddha's teaching has waned in strength. . . . On the whole, no one acts according to the highest code of discipline, meditation, and wisdom."[28] Thus begins *The Sadhana of*

Mahamudra, written on September 6, 1968, in the very place where Pad-masambhava "meditated and manifested as Dorje Trölö, his crazy wisdom form."²⁹

A "very special" place where, nonetheless, at first, during three very disappointing days, Trungpa had the experience of no-place. His retreat unfolded in a very ordinary way. It was like a "space between," before the return to England: "[I] thought about what I would have to do when I went back, so Tagtsang was just a resting place for me."³⁰

Disappointment, boredom, lost time. The "shabby" side of this no-man's-land: "The cave itself . . . is a dark little dungeon. It smells of moss and rotten wood and decaying offerings. . . . It's just like getting inside a garbage pail. . . . In spite of my respect for the place, it's still just a dingy hole."³¹

This experience of bardo put him in increasingly extreme and intense states of mind. Trungpa lived in expectation, hope, and then frustration, depression, all while being haunted by the question of transmission: "I kept thinking about how I could actually communicate what I knew to others."³²

The more the depression intensified, the more it collected the inner self into himself, to the breaking point where he opened up to the other: "At that time I started drinking more and more because I felt depressed . . . one night . . . I got extremely drunk and frustrated . . . it was a very intense and very personal experience. . . . It was an internal yell, and it created some kind of breakthrough, and some understanding of alcohol at the same time. . . . At that point, I very quickly attained some kind of realization . . . the headlines of this Sadhana just came up in my head, flashed in my mind . . . and the next day I woke up quite clear, without any hangover. I was very happy and joyful; my whole mood had completely changed. . . . I began to write the Sadhana on that day, and I completed almost the whole thing. . . . I didn't have to think about what I was doing; the whole thing came out very fresh."³³

It is in this way that Chögyam Trungpa describes how, in an instant "all experience becomes crazy wisdom," under the almost Dionysiac mask of an "extraordinary" drunkenness. This internal scream, which makes one think of the scream immortalized by Edvard Munch, came out like light.

It is the cry announcing the birth of a new lineage.

Trungpa fulfilled the idea of Khenpo Gangshar to stop the war between the different schools of Tibetan Buddhism (which had been the project of Jamgön Kongtrül the Great in the nineteenth century): "In writing the Sadhana, I tried to bring together the Nyingma tradition and the Kagyü tradition. That is the basic idea of the Sadhana: to bring together the ati and mahamudra traditions. There's no conflict at all between the two."[34]

Poetically, Trungpa created a "collage," superimposing on Padmasambhava, founder of the Nyingma lineage and master of tantra, the figure of Karma Pakshi, who "was just one of the crazy wisdom lineage in the Kagyü tradition."

"So my purpose in writing the Sadhana was to build a bridge between the two contemplative traditions . . . to bring together in a harmonious way the mahamudra language of the newer school of tantra and the ati language of the older school of tantra."[35] What makes this collage possible, he tells us, is "some kind of basic foundation: the practice of surrendering, renunciation and devotion. . . . Without that you can't see or hear or experience the real teachings properly and fully."[36]

By analogy, it is this role of "basic foundation" that the maitri practice of space therapy will play starting in 1972–1974—a role of discipline and harmonization.

Trungpa spoke of "experiencing the real teachings completely." Why this insistence on "reality"? Because of the problems he encountered coming to the New World. The meeting with Suzuki Roshi, who asked himself how to work "with the neurotic or psychotic elements of the students and of the world in general,"[37] made him relive his experience in Tibet, as if Suzuki Roshi played the role of Khenpo Gangshar for Chögyam Trungpa.

How does one transmit the dharma in the United States when those who are interested in tantra are druggies or "psychotics"? Faced with these detours, with this *escape*, the first possible response is to recall the weight and richness of the *reality* of *what is*. From this angle, what Suzuki Roshi wrote in 1970—"When we hear the sound of pines on a windy day, perhaps the wind is just blowing, and the pine tree is just standing in the wind. That is all that they are doing."[38]—complements the real subject of Trungpa's sadhana: *seeing the profundity of everyday experience.*

This recall of the shock of reality, its freshness, its nakedness, is essential.

It is in this context, and when Suzuki Roshi died at the end of 1971 without having achieved his project, that during December 1971 Trungpa abruptly had the "audacious" idea of the Maitri rooms, close to the retreat caves of Tibet, close to the cave of Tagtsang: "I suddenly remembered the bardo retreat techniques for relating with space. Relating with the light dawned on me."[39]

At the same time the idea came to him from "somewhere": "I realized myself in a box. . . . I felt it's a square world that you're living in and there is an exit of some kind."[40]

It was like a vague recollection. He wrote:

People with parental problems need a four-windowed house
People with drug problems need a long tunnel with windows
People with spiritual problems need underground windows
People with suicidal problems need a tower with windows
People with intellectual problems need a room without windows.[41]

This is reminiscent of classical Tibetan medicine, based on the *Gyü Zhi* (*Four Tantras*) of Chandranandana, which connects illnesses with the elements and with places. For example, wind is linked to the mind—placed near the heart—and to mental disturbances, so when there is a wind illness, one needs a warm, comfortable, dark room (a very bright room would stimulate wind). If there is a bile illness, one would need a cool place with calming colors; if it is a phlegm illness, one needs a warm, bright, and loving place.[42]

But, for Trungpa, the elements are replaced by "I" (there are only "I" illnesses), and these are the problems labeled "psychological" that need to be connected to ways of being-in-the-world, an originating spatialization. States of mind produce a placement in space; therefore, spatialization can in turn act on states of mind. From the nature of space, one can work out a path:

"Bardo retreats are measured by individuals' heights. . . . The taller the person, the higher one raises the pictures [which are on the walls] of all the corners so that they have more space to relate with despite the most total darkness." [43]

One must try to go toward that kind of space: "Also I began to realize the old practice of the other techniques of Maha Ati, the ultimate yana, the ultimate point of spiritual enlightenment, spiritual achievement, is based on a sense of space."[44]

"Space" can therefore illuminate.

But what is *this* space, and how do we connect with it?

Ordinarily, we are in relation with a pseudo-space that results from the manipulations of our ego and arises from our projections. These projections forge an external world, therefore also an internal world, and, between these worlds, they establish a dualistic separation, the territory of "neurosis."

We believe, then, that everything comes from a sort of battle between internal and external, and we never confront our projections; although it is in fact ourselves that we are fighting, we do not recognize this. Logically, we would have to untangle these hardened, frozen patterns that "territorialize" space, the better to dominate it; but since they result from the very makeup of our "I," to untangle them is also to undo the "I," and awareness, and therefore to increase "confusion" (which also produces a certain kind of "enlightenment," since as opposites they depend on each other). At the same time, all this work of undoing must allow us to meet the original space, limitless and indestructible—which is neither "I" nor "mine," rather "not-I"—and which relates to it *in another way*, since this space does not depend on a control center, and is not a rational space, but, in "the most total darkness," is nevertheless that which illuminates: through its utterly vast opening, its quality, its texture consisting of different intensities.

In essence, what does it mean to open ourselves to "other," to what is not "us"?

Let us take pain as an example:

If you become the pain completely, then without *you*, pain's function becomes nothing. It is just energy, just sharpness of something. It might still cut through, but it is no longer pain as we know it.

You see, the problem is that we do not experience pain as pain at all. We only experience the challenge of pain, the *challenge* of whether or not we are going to overcome the pain. That is why we feel pain—because we feel that we are going to lose our territory and the pain is going to take us over. That is where the real pain begins on an ordinary level.[45]

What is important is that we should abandon the struggle.

Likewise, we are constantly struggling with space, and we believe, for example, that in "relaxing," we can have another relationship to space. But this can only ever be a false space, since relaxation is the opposite of struggle, and therefore depends on it; up to the point of relaxation, it gives evidence of struggle.

To connect with space here means to connect with space that is not our property, with space as it is in itself, immense, indestructible. We must therefore learn how to harden our bodies, to *hold* it, to make it indestructible, so that we are this space, and it is ourselves.

This tension has nothing to do with the act of freezing the space around us in our efforts to conquer it, in fragmenting it. It is learned through special training.

At the beginning, the practice of Maitri "space therapy" was parallel to the training in the Mudra theater group (from 1972, Trungpa developed his Mudra Space Awareness project—awakened presence in the space of movement—inspired by the monastic dances of Tibet).

The more one intensifies the body, the more one connects with the space around the body, and *from there*, to the immense totality itself: "Pull your muscles as if space is crowding in on you. Clench your teeth and your toes. . . . Very strange to say, in order to learn how to relax you have to develop really solid tenseness. You can breathe out and breathe in but don't rest your breath, just develop complete intensification. Then you begin to feel that space is closing in on you. In order to relate with space you have to relate with tension."[46]

It is the only way of approaching a space that does not belong to us and, through that, to train in *nonmastery*, therefore in other ways of existing and feeling, more expansively open, and different. The Maitri space therapy practice teaches to live nonmastery to the point that it becomes our habitual way of existing. Such is the power of ordinary magic: From the way that a person pours a cup of tea, you can tell how preoccupied he is.

In a talk, Chögyam Trungpa remarked that there is no word in either Sanskrit or Tibetan that means what we understand by "therapy," and that it would be better to speak of discipline (*sila*), but that the most important thing is not so much the name but the *attitude* itself, which can either be "oriented toward a goal," or present as a "way of living." In the first case, one has a tendency to make use of things, and that which one does not make use of is not really part of one's life. By contrast, if discipline becomes an attitude and part of our life situation, then we can have a friendly relationship with it, which is to say, finally, complete. And "basic health" is the capacity to really identify oneself with one's actions, one's emotions, one's thoughts . . . *with life as a whole.*

"The purpose of living your life is not simply waiting to die, but to dance with it, to work with it."[47]

To learn to rest in the state of nonmastery, to "remain natural" (one of Atisha's slogans), makes it possible to feel the glow of friendliness, which is as much the space of friendliness as the friendliness of space.[48]

The challenge is to open to existence as a whole. Do we have *need* of such a whole? In a certain way, through negativity, the presence of neurosis, with its inevitable burden of complaint, demonstrates a need to exist in another way; neurosis is a call, a request for "basic sanity." Paradoxically, the need expressed by neurosis proves that we also need an openness to the whole.

In the Maitri room, the neurotic will encounter his own neurosis, his need, but above all the deepest need (the *necessity*), of which the neurosis is only the indicator. He encounters it in a way such that he cannot escape it, and he will finally connect with it, in a movement that will change him, since the mechanism brought into operation will make him discover his own projections. It is as if he witnessed, thanks to the intensification that the experience produces, the genesis of his "I," from his relationship to the world and to others, and noticed the limitations introduced, and therefore opened himself to the limitless.

If we equated "confusion," which is Buddhism's starting point and working basis, and "neurosis," the latter would be removed right away from the medical and psychiatric model, and understood as arising from a distortion of the original space, effected by projections too enmeshed with "I," which provoke ignorance, passion, suffering. And, just as confusion is the request for enlightenment, and therefore is already enlightenment, neurosis is interpreted as the request for energy:

"Ego is seen as a kind of filter network through which energy is constantly being channeled and manipulated rather than being able to flow freely in unrestricted space."[49] "The object of the space therapy . . . is to increase the energy of a person's neurosis by having a patient lie in a posture particular to his diagnosed neurotic style."[50] In increasing the speed of this energy, the neurosis will become more visible, and one can "work with it more easily."

Here Chögyam Trungpa set in motion what he learned during his stay in the cave at Tagtsang. Revisiting this experience in September 1975, he confided: "The basic vision of the Sadhana is based on two principles: the principle of space and the principle of energy. Space here refers to the ati principle, the ninth and highest yana of buddhist tantra. The energy principle, or mahamudra, is the second level of tantra: it is also a high level of experience. So we are trying to bring space and energy together."[51]

And he says this, with the intention of transmuting all the neurosis of the world: "This is a very confused world, a very corrupted world at all levels. I'm not particularly talking about the Orient or the Occident, I'm talking about the world in general. . . . The question we need to look into is how we can overcome spiritual materialism fully and properly, without just brushing it off as simply an undesirable consequence. . . . How can we work with those things properly, how can we transmute them into livable, workable, enlightened basic sanity?"[52]

One sees that the challenge is social, and historic: if the world is *perceived* as workable, it becomes "benevolent." There is therefore a way to construct an enlightened world, not by referencing an ideal (imaginary) "I," or an ideal of "I" (upon which every theism hinges), but by starting from that which is perceived, and remaining at a down-to-earth level.

It is necessary then to create a *direct* link with energy, which requires a decentralized process (eliminating "I" as direct center), since energy is openness and consequently extends everywhere.

Returning to the distance he covered in the epilogue "Planting Dharma in the West" in 1976, Chögyam Trungpa specifies: "The Maitri approach to therapy involves working the different styles of neurosis through the tantric principles of the five buddha families. Rather than being subjected to any form of analysis, individuals are encouraged to encounter their own energies through a meditation practice employing various postures in rooms of corresponding shapes and colors."[53]

This passage clarifies the mechanism of which we spoke. Tantra distinguishes five main energies, known as buddha families. Each energy makes the way of being-in-the-world (the primordial intelligence) resonate according to a certain *tonality*; and this tonality can present itself in a veiled, confused way, or in a fully open, enlightened way—from which come different ways of perceiving *what is* and also ways of projecting. From this in turn come different styles of neurosis, since we seek a reference point to prove to ourselves that we exist; we then create our style. These styles are like "the handle that. we want to hang something on"[54] (to know, the proof of our existence). This is why we cherish our neuroses so much. At the same time, even because of this, the chaos of the neurosis is the only familiar ground where a spark of sympathy can be established, which makes it possible to *order* the chaos by connecting the buddha families to the mandala principle.

Why *five* buddha families? As Marvin Casper recalled in 1992, the Buddha remarked of his enlightenment that his awareness was clear, even, discriminating, unobstructed, and all-pervading. He then spoke of five wisdoms: mirrorlike wisdom, the wisdom of equanimity, discriminating-awareness wisdom, the wisdom of all-accomplishing action, and the wisdom of all-pervading space. He also realized that each enlightened aspect could be transformed into a confused aspect, in an expression of passion, aggression, or ignorance. Everything depended on ego-fixation or its absence.[55]

Thence arise the five buddha families, which allow one to map the topology of energy.

The vajra family is associated with water, the color blue, mirrorlike wisdom, and, in its enlightened form or in its confused form, aggression.

The ratna family is linked to earth, the color yellow, and the wisdom of opening or a feeling of poverty and dissatisfaction.

The padma family is linked to fire, the color red, and discriminating awareness or an ambivalence toward the world through an excess of instability and intensity.

The karma family is linked to wind, the color green, and the wisdom of all-accomplishing action or an excess of control, through fear of being destroyed, and manipulation.

The buddha family is linked to space, the color white, and the wisdom of all-pervading space or a space solidified through an excess of anguish and ignorance.

Each person's style is a mixture of these energies. "Each of these neurotic styles presents a different way of relating to space, which influences how one relates to a situation."[56]

If one is thinking about building a place with the help of the Maitri rooms, it is important to add that, in tantric iconography, the five families are placed at the center and in the four cardinal directions of the mandala: the buddha family is at the center, associated with a wheel; the vajra family to the east, and linked to dawn; the ratna family to the south, and linked to midday; the padma family to the west, and associated with the moment just before the end of day; the karma family to the north, and linked to evening.

From this context, Chögyam Trungpa speaks about a meditative practice including a number of postures in rooms of corresponding color and form.

There are also five Maitri rooms, in different colors, around two square meters. In each case, carpet and walls are the same color; the form of the window is different each time.[57]

"The patient is asked to lie in this posture in a room designed to reflect the traits of the buddha family involved. For example, a person with a vajra neurosis is asked to lie in the vajra posture in a vajra room. The patient must remain in the room for two forty-five-minute periods each day, with a short break between periods, together with one of the staff."[58]

The staff person represents the community (the equivalent of the sangha) while also elucidating the daily life situation. We will see an example, which Trungpa Rinpoche discusses at length, of how the place can be made, starting from a change in the relationship to original space.

"The style of a vajra person in his relationship to space is that he wants to see everything, take in all the details. In the vajra posture, the patient lies on his stomach on the floor with the legs together and arms at right angles to the body, palms pressed against the floor slightly, and the head turned to the side. The position tends to precipitate the basic vajra neurosis because the patient is down on the ground and his vision is very limited. The desire to be in touch with everything visually is denied by this particular physical situation. Everything you would like to see is behind you or above you where you cannot see it. The tendency of a vajra type to fragment space is accentuated by placing many small windows randomly in the room. At first, this situation might seem extremely irritating or threatening to the patient, precisely because he feels threatened by his own style of relating to space. . . . As the therapy continues, the patient's relationship to space in the therapy room becomes less threatening."[59]

Why "less threatening"? Because, in the Maitri room, the person can face his or her own exacerbated neurosis and thus get to know it better, recovering, progressively, his or her "self" in its entirety.

The close connection with the floor anchors one to the ground, while at the same time there is a feeling of what is above, which is not usually the case. "You do not feel solid enough to feel the ground when you are lying down . . . you feel like you were perched on space. . . . And the reason that you feel that is that you do not have enough relationship with the space in front of you."[60]

Now, on the contrary, everything comes back to us in the face: "In some sense, the postures are a way of mocking you. You haven't seen your space, and you have to live with it, and you have your own expressions of your neurosis which come back to you, and you have to live with it . . . Usually what happens is that we look for entertainment of all kinds, to take our minds off that. But then it is necessary to come back to one's world, to redefine it properly . . . It bounces back on you as *you*. That's why it's a kind of self-exploration process."[61]

Nonetheless, Chögyam Trungpa does not call on the idea of interiority or of internal awareness: "It is not that something doesn't go in you like an interior organism, it's binding yourself to your projection that's a problem."[62] It is a problem because, if we have created an external world from such projections, we have then forgotten it; and we wanted to believe in the very existence of the external world to convince ourselves of our own existence. We then imagine a *wall* between the world and ourselves, whereas we have in fact made this wall ourselves.

The difficulty comes from the fact that the projections need to take form in order to become visible: "Space therapy is concerned with projections, how they project outside, and no one can have a response at least until the projections have taken a sort of form."[63]

This taking form requires space, an original space, before all this assemblage, an "inviting," "accommodating" space, a Maitri space—on March 31, 1974, Trungpa says "a place."

In the Maitri room, the projections bounce off the walls, so to speak, analogously to the imaginary wall that separates us from ourselves, and come to us from outside, but little by little, in such a way that we recognize them as our own and adopt them. The person "may come to realize that the 'external world' is always the same in these rooms and therefore his shifting perceptions of the room are his own creation."[64]

We become "friends" with the wall. We feel the spaciousness of its energy, that is to say emptiness and, at the same time, maitri, "a sympathetic attitude . . . an element of softness or warmth . . . the element of maitri, or loving-kindness, begins to produce a sense of texture and solid reality."[65]

We then connect to a "space [that] is self-contained. . . . It has the space to afford to be space, spaciousness."[66]

It is also a space where one can receive others as guests, as Trungpa likes to emphasize. Trungpa humorously invites us to a different kind of "conquest of space": "In the Maitri exercises, we try to conquer space. We develop new modular systems of missiles, rockets, space stations. In developing certain little gadgets, space can connect to us. It is altogether like a space odyssey from this angle."[67]

From another angle, it is the reverse, since it is the composition of a "solidness in relationship to the earth"[68] and to the world.

We learn to work with the *reality* of the intensity that is in us; we move toward the more real, the more ordinary, which now appears to us with an extraordinary brilliance and in all the richness of its many connections: "The world is jumping out at us." We enter into this immensity: the chaos orders itself according to the mandala principle: the confusion turns into enlightenment; transmutation begins; we perceive what is, *as it is*.

"When we realize the basic totality of the whole situation, then perceptions become extraordinarily vivid and precise. That is because they are not colored by the fundamental conventionality of believing in something. In other words . . . where there's no belief in the blueness of the sky and the greenness of the field—then we begin to see the totality. The reason that perceptions are much more spectacular and colorful is that we do not transmit the message of duality between solidity and spaciousness."[69]

Restored to the utter fullness of its display, the everyday becomes something *sacred*, which we feel as such and celebrate.

The "hardiness" of maitri becomes clear: "It is not sweetness in the sense of being nice. . . . It's basically being open. Extremely open."[70]

Open to a sort of message that transmits unceasingly.[71] Everything becomes precious: Each instant, each of our movements ordinarily possesses something to make us think.

Finally, that which we lived as "no-place" is revealed to be a "some-where." But this "somewhere" is not a "territory": "Understanding shun-yata means that we are beginning to realize that there is no ground to get."[72] This "somewhere" is where "a brilliant spark or flash happens," "within space or understanding of space."[73]

The *place* only lasts for a flash, but only this flash lasts; and to live in this place is to live in the interval between these two propositions. To explore the gap opens out onto this interval, which is of a spiritual nature: "The important thing, to begin with, is to have a blank sheet of paper in front of you."[74] Then the invisible trace of this interval can be inscribed.

Chögyam Trungpa responded to the uncertain situation of humanity by taking as a starting point a Tibetan Buddhism as if "finger-painted," and giving a way of thinking about place and its "need" that restores the earth to its dignity, while allowing humans to uplift themselves.

He understood that, now, what can create a place, for a person, is that which takes part in its *everydayness* to uplift him- or herself in a limitless space, while conserving solidity with respect to the earth. Both are necessary. Matisse had intuited it: our period in history requires a "limitless space in which for a moment we feel so free" (written after a Paris-to-London flight).[75]

This *need* belongs to our "now": "Each era brings with it its own light, its particular feeling of space, as a *need*. Our civilization, even for those who have never been on an airplane, has led to a new understanding of the sky, of the extent of space. Today one has come to demand total possession of this space."[76]

That which Trungpa saw very well is that losing oneself in space, or "extreme spacing," would be madness.[77] The counterweight of the down-to-earth, of the everyday, is necessary. And out of this need, one also finds an echo in Matisse, when he is faced with an empty canvas: "The characteristic of modern art is to *participate in our life*."[78]

Matisse spoke (February 3, 1949) about this acute perception of the everyday, the fully opened center of the Maitri practice: "My work consists in soaking in things. And afterward, it comes out." He called this work "prayer": "I don't know whether I believe in God or not. I think, really, I'm some sort of Buddhist. But the essential thing is to put oneself in a frame of mind which is close to that of prayer."[79]

What happens when one draws after being thrown into prayer? "These drawings, they must come to you from the heart."

To create a "spiritual" or "cosmic" space implies making the Maitri experiment of opening the heart ("love," says Matisse). But that heart that opens is also an empty heart, since it opens into a *nonapparent* space.

The most important thing today is not to flee the earth, but to perceive in the earth a "new land," simple and humble.

And this ordinary, everyday, banal space, which is *the space that will uplift us*, is felt by an *empty heart*.

The cave at Tagtsang, at first experienced as an "ordinary" corner, was revealed to have a "very powerful nature" as soon as it became a *place* for Trungpa: "You had a feeling of empty-heartedness once you began to click into the atmosphere. It wasn't a particularly full or confirming experience; you just felt very empty-hearted, as if there was nothing inside your body, as if you didn't exist. You felt completely vacant, without feeling. As that feeling continued, you began to pick up little sharp points: the blade of the phurba, the rough edges of the vajra. You began to pick all that up. You felt that behind the whole thing there was a huge conspiracy: something was very alive."[80]

When the earth is devastated, it is necessary to go "underground" to find the warmth of life, such a little flame.

A few years before his death, Chögyam Trungpa decided to move to a different place and live in Nova Scotia. In a poem written October 25, 1982, he speaks of this "new" land:

It is time for use to change to a new planet,
Fresh planet,
Extra planet.
. . . .
It is time to take pride in the small island,
It is time to be small.
. . . .
It is time to be a human being.
It is time to *be*.
. . . .

Let us be,
. . . .
We have discovered something very ordinary
. . . .
Let us celebrate that we have discovered insignificant island,
Let us appreciate the ordinariness of it,
Let us celebrate![81]

In the "no man's land" where we wander, there is, hidden, and never-theless present for all to see, a "little island," very ordinary, insignificant. Such is the place of our "need"—of our necessity.

Notes

1. See Hannah Arendt, *Between Past and Future: Six Exercises in Political Thought* (New York: Viking Press, 1961), preface.

2. Chögyam Trungpa, *Transcending Madness*, p. 73.

3. Ibid., p. 1.

4. See Pierre Jacerme, "L'Ébranlement de tout étant," in *L'Enseignement par excellence* (Paris: L'Harmattan, 2000), pp. 155–177. In English: "Is there an Ethics for the 'Atomic Age'?" in *Heidegger and Practical Philosophy*, ed. François Raffoul and David Pettigrew (Albany: SUNY Press, 2002), pp. 301–316.

5. Jeroen Brouwers, *Rouge décanté* (Paris: Gallimard, Collection Folio, 1997), p. 140.

6. M. Blanchot, *L'entretien infini* (Paris: Gallimard, 1969), p. 396.

7. Allen Ginsberg, *Spontaneous Mind: Selected Interviews 1958–1996*, ed. David Carter (New York: HarperCollins, 2001), p. 13.

8. Ibid., p. 16.

9. Ibid., p. 27.

10. Ibid., p. 29.

11. Ibid., p. 30.

12. Ibid., p. 31.

13. Henri Michaux, *Passages, 1937–1950* (Paris: Gallimard, 1950), "L'imaginaire," p. 49.

14. On this point, see Hannah Arendt: "The Conquest of Space and the Stature of Man," in *Between Past and Future*, pp. 265–280.

15. *Transcending Madness*, pp. 68, 108.

16. Quoted in Fabrice Midal, *Trungpa: Biographie* (Paris: Editions du Seuil, 2002), p. 93; emphasis added. English edition: *Chögyam Trungpa His Life and Vision* (Boston: Shambhala Publications, 2004), pp 87–88.

17. *Transcending Madness*, p. 180.

18. Ibid., p. 39.

19. Kyabje Kalu Rinpoche, *Luminous Mind: The Way of the Buddha*, trans. Maria Montenegro (Boston: Wisdom Publications, 1997), pp.132–133. Emphasis added.

20. *Transcending Madness*, p. 161.

21. Ibid.

22. The sadhana is a spiritual act that enables the realization of the deity. It is performed by the practitioner, in particular using visualizations and the recitations of mantras.

23. Chögyam Trungpa, "The Sadhana of Mahamudra," December 1975, in *The Sadhana of Mahamudra Sourcebook*, chap. 6, pp. 110, 112.

24. Chögyam Trungpa, *Born in Tibet*, in *The Collected Works of Chögyam Trungpa*, vol. 1, p. 122.

25. Ibid., pp. 122–123.

26. On these points, see Chögyam Trungpa, *Training the Mind and Cultivating Loving-Kindness*.

27. *Born in Tibet*, in *Collected Works*, vol. 1, pp. 153–154.

28. Chögyam Trungpa, *The Sadhana of Mahamudra* (selections), in *Collected Works*, vol. 5, p. 303.

29. Chögyam Trungpa, "The Embodiment of All the Siddhas," September 1975, in *The Sadhana of Mahamudra Sourcebook*, p. 2.

30. Ibid., p. 4.

31. Ibid., p. 5.

32. Ibid., p. 4.

33. Ibid., pp. 5–6.

34. Ibid., pp. 6–7.

35. Ibid., p. 7.

36. Ibid.

37. Maitri Conference, February 1973. Document courtesy of Fabrice Midal.

38. Shunryu Suzuki, *Zen Mind, Beginner's Mind* (New York: Weatherhill, 1970), p. 78.

39. Chögyam Trungpa, Maitri Conference, February 1973.

40. Ibid.

41. Ibid.

42. See Terry Clifford, *Tibetan Buddhist Medicine and Psychiatry* (York, Maine: Samuel Weiser, 1990).

43. Undated document, courtesy of Fabrice Midal.

44. Maitri Conference, February 1973. Document courtesy of Fabrice Midal.

45. Chögyam Trungpa, *Orderly Chaos*, p. 21.

46. Chögyam Trungpa, Mudra Theater Group talk, n.d.

47. Chögyam Trungpa, Maitri Conference, San Francisco, March 31, 1974.

48. Jean Lauxerois needed the French word *amicalité* (friendliness), instead of *amitié* (friendship) to translate Aristotle's idea of *philia* (*Nichomachean Ethics*, 8 and 9), since, as he says, "for the Greeks since Homer, the currency of *philia* says more than friendship in the sense that we understand it: it names a way in which every living being, man or animal, man and animal, is necessarily bound to other living beings as long as he is in the world." Aristotle, *L'Amicalité (Philia)*, trans. Jean Lauxerois (Garche: Éditions À Propos, 2002), p. 84.

49. Chögyam Trungpa, "Space Therapy and the Maitri Community," p. 566.

50. Ibid., p. 573.

51. Chögyam Trungpa, *The Sadhana of Mahamudra Sourcebook*, p. 1. Mahamudra attacks dualism in order to obtain a clear perception of the phenomenal world, thus to re-create all the richness of the world. The maha ati yana seeks to transcend reference points.

52. Ibid., pp. 1–2.

53. "Epilogue: Planting the Dharma in the West," *Born in Tibet*, in *Collected Works*, vol. 1, p. 272.

54. *Orderly Chaos*, p. 41.

55. Marvin Casper, "Maitri Space Awareness," *Shambhala Sun*, September-October 1992, p. 5.

56. Chögyam Trungpa, "Space Therapy and the Maitri Community," in *Collected Works*, vol. 2, p. 9.

57. See Fabrice Midal, *Chögyam Trungpa: His Life and Vision*, chap. 8, "Maitri: Opening Out to the Manifestations of Space."

58. Chögyam Trungpa, "Space Therapy and the Maitri Community," p. 573.

59. Ibid., pp. 573–574.

60. Chögyam Trungpa, talk on Maitri, n.d. Document courtesy of Fabrice Midal.

61. Chögyam Trungpa, San Francisco Maitri Conference, 31 March 1974, p. 10.

62. Talk on Maitri, n.d.

63. Ibid.

64. The interesting argument of Marvin Casper, in "Space Therapy and the Maitri Project," in *The Collected Works of Chögyam Trungpa*, vol. 2, appendix, p. 649.

65. *Glimpses of Space*, p. 27.

66. *Orderly Chaos*, p. 46.

67. Talk on Maitri, n.d.

68. *Transcending Madness*, p. 133.

69. *Orderly Chaos*, pp. 63–64.

70. Marvin Casper, quoted in Midal, *Chögyam Trungpa: His Life and Vision*, p. 174.

71. On this point, see *The Lion's Roar*.

72. *Training the Mind*, p. 14.

73. *Transcending Madness*, p. 3.

74. Trungpa, *Dharma Art*, in: *Collected Works*, vol. 7, p. 34.

75. Henri Matisse, *Écrits et propos sur l'art*, ed. D. Fourcade (Hermann, 1972), p. 236.

76. Ibid, p. 201. Emphasis added.

77. *Transcending Madness*, p. 133.

78. Matisse, *Écrits*, p. 308. Emphasis added.

79. Henri Matisse, quoted in Françoise Gilot and Carlton Lake, *Life with Picasso*, part 6.

80. *The Sadhana of Mahamudra Sourcebook*, p. 115.

81. Chögyam Trungpa, "Farewell to Boulder," in *Collected Works*, vol. 7, pp. 579–580. Used by permission of Diana J. Mukpo.

Getting to the Bottom of Things

Reading Cutting Through Spiritual Materialism

DZIGAR KONGTRÜL RINPOCHE

OFTEN, DESPITE OUR good intentions to truly develop ourselves as genuine Buddhist practitioners, we find ourselves trying to mold our path into something that serves us in an ordinary, conventional way. We may find ourselves expecting the dharma to make us feel good all of the time, to resolve all of life's challenges. We may use the dharma for worldly effect, to impress others with our uniqueness or to make a show of what a good practitioner we are. This "feel good" approach to spirituality is popular in this day and age. Usually this approach simply covers up our own egotism. In this way, as individuals and spiritual communities, we get sidetracked in the name of spirituality, never getting to the root of our suffering and confusion.

The Vidyadhara, Chögyam Trungpa Rinpoche, observed this, and so he wrote the book *Cutting Through Spiritual Materialism*. He knew that lifetime after lifetime we have been handing our precious human life, endowed with a mind of infinite potential, over to a thief. This thief—the ego—has done nothing but rob us of our noble qualities and kindest intentions. Even in the context of dharma, where we have studied the benefits of renouncing the ego, the exact same thing seems to occur: we blindly turn our heads as ego lays claim to even the smallest spiritual accomplishment.

In his book Trungpa Rinpoche alerts us to this very danger. He encourages us to examine ourselves closely, to investigate our mind and experience, so that we don't continue to deceive ourselves over and over again. He urges us to look for the true meaning of embarking on the spiritual path. He helps us to discover genuine discipline, practice, and the authentic lineage of spiritual masters. This is an invaluable reference and reminder for anyone looking for true inner freedom and transformation.

Working with ego-attachment is the constant challenge for all practitioners. Whether it be a lama sitting on a high throne or someone who receives an introduction to meditation practice for the first time, the challenge is the same: at some point we need to go beyond the limits of ego, whose basic function is to cherish and protect itself at all costs.

We have attempted in the past to achieve happiness through valuing this ego of ours. We have accumulated wealth and accomplishments and tried to cultivate feelings of respect in the eyes of others. We have sought peace and relaxation through trying to smooth out the hard edges of our personalities. We have joined a spiritual community to develop inwardly. But somehow none of it has worked. We still find ourselves bound down by our own hopes, fears and anxieties. This is because all of these attempts were focused on "I," "me," and "mine."

Cutting through spiritual materialism means going beyond ego-clinging, which means seeing through our own deception. In Tibetan Buddhist symbolism the female wisdom dakini, Vajrayogini, holds a hooked knife to symbolize cutting through deception. This image reminds us that we need to cut through the false notion we have about what brings us happiness and what brings us suffering. It reminds us of the true purpose of the path. We need reminding. So often we find ourselves sitting in a pile of hot ash, having been burnt by the fire of our own ego-driven passions. Our intention may have been noble; after all, we were only looking for happiness. But because of ego-clinging, our action was not able to meet our noble intent.

So our passion must be to see the truth and be honest with ourselves. This honesty comes when we begin to see that this self-deception has never served us. It has only caused us great sorrow, and it has made others around us suffer as well. To be so truthful takes daring. It takes daring to cut through this self-deception, and to do it again and again.

We may begin to feel a bit raw at this point. But this rawness, which comes from a sincere longing to get to the bottom of confusion and suffering, is strongly tied to liberation. That's what the Buddha did; he got to the bottom of this great mystery of suffering and happiness. This is how he and all the great sages of the past liberated themselves from suffering and attained enlightenment.

When we see the wisdom in honestly looking at our plight as human beings, when we see the wisdom of going beyond the confines of ego, the spiritual path is no longer child's play. Spirituality is no longer something we use to churn up our excitement with different momentary toylike ideas and feelings, which we can then simply dispose of when we feel bored. This kind of thinking fuels discontent. We usually find that we are never pleased, never still, but rather we move on to the next thing with tremendous restless energy. If we look closely at all of this, it would be really hard to not want to do something . . . something different . . . something a bit more intelligent. Don't you think?

Often people think that renouncing ego means renouncing your family, your home, and your material possessions. But these things are not a problem in and of themselves. In fact, the ego prevents us from enjoying them fully because the world has only one use in ego's eyes: to protect and cherish itself. Some things are a threat to ego. Someone is doing better than we are, or our state of mind is not as happy as we would like it to be. Ego wants to get rid of these bothersome situations or feelings. Then there are all the things the ego uses to cherish itself; things that make it feel special, good, or worthy. In the world according to ego, we are constantly on edge, controlled by our likes and dislikes, hopes and fears. We try to control our outer circumstances, and to some extent we can. But in a larger sense our happiness remains dependent on the ever-changing circumstances around us.

Trying to arrange the world around us in this way is like trying to arrange the furniture while our house is on fire. We are looking in the wrong direction for security and happiness. We are missing the greater meaning in life because we are focusing on petty, insignificant things. We are looking outward instead of inward toward our own mind. This is the larger deception of samsara. This dependency and vulnerability is really what we have to renounce. And we can only renounce it through cutting the tie to its root—the ego.

Trungpa Rinpoche is an example of someone who gained independence from ego-grasping altogether. He got to the bottom of things through cutting his ties with ego—by seeing through his own deception. Because of this he was able to teach of the dangers of ego-attachment. These teachings are essential. They concern all manners of practice. As it says in the lojong teachings, "All dharmas agree on one point." What is that point? That point is that ego-clinging causes pain. In order to reduce that pain, we need to reduce ego-clinging. All dharma practice, whether it be the practice of loving-kindness and compassion or resting in the nature of emptiness, is aimed at going beyond ego-clinging.

We need the information contained in this book as a thirsty person needs water, a hungry person needs food, or a sick person needs medicine. It is our key to a healthy spiritual life and genuine path. We need to identify the cause of suffering and happiness through questioning our usual approach. This kind of investigation is very important and very practical. Otherwise a book of this nature will just gather dust on the shelf. A great teacher like Trungpa Rinpoche may come into this world, but what difference will it make if we do not deeply examine and apply what he says? We may think, "Oh, what an amazing teacher he was," but a teacher is only a teacher in relation to his students. And a student is only a student when he or she is able to put the teachings into practice—to get to the bottom of suffering and confusion—and transform his or her mind.

You may have been a close student of Trungpa Rinpoche or a student who had little or no contact with him. You may have simply been introduced to his teachings through his books. But the meeting between teacher and student takes place not by how much *physical* closeness or distance we have with him or her. What brings us close to the teacher is our ability to take the teachings to heart and experience them directly.

So please take Trungpa Rinpoche's teachings to heart. Investigate your experience of them and see if they are true. If you find them to be true, then put them into practice. If you do this, you will receive the blessings of all the enlightened beings, manifested in the truth that liberates.

The Founding Vision
of Naropa University

"Let East Meet West and the Sparks Will Fly"

REED BYE

CHÖGYAM TRUNGPA RINPOCHE arrived in Boulder, Colorado, in
early 1970 to teach a course on Buddhism at the University of Colorado at the invitation of two faculty members who had read his first book,
Meditation in Action. Quite quickly, he began to attract other students who
wanted to explore Buddhist spiritual teachings under his guidance. It became clear to those living in Boulder at the time that there was a great
deal of energy and creativity in Trungpa's style of presenting the Buddhist
tradition to Western students. He had found receptive ground upon which
to create situations for teaching.

By early 1973, among other projects, Trungpa began to suggest to students the idea of beginning of a school where Buddhist teachings could
mix with Western intellectual and artistic traditions. Marvin Casper, later
to become a professor of psychology at Naropa, was one of those involved
in the initial conversations and described the inspiration for starting such
a school: "The basic idea was an institute that would create an interface, a
dialogue, between Buddhism and the intellectual culture of the West, as
well as with other spiritual traditions. . . . I remember at some point Rinpoche talked about creating sparks by juxtaposing different traditions.
The idea was that if you look at things from different perspectives, you can

get to their essence. If people from different traditions challenge and compare their approaches, they could go beyond conceptual mind to new perspectives."[1]

The colorful history of the birth and development of this idea—into what is today a fully accredited university with a four-year undergraduate college, six graduate departments, a school of extended studies, and numerous online degree programs—is a many-chaptered story beyond the scope of this article. Here I wish to simply shed light on the educational vision that produced Naropa University.

The Founding Inspiration

It is important to note that from its inception Naropa has grown quite literally from the ground up. There have been very few large donations that might have allowed it to skip any steps in the growing process, and step-by-step growth seems to have been an important part of its vision: that a timely idea can be realized from a simple inspiration, through cooperation and dedicated effort. An emphasis on process and journey, personal and institutional, was integral to Trungpa's teaching in all the endeavors he and his students undertook. "In his style, Rinpoche would just start something and then see how it developed, going step by step. We didn't have any great master plans in terms of how Naropa could evolve in time," Casper recalled.[2] Trungpa evoked the image of organic growth as follows: "The usual way of cooperation is based on the sense of sculpturing a product rather than just letting it grow. . . . 'Letting it grow' is not based on the end product, you are simply concerned with the developmental process. You nourish what needs to be nourished, care for what needs care, and destroy what needs to be destroyed. You are not particularly concerned with what the outcome will be or how long it will take. There is no need to dwell on the details of your own contribution. At the same time to let it grow does not mean total wildness in which everything is allowed."[3]

In 1974, Naropa Institute began its existence as a summer program, with a luminous visiting faculty of artists, intellectuals, historians, and psychologists, including Allen Ginsberg, Gregory Bateson, Gary Snyder, Anne Waldman, Ram Dass, John Cage, Herbert Guenther, Barbara Dilley, Joan Halifax, and Stanislav Grof. All were invited on the basis of life work seen as "resonating with the essence of dharma."[4] Although the operating budget and resources were very small, almost all of those invited to attend and teach accepted.

On June 10, fifty-five faculty and sixteen hundred students gathered at Naropa's opening convocation ceremony, held in a large auditorium on the University of Colorado campus. On that occasion, Trungpa spoke to the heart of the new project: "The Naropa Institute developed from the idea of working with what exists in this country and also with traditions around the world. . . . The basic point here is that we could work together, we could relate with each other on the basis of *trust*—which seems to be lacking enormously in the Western educational tradition."[5]

He went on to say that such a project did not require or imply a reformation of the Western educational tradition per se but rather a "new way of looking at education." One of the problems he found in U.S. culture as he was encountering it at this time was its attitude toward its own traditions. A large-scale rejection of what were felt to be outmoded societal mores and values spurred generational suspicion and cynicism about tradition altogether and doubt that anything vital and relevant to contemporary life could be found in established cultural institutions.

So, perhaps ironically, the first spark from the meeting of East and West in the vision of Naropa University was the suggestion that students should think twice about rejecting their own heritage: "We could reignite our pilot light by respecting, trusting, and acknowledging the tradition in which we have grown up. Whether it is Eastern or Western does not really matter, we could still do it. There are enormous possibilities in relating with the dignity of our culture, which we haven't acknowledged."[6]

Thus, Trungpa argued for recognition and appreciation of one's cultural heritage and its accumulated wisdom. Such wisdom, he explained, is held in cultural customs and practices, so that to ignore or reject them is largely to reject oneself and one's access to human wisdom. "We can regard tradition as the foundation and stepping stone for learning rather than something to be rejected. You cannot grow if you cut off your root."[7] In his later book *Shambhala: The Sacred Path of the Warrior*, he wrote:

> How to construct a building has thousands of years of history behind it. First human beings lived in caves; then they learned how to build huts. Then they learned how to construct a building with pillars and columns. Finally they learned how to construct a

building without columns in the center, with arches spanning the ceiling, which is a remarkable discovery. Such wisdom has to be respected. . . . Many people must have been crushed when they tried to build a structure without central columns and it collapsed. People must have sacrificed their lives until a model was developed that worked. You might say that such an accomplishment is insignificant, but on the other hand, the failure to appreciate the resourcefulness of human existence . . . has become one of the world's biggest problems.[8]

At the same time, to idealize or dwell in the forms of the past can lead to blindness to the circumstances of one's present situation. In order to incorporate both knowledge and respect for tradition and awareness of the particular present, Trungpa explained that we must learn to open our eyes to *nowness*, "the magic of the present moment, [which] joins the wisdom of the past with the present."[9] The nonconceptual experience of nowness keeps wisdom fresh and adaptable; without it, our inherited wisdom shrinks into cultural habits and dogma.

When corruption enters a culture, it is because that culture ceases to be *now*; it becomes past and future. Periods in history when great art was created, when learning advanced or peace spread, were all *now*. . . .

You have to maintain nowness . . . so that you don't corrupt *now*, and so that you don't have false synonyms for *now* at all. The vision of enlightened society is that tradition and culture and wisdom and dignity can be experienced *now* and kept *now* on everyone's part.[10]

The founding inspiration of Naropa University as an educational institution, then, involved the weaving of academic study and the practices of mindfulness and awareness. This was to be a school where scholarly disciplines would be pursued along with contemplative practices that uncover the direct experience of nowness. In this way, the wisdom within cultural traditions and academic disciplines could be received and extended into the world with fresh life.

Normally in secular academic study, one does not find much direct involvement with the wisdom traditions of cultures. Nonconceptual religious practice, for instance, is not often brought together with historical and doctrinal study. This kind of engagement, even at an introductory level, requires a depth of instruction and trust that purely intellectual study can only suggest. As a result, the Western academic tradition tends to look at religion from a scholarly perimeter. Perhaps the same generalization could be made about psychology, the arts, and other disciplines as well.

There are, of course, many challenges that arise when wisdom traditions are presented with attention to their spiritual as well as historical and doctrinal dimensions. The first is that of ensuring trustworthy and authentic presentation of the material, and addressing the question of how that authenticity can be gauged. Over the years, Naropa has had to work with a number of such challenges, while attempting to remain true to its specific educational mission "to encourage the integration of the teachings of world wisdom traditions with modern culture."[11] "Integration" implies more than the objective study of history and belief systems within such traditions; it involves inner or spiritual understanding as well. This kind of teaching demands authentic presentation and reception of living traditions in a world susceptible to materialism, fundamentalism, and various forms of aggressive factionalism and appropriation. Naropa's mission statement elaborates on this point: "The wisdom traditions of the world, which include the great religions, hermetic teachings, and shamanistic cultures, offer insight into and guidance for contemporary society. By bringing these traditions of wisdom into the curriculum of modern education, a student's self-importance and narrow perspective begins to dissolve. Thus, a ground is established for the examination and exploration of the diverse expression of human experience within modern culture as well as throughout the world."[12] A major challenge in the presentation, study, and practice of authentic traditions is the tendency of a student or teacher to treat such teachings as self-aggrandizing or ego-enhancing acquisitions. This had been a concern for Trungpa from the beginning of his presentation of Buddhist teachings in the West. He identified the problem as "spiritual materialism": "There are numerous sidetracks which lead to a distorted, ego-centered version of spirituality; we can deceive ourselves into thinking we are developing spiritually when instead we are strengthening our egocentricity through spiritual techniques. This fundamental distortion may be referred to as *spiritual materialism*."[13]

Naropa University has had to explore and assume accountability for its handling of sensitive and complex issues that arise in the presentation of the spiritual aspects of cultural traditions, especially in cases where the home culture of that tradition has been a historically oppressed or marginalized one. Here, too, informed respect and mindfulness together must explore the boundary between genuine presentation and engagement, and cultural misrepresentation or appropriation.

Discriminating Wisdom

In the Buddhist educational tradition, an important ingredient of wisdom is the critical intelligence that can discriminate particular qualities of phenomena accurately. Such intelligence is spoken of as a double-edged sword that cuts through both obscurations in the object of investigation and in the one who is investigating.

> When you follow these principles of education, you begin to use your logical or critical intelligence to examine what is presented to you. That critical intelligence is also critical intelligence about yourself. That critical intelligence is applied two ways; towards what is presented to you, the educational material, as well as towards who is going to be educated. So you work with yourself as well. The two blades of the sword work simultaneously. Then you begin to find yourself examining things constantly. The process of education becomes very precise and clear and absolutely accurate.[14]

In Sanskrit this intelligence is called prajna, and it is said to be awakened and nurtured by three activities: hearing, contemplation, and meditation. *Hearing* refers to listening and study with an attitude free of conceptual prejudice. What is being studied is received with as open a mind as possible. *Contemplation* involves reflection upon what one is studying beyond an informational grasp and examining it in light of lived experience. *Meditation* is practice in opening to nowness, relating with the immediate present mindfulness of life. Meditation develops mindfulness beyond preoccupation with internal thinking and reaction. Practiced together, these three prajnas complement each other by sharpening intellectual understanding along with intuitive self-understanding in the educational process.

The Naropa University logo has at its base the Sanskrit motto (written in Tibetan) *prajna-garbha*, which translates as "womb of wisdom." In the view of vajrayana Buddhism, the feminine principle of wisdom awakens the masculine principle of skillful means. Together these stimulate intuition and intellect to work together in the educational process. When this happens, wisdom enters into activity and activity takes on qualities of compassion, a real interest in "waking up" oneself and the environment in which one is present.

In the practice of sitting meditation, one's breath is used as a continuing reference for present attention, and this practice has been the foundation for the development of mindfulness at Naropa University. Although not required in all programs, meditation practice is integrated into many courses and programs, and every semester a Practice Day invites the community to gather and relate directly to mindfulness and awareness practices, first in group sitting meditation, and then through a range of sample workshops exploring contemplative disciplines associated with the Naropa curriculum. These have included contemplative prayer from various religious traditions, ikebana, various arts practices and panels, earth-based ritual, and so on.

The question of whether and to what extent sitting meditation should be recommended or required for students at Naropa has had a long history of discussion. Trungpa himself was characteristically ambiguous when asked this kind of question. His view seemed to be that meditation practice per se is not the point, but the mindfulness and awareness that meditation promotes are very much the point. Here is an excerpt from an exchange with a student at Naropa following a talk given in 1979:

Q: Do you think it's possible that through discipline in your own field you could still be a genuine person without sitting practice?

Trungpa: Well, that's an interesting question. I think that some kind of experience of sitting practice seems to be necessary. Which does not necessarily call for being a Buddhist, but some kind of meeting one's own mind and facing one's own face is necessary with any art.[15]

Mindful awareness is said to come from a "synchronized" body, speech, and mind, and sitting meditation, with practice, works to accomplish this synchronization. With one's body in an alert, upright posture, attention is placed on the breath going in and out, and returned to it when thoughts take that present attention away. In this way, mental distraction begins to settle down and one tends to feel more grounded in one's body. Of course, there are other methods of synchronizing body and mind and raising mindfulness and awareness, and, at Naropa, these are referred to as "contemplative" practice courses. They include yoga, t'ai-chi ch'uan, aikido, ikebana, poetry, and the performing arts of theater, dance, and music. There is a contemplative course requirement in all the academic programs at Naropa.

The Wisdom Lineage of Naropa

With its roots in traditional Buddhist epistemology, the "new way" of looking at education that Trungpa intended for Naropa University turns out to be a very old way at the same time. The particular educational vision and mission is identified with the wisdom lineage of the Indian pandit Naropa, a forefather in the Kagyü Buddhist lineage of practice and study. This is the lineage in which Trungpa was himself recognized as a reincarnated master and trained from early childhood. He makes it very clear that the vision of Naropa University is an expression of the accomplished wisdom and skillful activity of that particular lineage: "We are following in the footsteps of Naropa, a great Indian yogi who passed along his knowledge and wisdom. We are the followers of the Naropa lineage. And we have some clues as to that wisdom. We do have some ideas how they handled their world of wisdom, and we have some ideas how such a jewel came about and how such an inheritance can be worked with." [16]

There was a longstanding Buddhist educational tradition in medieval India that continued in Tibet. Universities such as Nalanda, which flourished in India from the fifth to the eleventh centuries C.E., and Samye, which developed in Tibet after Buddhism migrated there in the twelfth and thirteenth centuries, were international centers of study and learning inspired by the Mahayana Buddhist ethos of cutting through delusions based in dualistic conceptions of self and other. From the clarification of those delusions in oneself, unconditional compassion and skillful methods of working for the benefit of others are said to arise spontaneously.

Naropa was an abbot at Nalanda University in the eleventh century and renowned for his scholarship and meditative insight. A well-known story about him serves as an ongoing reminder of Naropa University's mission of bridging conceptual knowledge and self-understanding. Trungpa told this story at the initial Naropa Convocation in 1974:

> One day, Naropa was reading his books of logic and basic doctrine, when he was suddenly interrupted. An ugly woman appeared and asked him: "What are you doing?" The scholar automatically answered, "I'm reading these books." The woman asked another question, "Do you understand the words?" Naropa replied, "Yes, I understand the words." At this the old woman seemed overjoyed and danced around waving her walking stick. Naropa began to think that if she was so happy to hear this, he should tell her something more, but when he added, "I also understand the meaning," the old woman got very upset. She wept and threw away her stick, and became very angry.
>
> "How is it that you got so upset when I told you I understood the sense behind the words?" he asked. The old hag replied, "When you said you understood the words, I felt hopeful because you didn't lie to me. But when you said you understood more than the words, that you understood the meaning, I was very upset that such a great scholar and great person would lie to me."[17]

After relating this story, Trungpa told his audience: "Ladies and gentlemen, this is the basic situation we are facing. We have this particular example of Naropa happening in our lives. The purpose of the Naropa Institute is that we not only understand the words, but that we understand the meaning behind them at the same time. Because of this we decided to name this particular institute after Naropa."[18]

The old woman in the story is an embodiment of wisdom. She points at Naropa's ignorance of the difference between knowledge of relative signs and references (the "words") and knowledge beyond conceptual understanding (the "meaning" or "sense" to which the words may help lead us).

Both of these dimensions of knowledge are necessary, and Buddhist education values the realization of wisdom and compassion beyond conceptual
knowledge as the true understanding of mind and the ultimate goal of
learning.

In 1997, the Dalai Lama also emphasized this double dimension of
knowledge when he visited Naropa to participate in a conference called
Spirituality in Education. During the visit, he told an audience of university faculty and staff: "For the institution that is named after the great pandit Naropa, there are certain responsibilities to be able to really deserve
that honor and that title. The particular responsibility I see is to be able to
impart the insights of Naropa based on profound learning and scholarly
understanding. In addition, it should be able to impart to the students the
glory and power of the dimension of heart, a good heart, and altruistic aspiration. If you are able to achieve such a combination, then you are truly
worthy of the name."19

The classical system of Buddhist education involves ten aspects of
knowledge. These ten involve the five ordinary sciences (poetry, astrol-
ogy/mathematics, terminology/language science, dance and theater, and
"name," the study of mental imputation and conceptual labeling) and the
five extraordinary sciences (creative arts, medicine, grammar and philosophy, logic, and metaphysics).20 These are perhaps somewhat analogous
to the *trivium* and *quadrivium* of medieval Western universities (logic,
rhetoric, and grammar at the elementary level; geometry, astronomy,
arithmetic, and music at the higher level), which form the historical basis
of the Western liberal arts curriculum. In the Buddhist tradition (and perhaps to some extent in the medieval monastic educational system) there
is the understanding that learning must begin with cultivating the heart
and mind of the student, the receiver of knowledge, in order that she or he
may properly understand the words and then, through contemplation and
meditation, their intended meaning. Ponlop Rinpoche, a Tibetan scholar
and teacher, spoke of this preparation as necessarily including the synchronization of body, mind, and speech: "In this science of knowledge we
talk about synchronizing mind and body, synchronizing mind and speech,
synchronizing body, speech, and mind—all three together. It always goes
a little bit inside, and in a general sense, if you just present grammar or
rhetoric or anything like that, it can be very outside, very outer phenom-

ena. So I don't know how much emphasis is on going inside (in the Western medieval model), but I would think that that maybe one of the differences is that there is a strong emphasis to go more inside, more sense of contemplation in these Ten Aspects of Knowledge."[21]

Is Naropa a "Buddhist" University?

The question of whether and to what extent Naropa University (the nàme was changed from Institute to University in 1999) is a "Buddhist" institution has come up again and again throughout its history. The university declares its intention to be a "nonsectarian liberal arts institution" and to "exemplify the principles grounded in its Buddhist educational heritage." Trungpa addressed this issue in a public talk entitled "Why Buddhism in America?" given at Naropa in the summer of 1980:

> We are applying the Buddhist mentality or Buddhist approach to education at Naropa Institute, rather than purely taking a religious approach to education. We are not particularly talking in terms of converting people to Buddhism, but we are talking in terms of bringing the inheritance of Buddhist methodology into our system of education. . . .
>
> It's not Buddha-ism. The religion of the Buddha isn't necessary, particularly, but the disciplines that we have developed and learned from over 2500 years are necessary."[22]

The Buddhist inspiration of Naropa University is the human potential for growth beyond dogmatic ideas, beliefs, and concepts (while noticing the tendency to cling to them). Its intention is to offer a place where students and practitioners of particular disciplines can meet and teach, discuss and debate particular points and issues. Such meetings should produce sparks that open minds so that the teachings of any tradition may be experienced at greater depth, and so that the tradition itself remains viable within changing cultural conditions and open to the various needs and understandings of students. Trungpa referred to the unfolding nature of spiritual growth within a discipline or tradition in an early dialogue with Ram Dass and others at Naropa:

CT: Tradition provides you right in the beginning with a good setting and provides food, home, shelter, companionship and someone to look up to. . . . Then at a certain point you begin to find that tradition is entrapment, imprisonment. Then you begin to look at it twice, thrice, and find out more about it. Why are you imprisoned? Is it because the tradition is inadequate? [Or] because you are such a smart person?

Ram Dass: Or has your stance toward the tradition been inadequate?

CT: And then there is a strong possibility of a changing shift which creates a spark. And then again the tradition comes back. . . . It's rediscovering one's imprisonment as a sacredness of some kind.[23]

Such moments of rediscovery are moments of learning. Because they involve moving from a relatively known situation into a relatively unknown one, they may be experienced as embarrassing, insulting, painful. This transitional discomfort is inherent to the process of education (literally, in Latin, *educere*, to "lead out"), and it is not necessarily constructive to try to make learning painless: "Comfort is not in the best interest of student or teacher. When we begin to present education as a toy or a lollipop, we begin to devalue our wisdom, and we reduce school to a candy bar approach, as opposed to a university or a center of learning."[24]

The edge of concern and, occasionally, discomfort about whether and to what extent Naropa is a "Buddhist" school is an issue that continues to provoke discussion at the university. The common understanding is that Naropa is "Buddhist inspired" in its educational philosophy and basic pedagogy, but that part of this inspiration involves extending to meet other genuine scholarly, artistic, practical, and spiritual traditions. This conforms with Trungpa's larger vision for what he referred to as "enlightened society" as a whole, the vision and lineage of Shambhala, a legendary Central Asian secular/spiritual tradition whose teachings he planted the West. He spent a great deal of his time and energy in the last twelve years of his life adapting and passing Shambhala principles and practices to his Western students. In a course called "The Warrior of Shambhala," co-taught with his dharma heir Ösel Tendzin at Naropa in 1979, Trungpa began with the statement: "The vision of Naropa Institute, which we have founded, has been that of Shambhala vision—right from the beginning. . . . Shambhala culture, Shambhala tradition, is very closely connected with the principles and the vision of Buddhism. At the same time, it provides us with a secular notion of how we can actually commit ourselves into a particular type of world that is true and genuine and good for us."[25]

The basis of Shambhala vision supports all human wisdom activity and therefore accommodates any genuine human path or tradition:

> The Shambhala teachings are founded on the premise that there is basic human wisdom that can help solve the world's problems. This wisdom does not belong to any one culture or religion, nor does it come from the West or the East. Rather, it is a tradition of human warriorship that has existed in many cultures at many times throughout history.
>
> Warriorship here does not refer to making war on others. Aggression is source of our problems, not the solution. . . . Warriorship here is the tradition of human bravery, or the tradition of fearlessness.[26]

Judith L. Lief, a past president of Naropa, referred to the inclusive nature of Trungpa's educational vision for Naropa in a talk given to the University on Practice Day in 1999: "Even from the very early days of Naropa, the vision of Naropa was not to be a sectarian Tibetan Buddhist institution. . . . Trungpa Rinpoche wanted to include all the wisdom traditions. He wanted all the wisdom traditions to be genuinely alive at Naropa. It was not just a matter of having a department of Christian studies or Hindu studies or what have you, but of having an ashram or a monastery right on campus."[27]

Naropa's founding vision for an inclusiveness of wisdom traditions presented and practiced at the university is not simply a syncretic or even pluralistic one. The point, rather, is to create an institution where such traditions can present themselves and their teachings with full integrity, and evolve in their work in the world through contact with others:

> The sense of total commitment to one tradition brings about the perspective and wisdom to work with ways that have developed in other traditions. Other disciplines can then be seen as process rather than purely for their end product. Bringing various disciplines together has to be more than eclectic-minded. Merely collecting many ideas and methods and trying to find a common link seems to

bring only more confusion. It is more a question of providing an atmosphere of basic sanity in which all disciplines have a chance to
refine themselves. . . . The basic ground is nonaggression.[28]

Naropa's Ecumenical Vision in Practice

Between 1981 and 1985, Naropa Institute and its Religious Studies Department hosted a yearly Christian and Buddhist Conference so that contemplative practitioners from these two religious traditions could compare
and contrast their experience and views. Reginald A. Ray, a Buddhist
scholar and an organizing participant in the Naropa Christian and Buddhist Conferences, said that he and other of its organizers had not initially
taken much interest in the plan, which Trungpa had raised a number of
times. "As is typical of new converts," Ray said, "we shared a resistance
and lack of curiosity toward other religions, and especially toward those
with which we had grown up."[29] As the conferences and their conversations developed, however, he found this holding on to an "exclusive"
identification with religious affiliation breaking down: "The communication was often unexpectedly heartfelt. In particular we began to sense that
we Christians and Buddhists were on the same journey. . . . We shared the
same longing for the ultimate and yearning for fundamental transformation; we rely on the great contemplatives, past and present, of our respective traditions; and we see community to be fundamental, even as it
ironically highlights the solitary nature of the spiritual journey."[30]

The origin and development of the other academic departments at
Naropa followed a similar course of expanding engagement within their
larger scholarly or artistic traditions. Appreciating the "sparks" that may
fly in those engagements produces a natural receptivity to further communication as well as a broadening sense of one's own boundaries. Trungpa
said: "Having fully incorporated into one's own life-experience the knowledge and discipline learned through one tradition, you can then see the essential meaning of other traditions. When you are willing to let go and
relax with experiences, not holding on to the sense of security in what you
know, information becomes part of the learning process and cooperation
develops naturally."[31]

Allen Ginsberg and Anne Waldman organized the Jack Kerouac
School of Disembodied Poetics at Naropa at Trungpa's invitation during

the first Naropa summer of 1974. In 1976 they, along with poet and teacher Michael Brownstein, drafted a mission statement of "General Practice of the Jack Kerouac School of Disembodied Poetics at Naropa Institute," which expresses the spirit of contemplative engagement within the realm of poetic practice and study. (The term *poetic* here refers to all forms and genres of the literary arts.) This document begins: "Observing an interpenetration of Eastern and Western human arts, the Poetics Program at Naropa Institute combines study of traditional Western composition up to present century (with special emphasis of writing creation that reflects mind nature observed during composition time), with traditional Eastern meditation discipline, commonly sitting following breath."[32]

This statement of "general practice" goes on to list eight points of general practice that describe an approach to contemplative poetics within the particular historical perspectives of North American poetics with which its founding faculty were aligned. The first three of these points:

1. To link Western traditions of spontaneous composition with Oriental practice of the same—historically represented by the lineages of Milarepa the poet, Japanese Zen haiku, and the poetic sayings and writings of Indian, Chinese, and other spiritual poetics.

2. To reinforce the basic concerns of Naropa Institute in context of creative writing by grounding the student in practical observation of detail, attention to concrete particulars, and a sane relationship to the phenomenal world.

3. To influence both poetry teachers and students in the direction of classical meditation practices, and to influence the Naropa meditative community in the direction of practical poetic articulation of their personal experience.[33]

The final point (#8) of the statement reads: "There being no party line but mindfulness of thought and language itself, no conflict need rise between "religion" and "poetry," and the marriage of two disciplines at Naropa has survived four years and is expected to flourish during the next hundred."[34] For thirty years now, the school has sponsored a Summer Writing Program at which approximately forty writers from around the country and the world gather as visiting faculty to teach weekly writing workshops, discuss writing related issues on panels, and give readings from their work.

Likewise, Naropa's Contemplative Psychology Department, first known as the Buddhist and Western Psychology program, found purpose and inspiration in the contact between the Western therapeutic tradition and the contemplative practice of present awareness. The first issue of the *Naropa Institute Journal of Psychology* published a talk by Trungpa titled "Becoming a Full Human Being." It elucidates a simple but radical re-visioning of psychological treatment inspired by the meeting of Western and contemplative traditions: "Basically the work we are involved in is how to become full human beings and how to inspire full human-being-ness in other people, who feel starved about their lives. The notion of the full human being does not so much refer to someone who can eat, sleep, shit, and talk, but beyond that to a person with a basic state of wakeful-ness. We might seem to be asking too much in looking at this in terms of wakefulness, but wakefulness is actually very close to us. We are touching it all the time."[35]

In a question-and-answer period that followed this talk, there was an exchange between Trungpa and psychology faculty on the question of patients' and therapists' identification with autobiographical story as a source and site of mental problems and their treatment. At one point, the Program's first director, Dr. Edward Podvoll, says, "It seems to me that there is an obsession that we all have, and that all of our patients have, with how we became what we are. In some way it is necessary to hear that a little bit in order to communicate with them." Trungpa responds:

> That is true, but that can be done with a present orientation. It does not have to be purely a matter of retelling a story, but rather of see-ing that the present situation has several levels: the basic ground, actual manifestation, and where it is about to go. So the present has three facets. Once you begin to approach it that way, it comes alive. But it is not a question of trying to reach a conclusion. The conclu-sion is already manifest in the present. There might be a case his-tory, but that facet is already dying. Actual communication takes place on the spot. By the time you sit down and say hello to the pa-tient, that person's whole history is there, on the spot.[36]

In this perspective, a lot of information is proposed as accessible by means of simply being with the "present situation." Whether this kind of attention is called "mindful awareness," "nowness," "spontaneous mind," "basic sanity," or "wakefulness," the approach of "contemplative education" is to fearlessly enter the gaps in conceptually bound thinking, and thereby find one's mind to be more open and spontaneously intelligent than one had perhaps previously realized. In this sense, the envisioned inclusion of many academic and spiritual traditions at Naropa University offers ways for each of those traditions to stay in contact with its living spirit through engagement with others and avoid the tendency to settle into dogmatic ruts and sectarianism.

Thirty Years On

In the spring of 2003, John Cobb retired after ten years as president of Naropa and near the end of a personal reflection and report published in the Naropa community, affirmed the Buddhist inspired and nonsectarian nature of Naropa: "This work has no blueprint and is not static. Naropa is at once a Buddhist-inspired university and nonsectarian. One might say that Buddhism is ultimate nonsectarianism, and at the same time say unequivocally, as the founder did: 'The Kagyü lineage is the host of Naropa Institute. We can't forget that.'"[37]

Dr. Thomas Coburn, who succeeded John Cobb as president in 2003, made the theme of his inauguration, "Naropa University at the Confluence of Two Rivers." Dr. Coburn, the university's first non-Buddhist president, explained his metaphor further at the inauguration: "Naropa's approach draws, in a uniquely contemporary way, on two educational traditions, one deriving from classical India, the other from classical Greece. Like the confluence of two rivers, these traditions together are larger than either has been individually. Together they develop skills to gain access to the underutilized resource of the inner life of spirituality while fostering understanding and constructive engagement with the external world."[38]

In apparent agreement with the vision of the University's founder, Dr. Coburn proclaimed that personal and institutional development requires both internal and external growth. Such growth requires labor like a farmer's—seeding, watering, cultivating, responding to conditions, harvesting—and the patience and live attention that make those efforts effective. It requires discipline. Naropa at thirty years old is still young in cultivating an environment where people in diverse fields of study can grow in self-understanding as well as in knowledge, but the aspiration to do so was clear at the beginning and remains so.

> Naropa Institute has a long growing process. Maybe one hundred years, and we're not in a special rush. It's a long-term project and I don't expect to see the beginning of the end of it. But hopefully education could become a situation of practice and personal development, so education could be a powerful one, a tough one that imposes discipline on the student. And hopefully we could develop a greater contribution to not only America alone, but the greater universe."[39]

Naropa University's approach to education is based in the love of wisdom awakened through openness to personal experience. In the meeting of the visionary and the immediately personal, sparks will fly, provoking psychological and intellectual growth as well as confidence in the limitless potential, the basic goodness, of human beings, however we may struggle against it. At Naropa there is certainly struggle, but in most cases, the heart opens at some point in that struggle and so education continues. "Love of wisdom," as Trungpa said in an early meeting with Naropa faculty, "puts you on the spot all the time."

Notes

1. Marvin Casper, unpublished chronicle based on interviews conducted by Simion Luna in 1998–1999.

2. Ibid.

3. Chögyam Trungpa, "Transpersonal Cooperation at Naropa," *Journal of Transpersonal Psychology* 7, no. 1 (1975).

4. Marvin Casper, unpublished chronicle.

5. Chögyam Trungpa, "Welcoming Remarks," Convocation of Naropa Institute, June 1974, p. 1.

6. Ibid.

7. "Transpersonal Cooperation at Naropa."

8. *Shambhala: The Sacred Path of the Warrior* (Toronto: Bantam, 1984), p. 71.

9. Ibid., p. 71.

10. Ibid., p. 72.

11. Naropa University Mission Statement, point 5.

12. *Naropa University Course Catalog,* 2003–2004, p. 8.

13. *Cutting Through Spiritual Materialism* (1973), p. 3.

14. Chögyam Trungpa, "Why Buddhism in America?" Talk at Naropa Institute, Summer 1980.

15. Chögyam Trungpa, "Meeting with Naropa Institute," March 12, 1979.

16. "Welcoming Remarks."

17. Trungpa, "Welcoming Remarks," p. 4. Passage edited by Reed Bye.

18. Ibid.

19. His Holiness the fourteenth Dalai Lama, Address to the faculty and staff at Naropa, 2000. Quoted in John Cobb, *Lineage and Innovation* (Boulder: Naropa University Press, 2003).

20. The Dzogchen Ponlop Rinpoche, "Contemplative Learning: The Ten Aspects of Knowledge," talk at Naropa University, 1997.

21. Ibid.

22. "Why Buddhism in America?"

23. "Sparks" in *Loka: A Journal from Naropa Institute,* ed. Rick Fields (Garden City, N.Y.: Anchor Books, 1975), p. 19.

24. Trungpa, "Why Buddhism in America?"

25. Chögyam Trungpa with Ösel Tendzin. "The Warrior of Shambhala," course given at Naropa Institute, July–August 1979.

26. *Shambhala,* p. 28.

27. Judith L. Lief, "Womb of Wisdom," excerpts from Practice Day Talk, March 9, 1999.

28. "Transpersonal Cooperation at Naropa."

29. In *Speaking of Silence: Christians and Buddhists on the Contemplative Way,* ed. Susan Walker (New York: Paulist Press, 1987), p. 12.

30. Ibid., p. 13.

31. "Transpersonal Cooperation at Naropa."

32. *Talking Poetics from Naropa Institute,* vol. 2, ed. Anne Waldman and Marilyn Webb (Boulder: Shambhala Publications, 1979), p. 415.

33. Ibid., p. 416.

34. Ibid., p. 418.

35. Chögyam Trungpa, "Becoming a Full Human Being," *Naropa Institute Journal of Psychology* (Boulder: Nalanda Press, 1980), p. 4. Reprinted in Trungpa, *The Sanity We Are Born With.*

36. Ibid., p. 8.

37. Cobb, "Lineage and Innovation."

38. Dr. Thomas Coburn, in event program, Naropa University Presidential Inauguration, November 1, 2003.

39. Chögyam Trungpa, "Meeting with Faculty and Administration," July 18–19, 1975.

The Way of Basic Sanity

Chögyam Trungpa Rinpoche's Perspective on Sutric Buddhism

TRALEG KYABGÖN RINPOCHE

CHÖGYAM TRUNGPA RINPOCHE'S perspective on hinayana and mahayana Buddhist practices is unique. Summarizing his views, ranging as they do over so many profound issues, is not an easy task. (To include an overview of tantra would have meant writing an additional article of similar scope, so I have confined myself to presenting his views of sutric Buddhism.) The number of his books is already quite large, with more arriving. While Trungpa Rinpoche is a very organized thinker in one respect, with a masterly command of the English language, in another respect his teachings almost defy systematization; his spontaneous outbursts of poetic expression and brilliant insights into our human folly can appear at any instant in his discourse, making it very difficult for anyone to write about his work and do his thinking justice. I have tried to draw the reader's attention to certain salient features of his vast and profound teachings, selecting themes that I personally have found important and inspiring. As much as possible, I have also allowed Trungpa Rinpoche speak for himself, by including examples from his books to illustrate my points.

In these teachings, Trungpa Rinpoche presents a direct and explicit Buddhist method of discovering our own basic sanity. His writings provide a methodical approach for prevailing over our neurotic tendencies, for he regarded this as the fundamental method for realizing our basic sanity on the spiritual path. According to his understanding of the human condition, neurosis is the result of acquiescing to egoistic domination and the consequent entanglement in a variety of predictable self-deceptions. He highlights how calculating, shrewd, and resourceful the ego can be and how willfully we thereby misuse our emotions. He also clearly elucidates Buddhist methods for cultivating compassion and wisdom—the two essential qualities for attaining enlightenment, or for realizing the basic sanity that is our natural inheritance as sentient beings.

Basic Sanity

One of the central and recurrent themes in Trungpa Rinpoche's thought is this notion of basic sanity. Throughout his teaching career he tirelessly returned to this topic, emphasizing its significance for our times. Perhaps the best way to understand what Trungpa Rinpoche meant by "basic sanity" is that it is a particular attitude or distinctive state of mind—an unencumbered openness characterized by the absence of hope and fear. As he explains in *Transcending Madness:* "You could have a basic sound understanding of the logic of things as they are without ego. In fact you can have greater sanity beyond ego; you can deal with situations without hope and fear, and you can retain your self-respect or your logical sanity in dealing with things."[1] It should be acknowledged at the outset that the notion of transcending hope and fear is predominantly associated with the teachings of the Kagyü and Nyingma schools of Tibetan Buddhism. Trungpa Rinpoche made liberal use of certain fundamental concepts from these two schools to convey the principal Buddhist teachings, even when the subject did not directly involve Tibetan Buddhism. Something of the flavor of tantric Buddhism can also be detected in all of his discourses, such as this extract from *Cutting Through Spiritual Materialism*, which is typical of Trungpa's teaching style: "Somehow we lost the unity of openness and what we are. Openness became a separate thing, and then we began to play games. It is obvious that we cannot say that we have lost the openness. 'I used to have it, but I have lost it.' We cannot say that, because that will destroy our status as an accomplished person. So the part of self-deception is to retell the stories. We would rather tell stories than actually experience openness, because stories are very vivid and enjoyable."[2]

Basic sanity in Trungpa Rinpoche's thought represents the attitude of enlightenment, which is free from hope and fear. The implication here seems obvious enough: the attitude of ignorance, if it can be put that way, dominates our deluded, samsaric mind through the inveterate afflictions of hope and fear. In the idiom of Trungpa Rinpoche's teaching style, this would be termed neurosis. Trungpa Rinpoche's view was that in order to appreciate our basic sanity, we should not endeavor to disassociate ourselves from these afflictions or neurotic tendencies but learn to work with them as the actual basis of our spiritual journey. As he states in *Crazy Wisdom*: "Developing basic sanity is a process of working on ourselves in which the path itself rather than the attainment of a goal becomes the working basis."[3]

Spiritual Materialism

One of the fundamental ways we go astray and become engulfed in the currents of hope and fear is by succumbing to a malady that Trungpa Rinpoche famously termed "spiritual materialism." As Trungpa saw it, the American spiritual scene was going through a major upheaval; young people were leaving Judaism and Christianity in droves, experimenting with hallucinogens, and dabbling in a plethora of Eastern religions, mysticisms, and philosophies. He regarded this as a critical moment in American history, one that was pregnant with many spiritual possibilities. On the one hand, there was the ubiquitous danger of degenerating into spiritual materialism, seduced by the myriad spiritual promises that proliferated and still abound. On the other hand, there was the very real possibility of a proper and complete reception of Tibetan vajrayana Buddhism in the West.

Trungpa Rinpoche set himself the task of introducing young Americans to the authentic teachings of Tibetan Buddhism. He did so in his own unique fashion, creating a completely novel yet strictly traditional style of presentation. He was convinced that to make any spiritual progress we have to begin with ourselves, with what he characteristically referred to as "our own neurosis." In his inimitable style, Trungpa Rinpoche describes it this way: "If you are utterly confused, you are confused to the point of seeming to yourself to be unconfused. This is what we call 'spiritual materialism.'"[4] His enduring message was that it is only through meditation practice that we can entertain any possibility of eradicating our neuroses. Any spiritual journey has to begin with oneself and one's own neurotic mind, or else there is the danger of turning our spiritual yearnings into a form of materialism. He warns his students in *Cutting Through Spiritual Materialism:* "It is important to see that the main point of any spiritual practice is to step out of the bureaucracy of ego. This means stepping out of ego's constant desire for a higher, more spiritual, more transcendental version of knowledge, religion, virtue, judgment, comfort or whatever it is that the particular ego is seeking. One must step out of spiritual materialism."[5]

Hopelessness

Trungpa Rinpoche presented a unique and contemporary approach to dealing with our neurotic tendencies. For him, a truly spiritual journey toward basic sanity has to begin with a sense of hopelessness—the recognition of the complete and utter hopelessness of our current situation. He assured his readers that they are required to undertake a major process of disillusionment in order to relinquish their belief in the existence of an external panacea that can eliminate their suffering and pain. We have to learn to live with our pain instead of hoping for something that will cause all of our hesitations, confusions, insanity, and suffering to disappear. This theme is elaborated upon in *Illusion's Game:* "Creating this kind of hope is one of the most prominent features of spiritual materialism. . . . There are so many promises involved. So much hope is planted in your heart. This is playing on your weakness. It creates further confusion with regard to pain. You forget about the pain altogether and get involved in looking for something other than the pain. And that itself *is* pain. . . . That is what we will go through unless we understand that the basic requirement for treading the spiritual path is hopelessness."[6]

To make any advance on the spiritual path, according to Trungpa Rinpoche, we have to realize that there is no savior, no such thing as a divine hand that will reach down and lift us out of our malaise. In fact, he claimed that being hopeful is simply a form of neurotic confusion, a symptom of self-deception, of not being true to oneself. A fundamental sense of fear and dread lies at the basis of this approach, for to think that there is something other than ourselves, something to be found outside ourselves, that will rescue or save us from ourselves is completely misguided, to say the least. We are compelled to pursue this kind of intervention because of the painfulness of our existence. As Trungpa says in *Dharma Art*: "The experience of I, me, a personal existence, ego, self, whatever you want to call it, has a sense of immense fundamental pain. You don't want to exist, you don't want to be, but you can't help it. . . . We are allergic to ourselves; therefore, we create all kinds of sicknesses and pains."[7]

Throughout his life, Trungpa Rinpoche presented the Buddhist message in a challenging and uncompromising fashion. Even the central Buddhist notions of enlightenment, buddhahood, and nirvana were not to be treated as objects to be pursued and possessed as some kind of reward for our efforts. Trusting that such transcendental realities will allay our fears of neurotic confusion and samsaric suffering is something that Trungpa Rinpoche equated with using a carrot and stick to control a donkey. As he says in *Crazy Wisdom*, "in spiritual materialism promises are used like a carrot held up in front of a donkey, luring him into all kinds of journeys; in transcending spiritual materialism, there is no goal."[8] To use another Trungpa-ism, this is equivalent to grasping the wrong end of the stick. He alleges that we are driven to this kind of impulsive and humiliating behavior because "Nobody has given up hope of attaining enlightenment. Nobody has given up hope of getting out of suffering."[9]

From Trungpa Rinpoche's point of view, to be overly enthusiastic and enthralled by enlightenment is to begin our journey with the kind of subtle fallacy that guarantees bewilderment. This misconception arises because we have not confronted a genuine sense of hopelessness and we are still trying to escape our own condition for some more enchanted realm of existence. Trungpa demanded total, uncompromising honesty and authenticity with ourselves in this regard, more so than any other Buddhist teacher in the West. This requisite can be gleaned from the following assessment in *The Tibetan Book of the Dead*: "In other words, the whole thing is based on another way of looking at the psychological picture of ourselves in terms of a practical meditative situation. Nobody is going to save us, everything is left purely to the individual, the commitment to who we are. Gurus or spiritual friends might instigate that possibility, but fundamentally they have no function."[10]

A transformative sense of hopelessness is an essential element of the path for two reasons: the fascination with enlightenment and nirvana has the potential to become a dangerous distraction from our present condition, while the fixation on a god or divine being that will rescue us reduces us to a puerile state of dependency. Both of these approaches encourage the kind of wishful thinking that leads to spiritual materialism. We cannot use transcendental, nirvanic concepts to safeguard ourselves from the realities of conditioned existence, nor can we draw succor from thinking that a divine being will bestow salvific favors on us and release us from our imprisoned desperation. Buddhism, being nontheistic, does not hold out any promises of divine grace or supernatural intervention, as Trungpa Rinpoche makes clear in *The Lion's Roar*: "You see, Buddhism is the only nontheistic religion. It doesn't contain any promises, or doesn't permit any. It just suggests the basic necessity of working with ourselves, fundamentally, very simply, very ordinarily. It is very sensible. You have no complaint when you get to the other end of the trip of Buddhism. It's a very definite journey."[11]

Trungpa Rinpoche felt strongly that theism has the tendency to create a sense of dependency, which renders the individual perpetually hopeful but with no real certainty about his or her own redemption. He felt that this approach was both psychologically harmful and spiritually vacuous. The approach of nontheism, on the other hand, emphasizes a genuine sense of hopelessness that, in an ironic twist, produces real conviction in our own ability to secure liberation for ourselves and by ourselves. Trungpa Rinpoche could not stress enough that this genuine sense of hopelessness, along with trust and faith in oneself, are the real precondition for engendering authentic spiritual development.

The openness and lack of ground that this hopelessness engenders is not unworkable, but it has to be filled by faith. Trungpa did not mean faith in something external, but a trust or conviction in our own ability to liberate ourselves. In Trungpa Rinpoche's thought, genuinely experiencing a sense of hopelessness does not lead to despair or a sense of the meaninglessness of life; it gives rise directly to this trust in oneself. This is the natural result of genuine hopelessness, because of the attendant realization that nothing we can imagine or strive after will safeguard ego's territory. Something of our basic sanity will be allowed to surface as a result. A sense of meaning and faith will arise from this trust in ourselves and our own self-determination. Hopelessness and faith, Trungpa Rinpoche says, must coexist if we are to discover our basic sanity. As he says in *The Lion's Roar*: "We have completely tired ourselves out, exhausted ourselves beyond our hopefulness. We realize that life is hopeless and that any effort we put in to gain further experience is also hopeless. Then we get into a real understanding of the space between us and our goal. That space is totally and completely full. And that fullness is what is called faith. . . . Faith here means dedication to and conviction in one's own intelligence. . . . You have trust in the basic truth of what you are, who you are."[12]

In Trungpa Rinpoche's teachings, faith consists of seeing everything about ourselves as workable and salvageable. In this context, then, faith has to be understood in a different way from traditional religious contexts, where hope and fear go together and both involve placing trust in the unknown. For Trungpa, faith is a task that we can carry out by ourselves, because in spite of our neurotic tendencies, confusions, and bewilderment, we already possess the innate intelligence and ability to extricate ourselves from our samsaric entanglements. As he says in *Meditation in Action*: "You see, you are your own best friend, your own closest friend, you are the best company for yourself. One knows one's own weaknesses and inconsistency, one knows how much wrong one has done, one knows it in all detail, so it doesn't help to try and pretend you don't know it."[13]

This kind of conviction in oneself represents a tremendous act of courage. Being hopeful, on the other hand, only indicates a cowardice that is intimately associated with feeling helpless. By establishing trust in ourselves, we also simultaneously develop the ability to trust others, particularly our teacher, spiritual friend, guru, and so on. Not having faith in ourselves or trusting our own innate basic goodness only leads to a sense of desperation that is veiled in a thin layer of hopefulness and an obvious mistrust of others. All that we have is hope.

For Trungpa Rinpoche, this kind of hope is simply wishful thinking and should be rejected as useless and demeaning. Many readers may find this provocative, but it is worth pursuing Trungpa Rinpoche's explanations of how this lack of courage and trust in ourselves can manifest as arrogance and egoism, ensuring the interminable neurotic habits that conceal our vulnerability, meekness, and ultimate lack of faith. As Trungpa says, "Our problem all along is that we have been too smart, too proud."[14] We do not want to relate with anybody else because we have become completely fixated on enlightenment. In fact, we may eventually find any kind of trust exceedingly hard to generate.

These attitudes ensure that we remain in a state of perpetual immaturity. As Trungpa was fond of saying, we must take stock of ourselves and pull ourselves up by our bootstraps. Nothing external is going to come along and change things for us. While Trungpa was aware that this message might initially seem bleak, it is ultimately uplifting. Realizing that we can turn our lives around by accepting our utter hopelessness will bring joy rather than despondency and desperation. Once we have given up hope, we can really traverse the spiritual path instead of constructing fantasies or recoiling from doubts. As he makes clear in *The Myth of Freedom*, joy "transcends both hope and fear, pain and pleasure. Joy here is not pleasurable in the ordinary sense, but it is the ultimate and fundamental sense of freedom, a sense of humor, the ability to see the ironical aspect of the game of ego, the playing of polarities."[15]

A genuine experience of hopelessness, Trungpa assures us, is an unfailing defense against the dangers of spiritual materialism because it brings about fearlessness. Fearlessness is another essential element of Trungpa's vision, for both hope and fear must be confronted on the spiritual journey. The lure of spiritual materialism lies in its empty promises of an eternal, paradisiacal existence or of selection by a divine being for special favors. In the end, however, these ideas only create the conditions for a perpetual state of infantile dependency.

Hinayana

Tibetan Buddhism has always favored a more progressive soteriological structure than many other Buddhist traditions. All four main Tibetan schools accordingly have their own system of the "paths and stages" format of spiritual cultivation and development. These are typically presented in the form of three yanas, or three vehicles: hinayana, mahayana, and vajrayana (or tantrayana). These three yanas can be presented from many different perspectives—we can find the views of the historical, doctrinal, geographical, philosophical, and individual spiritual developments there. Trungpa Rinpoche, along with many of the great Kagyü and Nyingma masters, was not interested in Buddhism's doctrinal, historical, or philosophical perspectives in themselves, but in what spiritual bearings the three yanas have for the individual. Understood in this context, hinayana does not refer to a particular doctrinal school but to an individual with a specific mental disposition and character. Trungpa Rinpoche gives just such a definition of the hinayana: "*Hinayana* literally means the 'small or lesser vehicle,' but it would be more accurate to call it the 'narrow way.' The hinayana is small or narrow in the sense that the strict discipline of meditation narrows down, or tames, the speed and confusion of mind, allowing the mind to rest in its own place. The hinayana is also called the 'immediate yana' because hinayana practice allows simple and direct experience of our own minds and of the world. We begin to realize that whatever we experience—whether good or bad, positive or negative—is workable, tamable."[16]

Unlike many Tibetan teachers who have lived and taught in the West, Trungpa Rinpoche clearly saw the necessity of taking students through the three-yana perspective of Tibetan Buddhism in a very traditional way. Tibetan lamas have often been very liberal with tantric initiations, teachings, and practices, thus unwittingly helping to fuel their students' distraction and fascination rather than providing a solution to it. Trungpa Rinpoche was unique in taking his students step-by-step through the hinayana, mahayana, and finally vajrayana methods of Buddhist teachings and praxis. To begin the Buddhist path, the individual practitioner must first embark on the hinayana, or small vehicle, by dealing with his or her own mind.

The Four Noble Truths

The best way to manage one's mind is through contemplating the four noble truths: the truth of suffering, the truth of the origin of suffering, the truth of the cessation of suffering, and the truth of the way out of suffering. Typically, Trungpa Rinpoche presents these truths in an immediate and contemporary manner, whereby the everyday experiences of modern life are clearly related to the traditional teachings. In correlation with his statements on spiritual materialism and wishful thinking, Trungpa asserts that suffering is an all-pervasive feature of human experience because of our overwhelming desire to resist or deny the existence of our pain. He argues that this resistance is self-defeating because pain is not something we can eliminate through an act of will, and we only create more pain for ourselves by trying to do so. The variegated experiences of suffering that we are subject to are exacerbated by both the denial of suffering and the insistence that happiness is something we can obtain in the absence of pain.

While acknowledging that it is part of our deep-seated habits and cultural expectations to regard happiness as something that we have to obtain in the absence of pain, Trungpa clearly presents the Buddha's teaching that happiness is obtained through working with pain rather than trying to make it go away. In fact, it is predominantly our attitude toward pain and our responses to it that determine whether we have a happier life or an unhappy one. As Trungpa Rinpoche explains: "The problem seems to be the attitude that the pain should go, then we will be happy. That is our mistaken belief. The pain never goes, and we will never be happy. That is the truth of suffering, *duhkha satya*. Pain never goes; we will never be happy. There's a mantra for you. It's worth repeating."[17]

It is essential to the spiritual path that we wake up to this fact and realize the fundamental insight of the Buddha into duhkha satya, the truth of suffering. When examining this experience of suffering, argues Trungpa, we discover that there are elements of both intelligence and stupidity involved in denying our pain by "hiding our private parts," as he expresses it. What he seems to be suggesting is that we find our pain and vulnerability embarrassing and constantly try to hide our fundamental discomfort to the best of our ability, pretending even to ourselves that we are completely in control of our lives; or, in Trungpa Rinpoche's terminology, we insist on preserving our egoistic territory. Doing so is both intelligent and stupid, because our discomfort is transparently obvious to others. Denying our pain and finding ever more ingenious and sophisticated methods for hiding it from others only compounds our misery and intensifies our deluded state of mind. It would be far more intelligent to acknowledge the reality of duhkha and try to address it in a practical way. As Trungpa Rinpoche states in *The Lion's Roar*: "We should admit this infamous, familiar pain. This is the pain that is actually happening. We cannot say that it is just nothing. It is the biggest thing that we have to hide. We plan all kinds of ways to hide it, thinking that nobody will know. . . . It is really very, very embarrassing; and that embarrassment is pain, duhkha, suffering. Trying to hide our private parts does not work out the way we wanted it to."[18]

For Trungpa Rinpoche, the origin of the all-pervasive, ubiquitous suffering we endure lies in our restless nature: we never take a break from our drive to succeed, acquire, and experience all manner of objects that might enrich our lives. As a result, there is a tremendous sense of speed involved in the accumulation of the material and emotional things we seek in order to ease our pain, and we never allow ourselves the space to be with ourselves, even for a moment. Trungpa Rinpoche says that grasping after things only accelerates the speed with which we scour for an ever-increasing number of material acquisitions and psychological comforts. As he explains in The Lion's Roar: "The origin of the suffering of our thingness is circling with speed. The origin of the suffering is the speed. Graspingness, re-creating one karmic situation after another."[19]

The solution to this is revealed in the third noble truth: the truth of cessation. Trungpa Rinpoche consistently maintains that if we pay attention to our inner inklings, we will find that we already have a basic nature of sanity within ourselves. This discovery is what will allow us to stop our struggle. Instead, we can wake up to the present state with ourselves as we are. Trungpa has this to say about the innate quality of our basic sanity in Cutting Through Spiritual Materialism: "We begin to realize that there is a sane, awake quality within us. In fact this quality manifests itself only in the absence of struggle. So we discover the Third Noble Truth, the truth of the goal: that is, non-striving. We need only drop the effort to secure and solidify ourselves and the awakened state is present."[20]

The way to effect this shift from the struggle to maintain our solid ground to a state of nonstriving is laid out in the eightfold noble path. By following and engaging in the practices of this path, we can attain some understanding of suffering, impermanence, and egolessness based upon the hinayana path. As Trungpa Rinpoche explains: "It is this fear of exposure, this denial of impermanence that imprisons us. It is only by acknowledging impermanence that there is the chance to die and the space to be reborn and the possibility of appreciating life as a creative process."[21]

Refuge

In order to embark on the hinayana path, we have to assimilate the four noble truths and make a real resolve to follow the Buddhist path. At that point it is essential to take refuge in the Buddha, dharma, and sangha. By taking refuge in these three jewels of the spiritual path, we are transformed into homeless travelers. Trungpa Rinpoche describes the impulse to take refuge: "Since we are in an emergency situation, the first thing we learn is that our struggle to pull ourselves out of samsara has to be given up. Being engaged in a struggle may give us some sense of security, in that at least we feel we are doing something. But that struggle has become useless and irrelevant: it only makes things worse. However, the pain we have experienced in our struggle cannot be forgotten. We have to work with it. Rather than struggling to escape pain, we have to make it our path."[22]

As sentient creatures, we never really have a permanent dwelling place, but we injudiciously continue to seek one and thus inure ourselves to our ignorance by believing that we have found a home in samsara. Nonetheless, our experience of samsara itself is constantly evolving, which is why it is depicted in the Buddhist teachings as cyclic existence. As sentient beings, we are continually transported from one state of existence to another in accordance with our karmic inheritance. Sometimes we may be transported to elevated states of existence and other times demoted to lower states, but the process is continuous and unrelenting until we are able to liberate ourselves within our own basic sanity or enlightened state. As there is no permanent, secure home base to be found in samsara, it is necessary to simplify ourselves and our expectations by becoming a "homeless one." As Trungpa says in *Orderly Chaos*, "true homelessness is just giving up without taking on anything new; it is just simplifying yourself without questioning what you are going to get in return."[23]

For Trungpa Rinpoche, taking refuge and becoming homeless in no way entails relinquishing responsibility for ourselves. It means only that we give up the familiar ground that supports our ego and admit that our ego is incapable of controlling its world or securing itself. Trungpa, in fact, describes taking refuge as the most authentic way of becoming responsible for our own lives. For example, he says: "By taking refuge, in some sense we become homeless refugees. Taking refuge does not mean saying that we are helpless and then handing all our problems over to somebody or something else. There will be no refugee rations, nor all kinds of security and dedicated help. The point of becoming a refugee is to give up our attachment to basic security. We have to give up our sense of home ground, which is illusory anyway."[24]

The real essence of taking refuge consists of totally surrendering. Trungpa Rinpoche's conception of total surrender warrants a brief explanation, because it represents a very interesting notion. He says that we must not surrender our individual responsibility to an "other," yet he maintains that it is essential that we undergo a complete process of relinquishment. By "surrender," Trungpa Rinpoche means going beyond fascination and expectation, which is a continuation of the theme of hopelessness that he highlights so much. This surrendering is a way of extricating ourselves from the egoistic tentacles that keep us trapped in self-delusion. As such, taking refuge is done through this surrendering, this freeing of ourselves from egoistic control. By taking refuge we are availing ourselves of the opportunity to awaken, to become like the Buddha, in whom we merge as the embodiment of the path.

As he explains: "'Surrender' means opening oneself completely, trying to get beyond fascination and expectation. Surrender also means acknowledging the raw, rugged, clumsy and shocking qualities of one's ego, acknowledging them and surrendering them as well. Generally, we find it very difficult to give out and surrender our raw and rugged qualities of ego. . . . We *can* afford to surrender that raw and rugged neurotic quality of self and step out of fascination, step out of preconceived ideas."[25]

As I understand it, Trungpa Rinpoche is making a very helpful suggestion for modern-day Buddhist practitioners. He differentiates taking refuge in the Buddhist teachings from the kind of alternative refuges offered by the religious and secular traditions of the West, especially the kind afforded by Western psychotherapies. It is very common for people to come to Buddhism and take refuge in the Buddha, dharma, and sangha in the hope that they will quite literally be saved by them, or rescued by a Tibetan lama from whatever mental afflictions they may be suffering from. As Trungpa Rinpoche states, we should surrender such notions at the gateway to the Buddhist path: "All the promises we have heard are pure seduction. We expect the teachings to solve all our problems; we expect to be provided with magical means to deal with our depressions, our aggressions, our sexual hangups. But to our surprise we begin to realize that this is not going to happen. It is very disappointing to realize that we must work on ourselves and our suffering rather than depend upon a savior or the magical power of yogic techniques. It is disappointing to realize that we have to give up our expectations rather than build on the basis of our preconceptions. We must allow ourselves to be disappointed, which means the surrendering of me-ness, my achievement."[26]

Shamatha

In strict accord with the three-yana approach of Tibetan Buddhism, Trungpa Rinpoche began by training his students in the practice of sitting meditation. He placed great emphasis on the practice of shamatha, because it is only through shamatha that we can learn to confront our own minds. Sitting with one's mind is the best way to experience the sense of hopelessness that Trungpa Rinpoche never grew tired of emphasizing: "In sitting meditation, you don't trip out, but simply sit, identify with your breath, work with your thoughts. You do everything very manually, very definitely, constantly. But in postmeditation practice, you are here. You are definitely here: whether you are combing your hair, pressing your clothes, walking around, taking a bite of a peach, or whatever you are doing in your life."[27]

To learn to be genuine and authentic and not yield to our innate impulse to scramble after a dazzling array of spiritual attainments, lofty meditation experiences, divine encounters, and so forth, we must first find a method of nullifying this tendency to aggrandize our egos and simply learn how to dwell in peace. This is achieved through the practice of shamatha meditation. Trungpa Rinpoche defines shamatha as "dwelling in peace" but adds, "*Peace* here refers to the simplicity or uncomplicatedness of the practice."[28]

The mind has a tendency to be drawn to various sensory and mental objects. In our unreflective moods we chase after material things or emotional comforts such as love and companionship, while in more reflective moods we give rein to the same tendency by scrambling after spiritual things. Neither of these approaches allows us to be with ourselves. We are always stepping outside of ourselves, with what Trungpa Rinpoche described with provocative acuity as "a poverty-stricken attitude." Shamatha meditation, on the other hand, allows us the luxury of dwelling in peace with ourselves and our neuroses. It is this simple, uncomplicated, and nonduplicitous approach that constitutes the true spiritual path.

In this context, I would like to draw the reader's attention to one small but significant aspect of Trungpa Rinpoche's presentation of shamatha meditation. In many Buddhist traditions, shamatha is consistently presented as emphasizing the suppression of thoughts to a greater or lesser degree. As a consequence of Trungpa Rinpoche's impeccable training in the

Kagyü and Nyingma methods of meditation, from the beginning he discouraged his students from suppressing their thoughts during sitting meditation. Instead, he instructed them to deal directly with whatever arose in their minds, without employing any of the techniques for suppressing thinking or fabricating a peaceful state of mind. The following passage is typical of his shamatha meditation instructions: "All those things that happen in sitting meditation are relating with ourselves, working with ourselves, exposing neuroses of all kinds. After you have been through a certain amount of that, you master the experience of breathing in spite of those interruptions."29

As Trungpa Rinpoche pointed out, the cause of suffering is our speed, the ever-increasing acceleration of the tendency to chase after things with greed and grasping. In order to work with suffering, we need to slow this unbridled and undisciplined energy of the mind. Constant agitation is like looking through the windows of a fast-moving train, because everything is subject to the blur of our neurotic speed. There is no effective method for treating our neurotic speed other than the practice of shamatha. Having slowed the neurotic activities of the mind, we can see things more clearly. As Trungpa goes on to say: "It is important to remember that the practice of meditation begins with the penetration of the neurotic thought pattern which is the fringe of ego. As we proceed further, we see through not only the complexity of the thought processes but also the heavy 'meaningfulness' of concepts expressed in names and theories. Then at last we create some space between *this* and *that*, which liberates us tremendously."30

Mindfulness

Sitting meditation is the very foundation of Buddhist practice; everything else is built upon it. The core of sitting meditation is the practice of mindfulness. Trungpa Rinpoche's main theme when presenting sitting meditation as a mindfulness practice was as a way of making friends with ourselves, or, in his words, "making friends with one's own neurosis." A unique feature of Trungpa Rinpoche's teachings on shamatha is his insistence that meditation practice is a way to make us more acceptable to ourselves.

No other Buddhist teacher has drawn our attention to the need to find ourselves acceptable as a precondition for spiritual growth. Friendliness toward ourselves comes from the open space generated by sitting practice.

It is here that we allow ourselves to perceive our individual neurotic minds directly. While our natural tendency is to avoid our faults and short-comings, this evasion is transformed by the process of mindfulness, which allows us to observe our habitual tendencies without judgment or with-drawal. Trungpa points out that a sense of self-acceptance gradually arises as a result of that perception. The friendliness that develops in sitting meditation has to be contrasted with the more insidious affliction of nar-cissistic self-love, which is not based on genuine self-acceptance.

Ego has a way of placing tyrannical demands on us, with certain things designated as acceptable and other things censored, suppressed, or pushed out of conscious purview due to their potential to cause unease and even serious pain. In shamatha meditation, we can create the genuine experi-ence of space and get to know ourselves more thoroughly—warts and all, as the saying goes. Trungpa describes this process: "Neurosis in this case is in-ability to face the simple truth. Rather than do that, we introduce all kinds of highfalutin ideas—cunning, clever, depressing. We just purely bring in as much stuff as we like. And that stuff that we bring in has neurotic qual-ities. What 'neurotic' finally comes down to here is taking the false as true. The illogical approach is regarded as the logical one. So just relating with ourselves in meditation practice exposes all this hidden neurosis."[31]

Trungpa Rinpoche also maintained that shamatha should not be per-ceived as a special act we perform. There is tremendous value is seeing meditation as a natural thing to do, rather than something special or ex-traordinary. We are not trying to cultivate a particularly deliberate, pur-poseful way of being and acting, nor do we allow ourselves to succumb to a completely mindless, habitual way of behaving. By avoiding both of these approaches, we can settle into some kind of natural ground that is alert yet relaxed. As Trungpa states: "In this case, mindfulness means that when you sit and meditate, you actually do sit. . . . You don't try to formal-ize the sitting situation and make it into some special activity that you are performing. You just sit. And then you begin to feel that there is some sense of groundedness."[32]

Cool Boredom

Trungpa Rinpoche warns that while sitting meditation is rewarding in it-self, we should not become too excited about our meditation experiences.

Instead, we should concentrate on becoming aware of a less celebrated state of mind, which he terms cool boredom. This boredom is a sign that our meditation experience is developing and is something we should embrace with enthusiasm rather than growing dejected about a perceived lack of progress.

This seems to me a very helpful instruction, because many meditators understandably expect their meditative efforts to bring new experiences—if not continually, then at least intermittently. When we have the experience of cool boredom, we may interpret this as a symptom of reaching an impasse in our spiritual progress, because it has none of the characteristics of a good meditation experience. According to Trungpa Rinpoche, however, it is necessary for us to go through this kind of boredom. This experience is unique to meditation, and it is described as cool because it is actually quite refreshing and has many beneficial aspects. He explains: "Boredom has many aspects: there is the sense that nothing is happening, that something might happen, or even that what we would like to happen might replace that which is not happening. Or, one might appreciate boredom as a delight. The practice of meditation could be described as relating with cool boredom, refreshing boredom, boredom like a mountain stream. It refreshes because we do not have to do anything or expect anything. . . . As we realize that nothing is happening, strangely we begin to realize that something dignified is happening. There is no room for frivolity, no room for speed. We just breathe and are there."[33]

Lack of Credentials

It is a testament to Trungpa Rinpoche's integrity as a meditation practitioner and teacher that he emphasized the importance of eschewing credentials of any kind as an integral part of the spiritual path. He spoke of this as "buddhadharma without credentials," and no teacher before or after him has underscored this point so forcefully. Trungpa brings this issue back to meditation practice, explaining that it is the experience of cool boredom that will assist us to overcome this hankering after credentials: "Boredom is important because boredom is anti-credential. Credentials are entertaining, always bringing you something new, something lively, something fantastic, all kinds of solutions. When you take away the idea of credentials, then there is boredom."[34]

This seems to be an extremely important attitude, in light of the fact that most of the world's great spiritual traditions speak of levels of attainment, gradations of consciousness, and so forth. They distinguish between superficiality and depth, ascending or descending, and different paths and stages of development. One could therefore be forgiven for wondering, What stage of development have I reached? What level of meditative concentration have I developed? How close am I to attaining a particular level of spiritual realization? This is not to deny the importance or reality of some of these stages of spiritual attainment, but the obsession with credentials is an attitude we must relinquish for our own benefit, because it actually inhibits our spiritual growth. As Trungpa Rinpoche says, the search for credentials is a sickness we have to eliminate from our meditation experience, without while still fully experiencing our neuroses. He likens this process to having an operation without an anesthetic: "We begin meditation practice by dealing with thoughts, the fringe of ego. The practice of meditation is an undoing process. . . . So the practitioner who is involved with credentials begins with an operation. Credentials are an illness and you need an operation to remove them. . . . They prove that you are sick so that you can have attention from your friends. We have to operate on this person to eliminate the credential sickness. But if we give this person an anesthetic, he will not realize how much he has to give up. So we should not use anesthetics at all."[35]

This idea of no credentials figures significantly in Trungpa Rinpoche's thinking. He continually points out that we should always remember the importance of engaging in spiritual practice without the desire for any form of recognition or acknowledgment, because it only reinforces the deluded tendency to define our territory, solidify our existence, and prove our worth to ourselves and others. It therefore limits and corrupts any spiritual insight we might attain in ego's claustrophobic domain. The temptation to pervert our experiences with credentials arises from the fact that ego has no real solidity, as Trungpa Rinpoche accentuates in the following passage: "In order to cut through the ambition of ego, we must understand how we set up me and my territory, how we use our projections as credentials to prove our existence. The source of the effort to confirm our solidity is an uncertainty as to whether or not we exist. Driven by this uncertainty, we seek to prove our own existence by finding a reference point outside ourselves, something with which to have a relationship, something solid to feel separate from."[36]

Vipashyana

With the practice of shamatha meditation and mindfulness, where cool boredom prevents the mind from being trammeled by the constant search for credentials, we can begin to grapple better with our egos. While it is the proper establishment of shamatha practice that allows this to happen, shamatha alone is not sufficient to cut through ego. We must learn to practice vipashyana meditation if we are to gradually gain a real understanding of egolessness.

In the mindfulness practice of shamatha, the meditator is forced to deal with his or her subconscious gossip and discursive thoughts. While vipashyana practice is based upon this development of mindfulness, it is a far more powerful method for allowing us to cut through the mechanisms of ego. This is so because vipashyana meditation allows us to become more aware of the whole environment, as this "allows us to become less self-centered and more in contact with the world around us."[37] The awareness of our underlying mental habits and tendencies continues to grow, as we develop an expansive sense of clarity about our surroundings, which gives rise to a greater insight into the nature of existence. It is this understanding of the insubstantial nature of ourselves and our world that really transforms the well-entrenched delusions that prevent us from realizing our basic sanity. Trungpa Rinpoche often advised his students that to see that the phenomenal world has no more solid existence than we ourselves do will enable us to see the whole thing as a great display that demands nothing from us. This is an essential step in our spiritual development, as Trungpa makes clear: "With further practice, we begin to lose the reference point of self-consciousness, and we experience the environment of practice and the world without bringing everything back to the narrow viewpoint of 'me.' We begin to be interested in 'that,' rather than purely being interested in 'this.'"[38]

It is essential to combine both mindfulness and awareness in Buddhism, so shamatha and vipashyana techniques must be practiced with equal emphasis, because shamatha will give rise to vipashyana, and mindfulness will give rise to awareness. Trungpa Rinpoche's teachings were quite traditional in this regard. Mindfulness allows us to become aware during specific mental experiences or everyday activities, such as conversing with others, walking, sleeping, lying down, eating, and so forth, while vipashyana is a nondirectional awareness, because it takes in the overall spatial context within which these experiences occur.

According to Trungpa Rinpoche, this type of vipashyana awareness has to be precisely defined, because we can exercise awareness in many different ways. Often we have the experience of awareness that we might call "tacit awareness," such as when we go about daily chores such as driving. Then there is "focused awareness," which has to do with narrowing our focus on a deliberately chosen object, such as typing on a computer keyboard. Then there is another kind of awareness, which Trungpa Rinpoche called "panoramic awareness," because with it, "you see the whole scene. There are no sidetracks."[39] According to Trungpa, the ignorance responsible for throwing us into a state of samsaric confusion is the product of a mind with a unidimensional, narrow focus. It stands to reason, then, that the opposite of ignorance would be a mind that is panoramic, spacious, unrestrained, free flowing, and wide ranging. This panoramic awareness is developed by expanding on the awareness that we have already developed in mindfulness practice. It seems that there is a gradual development from mindfulness to awareness, to focused awareness, to panoramic awareness: "We begin to see the pattern of our fantasies rather than being immersed in them. We discover that we need not struggle with our projections, that the wall that separates us from them is our own creation."[40]

Prajna and Egolessness

The panoramic awareness that we develop in vipashyana meditation is directly related to the traditional Buddhist concept of prajna. Trungpa defines prajna as the mental power that is endowed with the dual faculties of intellect and intuition: "Prajna, or intellect, is completely intuitive as well as intellectually precise."[41] Intuition, in this context, seems to imply a certain instinctive sharpness of mind, the ability to spontaneously see things clearly with precision and directness. At the same time, prajna has the quality of intellect, which also involves a precise, subtle, fine discrimination. This discrimination is possible because it is no longer so closely tied to our egoistic sense of the world, to me and mine; it is unencumbered by our insecurities and territoriality. He explains: "Prajna is precision. . . . It is the precision or sharpness of intelligence that cuts off the samsaric flow, severs the aorta of samsara. . . . So the ultimate idea of intellect, from the Buddhist point of view, is the absence of ego, which is prajna."[42]

Vipashyana insight then brings about the realization of twofold egolessness: the recognition of the insubstantial nature of both self and the phenomenal world. We begin to understand that all the suffering we experience, the entire gamut of pain and misery that we endure, is brought about by an erroneous conception of self and other. In Trungpa Rinpoche's thinking, this brings about two distinct yet related revelations: the recognition of our fundamental aloneness, whereby no external savior can bestow liberation upon us, and a tremendous feeling of connectedness with our fellow creatures and the created world.

Again in Trungpa's vision, something that was initially fearsome and the cause of great anxiety can blossom into something positive—in this case, into an effortless connection with the world. Here he seems to be suggesting that a total acknowledgment of our own aloneness, coupled with seeing that there is no supernatural principle to be relied upon, allows a sudden insight into the real significance of the sentient and insentient things of this world.

As such, this realization of egolessness does not push us into an abyss of nothingness; it brings a positive and holistic perspective to the entire Buddhist path. Egolessness, in Trungpa Rinpoche's conception, opens up a new possibility of living and interacting with sentient beings and the created world. Trungpa Rinpoche is also emphatic that egolessness does not equate with nonexistence; it is simply a matter of living in a more spacious manner, a manner that is, in his phrase, "without reference points." To relinquish reference points is an act of courage and trust in our own existence, without the need to rely on safe and predictable definitions for ourselves. As he says quite clearly: "There is a state without reference point that is basic the way completely outer space, without stars and galaxies and planets, is basic. The stars, galaxies, and planets may be there or not, but still the space will be there."[43]

Our ability to interact with others becomes enhanced rather than diminished when we cease to employ our entrenched habit of relying on reference points. "Non–reference point" also means that having understood twofold egolessness, we do not then fixate on this as another kind of definition for ourselves. As Trungpa Rinpoche states: "Then we are not finding out whether we exist or not, but we are simply looking at ourselves directly, without any reference points—without even looking, we could say."[44] Whether we have ego or non-ego, we have to give up holding on to our conception of ourselves. Then we can see things directly and clearly and interact with others in a straightforward and responsive fashion.

Mahayana

Prajna leads to egolessness, and this realization gives rise to the possibility of progressing from the narrow view of the hinayana to the mahayana, or "great vehicle." Trungpa Rinpoche describes the mahayana path as a daring and heroic vision, which entails working for the benefit of all sentient beings rather than indulging ourselves in the idea of our own enlightenment. It is a wide path of warmth and openness. Mahayana practitioners have the confidence that we have been born fundamentally rich and that we must develop this richness, we must allow ourselves to be awake, to let our natural instincts emerge. Trungpa describes the mahayana path in these words: "In the hinayana the emphasis is on acknowledging our confusion. In the mahayana we acknowledge that we are a buddha, an awakened one, and act accordingly, even though all kinds of doubts and problems might arise. In the scriptures, taking the bodhisattva vow and walking on the bodhisattva path is described as being an act of awakening bodhi or 'basic intelligence.' Becoming 'awake' involves seeing our confusion more clearly. We can hardly face the embarrassment of seeing our hidden hopes and fears, our frivolousness and neurosis. It is such an overcrowded world. And yet it is a very rich display. The basic idea is that, if we are going to relate with the sun, we must also relate with the clouds that obscure the sun."[45]

In Trungpa Rinpoche's view of the Buddhist path, it is the realization of twofold egolessness that allows us to open ourselves to others without fear or trepidation. It was the obsessive concern with our ego that stood in the way of fully developing relationships with others. Through shamatha and vipashyana practice, our ability to appreciate others develops naturally and we find ourselves gravitating toward the bodhisattva path.

The altruism that is associated with the mahayana does not have to be forced or structured into our lives—it is the natural evolution of basic sanity once our egoism has been undermined through vipashyana. The mahayana path is based on the discovery that others are more important than ourselves. In a sense, we begin to discover that we do not really exist, at least not in the fixed, predetermined way that we imagined, and the result of this discovery is that we develop the space to take a real interest in the welfare of others. As Trungpa Rinpoche states: "At the beginning there is a vague idea that something is not quite right. There is something wrong with oneself. Things are questionable, and one begins to look into the question, to relate with the pain, the chaos and confusion. . . . Then at a certain stage some of the answers that arise out of the search begin to create further hunger, further curiosity. One's heart becomes more and more steeped in the teachings. Then the mahayana experience of intense dedication to the path begins to take place. Dedication to the path in this case also means compassion, a loving attitude toward oneself and others. One begins to find one's place in the universe, in this world."[46]

Bodhichitta

As we become acutely aware of others and the myriad ways in which they suffer pain and degradation, we are compelled to resolve to do something to alleviate their suffering and find a way to work for their benefit. In Buddhist literature, this impulse is called bodhichitta. As Trungpa Rinpoche explains, giving rise to bodhichitta does not simply require a good heart; it also requires good intelligence. It is our heart that generates the warmth associated with compassionate action; however, we need intellect to discriminate between actions that are truly beneficial for others and actions that serve our own self-interest or misconstrue others' needs. It is this combination of warmth and skill that constitutes compassionate action.

The best way to realize bodhichitta is to cultivate bodhichitta, for while bodhichitta is innate in ourselves as "awakened heart," it requires nurturing and training to fully materialize in our actions and minds. This is accomplished through the practice of shamatha and vipashyana meditation and by bringing mindfulness and awareness to all our activities. This is the practice of compassion, of expanding our concerns beyond our own egoistic territory and generating warmth and gentleness toward others. As Trungpa says: "In the mahayana, when we begin to realize the bodhisattva principle through practicing bodhichitta, our concern is more with warmth and skillfulness. We realize we have nothing to hang on to in ourselves, so we can give away each time. The basis of such compassion is nonterritoriality, non-ego, no ego *at all*. If you have that, then you have compassion. Then further warmth and workability and gentleness take place as well."[47]

Buddha Nature

Bodhichitta requires both warmth and intelligence, and this intelligence is also regarded as an innate quality. In its innate form, this intelligence is known as buddha nature, which is another term for our basic sanity. Just like the warmth that portends bodhichitta, our innate buddha nature can be harnessed and refined through the practices of the mahayana path. In an interesting analogy, one that reflects his Kagyü and Nyingma training, Trungpa Rinpoche highlights our basic sanity as a persistent reality by describing it as the other face of ego. He suggests that ego has a Janus face, a two-sided head, with one face fixated and territorial, giving rise to the samsaric experiences of entanglement, and the other face a clear and unencumbered one that critically surveys all of our samsaric experiences. Our territorial face thrives on having a narrow focus, its main task being the pursuit of security. The flip side is our basic sanity, or buddha nature, which is much more flexible and spacious and quite unconcerned with our narrow hopes and fears. Trungpa Rinpoche writes: "Ego is that which thrives on the security of your existence. Beyond that there is intelligence that sees the foolishness in trying to thrive on your security. It sees that insecurity is the ego's problem. The intelligence that sees that is called *tathagatagarbha* in Sanskrit, which means 'buddha nature.' Every act that perceives pain and impermanence and egolessness and the five skandhas, and even that which perceives meditation itself, is an act of non-ego. In other words, we could say that ego has two aspects: one is the honest and solid, sincere ego; the other is the critical surveyor of the whole situation, which is somewhat intelligent and more flexible and spacious. That aspect that is spacious and flexible, intelligent, is regarded as non-ego and called tathagatagarbha."[48]

The Bodhisattva Vow

In order to strengthen the resolve of the mahayana path, we need to take the bodhisattva vow, the commitment to put others before ourselves. This vow aids us in the stabilization of our bodhichitta, or benevolent heart, because it ensures that we maintain our focus on becoming open to the world by remaining aware of our own and others' suffering and confusion. It is based first and foremost on the commitment to take responsibility for ourselves and do something about our own confusion. Instead of being the cause of further chaos and misery in the world, we can work on ourselves as well as others.

Trungpa Rinpoche, however, makes it clear that the bodhisattva vow is not taken to shield ourselves from the confusion and chaos that surrounds us or the aggression, passion, frustration, and frivolousness that throw us off balance. We have to give up our privacy, give up our ideas of building our own credentials, by developing a greater vision and being willing to work with others. In fact, in his view, the essence of the bodhisattva vow is the commitment to work with the chaos and confusion of our samsaric mind until we attain enlightenment. As he explains: "The sanity of this tradition is very powerful. What we are doing in taking the bodhisattva vow is magnificent and glorious. It is such a whole-hearted and full tradition that those who have not joined it might feel somewhat wretched by comparison. They might be envious of such richness. But joining this tradition also makes tremendous demands on us. We no longer are intent on creating comfort for ourselves; we work with others."[49]

Compassion

Apart from the innate intelligence that we already possess in the form of buddha nature, or basic sanity, we also have what Trungpa Rinpoche often called a "soft spot," which inextricably ties us to the vulnerability and needs of others. In his view, this soft spot is the inborn capacity for compassion. Trungpa's insight into the human condition understood this soft spot as related to a sense of tenderness that we have toward ourselves. The unique perspective here is his notion that our soft spot grows out of resentment. In *Illusion's Game*, for instance, he says, "The resentment is an outward-directed defense mechanism for protecting yourself, which automatically suggests a sense of softness, a soft spot in oneself."[50]

Perhaps we should pause here to try to understand the connection between this soft spot, basic intelligence, and resentment. Intelligence here means something fundamental and primal, perhaps even visceral, rather than something cerebral. What Trungpa Rinpoche seems to be suggesting is that the very fact that ego is so vulnerable pushes it into adopting a defensive posture and a mechanism for self-protection and self-preservation. It operates this way because of an underlying fear of being usurped, overwhelmed, or even destroyed. The fact that ego tries to present itself as an invincible entity when it is really quite vulnerable is an indication of the presence of softness. Trungpa states this clearly: "Whether we are crazy, dull, aggressive, ego-tripping, whatever we might be, there is still that sore spot taking place in us. An open wound, which might be a more vivid analogy, is always there. That open wound is usually very inconvenient and problematic. We don't like it. We would like to be tough. . . . Our basic makeup, the basic constituents of our mind, are based on passion and compassion at the same time. But however confused we might be, however much of a cosmic monster we might be, still there is an open wound or sore spot in us always. There always will be a sore spot."[51]

The intelligence aspect comes about through employing resentment as a strategic maneuver of the ego for its own protection, and this, in Trungpa Rinpoche's thinking, is the major source of our neuroses. The conflicting emotions are also skillfully used in order to secure the ego's territory, whether this takes the form of anger, jealousy, or subconscious gossip. The main point is that all of our conflicting emotions come about because of our overwhelming concern for the health of our own ego and its mistaken attempt to solidify its position. Although misguided, says Trungpa Rinpoche, this is a way of showing kindness toward oneself and therefore an indication of ego's ability to be soft. According to Trungpa Rinpoche, we have to rely on this softness and basic intelligence in order to generate compassion. This innate sensitivity is what allows us to cultivate bodhichitta in the true sense and thereby develop the genuine compassion of a bodhisattva.

Another quality of compassion that Trungpa Rinpoche highlights is the notion of spaciousness, by which he means that compassion is not enacted for any specific goal. It simply wells forth from a spirit of generosity that does not focus on relative notions of either the recipient of that generosity or our benevolence in offering it. Such compassion arises from what he called spontaneously existing joy: "Compassion has nothing to do with achievement at all. It is spacious and very generous. When a person develops real compassion, he is uncertain whether he is being generous to others or to himself because compassion is environmental generosity, without direction, without 'for me' and without 'for them.' It is filled with joy, spontaneously existing joy, constant joy in the sense of trust, in the sense that joy contains tremendous wealth, richness."[52]

A further aspect of genuine compassion that Trungpa Rinpoche identifies is the impulse to be kind to oneself, one's problems, and one's neurotic tendencies; it is a compassion that we feel toward ourselves rather than others. While this is similar to his notion of developing friendship toward oneself in shamatha meditation, in the mahayana context of the bodhisattva it becomes an idea of the utmost importance. For here, it is not simply a matter of accepting our own neurosis; we must utilize that neurosis as an integral part of our spiritual growth. Trungpa Rinpoche coined another unique expression for the cultivation of bodhichitta in this context, referring to our neuroses as manure for the field of bodhi. He encouraged us to acknowledge the complete pattern of our experience in both its good and bad aspects and regard that as our inherited wealth, rather than something to be discarded. Cultivating this friendliness and sympathy toward ourselves is an important aspect of developing compassion, because it will allow us to transform our neuroses into basic sanity. As he says: "Through thousands and thousands of lives we have been collecting so much rubbish that now we have a wonderful wealth of this manure. It has everything in it, so it would be just the right thing to use, and it would be such a shame to throw it away."[53]

Trungpa Rinpoche cautioned that while compassion involves a willingness to work with others, we must not try to cultivate compassion in order to create companionship for ourselves. In fact, genuine compassion arises from the experience of loneliness or being alone. Having a willingness to be alone creates its own space, which is the fundamental space that makes the generation of compassion possible. As Trungpa explains: "I suppose, to begin with, in order to develop compassion you have to be willing to be alone or lonely. You are completely and totally in a desolate situation, which is also open space at the same time. The development of compassion is not a matter of acquiring a partnership with things, but rather of letting everything be open. So the sense of loneliness or aloneness is the real starting point for compassion."[54]

Genuine love and compassion is nevertheless difficult for us to practice and to receive from others. That is because our love and compassion usually suffers from the distortions and corruptions of our own neurotic tendencies. No modern-day Buddhist teacher but Trungpa Rinpoche has stressed distinguishing a healthy practice of compassion from a less salutary practice. We often think of doing something good for others, of being a good neighbor, and so forth, as a paradigmatic way to love our fellow beings and judge what treatment should be accorded to them. This has become the yardstick of our behavior and conduct toward others. Trungpa Rinpoche's rejection of this form of action is quite unambiguous. He says that trying to be a good neighbor or a good person is not genuine love and compassion; it actually falls far short of the really genuine and pure love and compassion that is demanded of us in the context of mahayana meditation. As he explains: "That is the basic openness of compassion: opening without demand. Simply be what you are, be the master of the situation. If you will just 'be,' then life flows around and through you. This will lead you into working and communicating with someone, which of course demands tremendous warmth and openness. If you can afford to be what you are, then you do not need the 'insurance policy' of trying to be a good person, a pious person, a compassionate person."[55]

Real love and compassion has to come from being who we are, not from trying to be who we would like to become. It is not about attempting to become someone we are not, trying to be a good, loving, compassionate person, but simply being one. A genuine ability to be compassionate, according to Trungpa, has to come from meditation experience. It will not arise only from interacting with our neighbors.

Idiot Compassion

In many of his writings, Trungpa Rinpoche makes a distinction between two types of compassion: genuine and nongenuine. Genuine compassion is an absolute form of benevolence, while nongenuine compassion he referred to as "idiot compassion." In fact, this expression has become a staple in many contemporary Buddhist books. Trungpa explains his position thus:

"There are two different types of compassion. There is actual compassion, direct compassion, absolute compassion. Then there is the other kind of compassion that Mr. Gurdjieff calls idiot compassion, which is compassion with neurosis, a slimy way of trying to fulfill your desire secretly. This is your aim, but you give the appearance of being generous and impersonal."[56]

What Trungpa Rinpoche is most concerned about in relation to a genuine practice of compassion is the fact that when we are trying to be pious, good, compassionate, and so forth, it is very easy to be drawn into a superficial form of kindness that is devoid of courage and intelligence. Our effort to practice compassion can be jeopardized by egoistic preoccupations and our tendency toward a territorial mentality, seeking credentials and falling prey to spiritual materialism, idiot compassion, and all the potential pitfalls that he has alluded to in his writings. It is worth quoting in full the following passage:

> It is perhaps most important in working with others that we do not develop *idiot compassion*, which means always trying to be kind. Since this superficial kindness lacks courage and intelligence, it does more harm than good. It is as though a doctor, out of apparent kindness, refuses to treat his patient because the treatment might be painful, or as though a mother cannot bear the discomfort of disciplining her child. Unlike idiot compassion, real compassion is not based upon a simple-minded avoidance of pain. Real compassion is uncompromising in its allegiance to basic sanity. People who distort the path—that is, people who are working against the development of basic sanity—should be cut through on the spot if need be. That is extremely important. There is no room for idiot compassion. We should try to cut through as much self-deception as possible in order to teach others as well as ourselves. So the final cop-out of a bodhisattva is when, having already achieved everything else, he is unable to go beyond idiot compassion.[57]

Emptiness

A genuine compassion that transcends idiot compassion is grounded in the realization of emptiness and twofold egolessness. Trungpa states that the appreciation of emptiness occurs automatically if we have clarity.

When we are no longer fixated on reference points or solidifying our frag-ile sense of self, we can afford to be expansive toward others. When our obsessive concern with ego's desperate need to secure its territory grows more relaxed and our basic sanity begins to prevail over ego's neurotic speed, we have reached the doorway to enlightenment. When we no longer have to struggle with ourselves and our world, we begin to find that our spiritual development has become a natural thing. The dark, narrow focus of ignorance diminishes, while the expansive vision of basic sanity heralds the dawning of the enlightened mind. Such a realization of empti-ness coupled with the development of compassion is equivalent to attain-ing basic sanity in Trungpa's thought. Genuine compassion and twofold egolessness complement each other, as Trungpa Rinpoche elucidates: "*Shunyata* literally means 'openness' or 'emptiness.' Shunyata is basically understanding nonexistence. When you begin realizing nonexistence, then you can afford to be more compassionate, more giving. . . . We have lots to gain and nothing to lose at that point. It is very basic."[58]

Conclusion

When I first read Trungpa Rinpoche in the late 1970s and early '80s, there were two main qualities about his work that had a great impact on me per-sonally. The first was his style of teaching. He had a rare gift for making the dharma come alive with his choice of English words and idioms. Although he presented Buddhism in a very simple fashion, it was clear that this veiled a deep knowledge of the Buddhist philosophical traditions and a profound personal understanding. He conveyed the power and importance of the buddhadharma through the English language and presented it in its most genuine form—as something that should be understood experien-tially. His choice of words and phrases was unparalleled, even in English, and far superior to anything other people were writing about Buddhism at the time. Rather than be content with just a working knowledge of the English language, I was inspired by Trungpa Rinpoche to go further in its mastery in order to present the teachings more comprehensively. The other quality that impressed me was Trungpa Rinpoche's total acceptance of his Western students. He really believed that his Western students were just as good as their Eastern counterparts, and he gave himself to them thoroughly and openly, without any hesitations or reservations.

To summarize Trungpa Rinpoche's presentation, we attain basic sanity by acknowledging our innate intelligence and learning and combining that with our soft spot. These two basically correspond to the development of prajna (transcendental knowledge) and karuna (compassion) in mahayana Buddhism. For Trungpa, prajna has to arise from our basic intelligence. That intelligence, along with our capacity for compassion, are innate qualities and do not need to be fabricated. It is a natural unfolding that is facilitated by and dependent upon the practice of shamatha and vipashyana meditation.

Trungpa Rinpoche clearly illuminates the innate quality of our warmth and compassion when he discusses the notion of our soft spot. He says that even in our most hateful states, our anger and aggression arise as a response to feelings of hurt and pain within ourselves; therefore the initial impulse of our aggression is sensitivity toward ourselves. It is this sense of tenderness and vulnerability that represents the potential for compassion. As such, Trungpa Rinpoche's instructions in Buddhist practice are designed to help us realize the reality of our innate capacity for awakening or sanity, without succumbing to any illusions, unrealizable expectations, or bogus spiritual promises. By simply allowing ourselves to feel our pain and continue to work with our discomfort, embarrassment, resentment, emotional conflicts, fear of existence, and so forth, we will assuredly transform ourselves over time. That seems to be Trungpa Rinpoche's fundamental message of basic sanity.

Trungpa called this approach "buddhadharma without credentials" because it enables us to be genuinely ourselves, without needing to fear our own pain or to hope for salvation from outside ourselves. We no longer require patches to conceal our insufficiencies or avoid challenging situations. If we acknowledge everything in our world as it is, without labeling something as good or bad, we can work with our immediate experiences simply and directly. We will have no need to aggrandize ourselves with credentials or bolster our failing spirits with unrealistic expectations. Thus everything goes toward enlightenment, according to Trungpa Rinpoche; nothing can obstruct it. Even our own neuroses hasten the dawning of basic sanity if we know how to regard all psychological and emotional states as workable. It is for this reason that the fearlessness of the lion's roar can be proclaimed.

NOTES

1. *Transcending Madness*, pp. 17–18.

2. *Cutting Through Spiritual Materialism*, pp. 67–68.

3. *Crazy Wisdom*, p. 15.

4. *The Lion's Roar*, p. 5.

5. *Cutting Through Spiritual Materialism*, p. 15.

6. *Illusion's Game*, pp. 61–62.

7. *Dharma Art*, pp. 46–47.

8. *Crazy Wisdom*, p. 15.

9. *The Lion's Roar*, p. 22.

10. *The Tibetan Book of the Dead*, p. 2.

11. *The Lion's Roar*, pp. 23–24.

12. Ibid., pp. 28–29.

13. *Meditation in Action*, p. 26.

14. *The Lion's Roar*, p. 23.

15. *The Myth of Freedom*, p. 45.

16. *Journey without Goal*, pp. 1–2.

17. *Illusion's Game*, p. 60.

18. *The Lion's Roar*, pp. 9–10.

19. Ibid., p. 18.

20. *Cutting Through Spiritual Materialism*, p. 153.

21. *The Myth of Freedom*, p. 13.

22. *The Heart of the Buddha*, p. 64.

23. *Orderly Chaos*, p. 22.

24. *The Heart of the Buddha*, p. 87.

25. *Cutting Through Spiritual Materialism*, pp. 24–25.

26. *The Myth of Freedom*, p. 5.

27. *Dharma Art*, p. 20.

28. *The Lion's Roar*, p. 92.

29. Ibid., p. 93.

30. *Cutting Through Spiritual Materialism*, p. 224.

31. *The Lion's Roar*, pp. 91–92.

32. *The Heart of the Buddha*, pp. 30–31.

33. *The Myth of Freedom*, pp. 56–57.

34. Ibid., p. 53.

35. Ibid., pp. 51–52.

36. Ibid., p. 19.

37. *Training the Mind and Cultivating Loving-Kindness*, p. 149.

38. *The Heart of the Buddha*, p. 134.

39. *The Lion's Roar*, p. 11.

40. *Cutting Through Spiritual Materialism*, p. 168.

41. *The Heart of the Buddha*, p. 16.

42. *The Dawn of Tantra*, p. 82.

43. *Illusion's Game*, p. 64.

44. *Journey without Goal*, p. 22.

45. *The Myth of Freedom*, p. 104.

46. *The Lion's Roar*, pp. 62–63.

47. *Training the Mind and Cultivating Loving-Kindness*, pp. 149–150.

48. *The Lion's Roar*, p. 101.

49. *The Heart of the Buddha*, p. 109.

50. *Illusion's Game*, p. 84.

51. *Training the Mind and Cultivating Loving-Kindness*, pp. 14–15.

52. *Cutting Through Spiritual Materialism*, pp. 98–99.

53. *Meditation in Action*, p. 24.

54. *Orderly Chaos*, p. 89.

55. *Cutting Through Spiritual Materialism*, pp. 213–214.

56. *Illusion's Game*, p. 29.

57. *The Heart of the Buddha*, p. 126.

58. *Training the Mind and Cultivating Loving-Kindness*, pp. 13–14.

At the Kalapa Court, Boulder, early 1980. Photograph by Liza Matthews.
Used with permission.

Chögyam Trungpa
as a Siddha

REGINALD A. RAY

H ow MAY ONE best understand the Buddhist teacher that Chögyam
Trungpa was? In the popular press and even in scholarly studies, one
finds a variety of answers. Most share a certain perplexity in the face of
two seemingly contradictory features: his profundity, creativity, and prolific accomplishments on the one hand and, on the other, actions that reveal unconventional, "controversial," incomprehensible, and even
apparently "immoral" aspects. Most authors tend to side with one or the
other of these two views, in which case he is seen either as one of the
greatest and most influential modern exponents of Buddhism or as an example of a wrong turn taken in the transplantation of Buddhism to Western culture. In this article, I want to suggest that there exists a very simple
and traditional alternative to these two views of Chögyam Trungpa, one
that resolves and transcends the apparent contradiction between them:
namely, that he is best understood as a modern exemplar of the ancient Indian ideal of the siddha, a fully enlightened tantric practitioner who
teaches primarily through "crazy wisdom," awakened wisdom in its purest
and most powerful form.

The Indian Ideal of the Siddha

Shakyamuni Buddha grew up in a social and religious world that was, in many ways, very traditional and conservative. People followed the well-trodden ways of the status quo, including the caste system with its inflexible brahmanical hierarchies, rigid and external ideas of purity and impurity, and reliance on rituals. According to the early Buddhist texts, people engaged in religious activities because they were told to, believed in things they could not see, and performed rituals with a mindless faith in their efficacy. The Buddha's message was that such conventional, conservative beliefs and practices were ineffective because they did not address the immediate human dilemma: all-pervasive suffering born of ignorance and wishful thinking.

The Buddha taught that complete liberation from the torment of samsara is not only possible but readily available here and now, through the path of meditation. He taught his disciples to accept nothing but to question and examine everything in order to ascertain for themselves its true value. The path to realization, he said, was through a complete separation of oneself from ordinary life and through intensive meditation practice in the wilds. His disciples loved him greatly and regarded him not only as a mentor but as their dearest and truest friend. Yet the Buddha was clearly a masterful and uncompromising guide, and he pushed his students hard. The early texts reveal that he was an unconventional, sometimes outrageous voice in his day and that there were many powerful people, both lay and religious, who regarded him as a disrespectful and dangerous troublemaker; such people sought to undermine and even harm him and his disciples. For all these reasons the Buddha might justifiably be considered the first crazy wisdom guru.

With an irony noted by Max Weber, Joachim Wach, and many other religious historians, Buddhism itself eventually became an established, institutionalized religion, rivaling brahmanism in its traditionalism and conservatism. The great monasteries of northern India became centers not only of learning and the arts, but also of great wealth, with vast lands, attached serfs, and their own hierarchies. Monasteries achieved long-term stability and success by maintaining a network of close relations with the wealthy and politically powerful families of their area. The princes and kings of the local region were typically given much say in choosing monastic officials and in monastic governance. Thus Buddhist monastic establishments often became not only centers and determiners of Indian culture, but representatives and protectors of the status quo. Textual preservation, study and debate, and the behavioral purity of the monks became the hallmarks of monastic life, while the actual practice of meditation receded into the background. Institutional Buddhism provided a focus for lay devotion and donations. While performing an important stabilizing function within Buddhism, the monasteries often became reflections of conventional social and religious values, with the attainment of enlightenment only a remote ideal. Where was the radical spirituality of the Buddha? Where the critique of conventional values, the emphasis on rigorous meditation practice in the wilds, the ardent pursuit of enlightenment in this life?

In fact, throughout the history of Buddhism and in all its major schools, there was another, much smaller contingent of the sangha that kept alive the uncompromising spirituality of the Buddha and his earliest disciples. These were the so-called forest renunciants (*aranyaka*), individuals who renounced the world but, rather than entering the relatively comfortable life of the monastery, repaired to the forests and jungles, the lonely deserts and mountaintops, in order to practice meditation and attain in their lifetime the complete freedom of enlightenment. Among these practitioners were the forest yogins of the various Theravadan traditions, the mahayana meditators of the Dhyana school (later to become Ch'an, Son, and Zen), and, most important in the present context, the early siddhas of the vajrayana. And it is the siddhas of the vajrayana who give us the best chance to understand the essence of who Trungpa Rinpoche was.

During the first centuries of Indian Buddhism, three classical lifeways emerged for practicing Buddhists. Individuals could follow the way of the Buddha as laypeople, monastics, or forest renunciants/yogins. The siddhas, as forest renunciants, spent much time in retreat in the wilds, but they also maintained a spiritual and practical connection with lay life. Among the siddhas, who appear in our evidence at least by the sixth or seventh century, we thus find a fourth lifeway emerging, namely that of the householder yogin or lay practitioner. The siddhas were like forest renunciants in that they were single-mindedly devoted to the goal of attaining complete realization in this life; but they did so, in many cases, by spending at least part of their time living in the world, raising families, and pursuing some line of work that was usually in keeping with their inherited social caste.

What kind of Buddhist ideal do the siddhas represent? Trungpa Rinpoche gave several early seminars on Indian siddhas—including Padmasambhava, Tilopa, and Naropa—in which we find an intriguing portrait of these tantric masters. Siddhas included both men and women. from all socioeconomic levels and all walks of life. Among them one finds not only brahman scholars and priests, and kshatriya kings, queens, and princes, but also people from the lowest castes and even outcastes including herdsmen, weavers, cobblers, street sweepers, fishers, butchers, hunters, and thieves. It is quite interesting that, among the realized siddhas, the lower castes are rather more represented than the upper, reflecting the nonscholastic, non-hierarchical nature of the early Indian vajrayana.

Like other Buddhist yogins before them, the siddhas typically came to the spiritual life because of some kind of crisis—the death of a loved one; intense physical or psychological suffering; social, political, or economic disaster. Such experiences provoked in them an awareness of the fragility and brevity of human life and its inescapable suffering, and set them upon an intense spiritual search. In the midst of such crises, they typically met a vajrayana teacher who, having assessed their readiness for teaching and their capacity for practice, would invite them to receive initiation (*abhisheka*) and to undertake the journey to complete realization. Themselves siddhas, these teachers set their disciples upon the same course of rigorous training that they themselves had pursued to enlightenment.

In most cases, the siddha-to-be would withdraw from ordinary life and go into solitary retreat in various locations in the wilds, sometimes for a dozen or more years. For example, the siddha Shri Simha, the great Nyingma progenitor with whom the Vidyadhara, Chögyam Trungpa Rinpoche, would later be identified, spent decades meditating in out-of-the-way places like forests, caves, and charnel grounds. In this way, the siddhas fulfilled the "forest" ideal of the early enlightened practitioners. However, realization would typically be followed by a return to the world in which they would either appear in the bustle of towns and villages as wandering yogins or yoginis, or return to lay life as husbands or wives and members of society. Trungpa Rinpoche commented that it was in this social "ordinariness" that the power of the siddhas lay; for by making their living in worldly occupations, they maintained a direct connection with the earth. Unlike their monastic counterparts, they did not suffer the compromise or corruption more or less inevitable for those who depend for their livelihood on rich, powerful, and politically motivated patrons.

In spite of their sometimes conventional demeanor, the siddhas were at heart unconventional people. Their aims included teaching, converting non-believers, and training disciples, all the while expressing in everything they did the dangerous, boundless, outrageous energy and insight of enlightenment itself. Like the Buddha and other forest saints before them, they did not hesitate to criticize ignorant, self-serving, religious posturing wherever they found it. However, now the targets of their critique were, as often as not, the rich Buddhist patrons and the Buddhist monastic establishment itself with its scholasticism, its emphasis on external ritual purity (*vinaya*), and its involvements with competition, wealth, prestige, and power.

To get the highest training in conventional Buddhism, aspirants usually had to go through a long monastic education. Since this was made easier by prior education and by financial support, higher-caste individuals—and men—were privileged in this process. The siddhas, however, taught men and women based on the disciples' spiritual readiness and openness, not their caste, gender, credentials, or religious position. Beggars, outcastes, prostitutes, and criminals were as likely—or more likely—to receive tantric initiation as the high and mighty. As the biographies of the Indian siddhas make clear, this kind of openhandedness often outraged the custodians of conventional Buddhism and their rich and powerful patrons.

The siddhas' unconventionality often brought social criticism, attack, and ostracism. For example, the king Dombi-heruka—one of the eighty-four siddhas of whom the Vidyadhara was later understood to be an emanation—took a low-caste girl, against all convention, as his spiritual consort and tantric wife. Although his motivations were the fulfillment of his own and his wife's spiritual practice and, beyond that, the benefit of others when he was found out, the kingdom was thrown into an uproar. Demanding a "dharma king" who played by the rules, the subjects drove Dombi-heruka and his consort into exile in the wilderness. Only much later, after a series of misfortunes befell the kingdom, was the spiritual attainment of the king and queen finally recognized. However, by this time, it was too late, and the enlightened couple never returned.

The unconventionality of the siddhas and its implicit or explicit protest against the shallowness of conventional values was an important teaching device not only for ordinary laypeople, but even more strongly for the siddhas' own students; or it is in the training of their own students that the eccentric creativity of the siddhas most strongly reveals itself. As Rinpoche explained it, disciples—and especially the high-born ones such as Naropa—often found themselves placed in situations of extreme social degradation and humiliation: brahmans were told to eat meat, drink alcohol, and live in charnel grounds, all thoroughly degrading for their caste; effete scholars were set to impossible manual labor or told to consume ordure; kings and government officials were sold into situations of servitude for years to low-caste individuals; fastidious religious types were catapulted into the most horrifying and polluting of life circumstances.

It is important to understand this kind of tutelage properly. The siddhas' aggressive antagonism toward order and conventionality was not manifested simply for its own sake. Rather, it was aimed at disrupting the creation of karma and perpetuation of samsara that result when people seek refuge in the limiting self-concepts and conditioning of their personal and social contexts. The gurus in these examples understood that only when their disciples were able to abandon their superficial ego-identifications, would they find their way to the utter freedom of the awakened state within. For this reason, they placed their trainees in situations where their former, conventional identities were utterly and irrevocably dissolved. Along with such flagrantly dislocating experiences, the disciples were told to carry out their vajrayana practice, which in a more structured way brought about the very same end.

All of this is in line with the basic tantric insight that—as Rinpoche taught over and over—only when the conventional identity loses its foothold can the inner fire of enlightenment reveal itself. For the vajrayana, liberation involves realization of our own unborn awareness, a state of mind that is unconditioned, free, and unreservedly compassionate to suffering beings. In such a realization, there is no room for attachment to conditioned identities or loyalty to conditioned and limited values, even—and especially—if they are respected Buddhist ones. The siddhas reflected the qualities of the awakened state in the way they expressed their realization. They maintained utter integrity, even amid threats of injury or death; they spoke the truth, even when lies were more convenient; they did not hesitate to lay bare corruption when they saw it, even among the most powerful rulers. They taught their disciples by unconventional methods, —using alcohol as a means to evoke the enlightened state, having intimate relationships with their disciples, and criticizing or flouting local customs that they deemed hypocritical or inimical to the path of awakening.

The conventional Buddhist world typically viewed siddhas as dangerous, unpredictable, and undesirable individuals. In the earlier biographies, one does not find any siddhas living within monastic confines, at least not for very long. When the great siddha Virupa attains realization through his vajrayana practice, he begins to perform actions that are inconsistent with monastic values; soon thereafter he is expelled from the order. The siddhas Nagarjuna and Shantideva leave the monastery voluntarily after attaining enlightenment; its values and way of life are clearly too limiting for the enlightened activity they must now perform. Other siddhas are similarly expelled from the monastery or leave it by choice, unable to remain within its prestigious but suffocating confines. Thus it was that the Indian siddhas had little to do with the conventional monastic establishment. In fact, it was only toward the end of institutionalized Buddhism in India—usually dated to the Muslim invasions of east India in 1192—that the vajrayana was studied and practiced within monasteries at all.

The Indian siddhas were particularly renowned for their "crazy wisdom"—dharmic teaching that passed beyond the bounds of the norms of conventional sanity. This "insanity" (*smyon-pa*) expressed itself at all levels of the path. At the beginning, especially for women, "madness" became a mode of egress from the virtual imprisonment of caste, family, and marriage. Many students on the path, including Tilopa and Naropa, were instructed to behave as if they were insane; the harsh criticism and ostracism they experienced as a consequence helped to purify any attachment they had to social approval, personal identity, or caste pride. And, upon attaining realization, siddhas expressed their realization in actions that, while "crazy" from a normal societal standpoint, showed the uncompromising wisdom and compassion of the egoless state of enlightenment.

Trungpa Rinpoche spoke often about crazy wisdom, especially in the early 1970s. In his two early seminars on Padmasambhava, the preeminent Indian siddha, Rinpoche taught at length on the crazy wisdom lineage of the siddhas, which he himself had received from his teachers.[1] Crazy wisdom, he said, is "the action of truth." "It cuts everything down" and "it is ruthless" in that it destroys any attempt to make an ego version of whatever arises.[2] The ruthless action of crazy wisdom is not intentional, deliberate, or contrived in any way. The self-serving, deceptive energy of ego itself provides the force of crazy wisdom, which is just the natural response of the awakened state itself; "it is ego's intensity" that provokes the ruthlessness of crazy wisdom. Confusion calls for, indeed demands, its own destruction.[3] The crazy wisdom person is just there, completely awake and utterly without agenda. From ego's point of view, this fact in itself represents the ultimate ruthlessness; for it does not go along with ego's agenda. Crazy wisdom is completely independent of conventional morality, ethics, philosophy, or religious motivations—it is "just being itself."[4] It is the ultimate expression of compassion and even love.[5]

Part of the crazy wisdom of the siddhas involved alcohol and unconventional sexual relationships, both anathema according to brahmanical religious values. The siddhas are often showed consuming alcohol, sometimes as part of their ritual "feasts"—performed in charnel grounds—or in their day to day lives as teachers. In a well-known story, the great siddha Virupa is depicted consuming one million cups of liquor on one occasion. The siddhas also took consorts, sometimes taught their disciples in the context of sexual relationships, and brought sexuality into the arena of yogic practice; this influence survives today within the most esoteric of Tibetan yoga traditions. Padmasambhava is said to have brought many female disciples to the path through his intimate relationships with them.

When we turn to the specific historical and cultural context of Tibet, we notice that the vast majority of Buddhists, including laypeople and most renunciants, followed the more conventional paths of the classical mahayana and monasticized versions of the vajrayana that had been brought from India to Tibet. However, the naked and outrageous spirituality of the Indian siddhas was also transmitted to Tibet, continuing its life among yogins and household practitioners—particularly those affiliated with the Nyingma and Kagyü lineages. The traditions of the Indian siddhas also survived, particularly among the Kagyüpas, in certain lines of tülkus, or "incarnate lamas," who were brought up and lived as monastics. It was through these lineages that Trungpa Rinpoche received much of his training in crazy wisdom. Although they were often criticized by the conventional Tibetan establishment for their unpredictability and un-conventionality, among these schools in every generation there were al-ways a few individuals, such as Trungpa Rinpoche and his crazy wisdom teachers, who followed the path to its fruition and were known and revered as fully realized siddhas following in the footsteps of the Indian tantric saints.

The Tibetan siddhas were every bit as accomplished, outrageous, and inscrutable as their Indian counterparts. A vivid and not at all unusual ex-ample is provided by Namkhai Norbu Rinpoche's account of a certain Sakyapa monk who was expelled from his monastery after breaking the vow of celibacy. He then went into retreat for some years. When he reap-peared, he seemed to go insane, throwing his books out of the window, burning them, smashing statues, even partly demolishing his retreat hut. At that point, people began to regard him as crazy. After this he disap-peared. Three years later, someone came across him living in solitude at the top of a remote mountain. They wondered how he could possibly sur-vive there, in a place that no one ever visited and no food could grow. Al-though he refused to talk, people sensed in him extraordinary realization and wanted to be near him. In spite of his remote and inhospitable loca-tion, they increasingly began to visit him and came to regard him as a re-alized siddha. He subsequently demonstrated miraculous powers that confirmed this view.[6]

Chögyam Trungpa's Path to Becoming a Siddha

THE CLASSICAL TRAINING OF A TÜLKU

Chögyam Trungpa's connection with the Indian siddha tradition was ex-plicit; even before he fled Tibet for India in 1959, he had been identified with siddhas such as Shri Simha and Dombi-heruka. During a 1972 visit to Sikkim, I encountered a Tibetan who had known Rinpoche prior to his escape from Tibet; he said that even when Rinpoche was a young tülku, there was something unpredictable, uncanny, and somewhat frightening about him.

As a Kagyü tülku, Chögyam Trungpa entered into monastic life at a young age and was given the classical training accorded to incarnations. His training was traditional, conservative, and conventional; later in life, he observed that the main concern of his tutors seemed to be that he behave himself, act like the high tülku he was supposed to be, and not offend lay patrons and donors.

Although Rinpoche learned and benefited from his training, somehow—as in the case of many siddhas before him—the conventional religious world and values did not completely "take." Rinpoche later commented that, decked out in his tülku robes, surrounded by attendants, and prostrated to by the laity, he felt like a "fraud." This realization precipitated a profound inner crisis. Where was the true spirituality that Buddhism was supposed to be about? Where was the allegiance to the awakened state?

A turning point came in Rinpoche's life when he met and began to study under three lamas, all of whom were tülkus who were themselves considered highly realized siddhas. The first of these was Jamgön Kongtrül of Shechen, a monk of great realization and a renowned crazy wisdom teacher. Rinpoche remarked that "he possessed all of the qualities of Padmasambhava."[7] Shechen Kongtrül took on the Vidyadhara as a "heart son" and, over the many years of their relationship, trained him—sometimes sweetly, sometimes wrathfully—with rigor, precision, and thoroughness. Rinpoche came to love Shechen Kongtrül greatly, observing that "to be near him was to experience unbelievable peace and joyousness."[8]

The second of these teachers was Khenpo Gangshar Rinpoche, who was first a monk and later a lay yogin. One of Shechen Kongtrül's principal disciples, he was an extraordinarily powerful crazy wisdom master. Dilgo Khyentse Rinpoche, the third of Rinpoche's great siddha teachers, was a lay yogin who had spent much of his life up to that point in retreat and who embodied the vajrayana dharma in an especially pure and profound way.

These three lamas had little use for the conventional Buddhist forms in and of themselves. Each manifested a spontaneous, earthy spirituality that sprang directly from the heart. They engaged others directly and without pretense, cutting through their defense mechanisms and connecting immediately with their inspiration and devotion. Rinpoche saw that these siddhas embodied the teachings rather than simply imitating them. Like siddhas-in-training of old, Rinpoche accomplished many retreats under these masters. One of these was the famed and feared bardo retreat, involving seven weeks in complete darkness during which one passes through the experiences of death—while still alive—with its process of dissolution of the personality. Studying under these three great lamas, Rinpoche was first in awe and then the dutiful and devoted student. Finally, after much study and practice and rigorous tutelage, he began to realize in himself the same boundless state that he encountered in his mentors.

In Tibet, the siddha tradition was more integrated with the monastic way than it had been in India. Reflective of this, Rinpoche's education continued in the more traditional aspects of Buddhism that tülkus were expected to master, including classical topics such as philosophy, logic and debate, ritual, calligraphy, painting, monastic administration, and service to the laity. Thus it was that Rinpoche was trained simultaneously in the uncompromising, inner spirituality of realization of the siddhas and the outer, more conventional methods and forms of his Tibetan context.

Among Rinpoche's three principal gurus, especially interesting and indicative was Khenpo Gangshar. Raised by Shechen Kongtrül, Gangshar was renowned as a young monk for his faultless observance of the vinaya and his deep scholarly training. At one point, however, he became extremely sick while at Surmang monastery, the principal seat of the Trungpa line of tülkus. Gangshar was given up for dead, and seemed to pass away. In a small storage area separated from a larger room by a curtain, his body was laid out and left for several days to facilitate the postmortem samadhi (meditative equipoise) traditional for accomplished people. At a certain point, the Vidyadhara moved the curtain to see whether Gangshar was still in samadhi. Something seems to have accidentally brushed against Gangshar's face, and he abruptly opened his eyes.

From this moment onward, Gangshar's personality completely changed, and he became wild and wrathful. He renounced his monastic vows, took a female consort, and began to behave in a bizarre manner. He was said to be able to tell what people were thinking instantly just by looking at them; and he had no hesitation in exposing the posturing and pretensions of those he encountered, however well born, powerful, or wealthy they might be, including important patrons of the monastery. The power and truthfulness of his words were incandescent and seemed to flow effortlessly from a completely awakened mind. In a poem to Gangshar, Trungpa Rinpoche wrote, "his deeds are legendary; his skill and determination to present the utmost profundity of complete realization were unrivalled."[9]

Many who met him found his attainment self-evident and became disciples and devotees. Others, however, were troubled and embarrassed by his strange behavior, felt uncomfortable in his presence, and avoided him altogether.[10] Gangshar was a true siddha in the full sense of the word.

When Trungpa Rinpoche was about seventeen, Jamgön Kongtrül sent him to study with Khenpo Gangshar, and the lessons he received were profound and life-transforming. In the poem just mentioned, Rinpoche tells us of his training under Gangshar, saying that "Tirelessly—day and night for a year and five months— / Lord Gangshar taught only the ultimate instructions. He recognized the demons of my untrained being churning within me. / He dispelled the corruption of the teachings."[11] In the same poem, he expresses great love and devotion for this teacher and the direct, uncompromising, often wrathful training that he received at his hands during this period.

Crisis, Conflict, and Realization

It is interesting how much Rinpoche's life paralleled that of the Indian siddhas who began their careers as monastics. Like so many other lamas of his generation, Rinpoche was violently dislodged from his Tibetan world by the Chinese depredations of the late 1950s. For him as for others, this precipitated a most profound crisis. His family was lost; his teachers imprisoned, tortured and killed; his culture and his Buddhist heritage abruptly torn from him and largely destroyed.

In India, Rinpoche worked with the refugee community and maintained his monastic identity, but things were changing. In 1961, he entered into a relationship with a young nun, a liaison that had tremendous power for both of them. From this union came the birth of the Sakyong Mipham Rinpoche, Rinpoche's first child and the current lineage holder of the Shambhala community. Rinpoche soon went to England on a Spalding scholarship and began to study at Oxford University.

During this time, Rinpoche and his close childhood friend Akong Tulku founded a meditation center in Scotland known as Samye Ling. During this time, a playful, unconventional, and sometimes outrageous side of Rinpoche began to emerge. The woman who later became his wife, Diana Pybus, recalls that, during meditation with his students, Rinpoche would often fall asleep, and people would honk car horns out front to wake him up, amid much laughter and gaiety. His budding outrageousness is reflected in his meeting at this time with the English nun Tsültrim Palmo, who reports that during the entire interview, Rinpoche kept reaching playfully under her skirts, in spite of her continually refusing his advances.

From an external viewpoint, things seemed to be going well; but Rinpoche felt discouraged, both about the English people he was trying to teach and the Tibetans he was working with. On one side, he saw that many of his English students were overly fascinated with his colorful robes, his exotic Tibetan identity, and the esoteric tradition he represented; he missed in them a thirst for the genuine spirituality that he felt was the only real gift he had to offer. On the other side, some of his Tibetan confreres were becoming increasingly uncomfortable with Rinpoche's openhanded attitude toward his students, his friendships with them, and his willingness to meet them more than halfway. They felt that the primary task of the center was to preserve Tibetan culture and traditional Tibetan ways intact, keeping the Western students at arm's length. Rinpoche felt the frustration of his situation intensely and, in 1967, journeyed to Bhutan to enter into a solitary retreat in Tagtsang, Padmasambhava's famed mountain retreat cave, in search of direction and inspiration. Like siddhas before him, when he could no longer see the way ahead, he withdrew to "the forest."

One of the marks of Indian and Tibetan siddhas is the direct visionary reception of revealed religious texts, or terma ("spiritual treasures") rather than exclusive reliance on past tradition. In the cave, in a dramatic and climactic experience, Rinpoche received a terma known as *The Embodiment of All the Siddhas*. This revealed treasure, which encapsulated the instruction he would give over the next two decades, directly addressed the spiritual materialism and religious territoriality he found all around him. Most important, it opened a spiritual channel to the enlightened energy of the greatest siddhas of the Nyingma and Kagyü lineages, including Padmasambhava and several of the most powerful Karmapas. Evoking the experience of all phenomena as charged with the splendor and power of the awakened state, it established Rinpoche's core teaching as the vajrayana dharma of the Indian and Tibetan siddhas. The answer that Rinpoche received in Tagtsang was that the only way to overcome the destructive materialism of the dark ages that he was meeting in the West was for him to identify himself wholly with the ideal and the teachings of the siddhas.

Rinpoche returned to the British Isles, pondering over his experience in Bhutan and trying to see how to integrate it into his work. For several months, he was torn with conflicts about what to do despite, as he says in his autobiography, repeated warnings and messages from the phenomenal world.[12] This period culminated in a serious automobile accident that left him paralyzed on his left side. Despite this trauma, he recognized with humor that his accident was a message that could not be ignored: in order to propagate the true dharma, he had to remove the final obstacle between himself and his students—namely his Tibetan monastic garb and status. He gave up wearing robes and decided to marry, meeting his students on their own level by completely adopting their lifestyle and their world.

His Tibetan partner, Akong Tulku, was outraged and is reported to have felt that Rinpoche was turning against his Tibetan heritage. Reports of Rinpoche's "apostasy" quickly traveled throughout the Tibetan world, and suspicion and criticism were directed toward him from all quarters. Many of his English students, themselves hesitant and afraid in the face of the naked dharma Rinpoche proposed to deliver, abandoned him. The seals and emblems of his Trungpa line of tülkus were taken from him. Some suggested that Rinpoche was unfit to teach and even that he might be mentally unbalanced. As a result of the opposition, Trungpa Rinpoche was, in effect, "silenced," and it became impossible for him to teach. It soon became clear that Rinpoche could no longer live at Samye Ling, and he left. His life as a tülku and a teacher had, it seemed, come to a dismal and ignominious end. Like that of so many siddhas before him, Rinpoche's uncompromising commitment to the tantric dharma of realization resulted in his being banished from the conventional Buddhist world he had grown up in and identified with. Rinpoche's reaction perhaps provide a glimpse of what it was like for his Indian and Tibetan siddha predecessors who went through similar experiences. He became filled with hopelessness and despair. He lived only to teach the immaculate dharma; if he was prevented from doing so, why live at all? His wife, Diana Mukpo, reports that he seriously contemplated suicide at this time and, one night, came right to the brink. Perhaps surprisingly, this is again traditional for siddhas: figures such as Naropa and Milarepa, when seemingly blocked from their dharmic paths, also brought themselves to the very verge of self-destruction.

In the midst of this ultimate crisis, as with the siddhas before him, Rinpoche attained a new level of understanding and realization. The experience of hopelessness, he has written, "is the preparation for crazy wisdom, which does not know any kind of truth other than itself. . . . It doesn't put you anywhere. You have no ground to stand on, absolutely none. You are completely desolate. And even desolation is not regarded as home, because you are so desolately, absolutely hopeless that even loneliness is not refuge any more. Everything is completely hopeless. . . . Any kind of energy that's happening in order to preserve itself is also hopeless."[13]

Such a moment of total crisis is repeatedly exemplified in the siddhas' lives: "Naropa's state of hopelessness . . . was absolute. . . . Understanding Padmasambhava's life without a sense of hopelessness would be completely impossible."[14] This moment of utter despair is a crisis in the fullest sense of the word: as Rinpoche said later—in what appears to be an autobiographical statement—there comes a moment on the path when one faces two, and only two, stark alternatives: insanity or enlightenment.

EMERGENCE AS A REALIZED SIDDHA

By coincidence, at this time, Rinpoche received an invitation to come to the United States. He and his new wife left the bankrupt English situation behind, buying one-way tickets to the United States and into the unknown. Here Rinpoche quickly found an ever-widening circle of inspired and dedicated dharma students. The horrors of his experiences in England somehow allowed him to jettison the last remaining baggage of his traditional past. Suspicions, doubts, and criticisms from the conventional Tibetan world continued unabated; but now, with nothing left to lose, Rinpoche began to teach the dharma in an extraordinarily naked, open, and direct way.

Diana Mukpo remarks that, in England, Rinpoche had a light, uplifted demeanor prior to his accident; he was beneficent and gentle. But after the accident and as things became increasingly unworkable, he began to emerge an extraordinarily uncompromising and wrathful teacher. This transformation continued when he arrived in the United States and, at Tail of the Tiger meditation center in 1970 and the following years, he could be terrifying indeed. He spent a lot of time in the common living spaces, and students could always "hang out" in his room after dinner. But to be around him was to take your life into your hands. He was always so extraordinarily present, direct, and intense. His gaze was like a laser beam that tore through any pretense or posturing and made one feel stripped naked and completely exposed. This is what you wanted most in the world and why you found Rinpoche so compelling; but it was also what you most feared. You couldn't be satisfied with just running away—though many of us often did—for you felt the tremendous compassion in his actions. It was clear that here was a bodhisattva who had no thought whatever for himself and lived only to benefit others.

However, Rinpoche certainly did operate outside the realm of conventional expectations. I first met him in 1970 shortly after he arrived in the United States. Among other things, I told him I was in a Ph.D. program working on my dissertation, and I said I wanted to be his student. Later that day, a few of us were hanging out in his bedroom talking; sitting on his bed on the floor, he happened to remark that he knew of a certain person who was working on his doctoral dissertation and that in order to enter the teachings this person would have to give his dissertation to his teacher and forget his academic career. Rightly or wrongly, I took him to be talking about me. After agonizing for a couple of days, I finally came to him and said, "Okay, I give you my dissertation; I give it all up. I want to be your student." He looked at me for a moment and then just laughed it off. After thinking this over for a few more days, I began to see dropping out of graduate school—which I had never given a thought to before—as an increasingly attractive option. I went to Rinpoche and announced that I wanted to abandon this path and move to Tail of the Tiger to be with him. Again he looked at me intently and then replied that, no, I had better stay in graduate school and finish my studies since one day my degree might prove useful. After a period of adjustment to this most dismal of all prospects—dismal because I had finally found the teacher for whom I had been looking my whole life, I gradually began to find some consolation in my projected life of scholarship and the learning I was acquiring in school. Just then, however Rinpoche began talking about "petty and tiny scholars" who think they know something but are in fact terrified of the teachings and are hiding behind their scholarship. Suddenly, I found myself utterly exposed. And so it went on and on. It was always like that with Rinpoche—whatever you thought, whatever you wanted, he somehow always managed to come in from a different angle and open your mind and your life in a completely unexpected way.

Like the siddhas before him, Rinpoche entered fully into the worlds of those he was teaching. He had married, and he and Diana had children.

No one supported him financially; he made his own living through his teaching. Rinpoche smoked cigarettes with his students, visited bars with them, and went to the movies that they were seeing. He also drank alcohol and tried the drugs of choice of his students, notably LSD. Of the latter, he reported that it intensified the samsaric state to such an extent that it could deceive one into thinking it was some kind of genuine real-ization. Of alcohol, following in the siddhas' footsteps, he described its grounding, earthy quality, which, while poison in the hands of one seek-ing neurotic gratification, could be opening, uplifting, and freeing for the trained meditator.

And like Padmasambhava and other siddhas before him, Rinpoche also had intimate relationships with many of his woman disciples, some-thing that provoked suspicion and even alarm not only among those who did not know Rinpoche personally, but also among some of his own stu-dents. Even today, the search goes on for some kind of reasonable explana-tion for this aspect of Rinpoche's behavior. The fact that many of the women involved treasured the intimate time they spent with their teacher and found in these experiences such depth of humanity and such true and affecting friendship, does not seem to be of much help. People seem to want some kind of logical account, some kind of reference to general prin-ciples. Tradition points out that the actions of a crazy wisdom teacher are, by definition, "incomprehensible"—at least when viewed from the out-side—meaning that they fall outside the arena of conventional judgments and expectations. However, when viewed from the inside of the experi-encer him- or herself, the compassion and transformative impact are com-pletely unavoidable. The power of crazy wisdom is that it is absolutely unique and individual to the situation at hand; it cuts through deception and hesitation and lays bare the truth. In the hands of an unrealized per-son, "crazy wisdom" could clearly become an excuse for immoral and un-scrupulous behavior. Such has happened all too often in the recent history of non-Western religious movements in the West. But, by the same token, authentic crazy wisdom is also the most powerful method of communica-tion for a realized siddha and the most direct expression of compassion.

It seems clear to me that, embodying the approach of earlier siddhas in working with his students, Rinpoche was guided not by the external rules and regulations of conventional Tibetan tradition, but rather by the openness and needs of those who came to him; he did not hesitate to bring his students as far as they could go and then a little or a lot further. Unwilling to be limited by convention, Rinpoche did not hold back in any way from communicating fully with those who surrounded him. As a typical example, I might mention a twenty-four hour visit Rinpoche paid to me in 1973 at Indiana University, where I had a tenure-track appointment in the religious studies department. Rinpoche, who had come to talk to me about the inception of Naropa Institute planned for the following summer of 1974 (in which I very much wanted to participate) and to deliver a lecture on Tibetan Buddhism to the university community, stayed with me and my wife.

I met him at the airport about midday, and from then until the following morning when he left, I alternately felt fear and devotion, breathing in the atmosphere of danger, excitement, and inspiration that seemed to surround him wherever he went. Before the lecture, he invited me to consume a large quantity of sake. At the lecture hall, my inebriated introduction of him was incoherent, and I don't remember anything of what he said. I was too far gone even to realize how completely I was humiliating myself before my professorial colleagues and my students. After the lecture, in a question-and-answer exchange, Rinpoche had me responding to questions as if I knew a great deal about Tibetan Buddhism and meditation, which at that point I clearly did not. To make matters worse, the great Tibetologist Helmuth Hoffman, on the faculty at Indiana University at that time, was present and taking everything in.

As the truth of it all sank in, I enjoyed a long and sleepless night. But I awoke the next morning extraordinarily refreshed and feeling as if I had shed a huge burden. I said goodbye to Rinpoche—with him looking closely at me as he always did to see what was going on with me—and went off to the university for a departmental meeting and class. Never before had I felt so awake and alive; nor had my mind ever seemed so crystalline and so absent of fear. Somehow—and I still do not know in quite what way—Rinpoche had in those few hours of his visit helped me to make a very long journey indeed, which I intuitively realized at the time but came to realize much more explicitly as the years went by. Rinpoche's secretary at that time, John Baker, who had accompanied Rinpoche on the visit remarked, "You know, everywhere Rinpoche goes he seems to bring chaos into people's lives. But it always seems to be true that, as he says, 'chaos is good news.'"

As I learned later, when chaos is brought into the mechanisms of the ego—in my case, the multilayered arrogance and pride of academic credentials and career—deeper levels of awareness can begin to make themselves known. The devastation, dissolution, and rebirth that I experienced were not so rare, but were the rather typical results of the openness, generosity, and abandon with which Rinpoche engaged his students.

There is no question in my mind that the vajrayana of the siddhas was the very heart of Rinpoche's dharmic soul and of his teaching in America from the very beginning. Even before he had given his first refuge ceremony, his instruction was imbued with the tantric teachings. He spoke often of the "awakened state" and in his teaching instructed students to pay attention to the "gap" in their thought process where the enlightened mind was shining through. In working with frightening emotions, he taught us to experience them and enter into them fully and directly, without hesitation or judgment, seeking their inborn wisdom. Reminiscent of dzogchen, his meditation instruction involved directing us to the space of mahavipashyana, the groundlessness of shunyata, and the brilliance of the mind itself.

In his early seminars on Padmasambhava, Rinpoche described the three major facets of crazy wisdom and, in so doing, provided a fitting summary of his own actions as a crazy wisdom master. First is the dharmakaya aspect—"basic being," the open and limitless dimension of awareness. "It is a totality in which confusion and ignorance have never existed; *it is total existence that never needs any reference point.*"[15] In Rinpoche, one felt this dimension of crazy wisdom moment by moment as an utterly open awareness in which anything and everything was possible without any limitation or restriction whatsoever. Abiding in his presence, one could feel peaceful, blissful, or filled with the terror of losing one's reference points.

Second is the sambhogakaya aspect of crazy wisdom, the continual flashing forth of energy—sparkling, alive, dynamic, ever unpredictable, "that which continually contains spontaneous energy, because it *never depends on any cause-and-effect kind of energy.*"[16] One felt this aspect as a kind of fearful foreboding of Rinpoche's own complete independence from anybody's expectations, his unpredictable playfulness and humor, and his constant readiness and unquenchable appetite for instant, abrupt, and unhesitating engagement with situations. Third, and finally, is the nirmanakaya aspect, where the bodhisattva activity of the siddha reaches its most concrete and practical form. In the nirmanakaya, the openness wisdom of the dharmakaya and the sparkling wisdom of the sambhogakaya are reflected in the pragmatic situations of our current life, "self-existing fulfillment in relation to which *no strategizing about how to function is necessary.*"[17] One experienced this dimension of Rinpoche's crazy wisdom in the endless procession of activity that flowed from his hand, activity that seemed infallibly powerful, creative, and exactly appropriate and which at the same time seemed to arise without forethought or agenda of any sort.

The nirmanakaya aspect of Rinpoche's manifestation in particular deserves further comment. In one of his early teachings, he talked about the nirmanakaya in detail, describing how, in order to implant the dharma into a human environment such as ours, various things are necessary. One of the most important, he said, is a clear, orderly, accessible path of training in the basic view of Buddhism as well as in the classical series of graduated meditation practices, including, in his words, "a firm footing in hinayana discipline" or "the strictness of hinayana," "the benevolence of the mahayana," and "vajrayana inspiration."[18] Further needed is the creation of environments in which this training can be carried out—institutions and organizations to house, protect, and facilitate the path. There must be a reliable teacher, one who is steady, committed, and accessible; this he offered in himself. And finally required are devoted students willing to put the teachings into practice, for which he looked to us.

It is interesting that, as Rinpoche's teaching in North America progressed, he put a great deal of time and energy into this nirmanakaya level of his crazy wisdom activity. He established the Nālandā and Mahavajravairochana translation committees to render the philosophical, hagiographic, poetic, and ritual texts of his lineage into English for his students. He worked to establish a clear, systematic, and comprehensive path of training spanning the three yanas, which is now taught worldwide. And he established many organizations and institutions where the training, in different contexts and for different kinds of people, could be pursued. Some of these include Shambhala International, a global network of major practice centers and regional meditation communities; Shambhala Training; and Naropa University.

Such apparently conventional forms might be viewed as a departure on Rinpoche's part from the essence of his activity as a siddha and his manifestation of crazy wisdom. However, such an impression would be quite incorrect. As we have just seen, one of the major and indispensable features of the crazy wisdom of the siddhas is just this compassionate willingness to create whatever needs to be created so that the dharma can survive within samsara. In my view, Rinpoche's tremendously prolific creativity can be explained in no other way than as a concrete, practical embodiment of crazy wisdom in our world. What makes the forms he developed different—and often markedly so—from those of more conservative and conventional approaches is that they were evolved or adopted not out of any blind acceptance of the past, but rather because they were precisely what was needed and called for by the situation immediately at hand. In this way, Rinpoche's nirmanakaya activity continued throughout as a living and evolving situation, inspired by the continual arising of the sambhogakaya compassion and responsiveness out of the naked, unbounded awareness of his dharmakaya mind.

Conclusion

During the latter years of Trungpa Rinpoche's life and in the years since his death in 1987, the wild, open style of his crazy wisdom teaching of the 1970s evolved into a dharma that gives the appearance of being far more regularized and conventional. His vast body of instruction is now loosely systematized into a formal curriculum; the training students receive is organized in a complex ladder of steps and stages; and the organization he founded has developed into a classical bureaucracy. His eldest son, the Sakyong Mipham Rinpoche, tends to emphasize more traditional Tibetan mahayana themes, as he seeks to spread the lineage of his father and look after its successful propagation in the world. Has this lineage become overly conventionalized to the exclusion of its original crazy wisdom energy? This is an interesting and important question.

In any case, one must ask whether any of us students of Trungpa Rinpoche have been able to fully appreciate the depth, integrity, and compassion of his more outrageous manifestations. I sense that for many of us, there is some relief at the increasing conventionality of the institution he left. Is it possible that at least part of this relief may be in reaction to the fear we felt for so many years in the face of Rinpoche's wild siddha heart? To illustrate, I report a most painful yet illuminating moment that occurred a few years after Rinpoche's death, when another Tibetan teacher, a respected lama who had not been close to the Vidyadhara, gave teachings in Boulder, Colorado. During the question-and-answer period, an individual who had studied under the Vidyadhara stood up and asked the lama why Trungpa Rinpoche had been an alcoholic. After a long silence, the lama responded in a low voice but one that sounded, at least to me, like the rumbling thunder of an approaching storm: "What is wrong with you? Don't you realize that Trungpa Rinpoche sacrificed his health and his reputation in order to try to help you? Don't you see that he came and met you on your own ground because that was the only way you would ever have any chance of hearing the authentic dharma?"

Trungpa Rinpoche was and remained a siddha whose crazy wisdom was unrelenting—assuming now one, now another manifestation, depending on the needs of the situation. He was, I think, a siddha of the highest order and, as such, taught a dharma that cut through all kinds of self-serving spiritual materialism, especially that found within Buddhism itself, and even through the outrageousness expected of crazy wisdom itself. In the early days, he taught "buddhadharma without credentials," buddhadharma that was raw and naked, that was the living truth of nonself, no territory, and "politics turned inside out," as he said. He criticized those who held tightly to a more hesitant, "reasonable," and, frankly, too easily self-serving Buddhism. The many forms of teaching, training, and organization that our sangha has inherited were developed by the Vidyadhara himself and emerged out of the fiery chaos, day in and day out, of his crazy wisdom. But it is clearly important that, in order to retain their integrity, they remain grounded in that very crazy wisdom. Their proper and intended role, not only in his day but now and into the future, must be to shield, protect, and hold that crazy wisdom within, as its living essence, sometimes hiding it, sometimes expressing it openly, as the situation may permit.

NOTES

1. *Crazy Wisdom*, p. 58.
2. Ibid., p. 12.
3. Ibid., p. 24.
4. Ibid., p. 59.

5. Ibid., p. 58.

6. Geoffrey Samuel, *Civilized Shamans: Buddhism in Tibetan Societies* (Washington, D.C.: Smithsonian Institution Press, 1993), pp. 304–305.

7. *Crazy Wisdom*, p. 67.

8. *Born in Tibet* (2000), p. 97.

9. Chögyam Trungpa Rinpoche, *Light Rays of the Sun and Moon*, trans. Vajravairochana Translation Committee (Halifax: Vajravairochana Translation Committee, 2001), p. 13.

10. Samuel, *Civilized Shamans*, p. 307.

11. *Light Rays*, p. 21.

12. See "Epilogue: Planting the Dharma in the West," *Born in Tibet*, in *The Collected Works of Chögyam Trungpa*, vol. 1, p. 264.

13. *Crazy Wisdom*, pp. 90–91.

14. Ibid., p. 94.

15. Ibid., p. 20.

16. Ibid.

17. Ibid.

18. Chögyam Trungpa, *Collected Vajra Assemblies*, vol. 1 (Halifax: Vajradhatu Publications, 1990).

Inaugurating the Shambhala teaching program, Boulder, Colorado.
Photograph by Robert Del Tredici. Used with permission.

The Highest
Maha Ati Teachings

Chögyam Trungpa Rinpoche in Great Britain

RIGDZIN SHIKPO

Introduction

In the early 1960s the young abbot of the Surmang group of monasteries in Tibet came to Oxford to study fine art. He was part of the diaspora of Tibetan teachers forced to flee their homeland by the invading Chinese. This young abbot's name was Chögyam Trungpa Rinpoche, and he was the first genuine teacher of Tibetan Buddhism to come to the West. He taught Buddhism at the highest level and was able to make the most profound teachings accessible to many people.

I was fortunate enough to meet him in 1965, and when visiting him in Oxford with a friend, asked him some questions concerning a particular Tibetan text. He exclaimed: "You have brought me my own text!" and apparently as a result of this he decided to introduce us to dzogchen, the great perfection, or maha ati as he termed it. He began by addressing some very simple questions, and used his answers as a basis for developing the theme of the maha ati teachings in an extremely inspiring way.

I asked Rinpoche whether life or existence had any meaning or significance and even why there was anything at all. He quoted from a text by a Kadampa master (a master of one of the oldest schools of Tibetan Buddhism), which stated that "there is no purpose." He said that to look for a purpose is always to look elsewhere, away from what he called the immediacy of Being. To him, Being was something primordial, timeless, and yet immediately present. Being was not to be found in anything other than the immediacy of experience, yet it had a dimension of vast vision not present in the momentary, passing aspect of experience.

He said that all true creativity and significance came from this immediacy and from nowhere else. There was a natural process of movement within Being, a central expression of fresh creativity that somehow presented the truth and value of Being to itself through the medium of the person. As to the question why there was anything at all, he said that if you were to try to describe the nature of reality, you could speak of it in terms of an ever-yielding space, movement within that space, and a quality of aliveness permeating both. These three qualities were really not independent of each other, only described separately for convenience. The ever-yielding space suggests an intrinsic quality of movement and a certain sensitivity to it; movement implies space in which movement takes place and an aliveness giving rise to it. To be alive always implies a sense of movement and unfoldment.

Rinpoche said that my very questions arose from the play of these three qualities, and that the three qualities were basic to the whole process of questioning itself. He said that within beings there was a great sadness and that the cause of the great sadness was the loss of awareness of our true home, going astray, losing our way in a jungle of confused emotions, projections and misunderstandings. The going astray occurs at some deep level where we have mistaken Being for our ordinary sense of self. It is as though the snare of our self-delusion has trapped us so completely that escape seems virtually impossible. Yet in another sense nothing has really happened at all; for we remain ineluctably embraced within the sphere of Being and can never be apart from the naturalness of its movement.

The essence of the problem could be summed up in the phrase "I can be liberated from the snare of delusion." This implies an actual state of delusion to which the self is subject, and a process by which the delusion can be removed. Feeling ourselves to be imprisoned in some way, whether by external or internal conditions, a primary question that needs to be answered is whether the self as we commonly think of it really exists or not. This is what we might describe as the first challenge to a developing sense of vision, the true vision of Being.

Rinpoche said: "Fundamentally there is no snare of delusion; never was, never will be. It is the desperate struggle of ego to free itself from a sense of imprisonment that creates all the confusion. There has to be surrender, but you can't surrender to yourself and you can't surrender to an external projection of goodness, like God. It has to be to another person."

Rinpoche said that one could meet in this world members of a lineage of wise and loving beings to whom this surrender could be made, a surrender which eventually would involve giving up ego. Rinpoche said that it was not necessarily an easy matter to find such a person and to make the right connection, and even if this were to occur, undertaking the necessary training was not itself without pitfalls and dangers. Nevertheless the student would have to follow the path to the end for the truth of Being to be realized.

This person of the lineage would be a teacher of meditation, but they would also have to be much more. They would have to be able to inspire in the student a way of living that penetrated all the activities of the individual so that the whole life, whether mental, physical, emotional, sexual, social, cultural, or even financial, had to be given over to the Way of Being and to appreciating its movement. Finally, the lineage person would have to appear as an embodiment of Being itself and all their actions taken to exemplify the natural, ungraspable movement of Being.

The sense of a developing vision of Being creates great sadness, and an intense distress comes from a sense of oppression by external and internal conditions, by delusion and by ego itself. This is felt not only personally but in relation to the fate of others. Maha ati was described by Rinpoche as having the power to cut through this oppression, showing the distress to be in fact a self-inflicted wound. However, the great sadness within beings can never be removed, even at the highest level of maha ati, since whenever there is a conditioned sense of time and space there is loss of awareness. It is like an irritant that acts on the natural responsiveness of sensitivity, giving rise to the pearl of great price, unending love and compassion.

To truly realize this in its full immediacy requires a complete openness toward the inspiration of the lineage teacher at the highest level. If you do not have this then there is the sense of a path to be followed rather than instantaneous accomplishment as is sometimes mentioned in maha ati texts. The touchstone is a complete faith or trust in the immediacy of the truth of the words of the lineage teacher. If you have this in full measure then truly the fruit is instantaneous. It is part of the tradition of great compassion of maha ati not to stop or not to remain at the Olympian summit of the ultimate view, but to show students how to enter and proceed along the path that leads to its realization.

It seems a good idea at this point to outline some of Rinpoche's teachings on this aspect of maha ati. In the beginning of this introduction I described how Rinpoche took my basic questions and used them as a basis for maha ati. In the next section I describe this same process in more detail and try to show how it concerns the relationship between views about reality and proceeding along the path. I then describe how Rinpoche developed the upaya tantra out of the basic realities of natural human existence and the meditative simplicity of formless meditation. This is astonishing, since the upaya tantra is the union of the higher tantras, and formless meditation is the most basic of all meditations. By doing this, Rinpoche shows the great profundity of formless meditation.

The Initial Appreciation of the Great Perfection

Trungpa Rinpoche said that the highest teaching of the Buddha was the great perfection, maha ati. He said that this was a teaching of great simplicity and accessible in some degree to everyone. It is from this great simplicity that all the basic questions concerning meaning and our own sense of wonder about existence arise. We feel that these questions must have answers and that somehow these answers are within our grasp.

In the first flush of enthusiasm we feel certain that answers are forthcoming, but then there is a sense of disappointment. It seems that the answers we were looking for never quite arrive. However, the reason for this seems to be that we are looking in the wrong place. The answers take the form of direct, life-changing experiences; so while there are answers to our questions, they are not at all what we had in mind. They are not some new theory about life or the universe.

From the point of view of the great perfection, which is the most basic form of simplicity, the answer to these questions is to be found in the same place from which the questions themselves arose, so we do not need to seek anywhere else than in the simplicity and directness of our own Being. However, due to the basic split in our own natures, the split between the ego as subject looking at the rest of the universe as object, or between the mind that seems to be internal and the physical universe that seems to be external, we become lost in a maze of conceptional complexity. This leads us astray into areas where the simple directness of the original home, where all questions are brought to rest and all answers are to be found, is lost.

Searching for the solution in experience itself is gradually seen as passing beyond looking for a solution in the internal or the external. No internalized process of self-annihilation or self-abnegation will help, nor will devotion to or reliance upon an external god or divine being.

It is gradually understood that a path evolves from the core of simplicity moving from a sense of not having understood the genuine significance of experience and what its fundamental nature is, to an evolution in the general direction of an understanding of both, until this evolvement is complete and full understanding has reached fruition. Thus the initial state of great simplicity from which the basic questions arise is the ground, the evolution toward the goal of compete understanding is the path, and the final state of complete evolvement of understanding is the fruit.

First Steps along the Path

Initially the person who is trying to reach this simplicity of understanding has to move away from the confused projections that act both outwardly and inwardly. There has first of all to be a focus on and an acknowledgement of the pure simplicity of awareness itself. To accomplish this, it is best to allow the mind to flow freely and to acknowledge the simplicity of awareness when the mind plays in its field of many projections. This process is what is called meditation.

Although the person walking along this path is still at this stage considerably fixated on internal and external projections, some understanding of the nature and omnipresence of awareness begins to dawn. The tight grip of ego begins to loosen its hold, and a certain appreciation of the irony of existence begins to arise. Nevertheless, the student of awareness may feel that traversing the path is like a kind of super-psychotherapy, particularly in the Western milieu. This may take the form of considering the path to be merely the promoting of emotional and mental health and gaining and increasing the stability of the personality.

Beginnings of Real Vision

Eventually awareness and understanding increase until there is some sense that both what seems internal and what seems external are really based on awareness itself. This represents a complete change in worldview. Up to this point the tendency was to think of awareness as simply of the mind or as the stream of thoughts. Now there is a recognition that awareness is vaster in scope than the thinking process, but this is at the level of an intuitive conviction rather than actual knowledge. The actual acknowledge is confined to experience of the mind and the world about us. However, there is recognition that there is much to do as regards traversing the path; fruition still seems far off.

We still feel that our love and hate are directed to external independently existing realities in the world, although at some level a conviction begins to grow that it is love and hate that create the apparently loved and hated objects as emotionally graspable entities. We then develop an attitude of attraction or repulsion to these objects. This is opposite to how we normally think, in which external objects are just given as externally and independently existing, to be grasped at or rejected according to how we feel about them. The idea that the objects arise as they do because of the grasping or rejecting mind is a drastic shift in the way we view the universe.

The Ungraspable Nature of Experience

As the student proceeds along the path, the central importance of awareness begins to grow and become more and more significant. It may seem paradoxical, but as this centrality is perceived more and more clearly, awareness and the multitude of projections naturally associated with it be-

come increasingly transparent and less real in the way normally considered. In fact, up to that point, there had been unthinking reliance on the
totality of projections as the real and true universe, both at an internal and
at an external level. It is a shocking revelation for the student of awareness
to realize the complete falseness of this unthinking, but strongly held,
emotional assumption. The universe is now experienced as ungraspable
and the apparent reality of projections begins to collapse.

We begin to realize that this is not just a particular view that the
mind has of the universe, but is a true seeing of the nature of the universe
itself. The universe will then seem to the student of awareness to be like
a great void and a source of terror, but persistence in the path of truth
eventually leads to the ability to rest in the primordial simplicity that
does not need the security of reference points. However, it is only when
the student begins to focus on experience that this truth of ungraspability
is seen. When this focus is not present, projections may appear as they
normally do. So, once again, there is still the sense of traversing a path;
although understanding is present, it is by no means complete and
fruition is some way off.

FREEDOM FROM VIEWS ABOUT THE NATURE OF EXPERIENCE

Proceeding even further the sense of emptiness grows within the student
and appears as extremely real, indeed, realer than any other experience
the student has had up to this point. It appears as it does because of the
tremendous contrast between the falseness of the projected universe and
the universe in its true nature. The falseness of the projected universe appears so complete as normally not to leave room for any doubt about its
being the truth, whereas the universe in its true nature has never before
been experienced. However, the true nature of the universe is the unrec-
ognized backdrop against which all the projections took place, which in
some sense gave them their appearance of life.

As time goes by and the student becomes more used to this true state of
affairs, the sense of emptiness begins to fade, for after all it was simply the
absence of falsity which hitherto had been taken to be real. As the real becomes more and more vividly present, the sense that there ever was a delusion at the heart of experience begins to disappear. The original craziness

of the delusive appearances was remedied by the medicine of emptiness, but this emptiness was not anything as such and must itself be abandoned when its work is done. Thus when reality is truly seen, the experience of emptiness vanishes.

On beginning to mature into this last stage, the student begins to see that all views about reality are false, no matter whether simple or complex, superficial or profound, narrow or vast, it makes no difference. Actions do not need to be linked to a particular view of reality. Actions that arise now begin to arise free of egocentric involvement, so naturally love, compassion and wisdom become spontaneous.

The student could be thought of as like a child seeing reality free from views; thus the student's vision has a supernal freshness about it, like the vision of a landscape just refreshed and cleansed by rain. Still, there is the sense of needing to be free of views concerning reality; there is a sense of suspicion that the grasping mind may be active, so some part of the path needs to be traveled.

REACHING THE FRUITION

The student has now reached the point of the utmost simplicity and directness, except that there is some sense that this position has to be maintained against possible invasion by views. It is only finally that there is the recognition that when abiding truly in this state of utmost simplicity and clarity, the arising of views is not itself the problem; it is the attachment to those views, the believing them to be real, that would cause the re-arising of delusion. It might appear that this is the end of the process of traversing the path. It is certainly true that the student may give rise to tremendous confidence in this way of considering reality, but it still seems that there is the possibility of views being taken as real and that delusion may re-arise.

THE NECESSITY OF BEING INTRODUCED TO REALITY

The traversing of the path has always required some kind of effort. Although this process develops understanding and gradual relaxing of the tight grip of ego, the very effort to practice the path still involves the student with some kind of ego-centered reference point. The closed system of ego-centered activity can only be broken from outside; in other words, some quality of otherness has to enter into it. Obviously this cannot be just any kind of otherness for something inanimate will not be able to make sufficient communication to the student for ego to be surrendered or transcended.

The otherness has to take the form of a living presence, and the most obvious source of this living presence of otherness will be some being in the external world. Again, because of the necessity of clear communication this will be another human being, but again, not any human being will do; this human being must be someone who has themselves traversed the path and so is able to genuinely inspire others to do the same.

Naturally the student will generally have had a teacher right from the outset, because there are various techniques of meditation and practice that are beneficial and need to be learned from someone who has already practiced them. However, for a student who has reached the stage mentioned above, the function of the teacher is rather different. The teacher becomes the living embodiment of the path and the fruition. The teacher as living inspiration is more important than the teacher as instructor of practical techniques.

Transforming the World of Experience

The student must have the confidence that ordinary views about the universe will not rise up again. The universe itself needs to be transformed in such a way that it appears only in an unconfused form. This is a process by which the confused universe is transformed into the universe of awareness. By basing oneself on the inspiration of the guru in this last sense, one practices by special methods, and the universe becomes transmuted into the completely awakened state. Sometimes this process is described not as one of transmutation, in other words not as if the lead or iron were transformed into gold, but rather that the removal of leadness or ironness would allow the true underlying golden quality to shine forth by itself.

Generally speaking, the effect of the guru's inspiration may not work all at once, so there is still some sense of traversing a path to the point where the transmutation or removal of the superficial dross is complete.

Passion as the Root of Experience

The whole of our world is based on passionate involvement: passionate involvement with ideas, emotions, particular ways of treating experience, particular ways of seeing the world, with parents, with children, with friends, relations, with politics, religion, ideas of race, cultural values, with emotionally held views of all kinds, because in fact all views are emotionally held.

But the subtlest forms of passionate involvement are those that involve convictions about the nature of reality, held so strongly that they are not so much viewed as passionate convictions but as the nature of reality itself. Examples of these are the belief in the self in the ordinary sense, the belief in the concreteness of the external world, notions of the three times, notions of far and near, and so on. All these are viewed as simple statements about the nature of reality, they are not really considered beliefs. However they are beliefs, albeit held with the uttermost form of passionate conviction.

It is this passionate aspect of reality, associated at its most fundamental level with creation and destruction, life and death, the one and the many, existence and nonexistence that is at the root of all our notions of causality. In other words, our ordinary notions of cause and effect are inseparable from our passionate involvement with the world. It is from this basic space of passion that our volition arises and then returns, dissolving back into that same space of passion. At this most subtle level of experience, there remains only the reference point of causality itself. From this basic passion all worlds, pure and impure, arise.

At this point the guru enables the naturally existing power of the student to focus so as to benefit others, to withdraw when such a presence is not necessary, and to appear when it is. This most subtle level of causality associated with the appearance or absence of what is of benefit to others in the world is the most profound reference point of all. Nevertheless, even this reference point could be thought of as an unnecessary complication of existence.

The Great Perfection

At this level there is the final abandoning of attachment to any reference point, however profound or vast. This should not be taken to imply that internal and external objects, the senses and mind itself, views, convictions, and reference points, including even the most profound reference point of passion, do not appear in some sense. However, when they do so there is no grasping present; to the Western mind this is usually taken to mean that there is a repulsion or revulsion from such things, that they are to be negated, their existence denied somehow. This is not implied by nongrasping here. There may indeed be exhibited a passionate involvement in a particular way of viewing the world but within this passionate involvement there is a cool center of dispassion, of indestructible Being. This means that although the passionate involvement is real, and indeed realer than any passionate involvement that the ordinary person may have, there is what we might term an inspiration or intuition of the intrinsic ungraspability of all apparent phenomena. Without the guru to finally introduce the student to the nature of this indestructible Being, no realization of the great perfection, the maha ati which is no different from enlightenment itself, would be possible.

This is the final stage of the path when the path has come to an end: the ground of the most basic and simple inspiration, the path which is a movement that never moves apart from the sphere of Being and the fruit as the sense of finality itself are all realized as one. This is why we can speak of everything being naturally perfect, everything remaining in its natural state just as it is. This is the state of complete openness to all apparent phenomena, a naturalness beyond grasping or attachment.

In this state of absolute spontaneity every volition that arises is part of the mandala of the great dance of all apparent phenomena. There is now no need to think of insufficiency or incompleteness; notions or thoughts such as "it is still necessary to progress further along the path" are totally beside the point and finally brought to rest. All activities which might formerly have been seen as contributing to progress along a path are seen now as simple, naturally arising volitions having no force of attainmentness behind them.

This is the guru's final gift to the student, the natural confidence that all actions, thoughts, concepts, and convictions, are part of the Tree of Life; everything that arises and all acts that are performed have the natural and profound significance of awakening itself.

Upaya Tantra: The Union of Natural Human Experience and Formless Meditation

THE GROUND OF THE UPAYA TANTRA

The ground of the upaya tantra is the ordinary reality of natural human existence: birth, growing up, sexual maturity, conceiving of children, birth of children, sickness, old age, and death. This is the round of life, the round of birth and death, the round of ordinary human existence.

Human beings are naturally passionate about many things: the personal relationships between parents and children, husbands and wives, brothers and sisters, pupils and teachers, the different levels of society and their members, and so forth. There is the life of the intellect and of learning, the life of physical activity, the world of art and science, and the process of discovery and exploration in all its senses. There is passion concerning mental, emotional, and physical health, the growth and nurturing of crops, the management of natural resources, financial, commercial, and related activities; all that is summed up in the phrase "making a living." Politics, religion, philanthropic activities, laws that govern human relationships such as marriage, property, and so on, the role of a police force and an army; it would seem that the channels for our passion are endless. Important, too, are the areas of play, entertainment, and enjoyment.

It should not be forgotten that passion also has a negative aspect that seeks to destroy or disrupt these activities.

Last but not least, dignity in the expression of these activities is a central theme of human society, as of course is any loss of dignity that might occur. All are natural to what it is to be human, and it is this maelstrom of passion that is the ground from which the true path emerges.

This round of birth and death is found at all levels of existence and even buddhas expose the cycle of existence to us. This is the natural expression of the whole of existence; supersamsara, as Rinpoche called it. This basis of the upaya tantra manifests primordially in all sentient beings and, as the potential for the path, exists in all beings equally.

In actually practicing the upaya tantra, the profound meaning of the formless meditation is the view, and merging this view of the meditation itself with everyday life is the activity. Thus it is formless meditation that is the primary practice in the upaya tantra, and its profound meaning is

the truth of the three spheres. At this profound level, the formless meditation is thought of as an expression of the natural path of spontaneity,
rather than a practice as such. The fruit is simply the recognition that
nothing further is to be added and nothing needs to be taken away from
the spontaneously existent state of Being, the movement within which
produces all the apparent manifestations of supersamsara.

At the level of the fruit, rest in the sphere of Being beyond notions
such as practice or any need of self-perfection. This is the ultimate level of
formless meditation.

The Profound Meaning of the Formless Meditation: The Truth of the Three Natural Spheres of Existence

Being can be said to have an inner sphere, an outer sphere, and a sphere
that mediates between them. The inner sphere is the source of both the
creativity of the person and all their qualities, radiating to the outer
sphere as a wave of action. Most importantly, it is also the source of the
indestructible sense of truth, called rikpa or vidya. The out-breath creates a connection going from the internal aspect of the individual to the
outer world, from Self to Other. This inner sphere should not be confused with mind in the ordinary sense, although perhaps this is a necessary starting point.

The outer sphere is the source of Other, the external world, mysterious
in the sense that it is beyond our personal control and can always surprise
us. The freshness of new experience flows from this outer sphere to the internal aspect of ourselves, just as the in-breath flows to us without any
sense of ambition on our part. This is the external world connecting to the
internal aspect of the individual, from Other to Self. In the ordinary conditioned world of experience, we tend to take the outer sphere to be the
external universe as we know it. Although tempting, and perhaps again a
necessary starting point, this misidentification may lead us to think that
the outer sphere is merely external space.

The sphere that mediates between the inner and outer spheres is the
person. The person is the dynamic play of awareness, the wisdom of Self
and the wisdom of Other, playing between the two spheres. It is both center and periphery of the mandala of formless meditation and in some sense

could be described as nothing whatever and yet in another sense the hub of the universe of experience.

In Buddhism we say that within ourselves we have three innate tendencies: to create an internal aspect called mind, an external aspect called the environment, and a mediator between the two, which we call the body. These three aspects, created by the appropriate tendencies, exist for all beings, and the three spheres are their profound meaning. This indestructible quality of the three spheres links directly to the upaya tantra; the outer sphere corresponding to mahayoga, the inner sphere to atiyoga, and the sphere that mediates to anuyoga. Actually these three yogas are a unity, and it is wrong to assign maha, anu, and ati to particular spheres; it is simply used as a device to promote understanding.

We might say that the upaya tantra is the union of mahayoga, anuyoga, atiyoga, and that maha ati is the essence of that union, in which all are able to express their appropriate functions harmoniously.

THE INNER SPHERE

The innermost essence corresponds to the principle, the touchstone of truth that exists within every person. This is misperceived because of our confusion but is always there and can never in the very nature of things be completely overlooked or hidden. This is what corresponds to the self-arisen wisdom as referred to by the great fourteenth-century Nyingma master Longchenpa; it is also referred to as the buddha nature, not fundamentally different from the awakened heart of Being in its absolute sense.

In the ordinary person this wisdom manifests as the search for what is real, the search for truth. Everybody has that, even if they are not looking for truth in some deep or profound way. A connection to this touchstone of truth is needed by everyone simply to know the difference between truth and lies and the difference between what is true and what is false with regard to appearances, and even at the grossest level it is still the touchstone of reality for the individual. We could say that in some fundamental sense it arises directly from what we are, from the deepest level of our Being, for without it, it would be impossible to survive in the world.

We may try to find truth in places of learning, meeting religious teachers, ordinary secular teachers, in the teaching we receive from mother and father. They may teach us many different things, but nevertheless it is the same process for determining truth that is going on continuously, and our sense of what is true and what is false in their teaching comes from the same profound level. This is all very fundamental to us. In some sense it is not really different from the deepest part of ourselves, not different from the real essence of our own Being. Yet, in spite of this, the nature of truth is not seen clearly because of our confusion.

The outer sphere corresponds to the environment around us, and that environment takes the form of the way we work with the world. We wish to control the world or at least bring it into harmony with ourselves; we wish to enhance our relationship with it, bringing added richness to our environment. We want to charm and attract things in the world to us, want to repel certain others, want to use our bodies to do this, along with our minds and the strength and power of our emotions. In these ways we want to influence the outside world, to gain knowledge from it, and to impose our will upon it, even if some kind of destruction is necessary. Concurrently we also have the desire to nurture and foster what we believe is congenial.

Thus the power to influence the external world or the environment is important for the wave of action that goes from the inner to the outer sphere.

Beyond this wish to manipulate the external world there is truth at a profound level that wells upward from the inner sphere as a search for truth in a more external sense, such as looking for a teacher or guru who will lead us to discover truth ever more deeply. There is a sense in which to reveal more of that profound internal truth connects us to truth in the outer sphere. It is perhaps not out of place here to recall Polonius's advice to his son Laertes in Shakespeare's *Hamlet*:

> This above all: to thine own self be true,
> And it must follow, as the night the day,
> Thou canst not then be false to any man.

The Flow between the Inner and Outer Spheres

So it is as though a wave of truth proceeds from the internal aspect through the body and out into the world, returning like a reflected wave on a lake, passing back through the body into the internal aspect, where the discrimination of truth concerning the outer world is made. This to and fro action of the wave of truth is the profound activity of the three spheres of existence, the profound meaning of the rhythm of the in-breath and out-breath.

Buddhism is based on this natural force of truth, which is both communication and action, for it is just the natural aspect of What Is, what corresponds naturally to mind, body, and environment at some deep level. Whether enlightened or unenlightened, pure or impure, there is always some kind of mind or internal aspect, some kind of environment or external aspect, and some kind of body that plays between them. This seems inescapable at all levels.

There is no doubt that we have our needs and our desires and that we wish to express them and that we do this through our sense of truth, and do it in a passionate way, and this passionate way involves us in life and death. The appearance of the world, the appearance of manifestation, involves us in life and death; we cannot avoid that. So once again all this is just given, we don't have to create it through meditation or practice.

Thus sexuality, birth, life, death, are all part of the inescapable play of reality which unfolds constantly from within ourselves, whether we like it or not. The painful quality of experience, the joyful quality, love and compassion, sadness and poignancy; all are also inescapably part of the nature of things, and nothing to do with subscribing or signing up to a system of beliefs. Passion flows between the three spheres, and the flow between the three spheres is passion itself. However, in the upaya tantra, passion has at its heart a cool, unbiased quality of awareness not to be found in the ordinary nature of passionate emotion.

We wish to try to control the environment by various means. This is perfectly natural to beings, and Buddhism can be seen in many ways as a natural and ultimate expression of this tendency. What could be more wonderful than controlling the environment by creating a world suitable for the benefit of others?

There is a cycle of inspiration and volition that goes from the inner sphere to the outer and creates, and comes from the outer sphere to the inner and informs and communicates; it is this that continually makes the new worlds of supersamsara. When the basic inspiration is that of benefiting others, then it truly creates the New World, the true Utopia.

THE WISDOM OF SELF AND OTHER

There are two natural, self-existent wisdoms: the natural wisdom of Self and the natural wisdom of Other. The natural wisdom of Self has already been discussed; it is nothing other than the touchstone of truth, the indestructible internal source of reality. The natural wisdom of Other is a wisdom that presents the indestructible reality of Other to the wisdom of Self; it is this wisdom of Self that knows the truth of Other, knows the external world as Other.

Rinpoche told me that Longchenpa had his own special logic, different from that of other Buddhist teachers, and that part of this logic was founded on the truth of the reality of Other. We cannot find an external world in any other place than in the natural wisdom of Other. Thus it is the touchstone of truth that enables us to know there are beings other than ourselves, that there is an external world, and that through this natural wisdom of Other we have access to it. These wisdoms emerge spontaneously from formless meditation and must never be rejected by yogin or yogini. To cling to the ordinary vajrayana view might lead to the Buddhist equivalent of a heart attack.

Naturally we all have our own experiences related to external objects, but those of sense perceptions are not the same as those apprehended through the natural wisdom of Other. We have direct experience of the truth of the existence of Other quite apart from the experience of sense perceptions.

In the basic inescapable ground of non-ego and emptiness there is no place left for the reference points of an ego-centered universe. This spaciousness allows the two wisdoms, the wisdom of Self and the wisdom of Other, to emerge naturally and self-existently. This is why there is no solipsism in Buddhism.

THE PROCESS OF PROJECTION

There is a natural flow of communication from the inner to the outer sphere and vice versa. Both the flow and the space are completely neutral since they are not biased toward enlightenment or unenlightenment, or toward Self or Other. There is a natural play between the two wisdoms, the wisdom of Self and the wisdom of Other, and formless meditation enables us to participate in this play.

There is also a confused view of the process, a process based on the three kleshas (emotional poisons) of aggression, grasping, and confusion. When the outer sphere is internalized it becomes aggression, when the inner sphere is externalized it becomes grasping, and confusion arises from uncertainty about the boundary.

Buddhism may be said to consist solely in making the distinction between truth and reality on the one hand and the projections of materialism and solipsism on the other. Solipsism is the projection of the outer sphere into the inner sphere, creating a sense of an ego-centered universe where my perceptions are all that exist; the wisdom of Other is denied and the wisdom of Self transformed into ego. Usually the projection of the external sphere into the internal is incomplete, some genuine connections remaining. It is important to realize that it is our solipsistic projections of the outer into the inner sphere that produce the sense that the realities of love, wisdom, and compassion are simply private, personal, internal affairs, rather than powerful, living qualities from their own side.

There is also the projection of the inner sphere into the outer sphere to be considered. This creates the belief in externally existing egos and a graspable external world. If we were able to rely completely on the wisdom of Self, the indestructible sense of truth within the inner sphere, there would be no problem. However, the sense of truth is not apprehended clearly enough and projections occur.

The seeming irreversibility of apparent confusion is inevitable, due to the natural power of conviction, coupled with one's own egocentricity. By means of this same power of conviction, liberation from projections also occurs. However, the conviction must be transmitted from the wisdom of Other in the form of an external wise and loving person, the guru. Enlightenment is simply allowing the projections to return to their own spheres, when of course they cease to be projections.

It is a sad thing to think that in some quarters the tantras, and in particular mahamudra and even maha ati are treated as merely one's own mind, and that the external world is viewed as an irrelevance. This one-sided approach bodes ill for the future of Buddhism, particularly in the West.

POINTING OUT THE TRUTH

Thus the nature of truth, called rigpa or vidya, does need to be pointed out. We have some ability to do this ourselves otherwise we would not be able to function at all, but we also need another person to point out the nature of that truth within ourselves. Sometimes we can be helped by something apparently external, even inanimate, perhaps by reading a book or seeing an image. There might in fact be many possibilities for inspiration, depending on the person and how much confusion is present.

But as human beings we need another person to help us; for example, we need mother, we need father, we need teachers. We need them to help us understand language, we need them to help us work with the outside world in a way which seems to be inspiring and links in a positive way to experience. All this comes from the necessity of working with others.

If the guru is a preceptor, as in hinayana, then we are practicing according to his instruction and have some degree of connection to truth. However, the guru does not relate to us intimately; there is a sense that the guru is still an external figure and apart. The idea of the guru being internalized, affecting us in a very profound way, has not yet really occurred. So there is a sense of path and a sense of distance and a sense that enlightenment may be some way off, but that eventually it will be realized. In hinayana the confusion seems so strong that the only way to become enlightened is by oneself, and it seems that others cannot be helped except in a minimal way.

In mahayana there is the realization that enlightenment is intrinsically involved with others. There is the view that we can help others in a very vast way because of the intense communication that exists between what is Self and what is Other, and because there is a play between the external universe and the internal aspect. This play is recognized and expressed by qualities of Being that everyone shares through the universal space of clarity, awareness, and emptiness. However, it is still true that there is a sense that this takes time to accomplish. In hinayana the guru is like a friend, but in mahayana the situation is more like that of a family, the guru being like a mother or a father.

If we now turn to the upaya tantra proper, then the way we relate to the environmental aspect is in terms of what might be called the Way of

Power. The passionate body aspect, which plays between the inner and outer spheres, the passionate aspect of sexuality and death, birth and death, life and death; all of these powerful energies we carry around with us continually within our own bodies. We have the power to link mind and passion to the external world in an almost magical fashion. Practicing this, based on the formless meditation, is the union of the upaya tantra.

MAHA ATI

The essence of this union is maha ati, which is the nature of Being itself, not a practice. How then, can we talk of realizing it? The question here is one of the removal of confusion, rather than attaining some kind of realization. However, this confusion does not really exist in a substantial way, but is simply a distortion of view that needs to be corrected. It seems to be almost nothing at all, but this infinitesimal difference is sufficient to create a distinction between enlightenment and a turmoil of confusion, a maze from which there seems to be virtually no chance of escape. The struggle to escape seems to draw us deeper into the quicksand of ego-centered ignorance.

There is only one means of recognition, and that is through the meeting of two minds: the mind of the student with complete faith and devotion and the mind of the guru with realization and a deep connection to the student. In terms of the three spheres, from the inner sphere arises the complete openness of unshakable faith, and devotion and from the outer sphere comes the presence of the guru with whom the student has a very special affinity. This affinity arises from past connections, devotion to the practice, and from the living quality of awakenedness between student and guru.

Meeting such a guru cannot be contrived by our own efforts, but comes as the gift of our past living connections with Dharma. The most that the student can do is to prepare the ground for such a meeting, but there are no means of predicting when this meeting will occur, and part of the training of the student is to rest in the spacious quality of what is, without hope or fear.

When such a guru appears, the flow between the inner and outer spheres is naturally without confusion and we can say that at this point recognition of the truth is instantaneous. It can also be said that at that time there arises from the inner sphere the ultimate wisdom of Self, which dissolves the facade of flickering thoughts and grasping at notions of prophecy concerning our future enlightenment. This ultimate wisdom of Self flows together with the ultimate wisdom of Other, which is the absolute guru principle, founded upon the true encounter with the personal root guru as Other.

This is the end of the path, fruition itself, the removal of all apparent confusion.

Conclusion

According to Chögyam Trungpa Rinpoche, the only purpose of the path of the Buddha is the search for truth; the truth about the nature of reality which is immediately accessible to us if we care to look for it in the right way. However, there is something special about this truth that is not immediately obvious; for it is a truth that not only leads to wisdom, but also to love and compassion for all our fellow beings. Since in their deepest nature all beings are alike, love enters them all equally and compassion arises naturally for those who have not realized the truth of what is. Thus wisdom, love, and compassion are not fundamentally distinct.

Buddhism is completely based upon direct awareness, which transcends the ordinary self-centered experience emanating from ego or from grasping mind. One would have hoped that philosophy still meant the love of such wisdom, but this seems to have long ceased to be the case. Since in the practice of modern philosophy there is no way of reappraising or deepening one's personal experience by techniques that open oneself to the immediacy of experience, the philosopher has no means of acquiring new experiential data, no advanced technology of perception one might say. Most modern philosophers are therefore not competent to understand Buddhism; their ideas about it are based purely on prejudice, just as someone in the past without microscope or telescope could not take the first step in making new discoveries about the physical world, relying instead on fanciful conjectures about nature, uninformed by real knowledge.

Rinpoche's great hope for the West was that the obvious wisdom inherent in the direct immediacy of experience would eventually prove so overwhelmingly clear that it would just be seen as a truism rather than some form of esotericism. As he said the first time we met: "The simplicity of experience is all that you have; everything else comes from this."

The Establishment of
a Pure Monastic Tradition
in the West

Pema Chödrön

M Y TEACHER, THE Vidyadhara, Chögyam Trungpa Rinpoche, is
known as one of the pivotal figures in presenting the buddhadharma in the West. Often, when people speak of him, he is recalled as a
very unconventional teacher of Buddhism. There are stories of his unconventional behavior and his willingness to present the teachings in a fresh
and directly relevant manner to the situation he found himself in. What is
not so commonly known, however, is that he is also the founder of a
monastic tradition, and people might be quite surprised to hear how traditional he was in his views about monastic life.

Trungpa Rinpoche was raised in a monastic tradition. Identified at an
early age as a reincarnation of the tenth Trungpa, he was taken from his
family and brought to the Surmang monasteries for training. Having
grown up in a monastery, he remained a monk when the Chinese invaded
Tibet, forcing him to flee to India. He continued to wear his monk's robes
until 1969, after a car crash in England, when he came to the realization
that his robes were an obstacle to people's hearing the true dharma. He
gave up his robes and began to dress like a Westerner. In 1970 he arrived

Based on an interview by Christopher Tamdjidi.

243

in the United States, where he began to teach in his characteristic style, presenting the dharma in an unconventional and fresh manner.

I understand from some of his early students in North America that he first talked about his wish to develop a monastery as early as the early 1970s, when he arrived in North America. I myself had been ordained at Samye Ling in England, by the sixteenth Karmapa, before becoming a student of Trungpa Rinpoche's. Following my ordination, I returned to the United States and started to study with Trungpa Rinpoche and finally requested permission to become his student. We had our first discussion on the setting up of a monastery in North America during the 1981 Seminary (an intensive three-month period of practice and study of the Buddhist teachings). He was sitting there looking very, very happy, and he said it gave him such pleasure to be in a place where everybody was completely committed and one-pointedly engaged in meditation and the study of Buddhist teachings. He said that this was the closest we have to a monastery, and if one day we could have such a situation on a permanent basis, that would be like a dream come true.

In the early 1980s, Tsultrim Tondrup, one of Trungpa Rinpoche's students who was also a monk, supplicated the Vidyadhara to establish a monastery. The Vidyadhara responded that that would be wonderful and that Tsultrim should look for a suitable place on Cape Breton Island in Nova Scotia. Tsultrim set out on the search, and in the meantime, Trungpa Rinpoche started to talk to me, initiated sometimes by me, sometimes by him, about what he would like the monastery to be.

Transmitting a View of Western Monasticism

During our meetings then, and in all our interactions over the years, there were two particular aspects that Trungpa Rinpoche always stressed about the Western monasticism he wanted to develop: returning to a pure vinaya (the monastic rules and vows that monks and nuns take) and at the same time keeping an open, flexible mind. He conveyed these two things to me again and again, in different ways and at different times.

In one of our exchanges during the 1981 Seminary, he stressed the importance of keeping vows purely. He had been giving a talk on the vajrayana teachings, teachings that outwardly do not seem to have a monastic flavor. He was speaking that evening of the "one taste" of all phenomena, and of never holding back. He used sexual activity as an example to illustrate his point. Following the talk, people asked questions, and I also took the chance to ask him a question. I asked, "What about me? It seems like I cannot really follow those teachings." He looked me straight in the eye and asked, "Do you keep your vows strictly?" I said, "Yes, I do." To which he responded, "You should always keep your vows strictly, and if you keep your vows strictly, then you will quickly come to understand what I am really talking about here."

That was very interesting to me: that the vajrayana teachings, which said that one should work with whatever arose and for which there are no fixed rules, and which he presented so unconventionally, could be understood through keeping the vinaya purely. He did not say that in certain instances you do not have to keep your vinaya; in that particular instance, he just emphasized very strongly that I should never break my vows, and that if I did that, that would be an excellent basis for understanding the vajrayana teachings as he presented them.

He returned to this point again and again. We were at another Seminary, and I requested an interview with him to talk about the monastery. I was astounded that the word came back that very day that he would see me, because usually it took quite a while before one got to see him, if at all.

During that Seminary, I had had a number of business meetings with him, along with other people who were running the Seminary, and we would always meet in his sitting room, and so I assumed that's where this meeting would take place. But instead, when I got there, I was ushered into his bedroom. His shades were still drawn, so the bedroom was very dim, and he was sitting up in bed, covered by a sheet but apparently stark naked. I remember thinking: this is so like Trungpa Rinpoche, to have this conversation with me about the monastery in this particular setting. I remember laughing, and then he gestured to me that I should come down and sit right next to him on the bed. I laughed and said something like: "Well, Sir, this is a very unusual setting for discussion on monasticism." But he didn't crack a smile, he was just very serious and looked me in the eye, and he just started talking about the monastery.

He reiterated again that we should have very pure vinaya, and I remember his telling me as I was leaving, "You know, they are all going to be looking at you, they are going to watch the way you walk, the way you talk, and the way you conduct yourself, and so you better do it right, you know."

Basically that's what he was saying, and my impression by that time was that doing it right meant to be very pure in my keeping of the vinaya but at the same time being extremely flexible and open in my mind.

There was never anything conventional about the way he taught. It was interesting to me that he was quite insistent that I should keep my vows so strictly. But at the same time we would have interchanges that always indicated to me that the most important thing for him, along with keeping the vows, was not to have an uptight or conventional mind.

During one exchange, he was sitting in the front of a somewhat small room where a group of people were about to receive some vows from him. It was a small room, and I had been helping to set the room up. He was alone in the chair at the front, and I walked into the room across the back of the room to get something, and he looked up at me and said, "Do you wear stockings?"

These kinds of questions came out of nowhere, and they were not exactly the traditional questions that you would ask a nun. It wasn't an outrageous question, but in the context it really caught me by surprise, and I said, "No." But he had completely stopped my mind and managed to convey that we aren't talking about any kind of rigidity or any primness or properness. I always got the feeling we were never talking about fixed moralistic mind that was rigid about the celibacy vow, or rigid about the drinking vow, or rigid about any precept. But at the same time, he stressed keeping them purely. This was the interesting kind of squeeze that was always there with him.

Another time I was having an interview with him. It was a business meeting. I had gone to him to ask him some questions, when all of a sudden, in the middle of the conversation about a ceremony, he asked, "Do you masturbate?" Again, I was floored by this question coming out of space. It left me once again with the feeling that what he cared most about was being free of fixed mind and being free from holding rigidly to opinions and views or a code of ethics or anything like that. But at the same time, I should be a model nun in terms of how I kept my precepts.

To this day, these two instructions continue to be the guiding principles in our development of the Western monastic tradition, and I myself am still trying to follow these instructions, to keep that paradox in my life. I think that when we look further into the characteristics and particular aspects of the monastic tradition that is unfolding at Gampo Abbey, Nova

Scotia, then we can see how these principles are beginning to manifest and come alive.

Characteristics of Western Monasticism

Trungpa Rinpoche had felt that the monastic tradition had declined somewhat in Tibet. In fact, he very much hoped that the establishment of a pure monastic tradition in the West could prove to be beneficial to Buddhist monasticism, and in particular to the Tibetan monasticism that formed the basis of his approach to Western monasticism. He was very keen also to not just transplant a Tibetan or South Asian monastic model into the West; he really was very interested in developing something uniquely suited to the West.

He asked Khenchen Thrangu Rinpoche, whom he knew from Tibet and whom he considered to be a great example of someone who holds the vinaya purely and still has an open mind, to be the abbot of the monastery and direct its development. I was to be the first director. With the blessings and support of Trungpa Rinpoche and Thrangu Rinpoche, and a number of other Kagyü teachers, Gampo Abbey was set up in 1984, and the form that Western monasticism is taking had begun to unfold.

Clearly, while trying to remain as traditional and pure as possible, our form of Western monasticism has some very different characteristics from the form that is practiced in Tibet. In particular, two aspects—not separating men and women, and temporary ordination—differ markedly from the model in Tibet.

One thing that was clear from the beginning was that the monastery was to be for both men and women. From the beginning of this project there were two of us involved: one monk and one nun. Trungpa Rinpoche said that because we just had one monk and one nun, we would establish this monastery for men and women. In fact, he thought that this was a good thing because in this way there would be no escaping working with our sexual energy. He felt this was important for us to really work with our vows as a practice.

Another defining characteristic that Trungpa Rinpoche felt strongly about was temporary ordination. In the early meetings, he said that felt that it would be primarily a temporary monasticism that would cause monasticism to thrive in the West. In explaining what he meant by that, he said that we should use as our model the Southeast Asian countries such as Thailand. There, almost all men take ordination, sometimes for as short a time as a weekend or a week. But at some point in their life they become a fully ordained monk.

Trungpa Rinpoche stressed that there would be some people that want to become monks and nuns for their whole life, taking the novice vows and then taking the full ordination of a monk and nun. But he said the majority would take temporary ordination. And this is what we are actually finding: a few people want to make a life commitment, but for the majority, even if initially they think they want to make a life commitment, it is just something they do temporarily.

It took us some time to develop this. Thrangu Rinpoche, who had been the abbot of the monastery from the beginning, initially didn't feel he had the authority or empowerment to allow for temporary monasticism. This was not a tradition that existed in Tibetan monasticism, a tradition he was the holder of. He said it would have to be someone higher then himself, such as the Karmapa or the Dalai Lama, who could make that decision. But every year I would ask him when he came, until finally one year he just said yes, that would be fine. I was astounded. I asked him what had changed. He replied that he had noticed that other rinpoches were giving temporary ordination now, so he felt it would be all right for him to do so also.

What he instigated was that actually people take what are called the upasaka vows. These are usually considered the precepts for laypeople, but here they take the five precepts and they keep them very strictly; in this case we interpret the sexual precept as celibacy. They also go through a ceremony where they formally take the vow, and they shave their head and put on robes. During that period of time, which is a minimum of six months, they live at the monastery as monks or nuns. We have a lot of people coming to take temporary vows, and usually they take them for a year. Then, if they really find it supportive, they keep extending their vows and their stay in the monastery. Some people are still extending, and we don't know if they'll end up being "lifers," as we call them.

Connected to this, Trungpa Rinpoche thought that it would be really good for young people to take temporary vows before they go to college, and that people at the end of their lives, as long as it was not an escape, would also benefit from monasticism. During our discussion in the darkened room, he said that this would be excellent—that people could experience the monastic life before they jump into the full chaos of living, when you have a possibility of moving out the other side.

So that is the solution Thrangu Rinpoche selected. We do not have people coming and taking full bhikshu and bhikshuni ordination for a weekend, so we are not exactly following the Theravadan model. But this wish of Trungpa Rinpoche for temporary monasticism is definitely being kept, and that's what people seem to have an appetite for.

Reestablishing a Pure Vinaya

We have been trying very hard to establish a pure discipline: that is, something that people take seriously and do their best to keep purely. But it is clear when one looks at the vinaya that there are certain rules that not only are not kept by Tibetan tradition, but are actually impossible to keep. These include rules such as not traveling in a vehicle.

Trungpa Rinpoche said that those of us who are fully ordained should go through our precepts (which number 348 for women and 253 for men) one by one and discuss the ones that we felt were impossible to keep in modern times. We should thus identify a list of ones we could keep purely and strictly and then pass it by Thrangu Rinpoche for his permission. That is what we did. There are some that we all are in agreement that we are not keeping because it is not possible to do so in modern times. But in essence, we are not changing the vinaya. We are just temporarily adapting it to the culture; there has been an agreement, and the blessing of the lineage, that we are not going to keep certain precepts. So this can serve as the basis for a living and realistic vinaya that we can keep strictly and purely. By agreeing on such a vinaya, we avoid immediately any gray areas, any precepts that we all just ignore, and we can then keep the ones we take purely and strictly.

Alcohol and Sexuality. Trungpa Rinpoche insisted on strictly keeping the vows relating to alcohol and sexuality. He felt that there was nothing per se wrong with sexuality and alcohol; however, he did feel that most people had deeply ingrained habitual patterns relating to them and used sexuality and alcohol as an escape from their reality. He emphasized it was important to be strict not because these activities were bad, but so that we can really see our minds and our continual search for entertainment. In this way the keeping the vinaya is a practice, not a moral code. He insisted on this, and also stressed the importance of being free of hypocrisy. It is sad to say, but in Southeast Asia, China, and Tibet, places where strict monasticism has remained to this day, one hears a lot of stories about the sexual precept being held very lightly. In other words, one hears of monks going out at night to brothels and also drinking, and that everybody just pretends not to know. They want the monks to stay monks and remain in the monasteries, and so they let people do things like that. There are a lot of stories like that in all monastic traditions.

For Western people, where monasticism is a choice, this just doesn't make sense. If one is not going to keep the celibacy precept while being a monk or nun, then one will not learn from this practice. The learning from it only comes to you if you actually keep the vows. Once you start to get into this gray area where you say that sometimes it's all right to have a drink, sometimes it's all right to have sex, it is not going to work. Sometimes you will hear that homosexuality is all right because Buddha was only referring to sexual relations between men and women. When a Western monk or nun starts thinking that way, then basically they are just conning themselves.

It has been interesting to really see how keeping what he asked us to do keeps a very healthy and sane attitude to our vows, our practice. It minimizes self-deception and definitively does away with trying to deceive other people, pretending to be one thing and actually doing other things. In fact, hypocrisy is something that Trungpa Rinpoche deplored; he stressed that we should be monks and nuns without hypocrisy. I remember once he said that lying to yourself is even worse then lying to another person. There is no way to take vows and then consciously break them without somehow lying to yourself about what it is that you are doing.

The Last Meal at Noon. Equally, while the starting point of Trungpa Rinpoche's approach to monasticism was the Tibetan monastic tradition that he had been raised in, he also felt that on a number of points the Tibetan tradition had declined. For example, he felt it was important that the noon meal be the last, although this was something not practiced in the Tibetan tradition. He did not want us to be rigid about this; it did not mean that we could not have a single thing after the hour of noon. But he felt that there should be no meal, nothing chewable after the noon meal.

Not Handling Money. Another thing he mentioned was not handling

money. We have tried to work with this, but so far it has been very difficult. We do, however, keep the attitude behind this precept, meaning that
we are not accumulating wealth and possessions.

Sojong Practice. Trungpa Rinpoche also wanted us to practice purely the
traditional sojong practice, the bimonthly formal confession ceremony.
We started doing this based on an explanation by Thrangu Rinpoche, but
Trungpa Rinpoche continued to show a great deal of interest in the proper
application of this practice. I remember in particular one translation meeting, when we met with him to work on the relevant texts for the sojong ceremonies. He was very intent on finding the right words for the practice. In
the Tibetan texts there is a word usually translated as "sin," but he definitively didn't want any words that were charged with lot of meaning from a
Western historical background and that transmitted the wrong meaning.
He came up instead with "an obstructive condition"—that is how he translated the word instead of "sin." I feel this is very interesting because in the
Western tradition, sin somehow implies that we have basic badness in
our nature, whereas in the Buddhist and Shambhala view, we speak of buddha nature or basic goodness as the ground. And so a mistaken act is an act
that obstructs the realization of this basic nature. That is the meaning he
wanted us to work with in the sojong practice.

We work regularly with the sojong practice now, primarily based on
the Tibetan model, in terms of robes that we wear and the sojong ceremony itself. But we have adapted it so that for part of the ceremony
laypeople may be included. Normally, temporary monastics would not go
to a sojong ceremony, only those at the novice level and above. Now,
when we do our sojong ceremony, all the fully ordained monastics, both
monks and nuns, are together for the fully ordained part of the confession
ceremony; all the novices, both men and women, are together for the
novice part; and all the temporaries, both men and women, are together
for the recitation of their vows.

Keeping an Open, Flexible Mind

At the same time that we have been trying to keep the vows purely, we
also are working very hard on keeping an open, flexible mind. Trungpa
Rinpoche emphasized again and again that we should not use the monastic rules as a way to close ourselves off from the world—the whole point

was to see them as a way to further open our hearts and minds toward the whole world.

He therefore said I had to really watch for people's motivation, why they wanted to become monks and nuns. He said that many people are going to want to become monks and nuns who feel, for instance, that their love affairs have gone bad, or they want to escape from the chaos and discomfort of their life, or that they had lost their sexual drive or they are getting old and they just want a place to retire to. He felt that all of these are not good motivations, and in fact he said that the monks and nuns should always be horny. That was the kind of message that he was giving us again and again—that you keep your vows purely, but on the other hand, you are full of life, full of juice, open and interested in the world, and not in any way rejecting life.

Simplicity and Personality. He also wanted us to be flexible and open-minded in the relating to each other. For example, in the monastic tradition, there is an emphasis also on living a life of simplicity. We try to simplify our lives, our minds, and therefore also simplify outer things and really be in touch with the way we use outer things as a way to get ground under our feet. We should wean ourselves from the false sense of security that we invest things with.

But we also have to be clear that different people live this differently. My idea of simplicity would not be another person's idea of simplicity. Somebody else might feel that my idea of simplicity is indulgent compared with his or her view of it. Trungpa Rinpoche emphasized that we should leave room for that kind of thing. So our rooms at the monastery are all somewhat unique, each person's room reflecting their own personality and their own buddha family, and that's fine.

Not Cultivating Critical Mind. Trungpa Rinpoche stressed keeping a pure vinaya, living by precepts, but not being uptight about it to the extent that you start criticizing other people. In other words, if the fact that people are living their vinaya purely starts leading to critical mind, judgmental mind, then obviously we are missing the whole point. At the monastery we actually work a lot with critical mind, judgmental mind, as a practice. Within that very tight container of the monastic setting and the vinaya, with basically no entertainment at all, we also try to be caring for one another, developing the ability to appreciate each other, and give each other a break.

Slow and Careful Development. In fact, his key instructions for the overall development of the monastery also mirrored this. His primary instruction to me was that I should not have too high ideals of what the monastery is going to be, but instead just make small moves and then watch what naturally evolves, and go with that. Don't have this big goal that you have in mind; instead work with where things are at that moment.

For instance, even though he emphasized the temporary monasticism that took six or seven years, and even though he indicated returning to a strict vinaya, we are only now, some eighteen or nineteen years after founding Gampo Abbey, beginning to be able to have the "no eating" rule after lunch. We always do it during the yarne season, which is the rainy season retreat that happens for seven weeks a year, and we always do it on sojong. We are also just beginning to make some headway in seeing that at a certain stage in the development of a monk or nun being trained at Gampo Abbey, they begin to keep that rule all the time, unless they have health concerns. But we've had to do it extremely slowly, even though it was one of the main things that Rinpoche said to do.

Monasticism as a Path

Overall, we can see that the monastic path is an excellent vehicle for genuinely training oneself in the hinayana, the mahayana, and the vajrayana, as presented by the Vidyadhara Trungpa Rinpoche. The Vidyadhara always emphasized that one must go through all stages of Buddhist practice, and one must therefore train deeply and fundamentally in the hinayana and the mahayana before entering into the vajrayana. In this way too he was a traditionalist, as he was very much opposed to introducing students to the vajrayana teachings before they were ready.

Hinayana. Trungpa Rinpoche always called the hinayana the narrow path, since it cuts down speed and begins the process of really taming a student. He placed tremendous emphasis on the sitting practice of meditation and on developing genuine renunciation. He pointed out again and again that we are continually obsessed with maintaining ourselves and our me-ness, and with re-creating our story lines. We are continually engaged in our search for entertainment of all kinds—shopping, working, sex, dramas, love affairs—and closing ourselves off from reality. He stressed that the spiritual path is about opening ourselves up to other people, to the world, to reality as it is. And this starts with our willingness to give up our entertainment.

This is why, despite his unconventional manner, he was so insistent that monastics keep the vinaya purely. In that way, the monastic path becomes the starting point to developing genuine renunciation—giving up our story lines.

Mahayana. In the mahayana, we work with opening our hearts to other people and to the world. There is a tremendous sense of expansion and being, a willingness to feel our own tenderness. This opening up is not always easy or painless. Trungpa Rinpoche put a lot of emphasis on the fact that rubbing up against one another is part of our training in the monastic sangha. How you rub up against others, and how other people in the community irritate you or fall in love with you or whatever it might be, reminds you of what you most fear in yourself, or connects you to your deep-seated anger or deepest desire. Only if we can connect to our pain and our tender hearts can we really develop genuine compassion.

So he wanted to put a lot of emphasis on the community of monks and nuns, which of course is also what the Buddha did, as part of our training. That's where the genuine development of compassion comes in. As a monk or nun in Gampo Abbey, you are going to find yourself irritated with somebody. How you then work with that determines whether it is a path of awakening or a path of strengthening the habitual patterns that keep you locked in self-absorption. We thus want to encourage people to really notice their pain and desire and irritation, so that they can then use what comes up as a way of undoing habitual patterns. In doing this, it is important that there is an emphasis on self-compassion and kindness, because in the West guilt is a big trip, and a monastic situation is particularly prone to arousing shame and guilt.

We are always try to have Gampo Abbey be a place where our emotions are not in any way repressed. We try to encourage people not to act out or repress in any way, but to stay in the middle place of openness. This open space is the beginning of understanding shunyata and the development of compassion. Being able to stand in other people's shoes is a big part of our path.

Vajrayana. The vajrayana teachings introduce us to the notion of working with the energy of all situations, seeing whatever arises as inseparable from the awakened state. By not grasping or rejecting anything, we can see the nature of all things as they are, understand the essential energy of it, and work with it. For someone like myself, being a monastic has honed my life. The precepts have given me a fundamental understanding of renunciation and brought me to the place where I feel I am always training in being fully present at all times and not shutting down to anybody. Therefore, that ground of being fully present and not closing down to anything allows you to actually experience something that you normally would have an aversion to, or normally would grasp at, and to experience the one taste of it.

If you have been trained all along in using your precepts to see your aversion and your grasping as simply that—not strengthening those aversions and graspings, not giving yourself a guilt trip about them, but simply seeing them—then the seeing itself is the healing. You are living in a situation where it is very easy to see your own prejudices, your own biases.

In the case of aversion, you see it coming up and you notice how it hooks you and how it starts you on a self-righteous tangent of some kind. Seeing that becomes your path, untangling that through meditation and with the support of the dharma. In the same way, if you find yourself grasping at something—people fall in love at the abbey all the time—the practice is that there is nothing to be ashamed about, yet you keep your precepts. So people work with it, they get into their food and other trips that bring up their grasping, and they work with it as the path, not shaming themselves or feeling guilty about it, but still keeping the precepts very purely. Seeing things as they are, directly, without judgment, we begin to see the fundamental intelligence or wisdom in all situations—that there is energy available in all situations that is a manifestation of awakened mind. By fixating, through grasping and aversion, we simply freeze that experience, and then we are unable to connect with or work with that wisdom.

This path has led me to what I feel is an experiential true understanding of one taste and of coemergent wisdom, the understanding of the energies of the buddha families. In this way we get to the place where we realize that, for example, there is a coemergence to what we commonly experience as anger. One can use this energy as anger to build up our ego and our sense of aversion and grasping and so forth, and then it is very detrimental. On the other hand, if we tap into the energy of it, we can find this creative energy and the one taste of it. I have found that the way to experience this is through working really carefully with renunciation of habits of mind and speech and body that cause us to strengthen habitual patterns of prejudice and bias and right/wrong, good/bad thinking. In a sense that is the fundamental precept: never to stray from seeing things as they are, without bias or hope and fear.

An Example of True Renunciation

As I see more of the profundity of the buddhadharma and understand the monastic way as a path to realize it, I often think of Trungpa Rinpoche. Despite his very unconventional style, I always experienced him as a true example of someone who had developed genuine renunciation, was open without bias to all, and took delight in playing with the energies of all situations.

I remember experiencing this vividly during one of our translation meetings. We were all in his sitting room, waiting for him to join us. Once again it was so typical of Trungpa Rinpoche: his bedroom was attached to his sitting room, and so eventually he comes out, and again you could tell that he was naked under his bathrobe, and he was with a consort who was obviously also naked but had her bathrobe on, and the two of them sat down there, and then we proceeded to have the meeting about vinaya and the sojong. And he was delighted, and just kept saying over and over: This is so wonderful that we are doing this, how amazing that this is actually happening, that this might actually exist in the West. It was very touching and inspiring to me because I saw him as a model. I began to see that although everyone saw him as outrageous, which indeed he was, he was the model of somebody who knew what it meant to keep the precepts. He had learned what you need to learn from the precepts about fundamental renunciation: how slowing everything down by keeping precepts mirrors your mind back to you, and you can actually see all the places in which you get hooked and all the places where your habitual patterns just take over. You could see that he had been trained that way deeply and completely, and that based on this training, he could enter into outrageous and shocking situations; yet at that very fundamental level of his mind, he never broke the fundamental precept of never straying from the nature of mind.

For him the drinking and the sexuality were never an escape from a wide-open, immediate relationship with reality. In his manifestation, he was always demonstrating that in the end the state of mind was the fundamental thing—beyond whether you kept the precept or didn't keep the precept. In such meetings, what he conveyed to me was that you can follow precepts without a rigid mind that's locked into right and wrong and good and bad.

Another time, I went to ask him some questions when he was on retreat in Nova Scotia, in Mill Village. I went with a Chinese nun who was helping us in the beginning of the monastery. Her name was Venerable Yuen Yi. When she met Trungpa Rinpoche, he was a little drunk, and he was also wearing a kimono. Perhaps he had underwear on, but his legs were bare. Rather than being shocked, she had no problem with that at all. Right away she felt the quality of his mind, and she was quite taken by him.

We then had a little conversation based on some of the questions that had come up, and one of them was about whether the laypeople should have something that they can wear in the shrine room. And there once again, sitting somewhat tipsy and basically naked in his bathrobe, he took delight and interest in the details of this, and he said that that was a wonderful idea. He looked at her nun's robe and said that we should copy this Chinese robe in maroon, and then the laypeople could put this robe on over their clothes when they go into the meditation hall.

The Shambhala Mandala as a Large Dharma Container

In all of his teachings, Trungpa Rinpoche placed a great emphasis on seeing yourself as you are, not running away from yourself, and using your whole life as an opportunity to wake up. In this way, the monastic tradition offers a real path and container for people. It is a place where people can see themselves completely as they are, where they can come and soak themselves one hundred percent in the dharma. It is a very tight container, a place where there is no real entertainment for ego's games whatsoever.

However, the monastic tradition is just one path. It is not for everyone. You can also wake up in your normal life. But at the same time, the lessons from the monastic experience apply. No matter what situation you are in, the precept logic of simplifying or slowing down to the degree where you see yourself, where you acknowledge hooked as hooked, you acknowledge stuck as stuck, and you don't throw paraffin on the fire in terms of justifying your habitual responses to things is very important. In acting out habitual patterns, there is no "one taste" involved at all, it is just old habitual patterns, and it is your way of trying to keep ground under your feet. So in a way the monastery is a very simple situation, in which your habitual patterns become more and more transparent, and you are not getting caught in righteousness about "My way is correct, your view is incorrect."

It is not by acting out your anger that you come to understand the one taste of anger. It is by actually going through the stage of refraining in order to get in touch with how you are using those things to try to avoid the fundamental truth of the groundlessness of our existence. In a monastery the groundlessness is very, very close, and therefore it is extremely important to work with things in that way as they arise.

All of Trungpa Rinpoche's teachings were like this. He always taught about using one's life to wake up—through the Shambhala teachings, the teachings on dharma art, and numerous other contemplative disciplines. He always encouraged us to meet the boundary of our minds, where we meet our habitual patterns, where we can apply our awareness and mindfulness in every situation. He gave so many teachings that we can use to connect to the wisdom and sanity of our lives—while working, raising children, eating, socializing. His main emphasis was on becoming completely awake within the secular environment, using our lives as they are as a path. His teachings, and the Shambhala mandala that he created, could be viewed as one large container in which one can soak oneself completely in wisdom.

At Seminary in 1981, when Trungpa Rinpoche joyfully said that he if we could do this 365 days a year, it would be like a dream come true, he wasn't just talking about a monastery where people take precepts. He was talking about a situation where the commitment is wholehearted and nobody is conning themselves or justifying their neurosis and therefore blinding themselves to the truth of samsara. That would be a dream come true for him—a situation where people were actually training properly and stepping more and more into the world and not closing their hearts and minds to anything. That was his wish, and the essence of the world he created.

Chögyam Trungpa and the *Tibetan Book of the Dead*

FRANCESCA FREMANTLE

IN 1971, ONLY a year after Trungpa Rinpoche had moved to North America, he gave three lengthy seminars on subjects relating to the *Tibetan Book of the Dead*. Looking back at those days, it seems astonishing that he was teaching on such a profound text, which refers to the most advanced and secret practices of vajrayana, to people with little or no experience even of basic Buddhism. Certainly no other Tibetan lama at that time would have done so; but it was typical of Rinpoche's approach, which was always to be direct, unconventional, and courageous in proclaiming the lion's roar of dharma. Just as the *Tibetan Book of the Dead* asserts that everyone who hears it will be liberated, in the same way Rinpoche had unshakable confidence that all who came into contact with him had established a connection that would be for their ultimate benefit, even if they did not fully understand him or respond to him positively in this life.

His choice of topic may simply have been because the book was available in English and had become popular during the 1960s—those years of spiritual exploration and discovery for young people throughout Europe and North America. But no text could have been more symbolic of his future work, since it contains the essence of the vision that inspired him and that he expressed throughout his life. It sums up all the important elements of vajrayana and all the fundamental Buddhist doctrines. So, in a certain way, everything that Rinpoche taught could be seen as elucidating the *Tibetan Book of the Dead,* which itself is simply a reminder, at the most crucial time, of one's previous meditational experience, inspired by the instructions of one's guru. The astonishing teachings he gave at those early seminars, and the effect they produced, gave us a foretaste of the methods he would employ in the years to come. For me personally that period was a turning point, as it was then that Rinpoche asked me to work on a new translation of the book with him. The *Tibetan Book of the Dead* became in my mind the quintessence of dharma and the symbol of my connection with him. So it seems auspicious to use it as a thread on which to link some memories and impressions of this extraordinary man and to illustrate a few aspects of his life and work.

I first met Trungpa Rinpoche at Samye Ling in Scotland in 1969. At that time I had no intention of becoming a Buddhist, as my greatest love was for India and the Hindu tantric traditions, and I had studied Sanskrit in order to read their sacred texts. Although I was also interested in vajrayana, the tantric form of Buddhism, somehow I had received the impression that it had become diluted and corrupted and could no longer be found as a genuine living tradition. However, I was working on a Buddhist text, the *Guhyasamaja Tantra,* for my doctoral thesis, and for this it was also necessary to read Tibetan. A fellow student had met Trungpa Rinpoche and suggested that I go with her to visit Samye Ling, as he might be able to help me with my research.

We arrived late in the evening, so my first sight of him was on the following day at the early morning puja. It was still dark, and we waited for his arrival in the shrine room, wrapped in blankets to protect us from the cold. Above the shrine was a large painting of Amitabha Buddha, its red and gold colors glowing in the candlelight. When everyone was assembled, a slim figure in monastic robes entered the room, looking so young that I could hardly believe this was really Trungpa Rinpoche. He moved like a dancer, silently and gracefully; and when he prostrated himself before the shrine, his simultaneous dignity and humility produced an extraordinary effect. There was something extremely touching as well as awe-inspiring about him, and I was deeply moved. In a way that is impossible to describe, he appeared to be the living form of the painted Amitabha. I had met several genuine and impressive spiritual teachers before, but as I watched Rinpoche, I thought that I had never seen anyone who radiated such presence and awareness.

When we met later that morning, I felt as though we had already known each other for a long time. He gave me a room to work in, and set aside some time every day to answer my questions. One day he asked me if I had read the *Tibetan Book of the Dead*. I replied that I had looked at the translation but was not particularly impressed by it, and he simply remarked that it would be good to read it in Tibetan. But I assumed that the book was only addressed to the dead and dying, and I was not really interested in the question of what happens after death; I had no premonition of the important part the book would play later in my life.

Soon our sessions together grew longer and longer, and we began to talk about all kinds of things. He had as many questions for me as I had for him. Since he had decided to live and work in the West, he wanted to learn all he could about its culture. He particularly liked the poetry of T. S. Eliot and had translated some of it (*The Waste Land*, I think) into Tibetan. He read me some of his own poetry in Tibetan. He had translated many of his poems with the help of his students and was also beginning to write directly in English. Sometimes we listened to music together. He was attracted by the passion and the haunting melodies of the Russian composers; Rimsky-Korsakov's *Scheherazade* was a particular favorite, perhaps as much for the stories it illustrates as for the music. He played the Tibetan flute very beautifully, and he was also an accomplished painter. Among the paintings he showed me, one of the most impressive was of a large dragon with gleaming, rainbow-colored scales, coiling through the clouds of a stormy sky. In later years he channeled his artistic talent mainly into calligraphy, for which he became renowned.

Rinpoche had spent several years in India after his escape from Tibet, and we found that we shared a love of its classical arts. I had been learning the dance form of *bharatanatyam*, and, to my embarrassment, he insisted that I demonstrate it for him. On my next visit I brought him recordings of Indian classical and folk music, which he had heard and enjoyed while he lived in India. He had met several Hindu teachers there too and said that he had interesting discussions with them about religious practice (just as later he was to engage in dialogues with Christian monks). Although he sometimes spoke out strongly against certain aspects of Hindu belief, he understood that its innermost essence transcends the concept of theism, just as Buddhism does. He was especially interested in its tantric traditions. He told me that at one point he had even considered joining a group of yogins in Varanasi, who lived just as they had for centuries, wandering around the holy places and practicing in forests, mountains, and cremation grounds. He had performed a divination to decide which path to take, but it indicated that he should travel to the West instead.

We both spoke a little Hindi, so we played a game of speaking it to each other, mixed with exaggerated Indian English. I was very impressed with the fact that he was able to appreciate the subtle nuances, and especially the humor, in the variations of a foreign language that he had only recently learned himself. He loved playing with words, transforming them, and making puns, which he would create visually as well as aurally, using letters rather in the manner of contemporary mobile phone text messages. For instance, he silently wrote down "Y †?" (meaning "Why cross-question?") when he felt bombarded by too much curiosity. This playfulness appears in some of his poems, especially among those that he composed later in America. He would also pick up unusual words or colorful colloquial expressions and use them as often as possible, but with complete accuracy.

He was fascinated by the characteristics of different languages. One thing that struck him as significant was the frequent use of personal pronouns in English (which applies equally to French and other European languages), compared with their rarity in Tibetan, where they appear only when necessary to avoid confusion (and not always even then). As he pointed out, it would be possible to write a whole letter in Tibetan without the word *I*. He said that the continual use of the first person had made him feel uncomfortable when he began to learn English, and he preferred the impersonal Tibetan mode of expression.

I was hoping that I might speak some Tibetan with him, but I soon gave up the attempt. His English was so good that I could not bear to waste time struggling with the difficulties of colloquial Tibetan (which is very different from the classical, written form of the tantras). However, when we worked on the Tibetan text, he seemed to enjoy getting glimpses of his own language through the eyes of a foreigner. When I came up with unexpected observations, perhaps something about the peculiarities of Tibetan spelling, Rinpoche would open his eyes wide in amazement and say, "Oh, I never thought of that!" Then he would explore this unfamiliar perception like a child with a new toy.

He was extremely interested in Sanskrit, the sacred language of the Buddha's homeland. Both in Scotland and later in the United States, he would frequently ask me about the Sanskrit equivalents of dharma terms, the names of deities, the correct version of mantras, and so on. Later on, when he produced texts for his students to use in ritual practice, he insisted that the Sanskrit be pronounced correctly. Although many lamas have a reverence for Sanskrit, not many take such care; indeed, such an attitude is quite unusual.

My original reason for approaching Rinpoche had been to receive assistance with my doctoral research on the *Guhyasamaja Tantra*. As it turned out, that tantra is not practiced in his tradition, so he was unable to answer all my questions on the text. What he gave me instead was far more valuable—a wide-ranging understanding of vajrayana. All the time, in some mysterious, unspoken way, he was transmitting an insight into the true meaning of the tantras, and I began to see him as my guru. Since I had arrived with no expectations, it appeared miraculous to have met such a master out of the blue like this. His dharma teaching at that time was informal and spontaneous, responding totally to the situation of the person he was with. This is very much in the style of the siddhas, the legendary tantric masters of medieval India. One night I had a vivid dream of him as a siddha, presiding over a ritual feast in a forest, surrounded by dakinis (embodiments of the feminine principle) and disciples. This vision remained in my mind as an image of his inner nature, and it is how I always saw him and continued to think of him.

Rinpoche had been brought up in both the Kagyü and the Nyingma traditions, whose styles of practice differ in some respects. The Nyingma school preserved the original teachings transmitted to Tibet from India in the second half of the eighth century, and is particularly associated with Padmakara (or Padmasambhava), who is known as Guru Rinpoche, the precious guru. Its highest practice is dzogchen, the "great perfection," which Rinpoche usually called, in rather unorthodox Sanskrit, maha ati. This is a teaching of direct recognition of mind, going straight to the heart of our innate awakened nature; and its spirit of directness, spontaneity, and simplicity pervades the entire path. Many of the great Nyingma teachers are householders or homeless yogins, as well as monks. Derived from later Indian developments, the Kagyü tradition is strongly monastic, and its style is more gradual and structured. Its essential practice is mahamudra, the great seal or great symbol. Through it, phenomena are seen in the state of openness as they truly are, and one's perception of the ordinary world is transformed into the pure vision of a sacred world.

Rinpoche perfectly united both strands in his teaching, while emphasizing one or the other at different times. He began his career in Britain by teaching in the Nyingma style, but only a few fortunate and well-prepared students were really able to respond to it fully. Then, in 1968, during his visit to the cave of Tagtsang in Bhutan, where Guru Rinpoche had meditated, he received a vision of the great Guru unified with the Karmapa lineage of the Kagyü, a sign that indicated the direction of his future work. He wrote down his experience in the form of a meditation practice, *The Sadhana of the Embodiment of All the Siddhas*, later renamed *The Sadhana of Mahamudra*, in which he combines both approaches, exhorting the meditator to "Fearlessly enjoy the mahamudra / And attain the experience of maha ati." After his move to the United States, he introduced vajrayana according to the Kagyü style; yet his way of life was that of a Nyingmapa householder, and everything he taught was flavored with the taste of dzogchen. The Shambhala teachings of his later years, too, are pervaded by the dzogchen spirit, which can be adapted to all sorts of conditions and appear in many different disguises.

At the time when I met Rinpoche, he was not yet famous and had only a few students, so he had the freedom to teach in a completely individual way. But unfortunately I was very slow and dull and was unable to take advantage of such a wonderful opportunity. I may have had some familiarity with the tantras, but I found his instructions, or rather the lack of them, very difficult to follow. When I asked him how to practice, he would often say, "But you know what to do, just go ahead and do it!" He taught through his whole way of being rather than just by what he said, and he used hints and symbols that one might misinterpret or even miss altogether. It was only after many years that I felt I could begin to understand some of his words and actions, a process that continues to unfold and reveal the unique quality of his teaching and the greatness of his being.

Already he was searching for a method that would reach a wider public and bring the dharma to a far greater number of people than was possible in his restricted situation at Samye Ling. About a year after I met him, he moved to the United States, and the following year I went there to join him. In America I saw completely different aspects of his personality. He was continually responding to demands on his time, meeting new students, traveling, and talking to large audiences. The display of his nature seemed to have no limits. He possessed an astonishing ability to communicate with everyone he met—scientists, artists, academics, dropouts, the whole range of humanity—in their own language, so to speak. The key to this diversity of his nature was his complete openness of mind and his curiosity about everything around him, which enabled him to reach out to all kinds of people and enter into any situation, no matter how strange it might seem. He could see into people's hearts and enter their worlds without preconceptions, recognizing in them the potential for awakening. Since all his relationships were driven by his total dedication to dharma, everything he said and did was a teaching for that particular situation, often in a very subtle way. His whole life exemplified the ideal of the bodhisattva, who plays whatever part is necessary to help all living beings.

Fortunately I arrived at Tail of the Tiger just in time for the seminar Rinpoche gave on the *Tibetan Book of the Dead*. The literal translation of the book's Tibetan title is *Liberation through Hearing in the Bardo* (in-between state). It is one of the "hidden treasure" texts *(terma)* of the Nyingma school, believed to have been composed by Guru Rinpoche himself and then concealed. It was discovered and written down by Karma Lingpa in the fourteenth century. In 1925 the first English version was published, translated by Lama Kazi Dawa-Samdup and edited by W. Y. Evans-Wentz.

During the seminar, Rinpoche translated from the Tibetan text and offered commentary while the audience followed along in the Evans-Wentz translation. But he found the translation very unsatisfactory and frequently disagreed with the editor's comments and interpretations. In spite of his criticisms, it is worth mentioning that Rinpoche understood the great difficulties faced by these pioneer translators, and he very much appreciated the contribution that Evans-Wentz had made to the spread of Buddhism in the West. However, he felt very strongly the necessity of a more accurate version and suggested that we should do one together, which led to the publication in 1975 of our joint translation of the *Tibetan Book of the Dead*. As Rinpoche remarked in the book's foreword, the Trungpa lineage has been involved in the transmission of the *Tibetan Book of the Dead* since shortly after its discovery. His very brief account raises some historical questions, but unfortunately none of us thought to ask him about it in more detail. However, it seems clear that his predecessors had a close connection with this terma and that it was particularly dear to his heart. Appropriately, it contains both dzogchen and mahamudra instructions, while being thoroughly pervaded by the essential dzogchen view.

Translating it was an extraordinary experience. To work intensively on such a text is wonderful enough, but to study it with someone who has realized its essence in his own life is an extraordinary privilege. Naturally quite a lot of our time was taken up with textual matters; and on this level, working with him was a delight because of his interest in language. He had an unusual ability to understand the problems faced by translators, such as the significance of grammatical details and subtle ambiguities of meaning. He also recognized the importance of being faithful to the text and avoiding the temptation to interpret or elaborate as part of a translation.

Rinpoche was extremely concerned about how best to present dharma without distorting or diluting it, yet in a way that would be relevant to the modern world. Unhappy with many of the accepted translations of Buddhist terminology, which often dated back to the early translations of Pali texts, he was experimenting with alternatives. We had fascinating discussions about the subtle implications of various words and phrases and the associations they suggested. He wanted to avoid words that he associated with Theosophy or with the New Age movement of the sixties. Equally, he rejected words that were strongly identified with Christianity. Some of these he felt could not be separated from a theistic attitude, while others conveyed the sense of guilt that he found to be so damaging in the lives of many of his students. He often remarked that Buddhism emphasizes basic goodness instead of original sin. In order to convey this concept, Rinpoche adopted some of the language of psychology in preference to religious language. He described the awakened state as basic sanity, and life in samsara as a condition of neurosis. But I never felt entirely happy with this vocabulary. Looking back, it seems to me that a psychological view of life was typical of the 1970s, just as what Rinpoche called "the love and light approach" was a feature of the previous decade; and it now appears equally dated. Rinpoche's choice of certain words could be startling and effective in his talks, but they are not necessarily always suitable for translating traditional texts.

When we came across particularly interesting passages, Rinpoche was always ready to go further than was strictly necessary for our work and to leap into the boundlessly fascinating realm of the text's inner meaning.

Then he would often become inspired and talk about his own teachers, his experiences, and the profound teachings of dzogchen. At such times I had the sense of entering the presence of a higher dimension of awareness. It seems to me now that he was continuously radiating the power of mind-to-mind transmission. This power, or atmosphere, that he created was the ceaseless, spontaneous communication of his essential nature. Soon afterward in India, a lama asked me (in English), "Does Trungpa Rinpoche give good initiations?" I was not quite sure what he meant, as *initiation* is sometimes used as a translation of *abhisheka,* the ceremony of empowerment into the practice of a deity, which Rinpoche had not yet performed in America (*initiation* is one of the words that Rinpoche disliked, and he was the first to use *empowerment* in this context). But *initiation* also is used to refer to less formal transmissions or pointing-out instructions, which can occur spontaneously at any time; and remembering those experiences of direct contact with awareness, I unhesitatingly answered yes.

Rinpoche's interpretation of the *Tibetan Book of the Dead,* right from the start, was to treat it not as part of a ritual for the dead but as instructions for the living, to be put into practice here and now. He referred to it as the "Tibetan Book of Birth," or a "Book of Space," because its teachings relate to the principle of birth and death taking place at every moment, within the environment of basic space. Here space does not mean physical space but the experience of openness, boundlessness, and absence of ego, containing all potentialities within itself. That which is continually dying and being born is the ego, along with its whole subjective world. Our awareness is continuously arising from and dissolving back into that spaciousness at every instant of our existence. Instead of perceiving the true nature of reality, we try to "solidify space," as Rinpoche put it, and thus we become entangled in a world created from our own projections.

The title *Liberation through Hearing in the Bardo* alludes to the promise made in the book that anyone who hears this teaching, even without understanding it, will be liberated. Rinpoche commented that even if one has doubts, or else if one simply has an open mind toward the teaching, a sudden glimpse of awakening is possible through its great power. And this liberation, this glimpse of the awakened state that is our own true nature, occurs during the bardo. Bardo is the gap between the cessation of one state and the arising of another. Rinpoche emphasized that it refers not only to the period after death but to each moment of our lives. He called it "the immediate experience of nowness," the present moment that continually exists between past and future. Traditionally there are six bardos, which define certain transitional periods or intervals of suspension. These are the bardo of dying, the moment between life and death; the bardo of dharmata, when the mind is absorbed in the true nature of reality; the bardo of existence (or becoming), in which we enter a new embodiment; the bardo of this life (or birth), the interval between birth and death; and within the bardo of this life, the bardos of dream and of meditation, both states of suspension from ordinary waking consciousness.

The book begins with the bardo of dying, when all the constituent elements of a living being dissolve until only the most subtle dimension of consciousness remains in its natural, fundamental state of luminosity. If one can recognize this and rest in it without giving rise to any new subjective fantasies or projections, one is awakened. Next, the bardo of dharmata is a description of the dzogchen vision of how phenomena arise from the basic ground of reality, which is continuously and spontaneously expressing its nature as energy. It appears first as light of five colors, the subtle form of the five elements, from which arise the deities of the five buddha families. Through ignorance of its own true nature, the individual consciousness perceives them as external. Instead of merging with them, it reacts with fear and tries to escape, resulting in ever more terrifying hallucinations. Finally, in the bardo of existence, if one is unable to recognize the deities as oneself, one is drawn back through the power of past actions into the cycle of the six realms.

Rinpoche was to develop all these themes much further over the next few years; yet even in the short space of that seminar, he revealed them in a totally new light—as vital and vivid aspects of our own experience. He had an unequaled skill in bringing to life the concepts and images of this strange new world, in demonstrating the connections among them and making them relevant to everyday life and practice. During these intensive periods, he made us live the teachings, not just listen to them. I particularly remember the powerful effect of his words when he described the process of dying—the total dissolution of the ego, which is actually occurring continuously here and now—and the state of confusion, panic, and uncertainty that follows. It immediately became apparent that, as he says in the Commentary, the book is not primarily about the death of the body but is concerned with "a completely different concept of death."

Very soon after the seminar on the *Tibetan Book of the Dead*, Rinpoche gave another, titled "The Six States of Bardo." It took place at a beautiful site in the Rocky Mountains of Colorado, where the participants slept in log cabins or tents around a large central hall in which the talks and meditation sessions were held. The setting was magnificent, simultaneously down to earth in its living conditions and tremendously inspiring in the midst of such glorious surroundings. But the teachings that he gave and the way in which he made them intensely personal were utterly unexpected.

In this seminar he related the six traditional bardos to the six realms: the spheres of existence of gods, jealous gods, humans, animals, hungry ghosts, and hell beings. He treated them not as external realms at all, but totally as states of mind, our various styles of confusion. In this context a bardo is like a highlight, an interval of suspension between two opposite extremes, resulting from the intensification of the emotions that characterize the six realms. He spoke of the very thin line between madness and sanity, the -sense of uncertainty, when one experiences these highlights, between the possibility of enlightenment and the fear of becoming insane.

Rinpoche devoted a day each to describing the six bardos and their associated realms. By some magical process, which far transcended the actual words he spoke, he enabled us to experience the particular emotion associated with each one. I do not know if everyone felt this to the same extent, or if some people were immune to the effect, but certainly many of us began behaving in bizarre and uncharacteristic ways. The peaceful, meditative mood of the first few days, which seemed like paradise, gave way to an atmosphere of uncertainty and frustration. Surges of suspicion and jealousy arose, and quarrels broke out over the smallest matters. This seesaw of emotional turmoil was shocking and at times terrifying. One day feelings of sexual desire seemed overwhelming, and the next was filled with anger and aggression for no apparent reason. Some people reacted with depression and refused to take part at all, while others became hysterical. Naturally much of this unrestrained emotion was directed toward Rinpoche himself, who remained absolutely calm and cheerful amid the turmoil that surrounded him. I can still remember the vividness of it all, and the bewilderment I felt until I realized what was really taking place: all this display was like a magic show, created before our eyes in order to demonstrate the illusory nature of passion, aggression, and delusion.

The essence of the bardo teachings is to recognize the gap, or moment of openness, that occurs at the extremes of these emotions. At that point we have the opportunity to let go into the space from which they arise and into which they dissolve again. And these sudden, illuminating glimpses of openness were also part of the experience that Rinpoche transmitted to us. These encounters with a totally different kind of perception brought home to us in the most direct way possible that the realms and the bardos are not external worlds but are created by our own minds. They imprison us because we grasp at them, we believe in their reality, we solidify them. Rinpoche would return to the theme of the six realms again and again in the course of his teaching, so that we came to know them as an intrinsic part of our experience.

The mandala of the five buddha families, which lies at the heart of the *Tibetan Book of the Dead,* became one of the most important components of Rinpoche's teaching. The energy of the five families is neutral; it pervades the whole of existence in both the confused and enlightened states. For buddhas it manifests as five modes of knowledge, known as the five wisdoms; whereas for ordinary sentient beings it appears as their distorted and confused emotions, the five poisons. Rinpoche applied the principles of the five families to every possible aspect of life and showed us how to recognize them in our states of mind, in nature, in activities, in art, and so forth. He had become enthusiastic about photography and would take photographs to illustrate the characteristics of the families: for instance, the sharp vajra quality of angular shapes outlined against the sky or the seductive padma quality of a sunset. But the most important application of this system is as a powerful tool for understanding ourselves and others. Combining it with the bardos and the realms, he created a complete spiritual psychology of transformation.

The vajrayana deities—male and female buddhas in their peaceful, wrathful, or passionate manifestations, bodhisattvas, dakinis, and all the other divine beings—became real and vivid presences in our lives, embodying the qualities and activities of the awakened state. When Rinpoche gave teachings on the dharma protectors or the feminine principle, whose energy can be dangerous and unpredictable, anything could happen. Natural phenomena, accidents, coincidences—all kinds of events—became significant, sometimes in striking and dramatic ways. This way of seeing opened our eyes to the reality of the sacred world around us.

Rinpoche's teaching never remained in the realm of theory; his presentation of dharma was unique, and one always felt that it flowed directly from personal experience. His way of conveying the principles of Buddhism was not always traditional in form, but it inspired great faith in its authenticity. Yet he never gave the impression of handing down the truth in a dogmatic or dictatorial manner. He always encouraged his students to read widely, to learn as much as possible, and continually to ask questions. In contrast to the disparaging opinions expressed about Western students by some lamas, he said that he preferred teaching them because of their curiosity and outspokenness; he felt that Tibetan students were inhibited by custom from asking contentious questions or freely expressing their doubts.

Above all, he emphasized the importance of meditation as being the only way to go beyond intellectual understanding to genuine realization. There are many different methods of meditation in Buddhism, and many techniques for dealing with the problems—sleepiness, restlessness, boredom, discomfort, and so forth—that arise while practicing meditation. Rinpoche made practically no use of these techniques but insisted on the direct approach of simply relating to the nature of mind. Nor did he ever encourage his students to perform any practices directed toward worldly aims such as health or success; rather, he taught that one's own mind is the source of all fulfillment and attainments. Realization of awareness, the true nature of mind, is the one and only thing that is needed—above all at the moment of death. When our body and our senses dissolve, and everything we are used to abandons us, then we shall have to meet the essence of mind face to face. From his own experience, Trungpa Rinpoche exclaims in his *Sadhana of Mahamudra:* "The joy of spontaneous awareness, which is with me all the time, / Is not this your smiling face, O Karma Padmakara?" His whole life was dedicated to helping others so that they could realize this joyful state of naked awareness for themselves.

The fundamental message of the *Tibetan Book of the Dead* is the recognition of our own mind as awakened mind, the mind of the Buddha. And the instruction that the book gives again and again is to let go—of grasping in all its forms, of our desire and hatred, of our hope and fear—and to rest in our own awakened nature. This is the essence of Trungpa Rinpoche's teaching, which he presented in many different ways to suit the capacities of his students. And it is the way he lived his own life: never clinging to the past, never held back by regrets, he was always ready to go forward into the next phase of his journey with the intention of benefiting all beings. Even now that he has left this life, his presence is still profoundly felt in the lives of his students, and his influence on the transmission of dharma to the West is becoming more and more evident. To quote the *Sadhana* once again: "the power of his blessing can never be diminished."

Transforming Psychology

The Development of
Maitri Space Awareness Practice

JUDITH L. LIEF

If we are willing to take an unbiased look, we will find that, in spite of all our problems and confusion, all our emotional and psychological ups and downs, there is something basically good about our existence as human beings.
—Chögyam Trungpa, *Shambhala: The Sacred Path of the Warrior*, p. 29

MAITRI, SANSKRIT FOR "loving-kindness," is the foundation upon which Chögyam Trungpa Rinpoche based his teaching, his view of human psychology, and the unique therapeutic form he created, called Maitri Space Awareness practice. *Maitri* is defined as both kindness to others and self-kindness; it is the quality of "basic goodness" that marks our experience at its deepest level. Trungpa Rinpoche developed Maitri Space Awareness practice as a tool for cultivating this kindness, based on the subtleties of vajrayana Buddhist psychology and meditation practices. Space awareness practice was initially presented in the context of creating a residential therapeutic community. Later, Maitri Space Awareness practice was adapted as a powerful contemplative training method not only for therapists, but also for artists, educators, and meditation practitioners.

Encountering Western Psychology

... we could say that the hospitality created by the interest and efforts of Western psychologists is what has made it possible for us now to present a proper and full understanding of Buddhism on this continent.

—Chögyam Trungpa, "Creating an Environment of Sanity,"
in *The Sanity We Are Born With*, p. 143

Throughout his teaching career, Trungpa Rinpoche met with psychologists and therapists of many traditions. Deeply interested in cognitive psychology, psychotherapy, and transpersonal psychology, he devoted considerable energy to comparing and integrating Buddhist and Western views of the mind and emotions. He saw a natural link between psychology and meditation practice in their common quest for self-knowledge and sanity and their shared emphasis on compassion and caring for others. At the same time, he was careful not to blur the boundaries between meditation practice and therapy, viewing each as a distinct approach with differing goals and accomplishments. Trungpa Rinpoche discussed the nature of mind and the therapeutic process with leading therapists and psychologists, including Bruno Bettelheim, R. D. Laing, Gregory Bateson, Ken Wilber, and Stan Grof, and cognitive scientists such as Francisco Varela, Humberto Maturana, and Eleanor Rosch. His integration of psychology and spirituality also attracted the attention of the early humanistic psychologists Tony Sutich and Sonja Margulies, who was the editor of the *Journal of Transpersonal Psychology*. In searching for a language and a metaphor that would speak to his Western students, and seeing the power of psychology in contemporary Western thought and in the worldview of the man on the street, Chögyam Trungpa settled upon the language of psychology as a skillful way to present the teachings of Tibetan Buddhism in modern Western culture.

The Psychological Metaphor

Basic sanity applies to every person, no matter how disturbed he or she may seem.

—Chögyam Trungpa, "Creating an Environment of Sanity,"
in *The Sanity We Are Born With*, p. 151

In 1968 Trungpa Rinpoche went on a meditation retreat in Bhutan, at a famous cave once used by the great teacher Padmasambhava. At the time, he had been living in Britain for several years, studying at Oxford, and beginning to take on Western students. After his retreat, Trungpa completely changed the way in which he taught. He systematically began to remove any and all barriers between himself and his students. He no longer wore Tibetan monastic robes or taught in Tibetan, but began to teach in English and dress in Western attire. He adopted the lifestyle of a householder, married a young student, and immersed himself in Western culture and its forms. Many early students were unable to weather such a change and left. Trungpa Rinpoche and his wife, Diana Mukpo, decided to move to the United States and make a fresh start.

In late-1960s America, there was rampant fascination with the cultural trappings of Buddhism, accompanied by a romantic view of spirituality and an attachment to religiosity, all of which Trungpa called the trap of spiritual materialism. He was deeply concerned that his Western students' attraction to Tibet, their rejection of their own culture, and their hunger for special experiences would cause them to miss the essential point of the teachings. To truly understand Buddhism, he thought, it was essential that students cut through this view.

In his search for a metaphor free from spiritual materialism, Trungpa Rinpoche began using the language and imagery of Western psychology, presenting the Buddhist teachings not so much as a religion but as a practice and way of life. For instance, in keeping with his intention to use accessible contemporary language, he preferred the psychological terms *sanity* and *neurosis* to more religious or doctrinal terms such as enlightenment and bewilderment. He described Buddhist path as a journey from neurosis to brilliant sanity, a rediscovery of the sun of wisdom that is our birthright; and he made it clear that the most effective way to uncover that inherent sanity was through the practice of meditation. So, rather than being presented as a religious exercise, meditation practice was taught as a powerful methodology enabling students to look directly into the nature of both wisdom and confusion.

In Trungpa's approach, topics usually presented in terms of Buddhist cosmology were instead introduced as subtle psychological processes or states of mind. For instance, Buddhism posits the literal existence of the six realms of suffering, which are inhabited by beings such as gods, jealous gods, humans, animals, hungry ghosts, and hell beings. Trungpa portrayed these states as mental/physical realities we create, inhabit, buy into, and endlessly cycle through. Likewise, he taught the famous text known as the *Tibetan Book of the Dead,* not only as a guide to be read to the dying, but as a complete map of the mind with its interplay of sanity and insanity, pointing out its relevance to how we live our lives, not just to how we die and what happens thereafter. In discussing the bardo, or intermediate state, instead of focusing only on the transition between death and rebirth, Trungpa introduced the various bardos as psychological experiences of potent uncertainty that occur throughout our everyday life. He presented them as unsettling and groundless experiences of no-man's land yet as powerful turning points that could be opportunities for awakening.

In his approach to psychology, Trungpa Rinpoche was careful to ground his students in an understanding of the development of ego-fixation and the different patterns that it takes. He undercut the common view that sanity can be discovered apart from neurosis, emphasizing the primacy of sanity and how neurosis arises from within sanity itself. This common origin of neurosis and sanity allows for the process of transformation to occur, so that the very energies that trouble us become the forces we use for awakening and insight.

Through his choice of language and skillful use of psychological metaphor, Trungpa Rinpoche was able to demystify Tibetan Buddhist teachings and make them accessible to Western students. His penetrating presentation helped students realize the essential point of Buddhist teachings and practice, which is to transform one's state of mind and become more self-aware, compassionate, and skillful, for the benefit of oneself and others.

Plans for a Therapeutic Community

It is important for the therapist to create an atmosphere which makes people feel welcome. That attitude should infuse the whole environment. That is the point.

—Chögyam Trungpa, "Becoming a Full Human Being,"
in *The Sanity We Are Born With,* p. 141

In 1972, during the early days of the Boulder sangha, Trungpa Rinpoche established a theater group and a psychology group. Community members joined one of the two, meeting weekly to study and practice. Rinpoche introduced students in the theater group to "mudra theater practice," a sequence of exercises designed to heighten and intensify one's awareness of space, form, and energy. He instructed students in the psychology group to examine in depth the development of ego-fixation, the five wisdoms and their corresponding neuroses, the six realms of existence, and the experience of bardo. Inspired by the idea of a therapeutic community—as envisioned in the writings of psychologist Maxwell Jones and others—students in the psychology group began to explore the possibility of establishing a therapeutic community informed by the Buddhist teachings they had received from Rinpoche on the nature of mind and emotions.

Meanwhile, Trungpa Rinpoche had made a strong connection with the Zen master Shunryu Suzuki Roshi. Both teachers had noticed that meditation centers tended to attract a number of students who were emotionally unstable. They began a dialogue on how best to work with such students, who were drawn to the dharma but, due to their psychological state at the time, not able to begin formal Buddhist practice. Although the two teachers had begun to discuss a way of working together to address this issue, Suzuki Roshi unfortunately passed away before any joint project could take form.

Trungpa Rinpoche continued exploring the possibility of establishing a therapeutic community, engaging the support and expertise of students in the psychology group, particularly psychologists Marvin Casper and John Baker. The idea at the time was to create a household in which meditation practitioners and clients would live together—sharing work, practicing, and studying. The goal was to create an environment that was solid, simple, and sane, so that the resident clients could be healed through the companionship, mindfulness, and earthy practicality of communal living.

Patterns of Space and Energy

We have to be brave enough to actually encounter our emotions, work with them, in a real sense, feel their texture, the real quality of the emotions as they are. We discover that the emotion actually does not exist as it appears, but it contains wisdom and open space.

—Chögyam Trungpa, *Cutting Through Spiritual Materialism* (1973), p. 236

In February 1973, two major events were convened by Trungpa Rinpoche in Boulder: a theater conference and a psychology conference. In attendance were meditation practitioners and students of Trungpa Rinpoche as well as leading figures in the fields of theater and psychology. The Psychology Conference provided an opportunity to advance both conceptual and practical plans for the therapeutic community, which was scheduled to open in the fall of 1973. Trungpa Rinpoche chose the name Maitri Therapeutic Community, since the approach would be grounded in the Buddhist principle of maitri, or loving-kindness, the central energy of awakening and healing.

It was at the Psychology Conference that Trungpa Rinpoche first introduced Maitri Space Awareness. This practice has its theoretical basis in the Tibetan vajrayana teachings on the nature of mind, particularly those addressing the relationship between enlightened (or awake) mind and confused (or neurotic) mind. According to these teachings, the same basic energies can lead to either confusion or awakening, depending on one's willingness to let go of ego-clinging and self-absorption, and enter into the greater space of nonduality. In other words, the energies themselves are neutral but can be expressed in both neurotic and sane ways.

The energies underlying both confusion and awakening are grouped into five categories, called the five buddha families. Each of these families of energy has a confused manifestation and an awake manifestation, which are like two sides of the same coin. On the confused side are the core emotional patterns of ignorance, aggression, greed, passion, and envy; on the awakened side are the wisdom of all-encompassing space, mirrorlike wisdom, the wisdom of equanimity, discriminating-awareness wisdom, and the wisdom of all-accomplishing action (see the diagram). The environment in which these energies operate is said to have three main characteristics: it is indestructible, it accommodates birth and death, and it creates obstacles. In *The Sadhana of Mahamudra*, Trungpa Rinpoche described this space as "boundless equanimity which has never changed," and as being "unified into a single circle, beyond confusion." At the 1973 Psychology Conference, he referred to space as "the most existent property of all." The Maitri Space Awareness practice is based on the interplay of energy and space, in particular, the five energies and the fundamental space that accommodates them.

The five energies manifest not only in psychological states of neurosis and sanity, but also are connected with the five elements: earth, water, fire, wind, and space. (Here space refers simply to one of the elements, not to the more encompassing notion of space as contrasted to energy, which accommodates all five elements.) In fact, all phenomena are pervaded by these energies. The five energies are associated with colors, senses, seasons, times of day, landscapes, parts of the body, musical

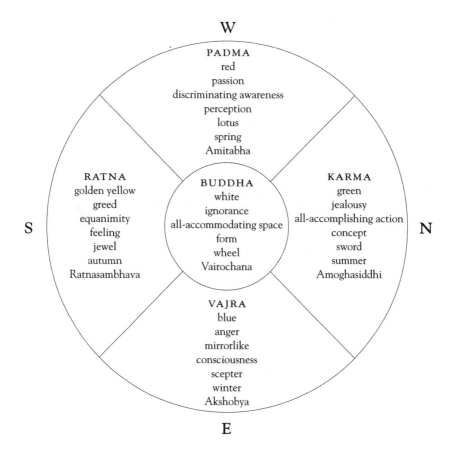

pitches, components of the self (the skandhas), styles of teaching, and stages of life. In Tibetan iconography, the pattern, or mandala, of the five buddha families is a central theme, represented diagrammatically (as on page 279) or by an array of deities.

The Maitri Space Awareness practice involves assuming particular postures in a series of five rooms, each room evoking one of the five basic energies. Four of the five rooms have windows that reflect the color of the room into the space within it. The fifth, windowless room is all white. A practitioner typically maintains each posture for about forty-five minutes. In describing the use of space, time, and energy in this practice, Trungpa Rinpoche said that the space accommodates sanity, the time duration is the healing mechanism, and the energies are the fuel of both wisdom and neurosis. The practice instructions are minimal. Students are advised that while in the room and maintaining the appropriate posture, they are simply to experience what they experience, without trying to make anything happen.

After practicing in a particular room, the practitioner exits the room and engages in ten minutes of "aimless wandering," during which there is no attempt to review the experience of the posture and room or to analyze the process intellectually. Instead, the student simply allows the energy evoked by the practice to flow as it chooses. As simply and effortlessly as possible, trying neither to think nor to cut off thinking, the student wanders about or sits quietly. The only stipulation is that the student must remain quiet and refrain from interacting or engaging in discussions. Between the practice session and later study and discussion, aimless wandering inserts a reflective pause, in which the student is a silent and lone wanderer within the energy and space of his or her immediate reality.

According to Trungpa, the idea of working with the energies of the five buddha families in this way came to him during a seminar on "crazy wisdom" held in December 1972 at Jackson Hole, Wyoming. As Trungpa Rinpoche was relaxing in his hotel room with a group of students, one student started frantically dancing about. Trungpa Rinpoche was quite fond of this brilliant but troubled student and on many occasions had gently helped him settle his rather manic energy. As the student's dancing and singing became more and more loud, complaints about the noise started to come from people in the hotel rooms above and below. Trungpa became acutely aware of the claustrophobia of being in a "box" stacked between other boxes. On the spot, he composed a spontaneous poem about the ways in which rooms, windows, and emotional energies are related to each other. He later connected this basic observation with his training in Tibetan yoga and psychology, in particular the teaching of the five buddha families. And out of that came the details of the rooms, postures, colors, and windows.

The first family, called the buddha family, is connected with the neurosis of ignorance and the wisdom of all-encompassing space. The corresponding room is small and cube-shaped, about seven by seven feet, and has no windows. It is white in color and soft white light diffuses into the room from the ceiling. In the buddha posture, one kneels on elbows and knees, head resting on hands, the gaze downward.

The second family, called vajra, or scepter, is connected with the neurosis of aggression and the clear reflection of mirrorlike wisdom. The vajra room is blue, with a series of slot-shaped windows. One assumes the vajra posture by lying prone with arms straight out and legs slightly spread, the gaze turned left toward the windows.

The ratna, or jewel, family is connected with the neurosis of greed and the wisdom of equanimity. The ratna room is yellow with a large circular window on one wall. The student lies supine with arms and legs spread wide, feet toward the window.

The padma, or lotus, family is connected with neurosis of passion, in the sense of seduction and clinging. Padma is associated with the wisdom of discriminating awareness. The padma room is red with a rectangular window on one wall. The prescribed posture is to lie on one's left side, with knees slightly tucked up and head resting on the left arm.

The fifth family—the karma, or action, family—is associated with the neurosis of envy and competitiveness, and the wisdom of all-accomplishing action. The karma room is green. Unlike the other rooms, which are cube-shaped, the shape of the karma room is like a cube topped by a pyramid. The ceiling of the karma room rises to a point at the center of the top; at that point there is a small window. The karma posture is arrow-shaped; one lies supine with legs extended straight and parallel, feet pointed and held together, and arms making a V shape.

The Five Buddha Families in Maitri Space Awareness

BUDDHA
Color: white
Neurosis: ignorance
Wisdom: all-accommodating space
Room: small white cube with no window
Posture: on elbows and knees, chin resting on hands

VAJRA
Color: blue
Neurosis: anger
Wisdom: mirrorlike
Room: blue cube with narrow window slats
Posture: on stomach, arms spread to side, facing window

RATNA
Color: golden yellow
Neurosis: greed
Wisdom: equanimity
Room: yellow cube with one large round window
Posture: on back, spread-eagled, feet toward window

PADMA
Color: red
Neurosis: passion
Wisdom: discriminating awareness
Room: red cube with rectangular window
Posture: on side, curled, facing window

KARMA
Color: green
Neurosis: jealousy
Wisdom: all-accomplishing action
Room: green cube with pyramid-shaped ceiling,
window at the very top
Posture: on back, legs straight and arms at angle
forming arrow shape

In the context of plans for establishing a therapeutic community, the introduction of Maitri Space Awareness practice was a completely unexpected development as far as the students were concerned. Participants at the Psychology Conference found the concept of space awareness practice was difficult to comprehend, and it was hard for them to see the value of holding odd postures in strangely designed rooms. Trungpa Rinpoche's earlier teachings on the fundamentals of Buddhist psychology had seemed so much more graspable and down to earth. It soon became evident, however, that practicing the five postures had the power to evoke a very personal, direct, nonverbal understanding of the five buddha families and to provide a clear glimpse into the nature and quality of one's own style of sanity and neurosis.

After the conference, the members of the psychology group continued their study of Buddhist psychology and went ahead with plans to establish a therapeutic community. Trungpa Rinpoche encouraged the study of the buddha families in depth. The instructions he gave for how to sense a person's particular pattern of energy were to run one's hands over that person's body, an inch or two above the surface, sensing the quality of energy present. Scanning a person in this way made it possible to diagnose his or her predominant buddha family energy and to assign the appropriate room and posture for Maitri Space Awareness practice. With varying degrees of success, the students in the psychology group practiced this technique on one another and used it in the diagnosis of early clients of the therapeutic community. This part of the practice was later discontinued, as few students felt confident in their ability to sense the energies clearly or make accurate diagnoses.

In the autumn of 1973, a group of students moved to a small farmhouse near Elizabethtown, New York, to establish the first Maitri Therapeutic Community, and began construction of the first set of maitri rooms. Clients were diagnosed with the scanning technique and practiced their posture once a day. Everyone there participated in the day-to-day activities of the community. Staff members also practiced space awareness daily. In these early days of the community, there were usually one or two clients and a staff of eight to ten. In the spring of 1974, the Maitri Therapeutic Community moved to a lovely piece of property donated by Lex and Sheila Hixon, in Wingdale, New York. The first set of maitri rooms, almost complete, was disassembled and taken to the new location to be reconstructed.

The practice of space awareness proved to be powerful and challenging, provoking the five basic energies very directly in staff members and clients alike. Each practitioner's predominant emotional habit pattern became more and more clarified and heightened, resulting in a highly charged "pressure-cooker" environment. After a time, it became apparent that members of the staff would need further training in psychotherapy, both Eastern and Western, before they could harness this intensified energy as a force for healing those with deep neurotic disturbances. Trungpa Rinpoche, in consultation with the Maitri staff, decided that further groundwork needed to be laid before the facility took on any more clients.

Psychology at Naropa

We should work with our neuroses, relate with them, and experience them properly. They are the only potential we have, and when we begin to work with them, we see that we can use them as stepping-stones.

— Chögyam Trungpa, *Journey without Goal*, p. 85

Initially, the Maitri experiment began to transform itself from a therapeutic community to a learning center, no longer taking on clients, but instead offering workshops in Buddhist psychology and training in Maitri Space Awareness practice. Here, too, the need for greater depth of psychological training became evident, training in which Maitri Space Awareness practice would be accompanied by the rigorous study of Buddhist and Western psychology. Trungpa Rinpoche had recently established Naropa Institute in Boulder, Colorado, as a summer institute, upper-divisional college, and graduate school. And it was Naropa that became the venue for the kind of in-depth training that Maitri staff members had sensed they needed. In 1976, Trungpa Rinpoche, together with Dr. Edward Podvoll and Dr. Antonio Wood, two leading psychotherapists and meditation practitioners, established Naropa Institute's master's program in clinical psychotherapy.

The master's degree in contemplative psychotherapy required coursework in Buddhist and Western psychology and internships in the field of mental health. In addition, students participated in an intensive three-month residential learning program in which they engaged in rigorous periods of meditation practice and Maitri Space Awareness practice. The self-knowledge and understanding generated by this intensive training provided students with personal resources essential to their work as therapists. The rigor of this training complemented their intellectual study in the classroom. To this day, Maitri Space Awareness practice, classroom study, and supervised internships remain the central components of Naropa's contemplative psychotherapy program.

In 1980, the *Naropa Institute Journal of Psychology* (later called the *Journal of Contemplative Psychotherapy*) began annual publication, addressing the theoretical and clinical dimensions of the encounter between Western and Eastern psychology. Through the efforts of Dr. Edward Podvoll and his student Jeff Fortuna, the program also gave birth to the Windhorse model of home-based care for psychotic persons. This model utilizes Eastern and Western modalities of care in the context of a compassionate and grounded household setting. Later, Dr. Fortuna founded the Windhorse Therapeutic Community, now located in Northampton, Massachusetts, based on the Windhorse model of home-based care and on his training at Naropa.

Maitri Rooms and Colored Glasses

Because Maitri Space Awareness practice is based on a set of five postures, each associated with a room of a particular shape and color, separate sets of maitri rooms had to be designed and built for the Maitri Therapeutic Community and the Naropa Institute to accommodate the practice. Naropa University currently has one set of maitri rooms on campus. Shambhala Mountain Center, a rural practice center in Colorado, houses a beautiful pair of maitri buildings, each with a set of five rooms. In addition, portable practice rooms have sometimes been used to allow programs to be offered in other locales.

Over time it became obvious that the paucity of rooms available for maitri practice severely limited the dissemination of these teachings. To remedy this, a portable variant of maitri practice was developed in which students assumed the postures while wearing glasses with lenses tinted in the colors of the five maitri rooms. With the specially designed rooms no longer a requirement, Maitri Space Awareness could now be taught and practiced virtually anywhere.

Maitri in the Arts and Education

Other departments at Naropa University also make use of Maitri Space Awareness practice and the maitri rooms. The creative arts faculty uses maitri practice to explore how color, space, emotional energy, and the creative process relate to one another. In Naropa's early childhood education program, the practice helps to elucidate teaching styles, learning styles, and patterns of classroom energy. Performing artists, musicians, and writers have also found inspiration in this approach, which evokes the very energies that fuel artistic discovery and expression.

Conclusion

> According to Buddhist teachings, although we acknowledge that people's problems may have been caused by their past upbringing, we feel that the way to undo problems is to cultivate that person's maitri on the spot.
>
> — Chögyam Trungpa, "Creating an Environment of Sanity,"
> in *The Sanity We Are Born With*, p. 146

Chögyam Trungpa Rinpoche pioneered the exploration of how Tibetan Buddhism's psychological teachings and meditative practices can creatively intersect with the insights of Western psychology. Rinpoche's primary interest in this regard was to develop a practical synthesis of the two traditions. From the early days of the psychology group to the establishment of the Maitri Therapeutic Community and the founding of Naropa University master's program in contemplative psychotherapy, Trungpa Rinpoche continuously mined the riches of the great Eastern and Western traditions, and valued their creative interplay.

Maitri Space Awareness practice is a powerful component of the psychological training offered at Naropa University. It gives rise to an often embarrassing recognition by students of their own pattern of neurosis, and offers a hint of the sanity lying underneath. Thus students begin Naropa's two-step educational approach of first looking into one's own patterns of heart and mind and then starting to work with those of others. As a result, when Naropa psychology students graduate and become therapists, they are able to connect with clients more genuinely and are less threatened by their own and other people's extreme states of mind.

Historically, the encounter of Trungpa Rinpoche with Western psychology and the development of Maitri Space Awareness practice has taken on many forms; but at its heart is the cultivation of loving-kindness and compassion. In the training of therapists, the self-knowledge gained by looking inward and exploring the nature of one's own mind in depth allows the therapist to develop greater acceptance, kindness, knowledge, and openness in working with clients. Maitri is what connects inner and outer understanding, therapist and client. Maitri makes genuine transformation possible.

With Tenga Rinpoche, with chakrasamvara, mandala model, Boulder, August 1986.
Photograph by Rachel Homer. Used with permission.

The Space Between

The Theater Legacy of Chögyam Trungpa

LEE WORLEY

Vajrayana: The Path of Skillful Means

Designed to be aids to the practice of meditation, hundreds of deities and mandalas mark the various vajrayana traditions of Tibet. By visualizing an image that represents one's basic nature, the practitioner tunes into that nature in its pure, nondistorted form. The mind reflects the mind back to itself. These ancient methods go directly to the heart of what meditation practice is designed to do—liberate the meditator from fixation upon and attachment to impermanent things, objects, people, or ideas. It is our attachment that causes our suffering. These deities and mandalas are "skillful means" because they have the potential to awaken us to freedom in this lifetime.

Chögyam Trungpa was a great master of these skillful means. When he met the Western consciousness, however, he understood that if students were to integrate the buddhadharma teachings into their way of being, rather than simply adopting external Tibetan forms and using these as further entertainment or what he called spiritual materialism, translations needed to be made. For example, he abandoned the life of a monk, married, and fathered children. He felt that the robes and all

that they implied were too exotic an attraction, that instead of support-
ing the message of shunyata or egolessness, they might become another
"trip."

During Chögyam Trungpa's years in the United States, he utilized
many Western forms and conventions, including business, education, and
the arts in his presentations of Buddhism. He used whatever he did as a
way to illuminate the nature of mind and phenomena. Among these many
skillful means that he designed for Westerners were several plays that he
wrote and a physical theater training that he developed for his performance students.

I first discovered this training in 1973 when I journeyed from Santa Fe
to Boulder to attend a theater conference hosted by Chögyam Trungpa
and his Mudra Theater Group. We had met once before in New York City
while I was still a working member of Joseph Chaikin's Open Theater. I remember seeing a short Asian man with a limp who spoke softly and almost
unintelligibly. Other than my impression that he could use some voice lessons, the meeting in New York was uneventful.

Around this time, one of his students visited the Open Theater Loft on
Fourteenth Street and told us a story about traveling with Chögyam
Trungpa in Bhutan where he and a Tibetan monk were serving as attendants. With Trungpa in the lead, the three of them were making their way
along the side of a cliff at night. As the student told it, the trail was very
narrow, the night quite dark, and he and the other attendant were quarrel-
ing over which of them should have the right to hold the flashlight to
light their guru's way. The disagreement went on for some time until finally Trungpa turned, snatched the flashlight from the one holding it, and
flung it over the cliff!

I was utterly intrigued by hearing about a teacher who would sacrifice
his own safety to teach his students. And so, years later, when I was invited
to the conference, I eagerly accepted the invitation. Since that time I
have studied, practiced, and taught the work that Chögyam Trungpa presented at the conference. In this article I wish to share some of the insights
into theater that I have gained through it.

Chögyam Trungpa's own performance training is briefly described in
Born in Tibet,[1] his autobiography of his early years as a young tülku, or
reincarnated teacher, his Buddhist training to become abbot of his lineage's monastery, and his harrowing escape from Tibet to the West. As

part of this education he was taught a monastic dance, a speciality of his monastery that accompanies a vajrayana sadhana, or practice. He writes that he did not consider himself a particularly good dancer, being more experienced in scholastic studies, but as abbot he was obliged to learn the dance so that he could lead the procession. The training is arduous and thorough, and the costumes lavish with heavy brocade, the dancers holding hand bells and drums. The "performance," which takes place within the monastery, is presented only for the monks. It was done only once every two years and goes on for twenty-four hours without pause. The dancers execute three hundred and sixty-five ritual movements indicating the days of the year as well as the three hundred and sixty-five obscurations that need to be overcome prior to liberation. Imagine the immense contrast between this definition of a performance and what Chögyam Trungpa encountered upon his arrival in the West!

Buddhism enters a culture subtly. Rather than imposing a set of liturgical or iconographical religious forms onto the new culture, Buddhism goes straight to the heart of the human condition and invites adherents of whatever culture to take a look at the nature of their minds. In doing so, practitioners begin to discover their culturally induced habits of thinking and assumptions about the nature of reality. As this understanding develops, practitioners are able to let go of preconceptions, becoming more adept at arising freshly in each immediate moment of nowness. They begin to shape their world from this liberated awareness. Artists may begin to find new creative expressions; teachers may begin to listen more carefully to their students; parents may begin to appreciate a child who seems "different" from them.

Chögyam Trungpa believed that art has the capacity to transform when used for purposes other than ego-gratification. His methodology included training the senses, training the mind by means of the body, and incorporating an understanding of space into the students' awareness. The Mudra training constituted skillful means for becoming aware of mind and also for becoming more embodied in performance. Buddhist concepts were thus incorporated into plays that he wrote as well as into his work with performers. Just as the peaceful and wrathful deities of Tibetan Buddhism mirror the mind, so does theater mirror society. As a master Buddhist teacher, Chögyam Trungpa aspired to hold a mirror up to the "enlightened society" within each one of us.

Space Is Outlined by Neurosis

"Fundamentally," Chögyam Trungpa says, "there is just open space, the *basic ground*, what we really are. Our most fundamental state of mind, before the creation of ego, is such that there is basic openness, basic freedom, a spacious quality; and we have now and have always had this openness."[2]

From Chögyam Trungpa's perspective, we are all neurotic. He attributes our neurosis to this very space: "We *are* this space, we are one with it. . . . But if we are this all the time, where did the confusion come from, where has the space gone, what has happened? Nothing has happened, as a matter of fact. We just became too active in that space. Because it is spacious, it brings inspiration to dance about; but our dance became a bit too active, we began to spin more than was necessary to express the space. At this point we became *self*-conscious, conscious that 'I' am dancing in the space."[3]

Out of oneness, we constantly manufacture the perception of duality. It is at this point that our neurosis begins. Because space has become other than "I," I must seduce it into dancing with me, and in doing so I solidify or fix it, denying it and myself the flowing qualities that are its nature. Chögyam Trungpa calls this event the birth of ignorance.[4] From there we build our sense of a solid, separate self and a solid-seeming reality "out there." The traditional Buddhist metaphor is of a monkey shut up in a five-windowed house (the senses) who restlessly jumps from window to window, fascinated by the exciting world "outside." As he becomes bored and desirous of new forms of entertainment, he cultivates his neurosis, attempting to seduce, repel, or ignore his world. Finally our monkey lives in a fabrication of his or her own delusion.

This view of ourselves might cause us to feel quite defeated. We might wonder what hope there is for reunion with the primordial open ground. According to the Buddhist view, at the moment of questioning we are beginning to deal with our neurosis; uncertainty begins our path toward clarifying our confusion about reality's true nature. In fact, from the vajrayana point of view, our neurosis and confusion are hardly problems. They keep us yearning for a more absolute truth. Chögyam Trungpa once proclaimed that confusion could be regarded as extremely good news! All of our chaos and confusion means that we are not fixed, not made of stone. We are alive and constantly moving, able to change and shed outworn patterns. Within the flux of our monkey minds, our open space shines forth.

It has been said that the Vajrayana teachings are especially powerful medicine in a culture in turmoil, where the intensification of the confusion surrounding self-identity leads people to question their assumptions. Thus it was that Padmasambhava brought the vajrayana dharma from India and transplanted it in Tibet, which was at the time a very rugged civilization looking for refinement. In the late 1960s and early 1970s, vajrayana came to the United States with Chögyam Trungpa, at a time when many Westerners were searching for truth, questioning their assumptions about the nature of reality. Even where no great upheaval is occurring, however, we still suffer from our attachments to the transient; our minds are still neurotic, still needing to be tamed. The dharma is always timely; space is always outlined by neurosis.

Sandcastles, a play by Chögyam Trungpa written in the early 1970s, is designed as a series of short scenes between two or three characters. Reflecting this era in North America, it echoes this searching and neurosis in absurdist form. In scene three, for example, a guru, "dressed in white and wearing numerous strands of wooden beads around his neck," is speaking with a student seated on the floor at his feet. The student, dressed in simple Western clothes, is complaining that while he has studied and practiced many sorts of yoga, he doesn't seem to be getting anywhere. He assumes that the guru can help him understand. The guru agrees, proclaiming that a good student proves that one is a good teacher.

> As the Holy Book of Cockrow says in chapter 1301 and as the Divine Book says also, "If you could balance yourself on one finger it is one of the most meritorious deeds that you could perform." After all we don't want to lay heavy burdens on our fellow beings. Your finger is the most generous outlet or crutch according to the Divine Book of Cockrow. "He who rests his divine attitude with his finger, he finds his way through the divine energy of the index finger as the Lord slew the Evil Ones through His index finger."[5]

Within this spoof on the pursuit of Eastern and Western holiness, some quality of space being outlined by neurosis reveals itself. Things are not only one way at all. There is a certain ambiguity that plays between our hopeful expectation that things will make sense and the ridiculous way things seem to appear. Nothing is spelled out for us, yet we continually suspect a message; by clinging to the anticipated message, we make our neurosis spin faster. Chögyam Trungpa once described his theater training as "harnessing the wild horses of neurosis." As in the practice of Zen koans, we wear out our conceptual frameworks until space, which has been there all along, miraculously appears.

The Step from Offstage to Onstage Is Only One Step

"The step from offstage to onstage is only one step" is one of the slogans from the Mudra Theater Group that I use in training young performers. It encourages approaching performance with a certain attitude of ordinariness, of "no big deal." Popular wisdom suggests that acting is a monumental achievement and attaining fame or wealth the goal, which only a few very special people will achieve. Thus, much of the benefit of studying and practicing art is lost. In the effort to reeducate young people so that they understand performance as a craft in which one hones one's tools, polishes one's role, and then gets out of the way, not being dependent on or discouraged by either success or failure, this slogan has been helpful. Returning playfulness to theater means that everyone on stage and off can enjoy the performance.

Taking this slogan in another direction, we could also say that the step from onstage to offstage is only one step. Trungpa's aspirations always included educating Americans about the possibility of a more sane society, a society where "there is no aggression and where people could discover their innate basic goodness and enlightened existence."[6] A senior student of Trungpa's said, "The Vidyadhara's message was that there is no time off from sacred view. All situations of gathering, meeting, and socializing were demanding opportunities for invocation, transformation, practice, and waking up."[7] In working on productions of Trungpa's plays, the rehearsal process might easily have been seen as a strong preparation for living a mindful life, if only the participants had been more aware.

Prajna is a play based on *The Heart Sutra*, a body of literature central to Mahayana Buddhism. *Prajna* is the Sanskrit word for the fundamental intelligence that sees things as they really are: empty, impermanent, and interconnected. The central idea of *The Heart Sutra* is "Form is emptiness, emptiness itself is form; emptiness is no other than form, form is no other than emptiness." The play begins with "six people dressed in white pajama-like clothing, holding brooms and facing each other at the center of the circle. They still sway to the recorder music even after it is finished. Their actions seem somewhat self-conscious and devotional. After a short time they turn outward as a group and begin sweeping the area in a choreographed pattern—out to the edge of the circle, in again, out again, and exit."[8]

This sweeping theme repeats at the end of the play, only this time by another set of people, who are dressed in maroon robes, possibly the same group now more enlightened. In an introduction to the play written by Andrew Karr, then director of the Mudra group, they are described as, "men and women who serve as uncompromising spokesmen for the teachings. Their behavior cuts through the neurotic trips of the people they confront."[9] The neurotic trips referred to include a man who is examining the solidness and stubbornness of a large rock, which he eventually lifts above his head with the aid of maroon-robed people raising and lowering long poles while they chant a portion of *The Heart Sutra*, and a ragged fisherman with an Irish brogue who reflects on the quality of his day and places small rocks around a blanket as he says, "This is for m'father. This is for m'wife. This is for m'husband," and so on. Again the maroon pole-bearers converge on him and continue the *Heart Sutra* chant. Two men enter and pull the blanket out from under the fisherman, who scrambles to collect his rocks but eventually joins in a dance with the pole-bearers. At the end, the maroon-robed pole-bearers "form a tight circle in front of the shrine. One by one they turn and sweep in a precisely stylized manner to the edge of the playing area, where each places his broom on the floor and sits facing the audience. Lights fade to black."[10]

Andrew Karr says that *Prajna* is "a simple play. . . . Our greatest problem was moving and acting with simplicity and directness—whether simply walking across the stage, lifting objects, or placing them on the altar—rather than trying to find a 'right' way of doing such things."[11] In Chögyam Trungpa's words: "The point is you don't have any philosophical background to determine how you should be acting before you act. It is quite different from getting a driver's license where you pass your training period, and then you know how to drive. In this particular thing you have nothing to relate to. You just act like any normal situation, the way any life situation happens. There's a door, there's a wall, there's a window."[12]

During the summer of 1974, while I was attending the first session of the new Naropa Institute, I was invited to watch a rehearsal of *Prajna* that the Mudra Theater Group was preparing for presentation later that summer. It was a hot and lazy afternoon, and the group was practicing in the meditation hall of their Buddhist center in downtown Boulder. I tucked myself into a corner, discreetly out of the way, and watched while eight or ten Mudra students learned to sweep the floor. Each student had a broom, and Trungpa directed each actor to first place the brush tips down at a right angle to the floor on the right side, then to pull the broom directly across in front to the left side, and then to gracefully lift the broom straight up from the floor, carry it back over to the right side, place the tips of the bristles gently down again, and repeat. This happened over and over while Trungpa moved among the group correcting posture, adjusting a grip on a broom handle, and, in one case, even demonstrating the stroke to a particularly clumsy young man. It seemed obvious to me that the group saw this exercise as a sheer waste of time but was willing to go along with what their teacher wanted them to do. As a well-trained, egocentric New York actress, I watched this extremely boring exercise with a quiet mental sneer. I felt that I could do a much better job than any of the people practicing, and I was intolerant of their awkward efforts.

At that rehearsal I myself received a teaching on simplicity and on form being emptiness, as well as on the attitude that I was manifesting (clandestinely, I thought). At one point during the sweeping exercise, Trungpa walked over to my corner with his right hand behind his back. Stopping in front of me, he brought forth his hand and, like a magician, displayed the heads side of a Kennedy half-dollar. I smiled, somewhat befuddled by the gesture, and nodded encouragingly. He then withdrew his arm once again behind his back. I waited to see what the point of this demonstration might be. Again he brought forth his hand and showed me the coin. I anticipated at least seeing the tail side, but no, JFK's head again appeared. I was without thought for a moment. Then Trungpa Rinpoche laughed, so I did too, although I was completely mystified. Later, in pondering the significance of this moment, I saw a link between my attitude toward the Mudra students and the teaching of this "magic trick." It remains a haunting reminder to me not to make judgments or think that I have the superior answer.

The Space between Audience and Performers

In addition to writing and producing a number of plays, Chögyam Trungpa created a series of postures for the Mudra Group. These provide a context within which "intensification" and "relaxation" of form and space are examined, experienced, and increasingly refined. I have been teaching these exercises as a foundation of theater training for almost thirty years. Since it is a group practice, this is the only way that I am able to maintain my own practice of them. They form a precious set of teachings within which I continually discover deeper truths about form and how it interrelates with space, while at the same time presence and confidence in my "performance" is strengthened. Over the years I've noticed that my students have become more appreciative of these seemingly boring, repetitive, and painful forms. Space is no longer the mysterious concept it was to the Mudra practitioners of 1972. Intensity is no longer something that happens to people elsewhere. As a species we are gradually becoming aware of space's significance as both our elemental support base and the interconnection that binds us uncompromisingly, inevitably, together.

When Chögyam Trungpa witnessed Western theater in the late 1960s, he saw acceptably coordinated people who, when placed in situations of pressure or "intensity," become spastic, dysfunctional, aggressive, or catatonic. He told the Mudra group that we become "hesitant . . . completely incompetent and lost, and don't know how to handle anything."[13] Under the pressure of a performance situation, reasonable folks suddenly lose their mindfulness. We who are accustomed to Western theater might think that what we are seeing is "acting." We do not know that there might be another, less distorted way to give a performance. "Time and space," Trungpa told us, "have to be a sympathetic environment for the activity to take place. A sense of generosity and compassion, so to speak, has to exist in the space as a mediator between the projection and the projector. And when that bridge begins to span, the gap begins to close, the performance, or any work of art for that matter, is no longer abruptly leaping off a cliff, out of nowhere into nowhere. It becomes a dance."[14]

The Mudra Theater Conference in 1973 in Boulder was the first exhibition of this Buddhist approach to theater that Trungpa's Mudra group was groping toward. In his key note address at the conference Trungpa said, "As I see it, the problem in acting doesn't seem to rely purely on body or voice, or being well trained, or having a highly skilled acrobatic style. The problem is not being able to relate with the space which surrounds the body. In other words: projector and projections. In this case the audience is the projection and the actor is the projector."[15]

Sometimes we witness a truly inspiring performance where the action, the actor, and the situation seem effortless and brilliant. In offstage life, however, we may learn that this very same person is frivolous, neurotic, or alcoholic. "The question of acting is not the point in this case," Trungpa told us. "What we are going to do, what is the important point, is to develop awareness while one makes a cup of coffee, cooks dinner, cleans the floor."[16]

The Mudra exercises challenge our cherished assumption that we understand the phrase "awareness of body." We think we have a fairly good awareness of our body most of the time. However, we fall apart in performance or high-stress situations due to our lack of awareness. Our panic hurls us upward into a thinking realm where we dizzily try to come up with ideas of "what to do next." Our first lesson in Mudra work is to discover how much of the time whatever body awareness we think we have is merely that: *thinking* about the body.

"The Intensification of Space," nicknamed, "The Lizard," is the first exercise that students learn. To begin, the performer lies on her back on the floor, arms along the sides, legs slightly apart, eyes open. She then opens her awareness to the space around her body and sequentially expands that awareness out to encompass the room, the building, the town, the state, down through the earth, toward the coasts and outward, the distance to the moon, and beyond. The human form, lying passively, becomes a small central reference point in vast space.

In this, as in almost all of the Mudra exercises, participants are guided by a person called "the Shadow." The Shadow does not execute the form but is responsible for the timing of the exercise and creating a narrative that describes the progression of the stages.

Once awareness expands outward into vast space, the Shadow suggests that the performers begin to notice the vast space becoming solid out on the farthest fringes. Solid space then gathers momentum, closing in on the body from "out there," encroaching on the soft and vulnerable reptilian form. As space rises up from underneath to touch the plane of the body, which is resting on the ground, the performers are asked to make the sense of solid intensity rising up from the earth as strong as their imagination can. In response, then, the Shadow asks the performers to intensify the back planes of their bodies. Initially this means tightening all of the muscles at one's command, solidifying them as much as possible, so that the intensity of space is matched by the intensity of their forms. Tightening all the back muscles, the performer then scans the back to see where there are gaps or soft spots. When the exercise is done properly, the Lizard's intensified body becomes definitely hard to the touch.

Next the Shadow suggests that the solid space is moving down on the top of the body. During this time, the performer concentrates on adding an intensified top plane while keeping the solidity of the bottom plane. Finally, intensity is built up on the sides of the body so that a completely intense, solid form exists in the midst of a totally intense solidified space. At the end of the exercise, the Shadow tells the performers to let go and release the intensity, after which they stand up and wander around the room randomly for a few minutes.

This practice reveals many assumptions about our relationship with our bodies. We discover body parts that we cannot intensify; that will not even stay in our awareness. We notice the urgency with which we try to escape from doing the exercise. We see how seductive it is to just hang out in vast space, or we notice how we painfully cramp up in one part of the body and ignore other parts. We can see quite clearly how our opinions about the exercise, or the Shadow, or entirely unrelated matters, undermine our ability to sustain exertion. Perhaps most profoundly, we discover the impossibility of ever completely mastering the exercise. Tension is limitless.

As we discover how little *awareness* we have of our bodies, we also begin to glimpse our utter lack of awareness of space. Practicing these simple Mudra exercises we start to recognize how useful space can be to us in creating a definition, a clear outline and limit to our form.

Voice Is the Communicator of the Mind

When I moved to Boulder in 1976, the Mudra Group asked me to work with them on a play by Chögyam Trungpa called *Water Festival*. In contrast to *Prajna*, this play has an air of celebration about it. The costumes of the large chorus are a pajama style in shiny turquoise satin, and that of the main character, Mr. Parchinson, has a decidedly comic flavor: "Black kimono with square Japanese hat and huge white earrings." The language is lighthearted despite the humorously desperate plight of Mr. Parchinson, who declares incessantly that he is "So thirsty. Utterly thirsty. I wish I could shed tears. I wish I could actually cry formally, as they say, spit on somebody. . . ."

Parchinson is spotted by an Old Lady (played by me in the original production) who, in her everyday persona wears a black jumpsuit and a Japanese tea-pickers' head-scarf, white with black polka dots. After some amusing exchanges about water and the lack thereof between Mr. Parchinson and a friend, the Old Lady enters with a pitcher of ice water and two glasses. Her intention is to serve them water until they tell her to just leave the glasses and not the water jar. She does so without first pouring them water from the jar.

In the next scene of this half-hour long play, the Old Lady turns out to be the preceptor for a festival of water, and Mr. Parchinson has volunteered to be the sacrificial victim "who will be willing to die in water, to be soaked in water, to quench his thirst in and out." Now the Old Lady has changed costume and wears "a large sleeved turquoise blue kimono with blue hat like a chef's hat." She is clearly in charge of the festivities, mounting a high platform atop which is a large water barrel. As a prelude to the ceremony, Mr. Parchinson, standing underneath the barrel, is invited to "make water" while the Old Lady pours a trickle of water from a pitcher onto his head. This, she says, is to express not losing water. Alas, despite the encouragement of both the chorus of turquoise pajama people and the Old Lady, Mr. Parchinson finds that he cannot leak. This is quite unacceptable to the Old Lady, who shouts, "You can leak! You can leak! If you don't leak, there's no water festival! Leak! It is my command!" The outcome is uncertain for a moment, but a solution to the dilemma is found while the chorus chants in praise of water and Mr. Parchinson's head is ducked into a bowl of water. As a result he discovers that he can drink through his nose, eyes, and ears, and can sing and dance. So doing, he joyfully joins the celebration, inquiring of the Old Lady whether he might perhaps leak on the festivities. Old Lady replies, "That would be unnecessary. I wouldn't do it." The water barrel is tipped, and all dance and sing.

The amount of work on all the technical aspects of this production was intense despite the slender plot. As with each of Trungpa's plays, the color of the backdrops, the designs of the costumes and props, and many other details are noted carefully in the script. For Trungpa these were not optional possibilities but integral to the design of the whole. Trungpa's emphasis in this production on sound and speech for both chorus and principles embodies what he had begun to communicate to the Mudra group two years earlier:

> The idea is that the visual perspective brings the vocal perspective simultaneously . . . when you look around you actually see the space very vividly and you know your sort of relationship with the space automatically. So the idea is that before you actually talk your eyes begin to talk and then you follow that sort of speech by saying things. First look and see your mind begin to react. And then after that you begin to use your voice. . . . It's not so much that you use your voice to reach large audiences particularly, but it is another kind of dimension of space, the space of the sound that does exist all the time anyway and what we are doing is trying to just spark that so that actually the voice is the sound of the mind.[17]

Training in this way requires the mind to slow down so that we can begin to see when a thought arises, and how a response to space formulates itself. It leaves most actors feeling vulnerable and unprepared. This is no doubt why the voice work had to wait until the Mudra Group had developed some skill in the more physical exercises. Chögyam Trungpa would applaud that sense of uncertainty, provided it is connected with the unconditional confidence that is trained through the body intensification exercises. In both the theater training and his plays (as well as his other art and his Buddhist teaching), it is clear that he sought an aesthetic that didn't boldly spell out everything but allowed a certain tentativeness to seduce the viewer into participation.

> If you write the textbook and also give commentary on the textbook and also interpret the whole thing emotionally, then there is no relationship left for the audience to work with. . . . On the whole, I feel that one's message should be communicated to people.

There's no harm in telling the world what you think it's all about without hiding or holding anything back. It's a question of the full moon being nice to watch, but maybe a crescent moon is more artistic. Suggestion can be more powerful than a bold statement because the layman has to take part in it. The audience has to take part in it.[18]

Writing in *Loka: A Journal from Naropa Institute*, theater director John Morrow fearlessly suggested that this new idea of "space awareness" might be just what the contemporary theater needed, having already journeyed through many phases from the emotional environment of the Actor's Studio, the sacred physical expression of Grotowski, an absurdist worldview, and the ensemble work of groups like the Open Theater:

So space awareness theater is growing out of the best of all the above, and focusing on space, wherever it may appear. And it appears in the emotions. The environment. The senses. The body. The mind. And it appears in the weirdest ways if one keeps watching it. It appears between the words when talking to another person. The meaning of the words seems to be formed more in the space before the word and after the word than within the word itself. So the actor gives the space at least equal meaning and consideration as the matter (the word).[19]

To this summary I would add that the space is not put in the composition for its own sake, but so that the viewers can begin to watch their own minds as well as the space and the objects "out there" within it. By practicing mindfulness and awareness, we develop the ability to maintain a steady, nonaggressive relationship with our perceptions and our world. Chögyam Trungpa believed that art as an activity can transform our lives and the lives of others. His theater training provides a truly skillful means with which to work. Carolyn Gimian writes: "Chögyam Trungpa was not primarily interested in creating a *philosophy* of art or a systematization of artistic theory. He was struggling to communicate the nuances of human perception: how intelligence arises in space, how it communicates with and grasps the sensory world and how a human being can provoke that fresh perception through artistic creation."[20]

A friend recently remarked that the idea of emptiness or space can often seem cold, distant, and lacking in the humanity of tenderness or caring. Perhaps the compassion of space awareness as it is transmitted through the theater methods and plays of Chögyam Trungpa requires a bigger understanding of the meaning of compassion than our busy lives usually give us time to ponder. This training is not seductive, kind, and gentle, and neither are these plays. In both, however, there is a sense of dignity arising from their unyieldingness. We are not being talked down to; we are asked to raise our consciousness up and out to include the highest understanding that exists. Whether we are actor or audience, Chögyam Trungpa expects no less from us than our ability to understand the totality of the situation, the inclusiveness of everything, neurosis and sanity all at once. We can be both the performer and the audience simultaneously if we bring unconditional compassion—compassion without a reference point—to what is happening all the time.

Being completely lost gives us direction because of the very fact that we are lost. That's how we begin our play with dark and light, our theatermanship.[21]

Notes

1. See *Born in Tibet*, chap. 8, "A Many Sided Training."

2. *Cutting Through Spiritual Materialism* (2002), p. 122.

3. Ibid., p. 123.

4. Ibid., p. 125.

5. Chögyam Trungpa, *Sandcastles*, ca. 1972.

6. In an interview about one of Chögyam Trungpa's Dharma Art installations.

7. Gina Stick, in an interview with Carolyn Rose Gimian, 2002.

8. *Prajna*, in *The Collected Works of Chögyam Trungpa*, vol. 7, p. 654.

9. *Loka: A Journal from Naropa Institute* (1975), ed. Rick Fields, p. 139.

10. *Prajna*, in *Collected Works*, vol. 7, p. 661.

11. *Loka* (1975), p. 139.

12. Mudra Theater Group Meeting. February 21, 1973.

13. Mudra Theater Group Meeting, December 18, 1972.

14. Chögyam Trungpa, Introduction to the Theater Conference, February 17, 1973.

15. Ibid.

16. Mudra Theater Group Meeting, April 12, 1973.

17. Mudra Theater Group Meeting, February 27, 1973.

18. Mudra Theater Group Meeting, February 17, 1973.

19. John Morrow, "Theatre and Space Awareness," in *Loka* (1975), p. 42.

20. Carolyn Rose Gimian, Introduction to *Collected Works*, vol. 7, p. xxix.

21. Mudra Theater Group Meeting, February 21, 1973.

Topsy-Turvy Times
with Trungpa

CHARLES S. PREBISH

IN THE SPRING of 2002, following a short bout with cardiac problems, I decided to move most of my books from my university office to my home study to allow me to work in a less stressful and more relaxing environ-ment. By some odd chance—probably karmically inspired—the very first books I grabbed down off the shelf were old, yellow, held-together-by Scotch-tape copies of Chögyam Trungpa's *Meditation in Action* and *Cutting Through Spiritual Materialism*. These were the first of his books that I read, and to me they remain his very best.

As I leafed through my tattered copies, I was propelled backward in time to the fall of 1973, when I was planning to teach a course called "East Meets West: Chögyam Trungpa and Carlos Castaneda." But I really wasn't so sure that I thought of Trungpa as "Eastern" or Castaneda as "Western." While students were walking around Penn State's campus with *The Teachings of Don Juan* or *Tales of Power* stuffed in the back pock-ets of their jeans—much the way I walked around ten years earlier with Kerouac's *Dharma Bums* stuffed in mine—I was still reading *Meditation in Action* and *Cutting Through Spiritual Materialism* again and again, finding something new and startling with each new reading. In my youthful naiveté, I even wrote to Trungpa, whom I had never met, and asked him if he would consider coming to Penn State to lecture in the course about his experiences in Tibet and in bringing the buddhadharma to America. I was shocked when I got back a handwritten note from him, saying simply: "Yes, if you think it's important." Overjoyed, I immediately went about the business of securing funding to pay for his expenses and an honorarium, and, when everything was in place, wrote back inquiring about his travel requirements. He never answered. Now, nearly thirty years later, I can just imagine Rinpoche laughing to himself and muttering something about expectations being silly and hopeless. Nevertheless, my course was held the following spring as planned, with *Meditation in Action* and *Cutting Through Spiritual Materialism* as its texts.

Eventually, a letter did arrive from Chögyam Trungpa, never mentioning the previous invitation to lecture but instead inviting me to teach Sanskrit during the summer of 1974 at the first session of a new institution called Naropa Institute in Boulder, designed to be a nonsectarian Buddhist university that would combine traditional studies with the practice of a "nonverbal humanity," whatever that was. The offer was enticing: a free place to live, some additional salary, and a chance to hobnob with counterculture heavies such as Allen Ginsberg, William Burroughs, Baba Ram Dass, and Gregory Bateson. Nobody could turn that down. Besides, it also created the occasion to make some sense of all the stuff I had been collecting on Buddhism in North America, and plans immediately began forming in my mind to write a book on "American Buddhism." At that time it never occurred to me to consider whether there even was such a thing as American Buddhism, but I intuitively knew there was. When the summer rolled around, I packed up my 1972 Pinto, and headed off for Boulder with my wife, two sons, and our dog—Buddha the beagle—to discover, or create, American Buddhism.

Apart from the professional benefits of the experience, the visit to Naropa provided another enticing feature: the opportunity to be around Buddhists, and that was something that was sorely lacking in my background. While my colleagues in graduate school went off to Dharamsala, Bangkok, and Tokyo to do their doctoral research, I sat in an office at the University of Wisconsin and translated Sanskrit monastic texts. While my colleagues were meeting bhikkhus and bhikkhunis, roshis and senseis, the height of my experience with Buddhists was seeing Geshe Sopa—the resident lama on the faculty—in a pair of Levis in downtown Madison one

Saturday morning. Despite my eagerness to meet masters and monks, I was more than a little edgy because I didn't know much about how to act in their presence.

I did get a bit of rehearsal not too many months before my departure, when my university was fortunate to have a visit from Sister Kechog Palmö, also known as Freda Bedi, an English widow who had become one of the first Western nuns in the Tibetan Buddhist tradition. She had worked extensively with Tibetans who fled to India after 1959, eventually becoming principal of the Young Lama's School in Dalhousie, where Chögyam Trungpa taught. She had even tutored Trungpa in English. Her Penn State visit was part of a fundraising tour to benefit the Tibetan refugee program.

It didn't take long for Sister Palmö to blow away whatever misconceptions I might have had about Buddhist nuns. She was polite but forward, literate but not snooty, and utterly forthright. And she was *big*. My first get-together with her was spent in a restaurant, during which time Sister Palmö ate far more than I had expected a renunciant to eat, and I was also surprised to see her eating meat. It must have been quite a sight for the locals: a big, bald-headed woman in maroon robes, traveling with a similarly dressed young Buddhist monk from San Antonio and a long-haired hippie professor. I was grateful for every moment I could get with Sister Palmö, and accosted her with questions about monastic discipline—my specialty—and all the little intricacies of the complicated practices of Tibetan Buddhism. Polite as ever, she simply wasn't having any of it. She wanted to talk about the four noble truths. I wanted to know about Vajrayana philosophy and tantric practice. What I got was right speech, right action, and right livelihood.

I made one final effort to get some sophisticated input on Tibetan Buddhism the following morning when Sister Palmö arranged a makeshift refuge ceremony for a few of my students. Before the ceremony, held in her hotel room at 7:00 a.m., I appeared and started peppering her with questions. "Tell me about the lineage system in the Gelukpa tradition. What about all the rinpoches in the West? Have you ever participated in the Kalachakra initiation? What's the Dalai Lama like?" She politely told me to shut up and went right back to talking about greed, hatred, and delusion, the "three poisons" of basic Buddhism. "Where is all the stuff about Nagarjuna, and Naropa, and wild yogis?" I asked. "In books," she said, adding: "And, in case you hadn't noticed, you live *in the world.*" Needless to say, this was very disconcerting to someone who thought he understood Buddhism. Just before she left on the next leg of her journey, Sister Palmö took me aside, privately, and told me that from this day on, much more was going to be expected from me, and made me recite the vows of the bodhisattva, after which she gave me a "bodhisattva name." Her last words to me were, "Now you can never turn back or renounce this vow."

Boulder wasn't like anything my family had ever experienced before. It seemed like a study in opposites: opulent, affluent houses at the base of the Rockies and barefooted hippie kids with patched jeans rambling around the Hill section of town near the Colorado University campus; bright, clean, blue skies overhead, and the faint smell of marijuana at street level. It seemed to reflect the familiar, progressive liberalism of Madison, minus the pervasive aroma of tear-gas, or the fear of being maced, that was only too familiar during the Vietnam War years.

I was eager to familiarize myself with the various locations around town that were being utilized by the institute, and to try and connect with other faculty members, almost all of whom were unknown to me. A couple of days before classes began, I wandered into the large building that was going to be used as the meditation hall, and for the large lecture course that was to be taught by Chögyam Trungpa a couple of evenings each week. It was a renovated old public service building, in which the main open space had been carpeted and a stage, or throne, had been erected in the front—giving credence to Robert Greenfield's later comment, in his book *The Spiritual Supermarket* (1975), that Trungpa was "trained to be a king and lost his kingdom. Now he's building another." In this building, I met several other faculty members who had wandered in just as I had, fueled by all kinds of probably wild expectations. As we were sitting on the floor chatting, I suddenly felt violently ill with the sort of urgency that usually necessitates a mad dash to a restroom or trash can. As I was desperately looking around for either, I noticed that Trungpa—whom I had never met but whose appearance I knew from photographs—had entered the building. It was an odd sight. Limping from the results of a stroke he had suffered in 1969 and dressed in a business suit, Trungpa made a rather cursory inspection of the building, followed by his entourage. Just as I was concluding that, in the absence of an available restroom or trash can, the floor was going to have to suffice for this now impending deposit, the nausea disappeared as if someone had flipped off a light switch. I looked back over my shoulder and noticed that Trungpa had, at that very moment, just left the building. Needless to say, the episode was very perplexing.

The next day, a lecture, followed by a rousing party, was planned to celebrate the opening of the institute. As everyone was milling about in the large fraternity house in which the post-lecture party was held, one of Trungpa's students appeared and asked me if I would like to meet "Rinpoche" (literally "precious one," Trungpa's title as an incarnate lama, or *tülku*). Remembering the previous day's experience, I started to decline, but with the realization that the disciple had a very firm grip on my elbow, I allowed myself to be led over to where Trungpa was engaged in an animated conversation with another partygoer. At first glance, up close, he wasn't anything like what I expected: he was portly, wore thick glasses, was impeccably dressed in a business suit, was smoking a Marlboro, and was drinking a glass of "Naropa punch" (grain alcohol with enough Hawaiian Punch to color it faintly pink). His disciple said, "Rinpoche, I'd like you to meet Professor Prebish from Penn State." Poor Trungpa. He never got to say a word. From the moment we shook hands, I started rambling off the most incredible string of nonsense imaginable. My wife later told me that it went something like: "Oh Rinpoche, I'm so excited to meet you. Your books have changed my life. What a great experience this is going to be. Garma Chang from Penn State sends his regards. I'm so excited to be here. What a great experience this is going to be. What a wonderful idea Naropa is. What a great experience this is going to be. I can't wait to get started." And on and on for a five full minutes. I stopped when Trungpa interrupted, shook hands with him again, and said, loudly, "Perhaps next time *we* should talk!" Then he immediately turned away and went back to his previous conversation.

My wife was mortified. She said to me, "Look at you; you made an absolute fool of yourself!" It was only then that I realized I was completely soaked, from neck to waist. My shirt was so wet I could have wrung it out. For my part, all I knew was that I was really light-headed and needed to get out of there, and that's what we did. We returned to our little rented house, and for reasons I still don't understand, I started to walk around the dining room table. It was some kind of Buddhist-inspired circumambulation, but for reasons unknown. My wife knew that when this kind of stuff happened, as it did every so often, the best thing to do was simply stay out of the way and let it run its course. I walked around that dining room table for *twelve hours straight*.

The first thing that occurred to me as I began circling the table was that I'd had two very short encounters with Trungpa, and each of them had produced outlandish, even bizarre results. I hadn't had a formal Buddhist teacher since my first teacher, Bope Vinita, went back to Sri Lanka in the late 1960s, and I wondered if some connection with Trungpa was beginning to reveal itself. I'd read lots of stories in Buddhist literature about the eccentric, unusual ways teachers revealed themselves to their future students. I myself had had only experienced something like this myself on one other occasion. As a first-year Ph.D. student at the University of Wisconsin, I repeatedly had inexplicable experiences whenever I was around the head of the Buddhist Studies Program, Richard H. Robinson. I didn't understand these encounters at all, but Robinson seemed to know exactly what was happening. Then, to my surprise, Robinson invited me to become his research assistant in the spring of 1968. From then on, it seemed as if Robinson took control not only of my academic training but also of my Buddhist training. What was so freakish about the circumstance was that Robinson never actually professed to being Buddhist, yet being and acting Buddhist was mostly all we ever talked about together, and we did so right up until Robinson's untimely death. I never shared any of this with my colleagues out of fear they would just laugh at me. Nevertheless, I privately believed that Robinson was functioning for me as the half-crazy yogi Tilopa did for Naropa.

As I continued walking around the table, I also wondered if I had finally found a sangha, or spiritual community, for myself. It was difficult being a Buddhist community of one at Penn State, as I missed the shared experience, and group ethos, that a sangha could provide. But the most important thing that happened during those twelve hours was the effortless fashion in which years of insecurities, unhappinesses, uncertainties, and simple little hang-ups just came tumbling out of their previously well-guarded hiding places in my mind. I felt as if I was seeing myself clearly for the first time since my father died in 1961. While this evanescent cascade of psychological revelations was exciting, it was terrifying as well. What's more, there seemed to be some unspoken imperative for action that I had never felt before.

The next day I was jarred out of my self-absorbed reflections when I received a telephone call from David Rome, one of Trungpa's close staff members. Rome called to say that Trungpa was granting all faculty private five-minute interviews during the summer, and did I want one? Truly, I didn't, or at least not one that would last five whole minutes. Thirty seconds seemed like a better, safer, time frame. Yet I didn't feel I could decline, so I agreed. I hadn't reckoned that the interview would be scheduled for the next day. Rome told me to appear at Trungpa's office at Karma Dzong, just a few doors down Pearl Street from the New York Deli made famous by the *Mork and Mindy* television show, at 4:00 p.m.

Since I hadn't had much experience with Trungpa yet, I didn't know that clock time and Trungpa time were two entirely different categories. When I appeared at 4:00 p.m., I was shown to a seat outside Trungpa's office and told that Rinpoche wasn't quite ready. Although I watched the door to Trungpa's office dutifully, nobody left or entered for the next *two hours*, so when I was finally escorted in at 6:00 p.m., I was thoroughly confused. This face-to-face visit was nothing like my other two encounters with Trungpa. I wasn't nervous at all, and Trungpa was wonderfully hospitable, offering me sake and a hearty thanks for coming to this experimental program. Yet, less than sixty seconds later, Trungpa leaned across his desk and said, "I have something I need to tell you."

For the next couple of hours, Trungpa engaged me in a rambling discussion about my "practice" that was nothing short of the most astounding spiritual diagnosis, and then prognosis, I could have imagined. Somehow—inexplicably—Trungpa knew everything about my spiritual history. This was not the sort of stuff one might read off someone's résumé, and that was about all Trungpa knew about me. But the most startling part of the discussion emerged when Trungpa said, "Charles, I think you should stop sitting in meditation." For someone who prescribed the basic Buddhist calming meditation practice known as shamatha for virtually everyone in his community, this was shocking, even heretical advice. But he went on to explain, "You've been sitting for almost ten years, and many hours each day as well. You've simply fallen into using sitting practice as an excuse to *withdraw* from the world rather than encountering it and experiencing it through the Buddhist principles you've learned. Get off your cushion and let the experiences of your everyday life be your guru. Only return to your cushion when you lose faith . . . and you will occasionally." He then went on to talk briefly about the efficacy of the wisdom inherent in the four noble truths. It was astounding advice, and accurate. Yet, during all of this miraculous encounter, he never suggested that *he* should become my teacher or that I should join his community. And there again were those persistent and seemingly inescapable four noble truths.

For the rest of our time together, we talked about everything from his community, and plans for the dharma in America, to his fabled drinking and sexual experiences. He held nothing back and made no apologies. When I left his office, nobody could figure out why Trungpa spent so much time talking to this guy who was merely a scholar. Just prior to my midsummer departure from the institute, I met with Trungpa one last time, and as I got up to leave, he pulled me into an incredibly warm, intimate hug and said, "Thank you so very much for coming; I do hope you'll come back again next year."

For most of Naropa Institute's summer population, the highlight of the powerfully packed menu of spiritual choices was Trungpa's twice-per-week evening course. Scheduled for 8:00 p.m., the class began whenever Trungpa arrived, and more often than not, that was around ten. As students began to catch on to the routine, they continued to arrive around eight, using the two-hour wait for a kind of spiritual party, in which rambling discussions occurred on topics ranging from the efficacy of zazen to the benefits of tantric sex. It would not be inaccurate to suggest that these conversions sometimes degenerated into a "my guru is better than your guru" competition.

Despite the advertised title of the course, whatever it was on any occasion, it seemed as if Trungpa's approach was always the same: basic Buddhism, and especially the ideas inherent in the four noble truths. At no time did these lectures ever go beyond the material presented in his book *Cutting Through Spiritual Materialism*, published in 1973 and edited from talks given at Karma Dzong in Boulder in the fall of 1971 and the spring of 1972. When questioned about his apparent overemphasis on the four noble truths, Trungpa simply made an analogy to the construction of a home, starting first with the foundation and concluding with the roof. By his own estimate, in 1974 he was still pouring the foundation, and that foundation—however boring it might have been to students yearning for more exotic teachings—was all they were going to get. It certainly represented a living lesson in the futility of expectations, but it was great fun anyway. Trungpa's humor was outrageous, his stories right on the mark, and his ability to field questions deft. Often, the after-lecture conversations spilled over into Boulder's bars and coffee houses and apartments.

True to his word, Trungpa invited me back to Naropa for the summer of 1975. My teaching responsibility was much different in the second summer. I was part of a "module" on Indian Buddhism in which the students enrolled in the module took classes together, ate and meditated together, lived in the same location, and hung out together in whatever spare time they could manage. It was planned claustrophobia, one of Trungpa's favorite teaching devices. For me, it was anything but fun. The module was cotaught by Reggie Ray, one of Trungpa's chief students and a good friend, which was fine, but the meditation instruction was delegated to one of Trungpa's disciples named Eric Holm, but who preferred to use his Dharma name of Lodrö Dorje. Holm and I were at odds from the very first day of the module. On his first lecture, focusing on the life of Siddhartha Gautama, the historical Buddha, Holm began badgering me about why Buddha's life and teaching should be revered as any more sacred and reliable than that of his teacher, Trungpa Rinpoche. Nothing satisfied Holm, and I knew that *everything* I said during the module was going to be held against the yardstick of Trungpa's teaching. The only satisfaction I got was by refusing to address Holm as Lodrö Dorje, so whenever we met at Naropa events, on the street, or at parties, I would always say, "Hi, Eric," and smile as Holm would fume and slowly say, "My name is LODRÖ DORJE, L-O-D-R-Ö D-O-R-J-E." "Right, Eric Holm," I would say as I walked away convinced he was trapped in his own spiritual materialism. The students in the module weren't particularly bright, or highly motivated, and I quickly lost interest. My one satisfying moment came when one of my students rather smugly asked, "Dr. Prebish, are *you* a Buddhist?" The affirmative answer, along with a description of my ten-year practice schedule, yielded instant acceptance. Without ever having been asked, "Have you ever *attained anything* in that practice?" I was instantly accepted as spiritually O.K.

In each of my two summers at Naropa Institute, I wondered a great deal about the attainments of the students who attended these interesting but sometimes outrageous summer sessions. That does not mean to say that I questioned the attainments of Trungpa's serious, ongoing students and disciples, or the followers of other Buddhist teachers, but I couldn't help wondering about the effectiveness of the many hours these summer

dharma-hoppers spent in private meditation, focusing with great seriousness on their out-breath while seated on brightly colored zafus in the large
meditation hall and elsewhere. They seemed to put in very many hours focusing on their out-breath, and with great seriousness while seated on
their cushions, yet they remained remarkably unchanged in their conduct
and moral behavior once they left the meditation hall. Viewed from the
outside, craving and grasping seemed reduced not at all, and the practice
of the eightfold path—the very cornerstone of basic Buddhist conduct—
was almost entirely absent. I once asked Trungpa if he had noticed this
too, and if so, what he thought about it. Trungpa nodded but then said, "I
think some of them are working through it." Just as I began cynically concluding that he was drowning in an ocean of nirvana-chasers, Trungpa
remarked that if only these young people would stop chasing enlightenment, they would be astounded to learn that nirvana was, in fact, chasing
them!

I didn't see Trungpa as much during the summer of 1975. He seemed
far less accessible, more guarded in what he said during his lectures, and
awfully tired. I and others thought he suddenly looked many years older
than a man in his mid-thirties. It appeared as if he needed a rest in order
to recharge himself physically. It wouldn't be long before Trungpa announced that he would begin a year-long retreat in March 1977, and it was
only a year later—on August 22, 1976—that he named Thomas F. Rich as
his "Vajra Regent," giving him the name Ösel Tendzin.

At the end of that second summer, my family got into the old Pinto
and headed back to Pennsylvania, where I would resume my secular life at
the university and my Buddhist religious life as a sangha of one. Although
I knew that some of my friendships within Trungpa's community were
solid and would endure, I also knew that I wouldn't be returning to Naropa
again. Now I had to finish the manuscript of my American Buddhism volume and resume my struggle with trying to understand why all the Buddhist teachers I had met placed so much emphasis on the first, and
apparently most simple, of Buddha's teachings: the four noble truths.

I bet I've read *Meditation in Action* fifty times over the years. One
wouldn't think an author could pack so much interesting material into a
tiny book that barely covered seventy-five pages, but Trungpa did—for me
at least. Each time I flip back through those turned-down pages, I find
something new. This last time I was struck by the simple purity and power

of the chapter on transmission. Trungpa says, "Transmission does not mean that the Teacher is imparting his knowledge or his discovery to you—that would be impossible, even Buddha could not do so. But the whole point is that we stop collecting more things, and we just empty out whatever we have." A little later he went on: "And when he has opened himself, the Teacher will say a few words, which probably do not mean very much. Or perhaps he will not say anything. The important thing is to create the right situation both on the Teacher's part and on the pupil's part. And when the right situation is created, then suddenly the Teacher and the pupil are not there anymore. The Teacher acts as one entrance and the pupil acts as another, and when both doors are open there is a complete Emptiness, a complete Oneness between the two."

One wonderful morning back in 1970, I'd had exactly the experience Trungpa described, at the conclusion of one of my weekly debates with my academic mentor Richard H. Robinson. Only this time, for some reason, Robinson had required that my wife and newborn son be present for our intellectual battle. Any grasping at permanence on my part was quickly dispelled, as that very afternoon Robinson was blown up in the house explosion and fire that ended his life about a month later. In 1974, when I told Trungpa about that experience, he simply smiled and hugged me.

The same continual lessons emerge from the chapter on self-deception in *Cutting Through Spiritual Materialism*. When Trungpa reminds us that "self-deception needs the idea of evaluation and a very long memory," he couldn't be smarter. I am always reminding myself of the immense truth of one small sentence in that chapter: "If we regard something as valuable and extraordinary, it becomes quite separate from us." He goes on to explain how we grasp after that inspiration precisely because we don't want to lose it. And over the years, I've learned again and again just how accurate and pervasive those two magical little books are, as goals, friendships, and even desires slip away with each new act of fear and grasping.

In recent years I've found a more portable little book to carry around with me, and I take it everywhere. It fits right in my jacket pocket, near my heart. It's John Daido Loori's *Invoking Reality: Moral and Ethical Teachings of Zen*. In it, Daido Roshi reviews taking refuge in the three treasures, the three pure precepts, and the ten grave precepts. I suppose it's no wonder I first met Daido Roshi at the first summer session of Naropa Institute.

Chögyam the Translator

LARRY MERMELSTEIN

THE VIDYADHARA CHÖGYAM TRUNGPA RINPOCHE had a great
passion for translating the dharma from Tibetan to English. By the
time North American students began encountering Rinpoche in 1970, his
command of the English language was already completely fluent, id-
iomatic, and intimate. It may be hard to believe, but his vocabulary sur-
passed many of his native English-speaking students. His English syntax
ranged from the extremely loose to near perfect at times, and this was always difficult to predict and seemed totally situational. But his command
and eloquence with all the skills English required was impressive.

He taught the dharma in English—directly and with penetrating precision and gentleness. Did he formulate ideas and dharmic concepts in
Tibetan and then translate them into English? Rarely, I think, and perhaps only when the topic was very technical or textually based. There
were often as many interpretations of what he had said as there were people who heard him, which I think reflects how intimately he connected
with his audience. And he used to amazing effect the fact that no one expected him to speak syntactically perfect English. Subtle, complex, and
mind-opening ambiguities, as well as multiple shades and layers of meaning emerged easily from his often slippery sentence structures. But the

teachings came out spontaneously, effortlessly—again, a product of his passion to connect with our world totally and without pretense. Dr. Alton ("Pete") Becker, professor of linguistics, commented after attending a lecture by the Vidyadhara in 1974, "Rinpoche did something I've always known was possible, but that I've never experienced before: he used language to destroy conceptuality."

Just as the Buddha Shakyamuni taught in the vernacular as he wandered the Indian subcontinent over twenty-five centuries ago, Trungpa Rinpoche spoke our language, with simplicity and directness. The kind of students he attracted never imagined they would learn his language, let alone recite liturgies or study commentaries in Tibetan. It had to be in English, and there seemed to be little effort needed, since he taught so completely in our language.

But, in truth, effort was required, especially as the students entered into the vajrayana disciplines of ngöndro (preliminary practices of tantra) and sadhana (yidam deity practice). Initially, Rinpoche composed his own liturgies in English, as he had left Tibet with only the smallest amount of his personal practice texts; and by the time he had journeyed to the United States, his books remained in Scotland, along with a number of important relics. But as we required more traditional liturgy, we began to obtain texts from other exiled lamas and scholars we encountered. Through the efforts of Tibetologist E. Gene Smith and his colleagues at the Library of Congress New Delhi Field Office, much of the wealth of the huge corpus of Tibetan literature slowly became available; in this way we began to acquire much of what Rinpoche needed—both for his more in-depth presentations and for his students' meditation practice.

Years before, in the United Kingdom, Chögyam the Translator emerged, working closely with some of his very articulate and literate students. With some works, he dictated a spontaneous translation in English, allowing his scribes to help him shape and edit the phraseology. His work with Künga Dawa (Richard Arthure) is perhaps the most notable; their translation of *The Sadhana of Mahamudra*, one of the termas ("treasure" texts) discovered by Rinpoche, is a beautiful and evocative practice liturgy, held very dear by all his students. With others who were studying Tibetan, he worked with Tibetan texts directly. Rigdzin Shikpo (Michael Hookham) was one member of the small initial group of translators who worked closely with Rinpoche in rendering the arcane language of another culture into their own. We look forward to seeing more of Rigdzin Shikpo's work with the Vidyadhara in the near future. Francesca Fremantle, who was completing a Ph.D. in Sanskrit at the University of London, was another early translator who collaborated with Rinpoche. She even crossed the Atlantic not long after him to teach Sanskrit at the University of Colorado and work with him to complete their translation of *The Tibetan Book of the Dead* (1975), which is still a classic in the field.

The Nālandā Translation Committee

In America, the translation effort developed slowly and organically, as a few of us who had the interest, though not necessarily any special talent, began to study Tibetan. The Vidyadhara himself taught a few actual classes on the Supplication to the Takpo Kagyüs sometime in 1973 and 1974, and this text, which we already knew well in English from his earlier translation in Britain, became a vehicle for teaching us aspects of Tibetan grammar. A small group emerged, with enthusiasm and some diligence, and Rinpoche began to meet with us periodically. We worked with him on songs of realization by some of the Karmapas and a beautiful sadhana he wrote while in the United Kingdom to his root guru, Jamgön Kongtrül Padma Tri-me of Shechen. This period was very much an apprenticeship for us in terms of education; and though it suffered from informality and lack of structure as compared with a classroom style, it gained much from the passion of both the students and their teacher working intimately together. And, moreover, it was "jolly good fun" at times, as he used to say.

The first project I was given by the Vidyadhara, at the 1974 Vajradhatu Seminary, was to prepare an edition in Sanskrit of the hundred-syllable Vajrasattva mantra, making sure that this was in accord with classical grammar. Sanskrit had been one of my main areas of focus while completing a B.A. in religious studies at the University of Michigan a couple of years earlier. The following year, this work became the basis for our first real group translation—the Vajrasattva liturgy of the ngöndro. A handful of students were completing their prostrations and refuge practice, and Rinpoche felt that it was important for them to begin to utilize the traditional ngöndro text. Up to that point we had been practicing based on oral instructions, and contemplating the four reminders with short verses spontaneously composed in English by the Vidyadhara.

The fact that Rinpoche was keen for his students to know this long mantra in a grammatically correct form in Sanskrit reveals his allegiance to providing as authentic and literate a transmission as possible, now that we in the West had access to such resources long forgotten in Tibet (since the days of the main translation activity of Tibetans had ended centuries ago). Not only did he want the mantra to be accurate in terms of its spelling, but he wanted us to be able to pronounce it as the Indians would their native classical language. This was in stark contrast to Rinpoche's Tibetan contemporaries, both his teachers and colleagues, who pronounced the Sanskrit syllables as if they were reading Tibetan—what we have sometimes referred to humorously as the "whores dew vrey" (*hors d'oeuvre*) style of pronunciation. He made great effort, though it seemed natural, to pronounce the many Sanskrit technical terms he utilized in his talks in the way these words would be said in India. However, when he chanted Sanskrit mantras encountered in Tibetan liturgies, whether during his own practice or reading transmissions, he would default to the ingrained Tibetan style of articulation, occasionally even poking fun at himself for doing so.

A related topic is the visualization of Sanskrit seed syllables and mantras, a common feature of tantric practice. In general, the Vidyadhara counseled us to follow the Tibetan tradition of visualizing such syllables using the Tibetan uchen (*dbu can;* "possessing a head") script. When asked why we couldn't use the Roman alphabet, he said, "I'm not willing to make that leap." He went on to discuss how important he felt it was that such visualizations be done using a syllabary (like those employed by Tibetan and Sanskrit) rather than an alphabet. The difference is that with a syllabary, a complete syllable is represented by one character, which contains both a consonant and a vowel. With an alphabet, the consonants and vowels are separate letters. Rinpoche thought it was important in one's visualization practice for the consonant and vowel to be inherently inseparable, and an alphabet cannot accomplish this as well as a syllabary.

As would be readily evident to anyone reading the Vidyadhara's books and teachings, his liberal use of Sanskrit and relatively rare usage of Tibetan terms again demonstrated his strong bias toward showing us the Indian roots of Buddhism, as well as the Indian vajrayana traditions, including the bodhisattva ideal of the mahasiddha lineage and their way of life as lay practitioners. We always attempted to find an appropriate

English word or phrase to translate the seemingly endless number of important terms. But if nothing suitable was found, we often preferred to employ the original Sanskrit, especially if this was not too difficult to pronounce or read for the English-speaking audience. Rinpoche wanted his students to develop a technical Buddhist vocabulary and required us to study the meaning of foreign terms. Using these somewhat unfamiliar words in a translation instead of always trying to coin English equivalents was meant to encourage further learning on the part of the reader. Perhaps it goes without saying, but we've found that most English speakers handle Sanskrit pronunciation quite well without any training; whereas the less familiar and linguistically unrelated Tibetan is often much more difficult.

When Rinpoche sought to name an organization or project, he often would turn to Sanskrit again—examples range from Vajradhatu to Shambhala, Nalanda to Naropa (all written without the more scholarly use of diacritics)—though he remained mostly in his native idiom for the names he chose for his military and service organization, known as the Dorje Kasung (Tib. *rdo rje bka' srung*), as well as for hierarchical titles within the Shambhala organization. Ultimately, it was a blending of several influences, but his hope was that many of the foreign words we used, especially the many important technical terms, would eventually enter the English language formally, as a number of Sanskrit words have.

For the Nālandā Translation Committee, the year 1976 was a watershed in many ways. We were joined by Lama Ugyen Shenpen, a longtime attendant and secretary to Dilgo Khyentse Rinpoche, a close teacher of the Vidyadhara, and among the very few to have escaped the Communist regime. Lama Ugyen proved to be an invaluable teacher and guide for us, and he assisted Trungpa Rinpoche in so many ways, being the only other Tibetan in our midst. Everything we translated was carefully reviewed with Lama Ugyen and often drafted with his help, though he too was engaged in learning a new language in order to improve what he could offer. After this draft was complete, we would begin again, reading the entire translation, line by line, to the Vidyadhara.

Our first project that included Lama Ugyen fully was our translation of the short and long Karma Kagyü Vajrayogini sadhanas. Some of the preparation was done before the 1976 Vajradhatu Seminary, held at Land O'Lakes, Wisconsin; but most of the work proceeded there, from working to complete a draft with Lama Ugyen to reviewing it all carefully with

Rinpoche. This process was very intense, usually involving eight to twelve hours a day, and the text demanded much more than our knowledge allowed. But our understanding grew, and Lama Ugyen's English improved steadily. At times it seemed magical, Rinpoche sneaking into our workroom while we pored over a passage with Ugyen; he would come just to check on our progress, prodding us along playfully and offering interesting details that transformed our understanding. Sometimes we were so immersed in our work that we wouldn't even notice him approaching, much to his mischievous delight.

It was during this intensive training program that *The Golden Sun of the Great East* was revealed to the Dorje Dradül, as the Vidyadhara was known in his Shambhala manifestation. This is the root terma text of Shambhala, the first of several mind termas he was to discover during his years in America, and these too required translating. (Years later, Rinpoche's discoveries were confirmed as authentic termas by his teacher Dilgo Khyentse Rinpoche.) As is the case with all such revealed treasure teachings, these were intentionally hidden centuries earlier (usually by Padmasambhava, but in this case, more likely King Gesar of Ling). A terma is hidden in order to benefit future generations, and the timing of its manifestation is an aspect of its prophecy. The Shambhala teachings are extremely important in the Vidyadhara's transmission of dharma. In fact, he once said that it was this intention alone—to propagate the kingdom of Shambhala—that provided the necessary inspiration to leave his homeland and make the arduous journey to India and the West.

Translation Methodology

From 1976 on, the annual three-month Vajradhatu Seminary, which included alternating periods of intensive meditation and advanced study, became for us a fabulous translation intensive and retreat. There were always at least two or three of us in attendance, sometimes many more, coming and going as our livelihoods permitted. Rinpoche seemed to have lots of time to work on our projects, and we sometimes met daily—rarely fewer than several times a week. Seminary was also his laboratory, where he would experiment with how to use our translations within his students' meditation practice. He sometimes spent hours in the shrine room with a handful of us, experimenting with different styles of chanting, drum patterns, gong ringing, and so forth. It was a very creative and fluid process of adapting the Tibetan ritual tradition to a new land and vocabulary, and every year there would be new advancements in our ritual and understanding.

Back home in Boulder, Colorado, the translation work continued, though generally at a slower pace. Meetings with Rinpoche were held once or twice a week when he was in town, perhaps more if a project was nearing completion. He once commented that the translation committee members were like "ladies to the court," connecting him to his mother tongue—no matter that most of us were male. Perhaps the translation work would have been easier without us, since for the most part he really didn't need us. But Rinpoche was training us, teaching us, and being so very kind to us. He was also building an institution.

As a translator, Rinpoche was both highly creative and meticulous. He gathered his students into a committee, usually at least a few of us at any given time, in order to develop a warm and collegial spirit of adventure and learning, always seeking to achieve just the right turn of phrase to ignite students' understanding of the text. In this way, Rinpoche was harking back to a very traditional time—during the transmission of the dharma from India to Tibet—when translators worked with accomplished scholar-practitioners. His resemblance to Marpa the Translator and to Padmasambhava is not lost on us. At first we were mostly his secretaries and editors, and were just beginning our journey into a different mind. A new mind was required, as Rinpoche explained, to learn a new language. It was the beginning of a long and rewarding collaboration.

Rinpoche composed much of his poetry in Tibetan, including tantric dohas and songs of realization, and frequently translated his verse into English himself. His private secretary, David I. Rome, and others would transcribe the spontaneous oral translation, editing somewhat on the fly, usually with Rinpoche's active participation. Occasionally these would be reviewed later by our committee, especially if they were to be included in an important publication. Most of his more extensive Tibetan writings, whether they were tantric sadhanas, treatises, or termas, were translated by the committee from the start in our usual fashion.

Rinpoche searched carefully for certain words, exploring with us how the intended reader might respond to a phrase. When we met at his home, the Kalapa Court, we always had the complete, thirteen-volume edition of

The Oxford English Dictionary nearby, and had great fun exploring the etymologies and nuances of a word. Clearly it was such a method that had resulted in Rinpoche's enormous vocabulary, and he often impressed us by knowing far more about certain words than we did. No doubt, Rinpoche would be so pleased and honored to know that the *OED* now cites his usage of the word *egolessness* as one of its historical references under the entry for *ego*.

Some words that might otherwise seem to be excellent choices were so heavily laden with problematic connotations that we found them unusable. Words such as *sin* and *prayer* came with too much of a theistic orientation and Judeo-Christian baggage; and so, after an initial trial of "neurotic crimes," we settled on "evil deeds" instead of "sin" for the Tibetan *sdig pa* and Sanskrit *papa,* and "supplication" and "aspiration" (instead of "prayer") for *gsol 'debs* and *smon lam*. Other words were not quite as problematic for a nontheistic connotation, such as "blessing" for *byin rlabs*. On his own, Rinpoche came up with some marvelous and inventive translations, though we did not always use these in our committee's work; to give just a few: "alpha pure" for *ka dag* (rather than "primordial purity"), the "eight logos" for *sgrub pa bka' brgyad* ("eight sadhana teachings"), and "the three lords of materialism" for *phyi nang gsang ba'i kla klo* ("outer, inner, and secret barbarians").

The group spirit was a very important component of our methodology as translators. Sometimes the work would go extremely slowly, when it seemed no one understood a passage, or when we each had to weigh in on our own way of reading or casting a line. At times there were effortless leaps or even flights of creative expression, and of course Rinpoche himself was often the instigator or articulator of these. The group process did seem to produce a much greater degree of care and consistency, even if it greatly increased the time involved. We were with our guru, a most precious opportunity, and time rarely seemed to matter, except when a deadline loomed. It was always a collaborative effort; discussions could become passionate, humorous, emotional, argumentative, but there was always a basic respect for each other and, of course, great reverence for our teacher. Looking back, I think we accomplished quite a lot during those formative years, especially given our lack of expertise. The committee approach may sometimes have squashed an inspired or lyrical turn of phrase one person offered, especially when it was far from the literal renderings we usually preferred. But the advantages usually outweighed the inevitable idiosyncrasies of the individual-translator method, and the group easily undermined individual ego trips. (There are, it is important to note, a number of exceptional dharma translators working individually as well.) If there is an example of the whole being greater than the sum of its parts, it is our Nālandā Translation Committee.

Our methodology also developed quite naturally, with everyone's participation. We strove to be as literal and accurate as possible, avoiding a more interpretive style of English composition. We viewed the Buddhist practitioner as our main audience, though we still made efforts to include some amount of scholarly reference and context for readers in the academic community. We crafted the language in a fairly simple idiom, avoiding overly complex or philosophically abstruse terminology. Rinpoche was concerned about the natural theistic and dualistic tendencies in language, perhaps somewhat more prevalent in English than Tibetan, and so we looked for ways to minimize or undermine this. One such example was our style of capitalization, which was as minimal as possible without becoming idiosyncratic. Only the most strictly defined proper nouns were capitalized, such as the names of people and places. The names of various yanas, or vehicles, were treated as stages on the path rather than as fixed schools or institutions. Important teachings, too, such as shunyata, mahamudra, and the four noble truths, were also written lowercase so as to deemphasize any substantialistic or static connotation. Rinpoche also minimized our personal pronoun usage whenever possible, though English demands these much more than his native Tibetan.

Improvement and refinement were constant aspirations. And so, as our translations were used by more and more practitioners, inconsistencies and obscure phrases surfaced, and we responded with corrections. In Tibet, there was the Old Translation school (*snga 'gyur*) and the New Translation school (*gsar bsgyur*). It seemed at times that we were developing the "retranslation school," but the Vidyadhara wanted it to be correct, and so improvements were made periodically. There was, however, very little time for such backtracking, as the work ahead loomed large indeed.

The design of our publications also was an area of exploration and experimentation, as this too was an important component of how the dharma was to be communicated. It had to be both dignified and functional. Long texts that served as liturgies to be chanted during one's meditation practice needed to be able to open wide and lie flat on the practice table, especially when the practice involved much ritual such as mudras (hand gestures) and music offerings (of bell and drum). With the help of graphic designers, we came up with a nearly square paper size that, when opened up, approximated the size of an open Tibetan-style book; however, the pages were to be turned like a Western book. This allowed for one's ritual implements to fit on a table nicely with the text, just as was done traditionally. The pages were left unbound, as they were in Tibet, which also allowed for easy rearrangement of liturgies at different times as required.

When playwright Jean-Claude van Itallie, a longtime student of Rinpoche's, became a sadhana practitioner, he urged us to consider including much more annotation of ritual instructions and commentary within the sadhana text itself. The Vidyadhara agreed that some amount of direction would be very helpful, especially for the first such practice text encountered; and so we republished the *Vajrayogini Sadhana* with a significant amount of marginalia, noting when to offer music, perform a mudra, or to use other ritual aids. The margins of such texts were purposely left very generous so that the students could include plenty of notes to facilitate their understanding. Rinpoche wanted us to do mostly our own annotation through personal study and practice of the material.

There was to be no hint of inferiority in our presentation of the dharma in English, a language that Rinpoche considered to be as suitable as any for transmitting the teachings. And so there was no interlinear Tibetan present, whether in the native Tibetan script or a pronounceable phonetic transcription (though such publications have proved extremely useful to students learning Tibetan). The practitioners were going to read and chant in English, and most of the Vidyadhara's students would have been completely lost if they were left to chant in Tibetan. For those few Westerners who learned the Tibetan language, the original text might suffice, depending upon their fluency.

Rinpoche once commented that it was not such a good idea to learn the dharma by means of learning the Tibetan language, and he had noticed that some strange or mistaken ideas seemed to creep in when that became the primary process of learning. Of course, we learned an immense amount about the dharma through our study of the language and the task of translating the texts for others. But Rinpoche's point was that it was best to learn the basic dharma principles in one's native language, without any additional cultural filters or projections beyond the usual.

Rinpoche delighted in word play of all kinds, and he apparently grew up writing clever little poems amid his lessons. (The eighteenth-century master Jigme Lingpa was his favorite poet.) In America, he also dabbled with translating English into Tibetan, with such forays as the opening sections of the *Tao Te Ching* and the Lord's Prayer. The latter text served as a terribly funny prank he played on us, giving it to one of our members as a small project to translate (back) into English. The translator quickly got the joke and burst out of his room laughing. The next "victim," of Jewish descent, was not so lucky, having never encountered this prayer before; and thus an entire translation was prepared for us to consider. The meeting to review this with Rinpoche was excruciatingly funny.

Tibetan Writings and Terma

Though the writings of Trungpa Rinpoche are not the main subject of this essay, I have alluded to various of them, some of which were composed in Tibetan, and some of which were also translated by him. As mentioned in his autobiography, *Born in Tibet*, Rinpoche wrote at least two sizable works while still in Tibet: a thousand-page treatise on mahamudra and meditation, "showing its gradual development up to the final fruition," and a two-volume "allegory about the kingdom of Shambhala and its ruler who will liberate mankind at the end of the Dark Age." Unfortunately, both of these works remain lost. However, we were excited to learn recently that a number of his other texts written in Tibet have survived.

Through discussions with Lama Yönten Gyamtso, an attendant of Trungpa Rinpoche from when he was still an infant in Tibet and a member of his escape party in 1959, we learned that Rinpoche began to discover termas at the age of six. Lama Yönten explained that often Trungpa Rinpoche would sit with his good friend Ugyen Tendzin (a tülku from Sip Dzokchen Monastery) and an older khenpo (senior philosophy teacher). The Vidyadhara would sometimes decode the terma finds orally, with Ugyen Tendzin often serving as scribe to record his pronouncements. Apparently, many of Rinpoche's termas in Tibet were what are called "earth treasures"—texts and ritual objects actually taken out of the earth or rock.

Before his recent death, Ugyen Tendzin—in compiling a table of contents of Rinpoche's writings in Tibet—wrote a beautiful essay about Trungpa Rinpoche as a tertön (terma discoverer). Trungpa Rinpoche's nephew, Karma Senge Rinpoche, who is from Kyere Monastery (a branch of Surmang), has spent many years traveling throughout Kham (Eastern Tibet) and beyond, in search of his uncle's writings. Thus far, he has collected over four hundred pages, and we were very fortunate to receive copies of these during his first visit to the West in the summer of 2003. We are now beginning to read and translate these texts, many of them termas, and so yet another chapter begins in our continuing work with the Vidyadhara.

The Teaching of Shambhala

SAKYONG MIPHAM RINPOCHE

What makes the lineage of Shambhala Buddhism especially relevant for the West?

Shambhala Buddhism provides the view and inspiration for how to deal with what's going on now. Even though Shambhala is rooted in a particular myth about an ancient kingdom in a particular place in Asia, its message is up to date. It is said that the Rigden kings will come to establish peace among beings, which is a story about the future. This teaching has to do with overcoming aggression here in the present.

Shambhala and the highest Buddhist teachings, basic goodness. Shambhala is connected with the vajrayana teachings, which are the highest Buddhist teachings; it's not a separate entity. According to the vajrayana view, the nature of all beings is indestructible compassion and wisdom. This is innate; fundamentally, all beings are good. In Tibetan the term is *döma-ne sangpo.* Döma-ne is the quality of beginningless, and sangpo is good, ground. So the basis of all things, down to the very smallest, is good and pure, in an unbiased, unconditional way. Human society is uncondition-

Interview by Fabrice Midal, edited by John Sell and Emily Hilburn Sell.

ally good—not in the sense of relative good and bad, but beyond good and bad. As we say in the vajrayana, it is beyond samsara and nirvana, beyond cyclical existence, and beyond aggression. Basic goodness really transcends the mind. It is beyond conceptuality.

A secular path. People generally say that those values are spiritual. But people also say that Shambhala is a secular tradition, a tradition based upon worldly needs, because it is grounded in doing what is best for society. The best thing for society, even in an everyday or a worldly situation, is the complete and individual fulfillment and happiness of the individual. This is really a spiritual pursuit. To look at the world in terms of basic goodness is related to sacred outlook: the world is good. In Buddhism, sometimes people think you should refrain from the world, not indulge in its attributes or pleasures. The world, according to the highest Buddhist teachings and Shambhala, is fundamentally workable and it's good, and therefore it's sacred, it's usable, it's understandable. At the highest levels of Buddhism, at the level of dzogchen in the Nyingma tradition and mahamudra in the Kagyü tradition, there is no separation. The view of basic goodness is beyond religion, beyond spirituality, beyond these conventions. Shambhala presents very practical details about how to live your life in the world, how to raise windhorse, how to have energy, how to work with your family. If you look at your experience as a necessary evil, something you just have to deal with it now, then you aren't really involved with a Shambhala path. At the same time, from a Buddhist point of view, the highest principle is having complete accomplishment spiritually, which includes temporal and secular accomplishment.

Universal monarch. In worldly terms, the Buddha is known as a universal monarch. In spiritual terms, he is the Buddha, the Awakened One. When Indra gave Buddha the great wheel of dharma, he said, "Please turn this wheel," which represents the power of a king; "You are not only the king of spirituality, but king of the whole world." That is really the notion of Shambhala Buddhism. We sometimes talk about the king and the Buddha, and in this particular time it's relevant.

When Trungpa Rinpoche was a young man, he had visions and insights about the necessity of Shambhala. His predecessor, the previous Trungpa, had also had such visions. Many people see right now that materially things aren't satisfying, and that there has to be something more to life. We have to look at the nature of things, and if we're able to understand how the world works, then at this particular time, we can have a society where people work together because they have a view of how to work together.

As Mipham's reincarnation, and having studied the teachings of Mipham, could you explain why this great master wrote so much about Shambhala?

The great nineteenth-century Tibetan teacher Mipham (1846–1912) wrote many works on Shambhala. He was one of the main people in Tibet to revitalize the Shambhala tradition. I think that this was a natural response to an increasing sense of aggression, an increasing sense that people's minds were getting exhausted, that people were stressed, and that compassion was waning. Shambhala is a place where everything—heaven, earth, and man—is in balance. Mipham also revitalized the tradition of Gesar of Ling. My father was a great reader of Mipham Rinpoche, so he became inspired by those teachings. The Dalai Lama and many other great lamas have studied Mipham Rinpoche's teachings on the Kalachakra, which is connected with Shambhala.

Do you want to comment on the relationship between Kalachakra and Shambhala?

Kalachakra is a tantra, a secret vehicle for recognizing the nature of mind and understanding basic goodness that is closely connected to Shambhala. It presents a complete world, including practice, view, and meditation. The Buddha was said to offer the *Kalachakra Tantra* as a way for the king of Shambhala to recognize his own enlightened quality. From that time onward, the *Kalachakra Tantra* has been associated with Shambhala and has been taught extensively. For the time we're in right now, it's a very auspicious tantra; it was one of the key tantras practiced in Shambhala. Both the Shambhala vision and Kalachakra are connected with bringing peace in times of aggression.

Certain teachings are made for certain times. The Shambhala teachings are here at this particular time to pacify aggression and agitation. Aggression produces fear. Fear produces cowardice, in that people are afraid even of their own thoughts and therefore are ruled by them. Shambhala is a place where people see the sacred element of themselves and the world.

They know how to work with their thoughts through the power of meditation. With this understanding, they overcome fear. In the Shambhala teachings we talk about having the confidence to overcome our own aggression, our own desire, our own jealousy and pride and so forth, which obstruct our ability to love and care for one another. So Shambhala is very much connected with establishing peace, because the teachings of Shambhala tell us how to do it.

Chögyam Trungpa also emphasized the relationship between Vajrakilaya and the Shambhala teachings. Could you comment?

In Shambhala the principle of the Rigden king, which is the totally enlightened, transcendent manifestation of enlightened living, is connected with Vajrakilaya, a wrathful deity who twirls a phurba—a three-sided knife—in order to overcome the three poisons. Shambhala also has a lot to do with kings and generals. Gesar of Ling is another wrathful manifestation. Wrath means being proactive, not waiting to act. It's too late to wait—we must do something now. After pacifying, enriching, and magnetizing, we need to destroy.

The deities are sometimes depicted in a black cloud or with a sword, which may seem like aggression. Wrathfulness doesn't involve aggression. It expresses a sense of urgency. Wrathfulness comes from compassion; if we don't overcome obstacles now, the world will fall into a degraded state. Vajrakilaya and the notion of cutting aggression is connected with Ashe—primordial confidence that has conquered aggression—a very honored principle in Shambhala. We are in a time where people have so much fear and mental agitation that they only act in response to very strong negative emotions. In Shambhala we uplift people so that they know their own wisdom and compassion, and act in response to positive motivation, putting others ahead of themselves.

As you've mentioned before, Chögyam Trungpa Rinpoche was related to Gesar. He dedicated his Shambhala books to him. You yourself have written a sadhana to Gesar, and have a very strong connection.

Gesar is our family ancestor. Mukpo Dong is a family lineage of Gesar of Ling, one of the greatest enlightened warrior-buddhas in Tibet. There are many songs about Gesar of Ling, who is sometimes presented as a folk hero, sometimes as a mystical figure. He is a very prominent teacher, just like Padmasambhava. In fact, he's said to be an embodiment of Padmasambhava. He is sometimes known as drala or werma, a being who overcomes aggression, the sense of poverty that exists in people's minds. We can invoke his buddha activity, his compassionate warriorship, in order to bring a sense of confidence and inspiration.

Gesar overcame a lot of obstacles. Since Trungpa Rinpoche also experienced great obstacles in his life, he used Gesar not only as a way of calling ancestors, but also as a buddha. He was inspired by Gesar's energy, because he also had difficulty. Gesar is a good example of a Shambhala warrior because he's a vajrayana buddha, Guru Rinpoche, and at the same time the king of Shambhala. The Buddha taught in many ways in order to help beings. Shambhala is here for our particular time, an inspiration that is in essence no different from the Buddhist teachings, but at the same time expresses itself in a slightly more personalized way. Enlightenment, like the sun, comes from one source, but it radiates to many different places.

Could you make a link between the image of the warrior and that of the bodhisattva?

Shantideva wrote about the notion of warriorship in his teachings on the bodhisattva, so in some ways you can say that Buddhism is borrowing that image of warriorship. Warriorship is courage—being able to offer our life, our ego, our attachment, for the benefit of others. In Shambhala we teach warriorship. Practicing compassion and dignity in a dark age like ours takes tremendous courage. It also requires thinking big. In terms of how his or her activity relates to a bigger picture, the bodhisattva is thinking much bigger than the ordinary person. Warriors going to battle also think much bigger. No longer fearing death, they can act in a courageous way. Their vast vision gives them tremendous courage. A person who has no fear is not reckless or suicidal; they've expanded their mind, so they're not held down in the same way somebody else is. They express a sense of tremendous confidence through their presence, and it brings fear into those of the setting-sun world, those who are still bound by self-absorption. The *Bodhicharyavatara—The Way of the Bodhisattva*—expresses the commitment to working tirelessly over as many lifetimes as it takes. That's warriorship: "I will work courageously and tirelessly forever for the benefit of others." The Shambhala understanding of warriorship has that quality of big vision.

Could we talk about Great Eastern Sun vision and setting-sun vision?

Setting-sun view comes from only looking toward our immediate satisfaction. We are only living in a world where we are encased in our own passion, aggression, and fear. Not seeing our limitless possibilities, our life-force energy is always diminishing. There's an immediate sense that our own power is diminishing. Our mind and body are not synchronized, because we are not relating to our own wisdom.

The notion of Great Eastern Sun is that we're relating to our inner wisdom. We know our basic goodness, which makes our own mind and heart very vast. "East" means that our wisdom is perpetually available and arising. It's consistent. There's a sense of perpetual awakening, shining, radiating. "Sun" means brilliance and lack of ignorance. Great Eastern Sun is the basic nature that we all possess. Setting sun is endless perpetuation of samsara, but it also has to do with how people's lives are not leading anywhere. In the setting sun, no matter what you do, it's a stale situation. It will eventually become dark. We will see less and less. We're not going anywhere. In Shambhala, every day, every situation, is a journey toward enlightenment, toward waking up.

Sometimes people feel threatened by the word *Buddhism* because of its religious connotations. But if you ask someone, "Do you want to be compassionate, courageous, or wise?" nobody's going to say no. Buddhism and Shambhala are ways to discover our own wisdom, compassion, and courage.

What is unique about Trungpa Rinpoche's presentation of the dharma?

Trungpa Rinpoche's expression of the Shambhala teachings is very fresh in terms of relating to what's happening in the world now. It's important to understand that he did not invent these teachings. He was very adamant about that: "This is what I learned, and these are the visions I had. I didn't come up with a new kind of Buddhism."

The notion of Shambhala is that we work tirelessly with the motivation of the warrior, which is to create an enlightened society for all beings. The view of a Shambhala person is to establish enlightened society. The community of Shambhala and of the Rigden king represents the vision of Great Eastern Sun, or wisdom. We want to establish a society that is the basis for enlightened activity. What is enlightened activity? The ultimate enlightened activity is to be engaged in virtue for the benefit of others.

Teachers like Trungpa Rinpoche and the previous Mipham Rinpoche, who also had visions, are coming out of wisdom, not simply out of writing books. These teachings have been handed down, showing how wisdom can be accessed. Rinpoche himself may have incorporated these principles as a way of trying to make them relevant to the West, but the nature of the realization has always remained constant. As he said, he wrote some texts on Shambhala, but there will be more texts written on Shambhala, there will be more commentaries written on Shambhala, and they will come from his future warriors.

The most important part of his legacy is not so much the uniqueness of the teachings, but rather that he worked at establishing an enlightened society. He was willing to actually do it, which is more important than that he came up with a teaching. This is what he told me: "This is why I'm doing what I'm doing, because it's needed. People need help, people need sanity, and this is the time to do it." There are traditions that teach how to raise confidence, there are traditions that teach how to understand wisdom—and we can show them to you—but the point is that we need to try to establish enlightened society. It would be no good if people thought he was just a great philosopher and that no one else had interesting things to say.

He himself was able to bring these teachings out of Tibet because he was having visions about this in Tibet. And I think that his seeing the destruction of Tibet added to his strength and his inspiration. The driving force toward the end of his life, and especially during the time we spent together, was to propagate the Shambhala teachings. He was adamant about why Shambhala is important. He is an example of a genuine bodhisattva responding to a genuine situation.

Teaching at the first Shambhala Training Level V in Boston, 1980.
Photograph © by Mary Lang. Used with permission.

From Cowards to Warriors

The Origins of Shambhala Training

CAROLYN ROSE GIMIAN

CHÖGYAM TRUNGPA RINPOCHE arrived in North America in early 1970. By 1976, just six years later, he and his students had created a sophisticated Buddhist world that showed all the signs of becoming an enduring tradition. He had founded more than fifty meditation centers, and he had started the first Buddhist-inspired university in North America, Naropa Institute, where he often lectured to audiences of more than a thousand. The faculty at Naropa included Allen Ginsberg, Ann Waldman, Joseph Goldstein, Sharon Salzburg, Jack Kornfield, Ram Dass, Maezumi Roshi, Gregory Bateson, William Burroughs, and many more spiritual and intellectual avant-garde luminaries. In cities around North America, on college campuses, in churches and town halls, Rinpoche had taught hundreds of seminars on meditation and the Buddhist path and given more than five hundred public talks. In New York, Chicago, Los Angeles, San Francisco, Boston, Toronto and other major cities in North America, he could count on an audience for one of his public talks of anywhere from five hundred to several thousand spiritual seekers. He had well over one thousand committed students who were undertaking the extensive practices involved in the Tibetan Buddhist path. He had started a three-month Seminary for the advanced training of his senior students.

He had appointed a Western student as his dharma heir, the inheritor of his Buddhist lineage. His books were best-sellers. By almost every measure, he and his work were already a huge success. Other than watching his world unfold and deepen, what more could he possibly need or want to do?

The scene around him seemed to whirl at terrific speed much of the time, punctuated by the silence and emptiness of the meditation hall and the absolute stillness and absolute force of the man at the center of the scene. In 1976, Chögyam Trungpa announced that he would spend the next year in retreat. It was a well-deserved break for him to refresh and renew his energy, and it also provided an opportunity for him to see how his students would do in his absence. Surprisingly, perhaps, it also marked the beginning of a new emphasis in his work. Never one to rest on what he had already accomplished, he began to develop a second and equally complex group of teachings. From late 1976 until his death in 1987, the propagation of the Shambhala teachings and the sacred path of the warrior was his passion.

In 1977 he spent the year in retreat, living in an old farmhouse near Charlemont, Massachusetts, where he received frequent updates on his students' activities. While on retreat, he asked a group of senior students to initiate Shambhala Training, a program for the general public that would bring the Shambhala teachings and the practice of meditation to a whole new audience.

In the Buddhist community that had grown up around Rinpoche, there was at this time a slight tendency toward Buddhist and vajrayana chauvinism developing among his students. As well, there was a particular version of Buddhist jargon that dominated the presentation of the teachings by senior students. When we were asked why we practiced or what Buddhism was about, a stream of foreign words and concepts often issued forth from our lips. We talked about becoming bodhisattvas, developing maitri and karuna, experiencing shamatha and vipassana, mahamudra, maha ati, sampannakrama, and you name it. We were energized and inspired by the practice of meditation and by our contact with Chögyam Trungpa himself, but unfortunately we were also often too full of ourselves, sure that we were the very best of the best of the new American breed of Buddhists. In many ways, we were! We were riding on the coattails of a man who cut a powerful figure through the American continent. He spoke to our hearts and minds with an impressive command of the English language. He encouraged us, not only to learn about Buddhism and to undertake the practice of meditation, but also to begin presenting many of these teachings to others, although we had only a few years of training. Our attempts were often more a mimicking than a reflection of a full understanding. Not having realized the depth of the teachings, our presentations often employed a kind of pidgin Sanskrit, or fractured phrases that we didn't fully understand.

I don't mean to belittle the efforts of Trungpa Rinpoche's students, because in fact we were trying to accomplish something quite new and without precedent. We had few if any examples to follow of Westerners who had undertaken and completed the journey that we were embarking on, so hesitation and mistakes, as well as false pride and imitation, were to be expected. As well, we were often in over our heads when it came to the presentation of the buddhadharma. Rinpoche may have had faith in our abilities, but I think we frequently felt extremely challenged by his expectations. Medical doctors have an expression: "See one, do one, teach one." That often seemed to be the protocol in Rinpoche's world as well!

Looking back, it seems that Trungpa Rinpoche's introduction of the Shambhala teachings and Shambhala Training was not just an "outreach" program but an integral way of training the students he already had. By introducing Shambhala Training, Rinpoche was forcing us to go further and deeper with our own training. To present Shambhala to others, we could not use our treasured Sanskrit phrases. Rinpoche gave instructions to us that in Shambhala Training, we should present the teachings without foreign terminology, without any linguistic or religious credentials, one might say. So we had to learn to present the teachings in English and to present the teachings not just with our intellects but also to speak from the heart.

In the fall of 1976, Trungpa Rinpoche had received a terma text presenting some of the most important Shambhala teachings on warriorship and confidence, entitled *The Golden Sun of the Great East*. Terma are considered to be teachings of the great Indian teacher Padmasambhava, which he concealed for the use of future generations in physical locations throughout Tibet and in the realm of mind and space. Padmasambhava "had various writings of his put in gold and silver containers like capsules and buried in certain appropriate places in the different parts of Tibet so that people of the future would rediscover them. . . . This process of rediscovering the treasures has been happening all along, and a lot of sacred teachings have been revealed. One example is the *Tibetan Book of the Dead*. Another approach to preserving treasures of wisdom is the style of the thought lineage. Teachings have been rediscovered by certain appropriate teachers who have had memories of them and written them down from memory. This is another kind of hidden treasure."[1] *The Golden Sun of the Great East* is such a mind terma. While still in Tibet, Chögyam Trungpa was recognized as a tertön, a teacher who "finds" or reveals terma.

In this text, there is a great deal of discussion of the idea of *zigi*, translated as "confidence" or "dignity," depending on the context. Confidence, in the sense that it is used in this text, refers to an intrinsic state of being that we uncover, rather than something that we pretend to have or that we build up or inflate. There is indeed a sense of rousing oneself, but one is rousing one's unconditional conviction in the strength of one's being, rather than trying to be something that one is not. This Shambhala text was the main study material to prepare ourselves for the presentation of Shambhala Training. About fifty of Rinpoche's students living in Boulder in 1977 had been selected as potential teachers for Shambhala Training. Twice a week, we met after work to review these Shambhala teachings, to give mock talks and discuss strategy for the presentation of Shambhala Training. In our mock presentations to one another, in which we visualized ourselves speaking to a large public audience, we were told by our instructors—other senior students—to be as overwhelming as we possibly could be and to belt out the reasons why Shambhala Training would be great for everyone to embrace. Many of our trial talks had very little content but were delivered with an almost evangelical zeal. We exhorted others to realize their potential for confidence and dignity, and dignity and confidence, ad nauseum at a fevered loud pitch. Most of us seemed to have a very limited understanding of the material that we were presenting. For many of us the confidence we were trying to instill in others was either quite abstract or quite foreign to us, a posture to be assumed rather than an inner quality to be discovered and embraced.

However, after several months of practicing our delivery, a few students from the group were selected to direct the first actual Shambhala Training programs, which took place over a weekend. Many of the rest of us were invited to be the assistant directors for these programs.

In general, our approach to the "real thing." the actual weekend programs, was very similar to our training sessions. The directors tried to
exude confidence and overwhelm the participants with their cheerful authority and charisma. As an assistant director, I was trained to cross-exam-
ine my students in their individual interviews, to ask them a cryptic
question such as "What is Great Eastern Sun?" and never, never to accept
their answer as good enough. We talked about approaching these interviews "dokusan style," but we were only imitating, indeed caricaturing,
the intense encounters between Zen masters and their students, rather
than reflecting actual insight. We had two interviews a day with our students, and in the second interview, I found that one of my interviewees
was furious because I was "laying a trip" on him. I had to agree with him; I
was, and I apologized. At the end of my first weekend as an assistant, I felt
depressed rather than elated by this new approach.

Apparently, I was not the only student who had such experiences. On
retreat in Massachusetts, Rinpoche got reports about the weekends that
had taken place. The feedback he received could not have been very positive, for after a few months of these floundering attempts, punctuated by
occasional brilliance and true heart, we—the first and future directors of
Shambhala Training—received a letter from him from his retreat. Rinpoche directed this letter to the head of the office of communications
within the organization, but it was clearly meant for all of his students
working on Shambhala Training, and it was read to us in one of our last
training sessions before his return from retreat. We were devastated by
what he said.

Nevertheless, to my mind, this letter still contains some of the best advice on teaching—and on genuine confidence—that one could receive.
Prior to receiving this letter, we thought that Shambhala Training was
about convincing others that we had something great to give them. In
looking back, such efforts seem to have been a misguided form of spiritual
salesmanship. What Rinpoche was offering us, instead, was a chance to
communicate and genuinely open ourselves to other human beings.
Somehow, we couldn't see that until we had gone through the bluster and
the posturing. We had to pump ourselves up with false confidence so that
we could discover the real thing. When I look back at this early period, it
seems to me that with this letter came the real beginning of Shambhala
Training.

Chögyam Trungpa writes:

People have been told to create Shambhala Training but instead they are just groping about and mimicking Shambhala Training. . . . As we know, the term "confidence" doesn't mean anything if we can't be sane in accordance with the buddhist doctrine. The term "dignity" doesn't mean anything if we can't observe the English table manners. It is useless to talk about the Great Eastern Sun unless we know how to make our own beds and be cheerful about the day's work ahead of us. . . .

We should pause for a moment and think about how fortunate we are to have the opportunity to bring about the Great Eastern Sun vision. We shouldn't constantly worry about our presentation of Shambhala Training. First we should appreciate how fortunate we ourselves are; then we will have something to say, some message to proclaim to the world. . . .

Shambhala Training can become a very powerful landmark in history only if we have a message to proclaim—and so far we don't have any message. All that we have said is that we are going to be secular rather than spiritual. This is a weak point which will cause us to cultivate jerks, artificial people who don't want to sit, who instead want to proclaim their personalities and say that they have ultimate confidence because their ambition to be powerful and sybaritic people is accommodated by their pseudo-spirituality. . . . Buddhism going secular is the best possible news for those people who just want to indulge themselves. . . .

We have to develop wholesomeness in the Shambhala Training administration, and our people have to be genuine—otherwise there will be no possibility of creating an enlightened society. Genuine means being without deception and without aggression. Genuine individuals do not build up their own personality cults, but are purely dedicated to their own mutual sanity.[2]

This excerpt communicates, I think, why you could be terrified by this man: his bluntness, his insight, his razor-sharp cutting through of deception. It also communicates why he attracted so many committed students and why you could fall in love with Chögyam Trungpa for all the same reasons plus a genuineness that knew no bounds. His criticism was at the same time his endorsement: he expected great things of us—and by us I mean all sentient beings—and he was unwilling to settle for anything less than the real thing.

When Rinpoche emerged from his retreat in December of 1977, he called together the now-deflated Shambhala Training directors' group, and he began to give us an extraordinary series of lectures on the principles of genuineness and meekness, which are the ground for the development of any further warriorship and which, he told us, were the ground for our presentation of the teachings to others. I remember the feeling in the room, or at least my own feelings at the time. While there was some fear, I also felt, as much as any other time I can remember, the sense of being a humble empty cup into which I longed for the teacher to pour the essence of the teachings.

As part of the sessions that Rinpoche conducted for the Shambhala Training directors, he also gave us a transmission for generating, or raising, our *lungta*—which he translated as "windhorse." This was the first time this transmission was ever given. This powerful wind or burst of energy unlocks our innate or primordial confidence, and it also teaches us to project that confidence to others, so that they too can be inspired into the wisdom of warriorship. In order for him to give this transmission and for us to genuinely receive it, it was necessary to prepare the ground, to break up the hardened clods of arrogance and false confidence and to water the ground with the genuine tears of longing of future warriors. This had been accomplished when he returned to Boulder from his retreat. As he wrote in a chant to the Rigden kings of Shambhala: "O Rigden Father, Your grace and gentleness have saved us from the depressions of the barbarians, and your sweet smile has produced chrysanthemums. / As we watch each petal grow, we rejoice and cry, and the tears of our crying produce future warriors."[3]

Almost all of the people from that original group trained by Chögyam Trungpa have gone on to become senior teachers in the Shambhala Training program. They, along with many others, are, in a real sense, the inheritors of the Shambhala wisdom that he proclaimed. The training program itself has been immensely successful, having presented meditation and the path of warriorship to many thousands of students. By and large, the program has kept at its core the message of humble meekness combined with glorious confidence that its founder personally conveyed. He taught us that real confidence, which we could also call bravery or fearlessness, comes from the softness of the human heart. It is the true art and the expression of being human.

When I look back, I am so grateful that such an uncompromising person as Chögyam Trungpa came to North America and presented the teachings here. Because of his tough but compassionate example, the genuine tradition of the Practicing Lineage and the true meaning of the Shambhala teachings can be realized in our lives. Although he has been gone for almost twenty years now, I think it is only recently that I have begun to take the nontheistic message of the teachings personally, realizing that, indeed, it is up to us. (I may be a particularly slow study!) There is no magical saving grace that will ensure that what he started will actually take root and flower. Although he planted the seeds of warriorship in the Western soil, it is up to each of us to nurture those seeds.

We have the confidence and the bravery within us to do so. Chögyam Trungpa wrote the lyrics to a number of Shambhala songs. One of them begins: "True command is the Great Eastern Sun / Confidence beyond hesitation / Just command is the warrior's sword / genuine and merciful."[4]

Will we use these tools—confidence, genuineness, and mercy—to build a warrior's world? Each of us has to answer that question for ourselves, not just once but on many occasions in a lifetime. In that sense, the origin of Shambhala Training is discovered over and over, here and now, in the choices we make, minute by minute, either to live in the warrior's world, meekly, without deception, or to indulge in the bloated arrogance and ego-clinging of the coward. As Rinpoche says: "There is no such thing as a failed warrior. Either you're a warrior, or you're a coward. . . . On the other hand, not succeeding is the warrior's staircase to discovering further bravery. Cowardice provides all sorts of challenges. . . . Rather than frightening you away, cowardice becomes a staircase. That is how a warrior is made out of a coward."[5] There is no praise or blame here. Long ago, when Chögyam Trungpa introduced his students to confidence and windhorse, he made use of our egotistical pride, confusion, and aggression as the good manure to fertilize the transmission. If we ourselves can use these plentiful materials within ourselves, we could have a bumper crop of meekness—which is the source of the warrior's genuine pride and dignity.

Notes

1. *Crazy Wisdom*, pp. 177–178.

2. From a letter to Joshua Zim, 1977. Used by permission of Diana J. Mukpo.

3. "Invoking the Rigen Father," in *Timely Rain* (1998), pp. 179–180. Reprinted courtesy of Diana J. Mukpo.

4. Excerpted from *True Command: The Teachings of the Dorje Kasung*, vol. 1, *The Town Talks*, ed. Carolyn Rose Gimian (Halifax: Trident Publications, 2003). Used by permission of the publisher.

5. *Great Eastern Sun: The Wisdom of Shambhala*, pp. 64–65.

The Influence of the
Epic of King Gesar of Ling
on Chögyam Trungpa

Robin Kornman

CHÖGYAM TRUNGPA RINPOCHE was an important figure in a movement of Tibetan Buddhist thought that flowered in the late nineteenth and early twentieth century, the Ri-me (*ris med*), or Eclectic school. The leaders of this movement, scholars and masters of meditation, came from different lineages or sects of Tibetan Buddhism. One even represented the native, non-Buddhist religion of Tibet, Bön. They combined the teachings and practices of their different lineages to produce a new synthesis, one that allowed followers of any school to use the best teachings from the other schools. In his eleventh incarnation Trungpa Rinpoche was groomed to be a leading spokesman of this movement and to advance its program in the monastic/academic society of Northeastern Tibet, a region that borders China.

As we will see, the Eclectics were not just a syncretic philosophical movement; some among them seem to have had a sociopolitical vision as well—a vision of how mundane society and mystical religion should be united. We will find this program in no political text, for the study of politics, as we have it from Plato and Aristotle, did not exist in Inner Asia. In that arid and sparsely populated region where nomadic pastoralists predominated, there was no such thing as a polis, a city, as we know it. There was no such geographical entity that could have generated a government one would theorize about. Whereas Greece had city-states or empires, Northeastern Tibet had nomadic groups and centers of trade, the Chinese empire to the east, and examples of burgeoning nomadic confederations such as the Mongols along the Silk Route.

The Tibetan oral epic of King Gesar of Ling presents an extensive and detailed description of an idealized nomadic government formed by a Tibetan tribe known as the Mukpo clan, which gradually expands to become an empire-sized nomadic confederation. The Eclectic movement used images from this immense corpus of oral and literary materials to construct its views on the nature and function of government. Trungpa Rinpoche in his Western mission called this "enlightened society"—the theory that there is a certain good way to combine religion, government, and society.

Enlightened Society

Chögyam Trungpa Rinpoche was not only a Buddhist religious teacher but a cultural leader. He devised a set of teachings on how Buddhist culture could apply to the first and future generations of Western Buddhists and outlined a philosophy to describe what he thought Buddhist cultural influence on the secular West should be. These ideas were presented to the public in museum shows, poetry readings, and performance situations at Naropa Institute, the university he created in Boulder, Colorado. To his students he delivered his ideas on the role of Buddhist culture in society in a more systematic form under the rubric of enlightened society.

The idea of enlightened society is that the Buddhist path is not simply a way to escape suffering and the wheel of rebirth and not simply a way of helping others to do this, but also a way of life reflecting the vision and values (if I may use that term) of the buddhas.

Those of us who are not yet enlightened live in samsara, cyclic existence, the realm of illusion. Samsara is one shore—"this shore"—of a river. On the "other shore," beckoning us to cross the flood, are the enlightened ones themselves, the buddhas of the three times and ten directions—a universe of beings who have transcended samsara, time, and space. Standing on this shore, we confused beings have our own point of view. When we look to our left and right, we see our fellows in samsara and the confused world we have built—a world where, as Marcus Aurelius might have said, we assent constantly to false judgments about phenomena and our own mental life.

Across the waters we see the tiny, distant figures of the buddhas calling us to join them. When we climb into boats and row across the river toward the buddhas, the figures of our fellows in samsara become gradually smaller and smaller, while our fellow travelers stay the same size, and the buddhas gradually grow in our vision as we approach their shore. The ship rocks, and we must row constantly. However it is worth the effort, because in the end we will find ourselves in the society of enlightened ones, who "go from bliss to bliss," whereas the samsaric people "go from from suffering to suffering."

The life we lead in the boat crossing the river of suffering to gain the other shore of enlightenment is what is meant by enlightened society. In developing a visionary sense of how this enlightened society will be, point of view is everything. We cannot truly occupy the point of view of the buddhas, for we are still confused beings. But we no longer see our lives from the point of view of those on "this shore," the samsaric shore. The virtues we develop and attempt to practice are based on the "other shore" of the buddhas.

There were several components to Trungpa Rinpoche's vision of the possibility of an enlightened society. The moral code had its grounding in conventional Buddhist ethics. For example, the first principle one absorbed to regulate action in society was the hinayana precept, "First do no harm." This means that the beginner or intermediate student may not be able to tell what is precisely the right thing to do in a given circumstance, but at least one can make sure one's behavior harms no one. In his play *Strange Interlude*, Eugene O'Neill wrote, "We must all be thieves where happiness is concerned." "Do no harm" prevents a principle of selfishness such as this from being put into action, no matter how it seems to coincide with what Western materialists would call, ironically enough, enlightened self-interest.

The central conception of enlightened society is the set of mahayana ethical principles known as the six perfections, or more literally, the virtues of "having gone to the other shore" (*paramita*). These were practiced by knights of enlightenment called bodhisattvas. Trungpa took the Tibetan translation of the Sanskrit term term *sattva* (Tib. *sems dpa'*) to be "mind warrior," *pa* being the word for a warrior or knight. He said that the central virtue of the bodhisattva path was the courage such a warrior must show.

Trungpa Rinpoche's strict definition of the six paramitas was based on Chandrakirti's *Madhyamakavatara*, which he obviously used for one of his greatest early seminars in America, "The Ten Bhumis." But beginning in the 1980s, he reformulated these ethical principles using a different set of metaphors and systems of signifiers, drawn from the *Kalachakra Tantra* and the *Epic of Gesar of Ling*. The epic was a work that drew upon teachings native to Inner Asia and influences from Chinese thought and literature.

In its modern forms the Tibetan epic shows vast influences from the syncretism of the Yuan dynasty, which combined what we might call Mongol multiculturalism with the philosophical language and bureaucratic infrastructure of the Confucian state. This influence followed quite naturally from the patron-guru relationship that Tibetan high lamas had with the Yuan emperors. It can be seen in the performances and visual representations of the Tibetan oral epic, wherein the warriors wear the armored uniforms and bear the panoply of heroes from Chinese novels, particularly *The Romance of the Three Kingdoms* (*San guo yen yi*) of Luo Guanzhong. The Kangxi emperor explicitly associated this novel with the Gesar epic in the Mongol translation of the epic he published.

The Qing dynasty was also ruled by the descendants of an Inner Asian nomadic confederation, and so the syncretism of the epic continued to have state support in modern times. In the 1950s, when the Communists began to exert their influence on studies of the Tibetan epic, they regarded it as a valid folkloric composition of the Tibetan and Inner Asian minorities of China. In this way, they continued the theme of multiculturalism, which favored the literary, political, and religious syntheses shown in the epic.

Thus, when Trungpa Rinpoche used the language of the Gesar epic to characterize the political and cultural philosophy he taught in his lectures on enlightened society, he was following a venerable tradition of the post-antiquity period in Sino-Tibetan thought. Therefore, he deployed in his political theory the Confucian ideals of natural hierarchy, heavenly mandate, and heaven, earth, and man. Without using the word itself, he presented a Buddhist theory of the Confucian notion of "humanity."

In enlightened society as Trungpa envisioned it, leadership would come from philosopher kings who possessed the mandate of heaven because of their wisdom. These kings were able to unite philosophical ideals with practical politics by having the principle of man uniting heaven and earth. The king was the man principle, which joined heaven as ideal with earth as reality. Following that logic, every person in an enlightened society who was trained in political leadership or who provided cultural leadership performed the same function of joining heaven and earth.

The deities that enlightened society would rely on were organized according to heaven, earth, and man as well. They were ordered according to heavenly gods called *lha*, gods of mountains and natural geography called *nyen* who joined heaven and earth, and gods of the waters called *lu* (Skt. *naga*), which were the earth principle. Lha, nyen, and lu matched heaven, earth, and man and numerous Buddhist metaphysical triads. The rituals of enlightened society included the *lhasang*, smoke-offering rituals in which a column of smoke joined the earthly world of the altar with the divine world of the skies. Even technology, the arts, and artisanal products were analyzed according to this principle. Trungpa thus evoked the Confucian classics in his political philosophy and invited into his theory the ritual system, the calendrical astrological theory, and the alchemical science of classical Chinese philosophy.

This fit well with Tibetan medicine, which involved a vast amount of Chinese medicine, native Tibetan religion, and, as we shall see, the cosmology of the Gesar epic, where the most elaborate image of enlightened society was found. It also fit with the calendrical culture of the Kalachakra, which included the Chinese system of elements.

Northeastern Tibet was not a land of cities and political centers, but a vast alpine pastoralist economy on the border of a huge agrarian empire. The Gesar epic in the edition that Trungpa probably knew depicts the region of Golok in Amdo/Qinghai as a place that developed a model for an enlightened society. The epic, in fact, is an idealizing narrative describing the founding of such a society in the course of a series of epic wars.

Many epics, of course, perform a similar function, depicting an ideal society at war or being given birth to by war. Eighteenth-century European literary theory regarded the *Iliad* in this way, Voltaire claiming that Agamemnon, for example, was the image of an ideal king. Virgil's *Aeneid* is still seen this way in contemporary criticism, and all the conscious descendants of these two epics continue the theme of idealizing the political

identity of a people. Presenting an ideal politic is one of the epic's methods of delivering to its natural audience materials for their sense of self-
identity. We learn who we are by reading the epic of our people. The Gesar
epic, as we shall see, was used in its home province as a basis for constructing religious and political identity.

The Eclectic school's version of the Gesar epic was thus available to
Trungpa as a political model, and he used this school's theorization of the
Gesar as a basis for his own missionary dispensation of mystical religion as
a public religion, attempting to re-create in the West the cultural program
that was being born in Eastern Tibet just as the Chinese invasion began.

The Gesar Epic as a Popular Mystery Text

The version of the Gesar epic that Trungpa used is today read by all Tibetans, but it was closely connected in his youth with a region of pastoral
nomads just adjacent to the area of influence of Trungpa's monasteries.

A public text may be universally available and part of a national discourse and yet at the same time have a special and peculiar life in a particular region. This is so for certain biographical texts in Tibetan esoteric
Buddhism. Even though the teachings and practices of Tibetan tantra are
secret, in a given region there are sometimes a set of texts that exist to
make the secret public property, so that an esoteric religion, a religion
whose practices and teachings are secret, may nevertheless be in one place
the public practice of all the people.

I am thinking here of texts that the great American Tibetanist E. Gene
Smith calls *rgyab* texts, literally "back" texts. These are narratives that feature tantric heroes undergoing spiritual training and gaining enlightenment through esoteric techniques. Smith calls them back texts because
they serve as general background reading for the study of the secret materials. They are public in themselves and very popular: songs from these
texts are on the lips of the common man, and famous passages are known
by the public. Nevertheless, in seeming violation of codes of initiatory secrecy, they give a public key to secret teachings.

For example, any literate Tibetan can read *The Life of Milarepa* by
Tsang Nyön Heruka and the collection of autobiographical songs that accompany it, *The Hundred Thousand Songs of Milarepa*. These two narrative
works show how an ordinary man gained enlightenment through the prac-

tice of the tantric system of meditation known as *mahamudra* (great symbol). The system of mahamudra exercises is complicated and must be performed stage by stage over a lifetime of asceticism, yogic exercises, subtle rituals, and meditation practices. Every stage is preceded by initiations that are given only to the faithful after they have proved themselves to their guru and taken vows of obedience and loyal commitment. Stage after stage the disciple journeys from one secret to another in this path, secret within secret, mystery secreted behind mysteries.

Actually, however, it seems that every secret teaching of mahamudra is mentioned, described, and illustrated in the course of Milarepa's two-volume biography, a perfectly public document. The songs describe something of how Mila visualizes tantric deities, even though in theory one must receive an abhisheka or initiation in order to have the right to do those visualizations. They describe Milarepa's experience in doing the inward yogic exercises in which one controls the energies (Skt. *prana*; Tib. *rlung*) that run along channels (Skt. *nadi*) in the subtle body. In general a person must do a three-year retreat in order to receive instructions in these yogas; the manuals that describe the exercises are extremely hard to obtain. But the songs of Milarepa are a rgyab text, a back text, to this tradition, and so the songs mention the yogas and describe them a bit. There are even sections where Milarepa describes his experience in the supersecret and controversial tantric sexual yogas. The most profound and advanced formless meditation practices are also described, even though some gurus refuse to give these teachings in public.

The songs of Milarepa are a public background text for the system of practices connected with mahamudra, and there are places in Eastern Tibet where they are so widely sung and generally studied that one could well say that through this background text an esoteric religion has been been moved into the sphere of public practice.

In this sense the background texts for the Nyingma lineage's tantrism are the biographies of Padmasambhava, whose verses provide the lyric material for the foundational Nyingma chants. In the same way, the advanced and secret Nyingma and Bönpo teaching known as *dzogchen* (great perfection) has its background text in certain editions of the Gesar epic and for the region of Golok in Amdo/Qinghai, this esoteric system of practices is indeed the public religion.

For those who have studied Tibetan Buddhism, it is strange to think that dzogchen should anywhere be common property. The Nyingma philosopher Jamgön Kongtrül the Great listed dzogchen as the last and highest of the nine *yanas* (vehicles). It is even stranger to think that the Golokpas, who are more more famous as bandits and fiercely independent rebels than as philosophers, should hold this as their common thought. It is strange to think that the wild, nearly lawless regions around Mount Machen Pomra are a homeland for some of the most profound philosophical ideas ever mentioned in human speech.

And yet some of Tibet's greatest thinkers have come from this region on the Sino-Tibetan marches, including Do Khyentse Yeshe Dorje, who was a reincarnation of Jigme Lingpa, and Mipham Gyatso, the great systematizing polymath of the nineteenth century, whose collection of commentarial works forms the heart of the modern Nyingma academic syllabus. In fact, many of the leaders of the Eclectic movement were connected in some way by family, proximity, or dharma lineage with the tribal nomads of Golok. There seems to have been some connection with Golok for Chögyam Trungpa as well. He initiated his students into the cult of one of the presiding mountain deities of the region, Magyal Pomra. He placed one of his principal American retreat centers under Magyal Pomra's protection and spoke of the oral epic of Gesar, which we now know was composed by Golok-speaking bards.

Enlightened Society and Mystery Religion

In Chögyam Trungpa's thought there is a strange mixture of religious secrecy with broad sociopolitical notions of the possibility of what he called an enlightened society. "Enlightenment" in this case refers to the Sanskrit term *bodhi*, the complete mystical realization of a buddha. Every institutionalized religion is at some point seduced into the notion of becoming a national or imperial religion, of becoming one with political leadership. The French policy of *laïcité* and the American doctrine of separation of church and state are testimony to the Western experience of the dangers of such a religious policy.

But our experience in the West of the dominance of a single religion over a society, the pervasive union of a religion with a government and social order, is fundamentally different from the Tibetan one. In the West, mystery religions do not dominate society, but only the public, common, and exoteric aspects of a religion. In Tibetan so-called theocracy, the leaders are not ordinary churchmen but mystics who seek to propagate their mysteries among the common people, even though the teachings are held to be secret and initiatory. It is as if Böhme or Eckhardt or John of the Cross or Teresa of Ávila or Thomas Aquinas in the late contemplative period of his life had sought to become Pope and exercise political power for their private mystical paths.

In a sense this notion of mystery religion as public path is close to Plato's *Republic*. The philosopher king and the political leadership of his idealized society were people who ruled by virtue of private mystical realizations. The one who sees the phenomenal world as mere appearance and reality as a transcendent other, rules the country and introduces the citizens to his private mystical world. To use tantric terminology, the leader expands the boundaries of the mandala, the private society of his personal students who share the initiatory mysteries, to the entire nation.

This was the theory of the relationship between religion and society that Trungpa Rinpoche elaborated in the West. Its metaphysics was based on the philosophical syncretism of the Eclectic movement, which evolved an almost Neoplatonic emanational version of Buddhist mysticism. The mythological machinery, the cosmology of his system, was based on the most complex of all Buddhist tantras, the *Kalachakra (Wheel of Time) Tantra*. But textually it was based on the Tibetan oral epic of King Gesar of Ling, which deployed a non-Buddhist divine machinery based on native Inner Asian shamanistic and animistic religion. The "back text" of Trungpa's socioreligious system was the Gesar epic. This meant that his model for the relationship between religion and society was what he saw in his region of Tibet, the Sino-Tibetan marches of Kham (Eastern Tibet) and Amdo/Qinghai. In particular, he pointed to the Goloks, nomadic pastoralist warriors, who made the mystery religion of dzogchen, the great perfection, their public religion through, among other things, the propagation of the oral epic.

The Regional Belief System of the Gesar Epic

In the imagination of Trungpa Rinpoche, the Goloks were fiercely independent and battle-hardened, living a romantic and adventurous life of banditry and pastoralism. It's probably true; but true or not, they were represented in the Gesar epic this way. So the cultural life of the regional nomads became an aura which surrounded Chögyam Trungpa's thinking about the dzogchen teachings.

The Gesar epic in the form he knew syncretically combined elements of Chinese alchemical Taoism, Inner Asian shamanism, and tantric Buddhism with the geopolitics of the Silk Route, with the oral literary materials and epic rhetorical values of pastoralist nomads, with the cosmology of the *Kalachakra Tantra*, and with the special Sino-Tibetan love of the implements of horse-mounted warfare. All of these elements in the thought of Trungpa Rinpoche can be traced back to the influence of the Gesar epic as a background to his most sophisticated thought and most elaborate cultural visions.

The Gesar epic itself is quite a rich and multifaceted literary phenomenon. It is the largest extant oral epic in the world. There are still bards in Tibet and China who can sing from memory many volumes of the Gesar. One female bard claims to be able to sing more than a hundred volumes, and a small army of Sino-Tibetan scholars now devote themselves to recording and studying these modern epic singers.

The epic tells the story of a martial bodhisattva who incarnates in Tibet along with a retinue of Buddhist and native deities to save the Buddhist religion from destruction at the hands of the armies of surrounding Asian kingdoms ruled by anti-Buddhist demon kings. These encircling enemies are the great kingdoms and ethnic groups of the Silk Route. At the beginning of the epic each of these kingdoms is ruled by a monster who was once a man, in fact once a great tantric Buddhist practitioner. They were superior Buddhist yogins in their previous lifetimes, but developed such great power and confidence through their tantric meditations that they became arrogantly opposed to their own gurus and turned against religion itself.

It is a key point in the worldview of Trungpa Rinpoche that negative power comes from a thwarted attempt to realize the positive. The demon kings are *dam sri*, vow violators. They took vows to perform vast positive acts and began on a career of becoming great bodhisattvas who would help many people and perhaps save whole societies. Their virtuous meditation practice and good intentions accumulated for them vast merit and magical powers. But at some point they took a wrong turn and their character changed from positive to negative, from bodhisattva to demon.

Now, as demons, they still retain the powers their previous virtuous deeds gained them.

Thus, in the anti-Buddhist enemies of Ling we see evil not as a self-existent substance distinct from the good, but as an impulse for good that retains its basic nature but has been twisted into evil. It is a thwarted attempt at transcendence. Since it arose from the universal ground of buddha nature possessed by all beings, it still retains its primordial character of goodness.

This is an example of how the epic fits itself to the dzogchen mystical system. The primordial nature of consciousness is the undetermined, unreified, transcendent All-Good (the Buddha Samantabhadra), beyond phenomenal manifestations of either good or evil. The positive instincts of bodhisattvas come from their inborn sense of the common ground and produce their aspiration to return to it by the most direct method. Evil demons base their negative paths on the same basic instinct, a sense of the common ground of existence. Like the bodhisattvas, they see the return to that ground as a transcendent move, but they mistakenly make their move in the opposite direction, fleeing the ground as if it were bondage rather than freedom.

The epic describes the creation of an enlightened being who, like the demon kings, is powerful with magic, but who, since he is enlightened, has the subtlety to see the positive roots of the kings' negative natures—or, to put it more precisely, to see their positive nature bent by subtle twists into a temporarily evil manifestation.

Chögyam Trungpa's teachings about the nature of this subtle twist became the foundation for his entire presentation of the path in America. He expounded this doctrine in a negative way in *Cutting Through Spiritual Materialism*, particularly in the first chapter, "Spiritual Materialism." The title of the book reveals the lineage sources of these ideas, for "cutting through" is Trungpa Rinpoche's translation of *trekchö*, the dzogchen term for teachings on meditation without characteristics. Trungpa Rinpoche's positive presentation of this doctrine appears in many places, but particularly in his Shambhala teachings.

Returning to the epic, we see in the first volume that Gesar is born in the midst of an auspicious magical display of good auspices among the culturally colorful and extremely warlike nomads of the Northeastern Tibetan marches. These people are wild but faithful to the buddhadharma.

At the crossroads of Chinese and Central Asian civilization along the eastern terminus to the Silk Route, they follow their herds of yaks, sheep, and cattle through vast, treeless meadows lush with mountain wildflowers and the treelike rhododendrons of the Himalayas, living as nomads in the alpine fastnesses of a land Tibetans call Amdo and Kham and the Chinese locate principally in Qinghai and Gansu. These nomads are superb horsemen and doughty warriors. They live in black yak-wool tents surrounded by the the giant killer mastiffs that Tibetans use as guard dogs. Their lamas are hearty and earthy but extremely learned. Their political leaders are wise, full of proverbial wisdom and copious formal speech, and, when it comes to tribal matters, capable of extremely nuanced political views.

The Gesar epic exists in many editions and in many literary forms. First of all, as a purely oral phenomenon, there are bards singing or telling the tale. Some bards are actually storytellers and their versions of the Gesar are pure prose. Others sing the traditional prosimetric epic form, which alternates prose story narration with a sort of folk aria sung by one of the characters. As Mireille Hellfer has shown, each character in the epic has his own particular melody and all of his, her, or its (for the horses sing as well) songs are sung in their distinctive melody.

The poetic form of the songs is very specific and stands in marked contrast to the elegant Sanskritic kinds of poetry favored by the Buddhist clerisy. It is full of nomadic proverbs, sarcasm, humor, and lyrical pastoral evocations. Like classical Buddhist poetry, the songs are often expected to have a subtle meaning that must be figured out by the hearer. This intellectual complexity usually comes from the need to figure out the relationship between the proverbs and the argument of the whole song, which is often no simple matter. Usually the songs are argumentative, not narrative. A speaker urges the other characters to a specific action or criticizes another character's thought or behavior. Although it is too early in our data collection to confidently generalize, it appears that the songs change from performance to performance less than the prose narrative.

Virtually every Tibetan knows the entire plot of the epic from childhood. The stories are absorbed from the general cultural milieu, and it does not really matter whether one has heard a bardic performance or not.

An Outline of the Epic

The story begins with the discovery by Avalokiteshvara or some other high deity that the land of Ling in Tibet is surrounded by the enemies of the four directions or the four demon kings.

There follows a council in heaven very much like the scenes in Homeric epics where Zeus consults with the gods about affairs on earth. At this council it is determined that some divine being must incarnate as a human and lead the armies of Ling against the four kings.

A great bodhisattva is chosen, but he refuses to take on human form unless he is accompanied by a team of other gods who will become his comrades in arms. He secures in advance the collaboration of a number of local Himalayan deities, as well as certain buddhas and famous gurus. For example, the horse-headed tantric buddha known as Hayagriva must promise to incarnate as the hero's future horse. Padmasambhava, the deathless guru guardian of Tibet, must promise to find Gesar a suitable mother and for his family a tribe of fearless warriors faithful to the buddhadharma. Mountain gods must forge magical armor and weapons for the future Gesar and his comrades. A native Tibetan goddess called simply Auntie (Manene) must appear to him constantly as his close adviser. The list of prerequisites the bodhisattva presents tells us much about the culture and religion of Northeastern Tibet and the way of life of the alpine nomads there.

The epic continues from here with descriptions of how the people of Ling and the animistic gods associated with Ling prepare to receive the incarnation. The birth of Gesar is itself an entire volume of the epic and reads in many respects like the accounts of the birth of divine heroes already familiar in the West. In fact, the birth stories of famous Buddhist lamas often follow a similar pattern: prophecies by diviners of the coming birth, the unique status of the mother and her dreams of a special impregnation, miraculous signs at birth, the investment of the tribe of the mother with a special destiny, general rejoicing that a savior has come to the tribe, and contemplations on the mystery of incarnation itself.

After the birth, there is a section of the epic of flexible length that describes the adventures of Gesar as child and youth. It is reminiscent of the Indian Puranas, stories of the child Krishna, a youthful trickster who is a god in disguise. There is no doubt that the Gesar epic contains influences from Indian epics, particularly the *Ramayana*.

However, the real source of the stories that make up the youthful Gesar section are probably Turkic narratives about Central Asian nomadic or tribal warriors. For example, young Gesar possesses the mental and magical powers one would expect from a bodhisattva, but he also has the distinctive abilities of a shamanic magician: the ability to use power objects and to deflect magical attacks of other shamans, the ability and propensity to change shape for purposes of deception, mastery of shamanic energy systems that, as we will see, are quite different from the systems of prana, nadi, and bindu central to Indic forms of yoga.

Immediately upon birth, the baby Gesar sets about the task of defeating the particular divine enemies of his tribe. For example, hardly is he out of his womb before he kills with a bow and arrow a demon who represents the power of a local marmot-like creature whose holes and tunnels plague nomadic shepherds. It seems odd that the first act of a Buddhist god would be to go off and kill an animal—in fact, a number of them. But it fits perfectly as the appropriate beginning to the career of a shamanic tribal protector. We will examine this point in more detail in a moment when we look at the influences of the Gesar epic on the thought of Chögyam Trungpa. But let us continue now with our rapid summary of the epic itself.

As a child our hero is not actually called Gesar—a noble name derived from the Byzantine title Caesar, which entered into usage among Mongolians as Kesar and evolved finally into the Tibetan Gesar. He is called Joru, a childish nickname. Joru is actually the image of a nomad juvenile delinquent. His body seems deformed. His clothes are made from uncured skins. He is stunted, dirty, and rough-mannered. He is the opposite of the nomadic ideal of the "young tiger" or "brave son"—the elegant, jauntily dressed, strong, hearty, clean-living young man that nomads present as their ideal, a noble youth who is strong, handsome, courageous, independent, and armed to the teeth.

Instead Joru is stunted, ugly, poorly dressed, unarmed except for the shepherd's weapon, a slingshot: he is deceptive, disagreeable to his elders, and constantly involved in mean practical jokes. At a certain point Joru actually pretends to be a serial killer, kidnapping Tibetan merchants and making it appear that he has murdered them. He is ostracized from the Mukpo clan into which he is born and must go off with his mother to live alone and friendless in the wild, unpeopled land of Ma. There he consorts exclusively with mountain gods and local spirits and grows up secretly, unfettered by politics and social obligations. The only human in his world is his mother. As far as his relatives and friends are concerned, he is an ugly boy who turned monster and was expelled from society.

From an anthropological point of view, he shows the form of an accomplished shaman who spends his youth on an extended shaman's journey through the invisible world of gods—demons, and local and ancestral spirits. From the point of view of a few discriminating Lingites such as the minister Denma, the epic's Ulysses; Chipön, the epic's Nestor; Drugmo, the epic's Helen; and Gyatsha Zhalkhar, the epic's Achilles—he is a enlightened guru whose ability to change form and disguise his true nature is a sign of buddhahood.

From the tribal point of view, Joru is at all times an object of suspicion. His mother claims to be the daughter of the king of the dragons, but she is taken into the tribe as the second wife of a leader of the Mukpo clan—a woman of doubtful origins and doubtful parentage. Joru seems to be a dangerous juvenile pest with the power of black magic, almost a demon. The different reference points are a mark of the Buddhist oral epic. Since Gesar sees the world of mere appearance as based on a dream, insubstantial when compared with transcendent reality, his attitude toward everything, even his relatives and close friends, is seasoned with irony and a sense of the inscrutable and the strange humor of the enlightened gods who, moving from bliss to bliss, see the life concerns of sentient beings as they move from suffering to suffering, as both a matter for compassion and a cosmic joke. There is thus always a play of different points of view.

In the third volume of the epic, the moment finally comes when Joru must transform from a monster boy into a glorious dharma king. The most beautiful maiden in Ling will be the prize in a horse race. The winner of the race will gain her hand in marriage and rulership of Ling. This is a recognizable motif from Turkish epic literature, where a hero must win one of three contests: a wrestling match, a deadly archery contest, or a horse race. Gesar joins the race and when he wins is transformed into an effulgent youthful prince. All the magical beings who agreed to incarnate with him gather around, and the entire tribe of Ling is led into the recesses of Magyal Pomra Mountain, where magical weapons have been left for them by gods and buddhas.

There is a great celebration, and the rough but honest and faithful tribe of Ling begins its journey to becoming an enlightened society.

The events narrated thus far take up the first three volumes of the epic in its currently most popular edition, a nine-volume work edited under the direction of the great Eclectic philosopher Ju Mipham himself.

In the middle episodes of the Mipham version, Ling is attacked by great empires in the four directions, the famous enemies of the four directions. At one point Gesar's consort, the lovely Drugmo, is kidnapped in a passage reminiscent of both the *Ramayana* and the *Iliad*. Wars are fought successively against each demon king. Each victory expands the political reach of Ling and gains for its tribes some unique cultural treasure or piece of science held by the defeated kingdom. These treasures become part of the patrimony of Ling and lead it step by step toward the greatness and sophistication of an empire. But we must note here that the ever-increasing sovereignty of Gesar and the Lingites is not like that of China's great agrarian empire or the Roman empire. It is the story of the step-by-step creation of a world-conquering nomadic confederation, like the empires created by the Mongols. The difference between an empire and a nomadic confederation is key for understanding the political theory of the Gesar epic.

The ninth and last volume is actually called *Gesar in Hell*, the *Great Perfection*. In it Gesar harrows hell and actually instructs the damned in dzogchen, the highest form of meditation practice in Tibetan Buddhism. They are liberated and leave the wheel of samsara. Gesar dies and transfers his consciousness to the Kingdom of Shambhala, where he exists to this day, waiting for the Buddhist apocalypse. You could say that this last volume occupies the same place in the overall epic as the *Bhagavad Gita* does in the Indian *Mahabharata*, for it is more a philosophical and contemplative manual than a battle saga.

There are many other versions of the Gesar. Sino-Tibetan scholars have collected more than a hundred volumes of published chapters and many times that of recorded performances of chapters in the epic. Like the *Mahabharata*, it is a huge, unwieldy corpus. We do not know what bardic performances Trungpa Rinpoche heard, but it is fairly certain that the written version he saw was one edited by Ju Mipham Gyatso, for Trungpa had his disciples translate and chant the Gesar rituals Mipham wrote to accompany this edition.

As we will see, Mipham created a sophisticated philosophical structure in his edition of the epic, and this structure provided a program for Trungpa Rinpoche's later dispensations in America and Europe.

The Tracks of the Epic in the Oeuvre of Chögyam Trungpa

As we have learned recently, Trungpa Rinpoche left a prodigious writing behind when he escaped Tibet, the remarkable product of the first nineteen years of his life. Ancient *termas* (found texts) that he discovered and transcribed, rituals he composed, his records of visionary revelations, meditation manuals, and works of poetry were scattered across Eastern Tibet in the area where he wandered as a young meditator and student and taught as a reincarnated lama (*tülku*). These works are being collected now by Karma Senge Rinpoche, a nephew of Trungpa Rinpoche's.

One work from Chögyam Trungpa's early period about which we know a great deal, but which has not been recovered, is a verse epic of several hundred pages probably titled *The Golden Dot: The Epic of Lha, the Annals of the Kingdom of Shambhala*. Trungpa Rinpoche began to reconstruct his original composition after escaping Tibet, and it is this later work to which we refer. The first chapter describes the creation of the world by nine cosmic gods (*srid pa'i lha*) who appear in the form of native Tibetan deities known as *drala* (*dgra bla*), or war gods. These gods represented primal and originary aspects of the phenomenal world. For example, one of these lha stood for all kinds of light. Glancing in many directions, this deity created all the lights that exist in the world, including the sun, the moon, the light of planets and stars, and the inward luminosity of consciousness itself. Another represented space and the sense of direction; by gazing and gesturing in different directions, this primordial god created every sort of space, including physical space, which is given an interesting definition: "the ability to separate two things." One goddess created all forms of water and every body of water in the world. Another was responsible for all mountains and hills.

In Trungpa Rinpoche's epic these deities were directed by a ninth lha called Shiwa Ökar (zhi ba 'od dkar), Peaceful White Light, a sort of absolute principle behind creation and the nature of reality. After these nine cosmic deities have created the world, Peaceful White Light goes to the things they have created and invests each one with an animistic spirit, a drala. So, for example, each of the bodies of water is given a *lu* (*klu*), or dragon spirit. The mountains are given *nyen* (*gnyan*), or mountain spirits. The highest bodies are given *lha*, or ouranic deities.

The *Epic of Lha*, so we are informed, proceeds in this way at great length. Unfortunately, this work was lost during Trungpa Rinpoche's flight from the Chinese. When he arrived in the West, he rewrote the first two chapters, but no more.

One of the really striking things about the two chapters we have of the *Epic of Lha* is that its previous texts, the literary tradition upon which it is based, are not, as one would expect, the Indic texts of Tibetan Buddhism (the tantras, sutras, and commentaries), but rather the creation myths found in Tibetan royal chronicles and in the *Epic of Gesar of Ling*. These literary works evoke the cosmology of native Tibetan religion, not Buddhism. They record first the creation of the world and then the creation and evolution of the tribes of Tibet: tribes from which the kings of Tibet are descended as well as Gesar of Ling.

In contrast to most Buddhist literature, this native Tibetan style of literature expresses notions of transcendence, not in metaphysical terms, but in terms of ancientness and primordiality. Religious ceremonies are likewise typically Inner Asian. Whereas a Buddhist work would describe sacrifices and fire offerings, here one finds instead the characteristic ceremony of the nomadic highland steppes of Inner Asia—the lhasang, or smoke purification. Royal families originate when the lha descend to earth or when mountain gods mate with humans. The inner physiology described in this genre evokes the same non-Buddhist cultural paths. Thus, while a Buddhist work would describe the body as containing a central channel and subsidiary channels and say that the channels carry different kinds of "wind" (Skt. *prana*), these Sino-Tibetan works describe officers, guardian deities, and different kinds of souls, in a manner reminiscent of alchemical Taoism.

Auras of defensive energy play about the body and guard the warrior in battle. The energies have colorful names that also remind us of Chinese cosmology: windhorse (*rlung rta*) and field of power (*dbang thang*), life force (*srog*), and life-duration force (*rtse*). These energies, this sort of cosmology, and this approach to tribal annals are all native to the epic and martial literature of the Eastern Terminus of the Silk Route. They are found in Mongolian annals, in Tibetan oral literature, and even in Chinese classical novels like *The Romance of the Three Kingdoms* that I mentioned earlier.

When Trungpa Rinpoche evoked this diffuse cultural tradition in his literary works, he was associating himself with a rising school of Tibetan thought which we call today the Tibetan Renaissance—the Eclectic or Ri-me school. The founders of this school were nineteenth century polymath Buddhist scholars Jamgön Kongtrül the Great, Jamyang Khyentse Wangpo, and Ju Mipham Gyatso. The Eclectics sought to unify the four principal sects of Tibetan Buddhism, the institutionalized non-Buddhist religion known as Bön, and the shamanistic and animistic teachings of native Tibetan religion into a single system.

This meant that they had to reconcile Inner Asian shamanism with the high scholastic metaphysics and epistimology of Indian Buddhism. The place where this theoretical work is done most explicitly is in the writings of Mipham. His version of the Gesar epic presents the general principles of Buddhist tantra and mahayana quite explicitly. But it is also a manual of shamanistic and magical lore. Unlike the usual bodhisattva, Gesar is a sorcerer and illustrates in his skillful means a particular sort of warrior's magic. His companions wisely comment on these practices and the epic, at least in Mipham's version, becomes a practical manual of Tibetan shamanism.

Earlier I noted E. Gene's Smith's extraordinary comment that dzogchen, although in general an esoteric tradition, is in effect the public religion of Golok. The same could be said of the Gesar style of shamanism. Every warrior in the epic is in some degree a magician. All of them have talking, flying horses. All of them perform lhasangs and use magic in battle to increase their personal defenses. Most of them have patron deities who appear in complex forms mixing aspects of a classical Indic tantric machinery with those of a wild, colorful local animistic deity. As in many Turkic epics, when warriors contend, they use magic on each other as a matter of course, combining arrow, spear, and sword work with energy and deity work.

In this way Mipham made his edition of the Gesar epic a hybrid of Buddhist and local ideas. He made sure that it would be read in this manner by writing a parallel set of Gesar chants that mix religions in the same way. These ritual practices may be found in the Na chapter of his collected works. One of the most famous is the "Long Werma Lhasang," an invocation of Gesar and his entire court as a sort of epic mandala. Here we see a careful combination of Buddhism according to the Nyingma sect with local religion. For example, Padmasambhava is invoked along with various buddhas; but then attention moves to Gesar and his court and companions, who are stationed not around Gesar in the four directions, but before him in the manner of the council meetings that occur in the epic when the Mukpo clan gathers. The figures in Gesar's courtly mandala are themselves surrounded by dralas, local deities, and figures of relative power.

Mipham's edition of the epic provides a systematic justification for the syncretic form of the mandala of deities that appears in the lhasang. Gesar is presented as a creation of the enlightened Buddhist tantric guru Padmasambhava collaborating with Amitabha, Avalokiteshvara, and a number of local Tibetan deities. He is literally formed from rays of light that emanate from Amitabha and Avalokiteshvara, dissolve into Padmasambhava, are radiated by him into the bodies of local deities, and transform them into a male and female tantric Buddhist tutelary buddha. These buddhas unite and give birth to an enlightened deity named Joyful to Hear, who agrees to reincarnate as Gesar. Joyful to Hear is partly formed from local deities transformed into buddhas, but he also carries upon his reincarnated body a number of native Tibetan animal-headed dralas who agree to co-incarnate with him. They live inside Gesar's body, secretly investing the power spots on his body—not the chakras that Indian Buddhism believe are located along the spinal column, but the places on the head, shoulders, and torso where the patron deities of native animism are believed to dwell in a fully functional warrior.

A careful reading of the first chapter of Mipham's epic will explain the spiritual technology of the Gesar *sadhanas* in volume Na. But Mipham did not invent this syncretic system. It is present in a world of Nyingma philosophical and chanting texts going back to the very foundations of Tibetan Buddhism. For example, there is a very extensive lhasang called the Mountain Purificatory Offering (*Ri bo bsang mchod*), which contains in the chanted text itself stages in the emanation of the absolute principle into the level of relative deities such as drala.

The "Long Werma Lhasang" is practiced in Golok, in Tibet at large, and among Tibetan refugee communities. In fact, the Dalai Lama's government in exile included it in a set of lhasangs that were distributed to Tibetan emigrés so that they could continue to perform culturally Tibetan rituals in their homes.

Another very popular Mipham chant in the same tradition has no title, but is actually a chant inscribed on prayer flags. This chant mentions gods who appear in what I would call an emanational order. It begins by calling on deities who represent the absolute, then moves on to enlightened individuals and teachers, and then invokes the Indian god Ganesha, who leads a divine army of dralas. Then it mentions gods who have to do with the manifest world and relative truth: gods of the cosmic lineage who command causality (or coincidence, karmic cause and effect).

In the Na volume of Mipham's collected works one finds numerous very short supplications to Gesar as well. There is even a Gesar Seven-Line Supplication to match the famous one to Padmasambhava.

Trungpa Rinpoche lifted the above chants from Mipham's Gesar cycle (*ge sar skor*) of practices and gave them to his advanced students to chant.

All of the above works by Mipham were translated by the Nālandā Translation Committee with Trungpa Rinpoche and given to his advanced students to chant.

The most interesting practice of all in Mipham's Gesar cycle is the Supplication to the Horse Race. *The Horse Race* is the third volume of the epic in Mipham's edition. For most of *The Horse Race*, Gesar appears not as a godling or divine prince, but as the ugly and ill-favored Joru. He is invited by Drugmo, the lovely princess who is the prize in the race, to come back to Ling so that he can enter a race to win her hand.

This chapter is full of messages about the epic's enlightened view of the conventional reality of the relative world. Some of the messages are ironic, criticizing the hollowness of life on the relative plane. Others are heroic, showing the powers and splendors of a phenomenal world that has devolved from the absolute.

In one chapter, for example, the lovely Drugmo goes to visit Gesar in his terrifying fortress of solitude in the land of Ma. On the journeys to and from Ma, Gesar plays vicious practical jokes on Drugmo and tortures her with Coyote-style tricksterism while simultaneously wooing her in many different disguises. This chapter is called "The Precious Queen," and it is a strange Buddhistic examination of femininity. Drugmo's overnice feminine egoism, her preciousness, is ruthlessly attacked by Gesar, who even temporarily disfigures her. And yet at the same time he praises her for being his indispensable complement in the world of manifestation.

Gesar's criticisms of and attacks on Drugmo seem unfair to the reader. But from the point of view of an enlightened trickster, they are a just critique and appropriate punishment for Drugmo's conventional feminine moral weakness. A Tibetan aristocratic woman must use a certain disingenuousness as she negotiates the conflicting forces that sway her life: her demanding brothers, her scheming father and uncles, the envy of other women, and the likely hostility of her future husband's family: the very numerous societal pressures tribal life brings to bear on beautiful young women. Drugmo is shown trapped in a web of these forces, and Gesar criticizes the hypocrisy that these kinship relations force upon her and the transparent feminine machinations that the conventions of human society impose on her.

The tricks are grotesque, at times quite violent and full of Buddhist irony. At one point Gesar even kills himself in order to test Drugmo's faith. Sobbing, she buries his body, bewailing the fact that her brothers will punish her if she comes home without the hero. She decides to commit suicide and begins to ride her horse into a river. She says melodramatically that this way she can at least be with Gesar in the afterlife. Gesar, however, comes back to life and derides her for improperly burying him. He scorns her conventional compassion, pointing out that she could not be manifesting true charity, for she was willing to let the horse drown with her.

In another chapter of this volume, Drugmo and Gesar's mother go off to catch his magical horse, who is a reincarnation of Hayagriva, the horse-headed tantric buddha. The horse is described muscle by muscle as the ideal creature, and we see the nomad's love, indeed worship of horses as a figure of divine energy.

Finally, in the last chapter of *The Horse Race*, Gesar arrives in Ling, and the race begins. Gesar's hijinks during the race are hilarious, but frightening to his supporters. For example, for much of the race he rides in the opposite direction from the finish line. During the race he constantly stops to engage other racers in metaphysical conversation. Observers complain that Gesar's childish pranks will prevent him from winning the race and realizing his destiny. But the sage chieftain of the Mukpo tribe replies, saying that if you understand the way worldly and enlightened energies work, you will realize that nothing can prevent Gesar from realizing victory, for the destiny generated by one's karma and field of power determine outcomes more than strategizing and hard work.

Thus, each chapter becomes an analysis of tantric and shamanistic energies: the metaphysical completeness that union with the feminine brings, the magical vitality of the horse principle, the way destiny is inscribed in one's karma and field of power.

In fact, the third volume, *The Horse Race*, is organized in order to have many levels of esoteric meaning. Each of the chapters is named by Mipham after one of the treasures of a Chakravartin, a universal monarch: the precious queen, the precious minister, the precious elephant, and so on. This is a very ancient, Indian list. Trungpa took up the list and used it in his American teachings, giving it esoteric meaning as a tantric iconographical map of relative energies that must be mastered by the adept in order to live ecologically in the world.

Every individual in society must be like a universal monarch to know success in the world: one must have a precious queen (that is, a sexual consort), a precious minister (a friend who is a sound adviser), a precious general (a friend who will help you get things done), a precious elephant (that is, a successful solution to the problems of traveling and moving about), and so forth.

When Mipham had his student, Gyurme, reorganize the *Horse Race* chapter into this structure, he brought out the teachings already inscribed in the oral epic on these subjects and made them evident to the thoughtful reader.

His method was strange and tantric. Before Mipham had his student edit this volume, Mipham wrote "The Horse Race Supplication," a ritual actually worshiping the text itself. The supplication is fairly lengthy and written in symbolic language reminiscent of the cryptic statements of oracles. Mipham gave this chant to the editor, taught him its inner meaning, and then told him to reedit the *Horse Race* chapter to fit the symbol-laden, oracular, inscrutable sections of the chant. This was his method of imposing religious and philosophical order on a naturally occurring oral folk phenomenon. Henceforth, the Gesar rituals would perfectly complement the epic, and as the epic continued to propagate itself naturally in the way that very good stories do, so would Mipham's particular religion of Gesar.

This is a good example of the technique the Eclectic school used to create a systematic interweaving of native shamanism, oral epic, and Buddhist tantra, alchemical Taoism, dzogchen, and the strange, vast *Kalachakra Tantra*. The textual sources for this syncretism are found in

Mipham's writings on the Gesar epic and in rituals and philosophical presentations from the Eclectics. Trungpa Rinpoche wrote his *Epic of Lha* within this tradition, conscious of the synthesis his gurus had effected. He became in effect the chief spokesman in the West for this syncretic system.

The key point here concerns emanation, a notion that may be more familiar to the reader from Neoplatonism:—the emanation of the relative world with all of its distinctions and individualities out of the undetermined absolute ground of reality, a concatenated chain of cosmic events that Arthur Lovejoy, the American intellectual historian, called the Great Chain of Being.

Buddhism is not always or even usually an emanational system, and it is usually better not to compare it with Platonic idealism. But in the world of tantric philosophy, this approach works. There is, in effect, a sense of the emanation of relative truth from ultmate truth.

Buddhist philosophy begins with the doctrine of the two truths. To put it simply, relative truth (Skt. *samvriti satya*) is truth as confused beings see it. Ultimate truth (Skt. *paramartha satya*) is what the buddhas, who are unconfused and undeceived, see. Relative truth is the world of things and persons. Ultimate truth is emptiness of self-nature, the lack of solidity of every apparently existent thing. Relative truth is appearance, and ultimate truth is reality.

The metaphysics of various Buddhist systems are distinguished mainly by their different positions on the nature of the two truths. The most common position is that relative truth is entirely deceptive, that there is no truth of any sort in it, or even, as in some readings of Nagarjuna and Chandrakirti, that there is no relative truth at all.

The philosophy both implied and explicit in Mipham's version of the Gesar epic relates to a philosophical debate alive among the Eclectics. All Tibetan schools of mahayana Buddhism take Chandrakirti's *Madhyamakavatara* (Introduction to the Middle Way) as a foundational text for their philosophical view. It is an introduction to Madhyamaka, the Middle Way, an approach developed by the great second-century Indian thinker Nagarjuna. Nagarjuna's work is itself an interpretation of the mahayana wisdom scriptures known as the *Prajnaparamita Sutras* (Perfection of Wisdom Sutras). Nagarjuna proposes a set of dialectical exercises by which one can arrive at a direct experience of the perfection of wisdom and a direct insight into the empty nature of reality. No matter how ineffable this mystical insight may be, no matter how impossible one might think it is to describe it, through this dialectic one can arrive at the correct experience of it.

Half of mahayana philosophy is simply a question of proposing different readings or interpretations of Nagarjuna. For example, Chandrakirti's reading, given perhaps a century after Nagarjuna's works were published, holds that relative truth is deceptive to the point of not being a distinct truth at all. So it is impossible to make any true statements, for any statement implies the solidity, the reification of relative or deceptive truth. One can, however, arrive at ultimate truth through a critique of relative truth, in which the spokesman for Madhyamaka never makes an independent statement, but only refutes the position of his opponents. This is called Prasangika Madhyamaka. *Prasanga* is Sanskrit for the argument form reductio ad absurdum, Chandrakirti's principal method of critiquing his essentialist opponents.

When Buddhism first arrived in Tibet it was connected with another reading of Nagarjuna, called Svatantrika Madhyamaka, whose chief representative was Bhavaviveka. *Svatantra* means "independent statement." According to this system, it is indeed possible to make some positive statements about the nature of reality, and these positive statements are beyond the reach of the all-destroying dialectic. In the Middle Ages the Svatantrikas had been overshadowed by the Prasangikas, and this raised a problem for the interpretation of tantra.

Tantra expresses itself through complex allegorical pageants known as mandalas. The mandalas are palaces or courts or, if you will, societies full of deities. Each mandala seems to describe an ideal world. Contemplation of a mandala and the deities within it presents to the meditator in a single, unified iconographical form an entire system of mystical philosophy.

Now, since mandalas contain deities who have many qualities, aspects, and attributes, they seem to be creatures of relative truth. It is thus difficult to find a metaphysical basis for such busy and colorful representations in the austere Prasangika system. Difficult, but not impossible. One must be careful not to interpret the deities allegorically. One must be careful not to use them as a basis for making independant statements, which are bound to be false, according to Prasangika Madhyamaka.

The Svatantrika system gave a richer interpretation of tantric symbolic texts, because now with it, it was possible to entrust a nondeceptive relative meaning to the tantric symbols. By the nineteenth century, however, Svatantrika Madhyamaka had gone out of fashion. The Eclectics brought it back into fashion, for they were very open-minded and were willing to deploy different philosophies on different occasions. Mipham himself provided new commentaries on the whole range of Indian scriptures, giving a rigorous basis to this sense of multivalency. Some Buddhist practices called for a Prasangika interpretation. Others worked better if you switched metaphysics temporarily and thought like a Svatantrika. In fact, each position in the history of Buddhist philosophy found its place in this graded practice system, which Trungpa Rinpoche passed on to his students from the Eclectics.

Thus he prescribed a variety of approaches to the two truths depending on what ritual and meditational practices were being done. For example, in his rigorous presentation of tantric skillful means at the 1973 three-month retreat for his Western students, he announced that during the section where he taught the visualization of mandalas, he would rely specifically on the view of Svatantrika Madhyamaka. This despite the fact that just a year earlier he had given an extensive lecture program at Rocky Mountain Dharma Center, called "The Ten Bhumis," based on Chandrakirti's *Madhyamakavatara*.

Later he set the Nālānda Translation Committee, his private translation group, to work producing an English version of two texts by Mipham that sponsored yet a third approach to Madhyamaka, called Zhantong, or Other Emptiness. The two texts in question were polemical treatises entitled *The Lion's Roar That Proclaims Other Emptiness (gzhan stong khas len seng-ge'i nga ro)* and The *Lion's Roar: The Great Essential Exposition of Sugatagarbha (bde gshegs snying po'i stong thun chen mo seng-ge'i nga ro)*. He said that contemplating these texts had brought him special moments of great realization.

The foundational text for the Other Emptiness school was a mahayana commentarial text entitled the *Mahayanottaratantra Shastra*. It was written by Asanga. Asanga's brother Vasubandhu wrote a prose commentary on Asanga's root verses. The English title in English would be *The Commentary on the Peerless Continuum*. The peerless continuum was the buddha nature, a deathless, undeceived consciousness that is the potentiality for enlightenment existing in the heart of every sentient being and, in fact, in all nature. Ordinarily, buddha nature philosophy is taken to be logically opposed to Madhyamaka, for it posits a positive reality, the buddha essence in everyone's heart. However, in Tibet there was a school of thought that reworked this philosophy into a form taken to be noncontradictory to Madhyamaka. The school was called Jonang, and its founder was the great scholar Dolpopa.

The monasteries of the Jonangpas were actually destroyed by the armies of the fifth Dalai Lama, and the school ceased to exist—that is, until the Eclectics quietly took it up and made it an essential part of their system. Like Svatantra, Zhantong (Other Emptiness) could be used to positively explain the nature of the gods who appear in Buddhist mandalas. In fact, it provided a unique ontological basis for Buddhist cosmology—a way of even explaining the existence of the lower gods, the nature gods and local deities featured in the Gesar epic and its related rituals. In Mipham's hands the meaning of the cosmology of the epic and the spiritualist and shamanistic practices in it took on new life. There was now a way of understanding relative truth not simply as a mistake in perception, but as an emanation down from the formless absolute. The emanation would reach down as far as the classical Indic deities of Buddhist tantra and then would reach down even further to embrace local deities and nature spirits who express Tibetan ethnic identity—all would now be considered to have a connection to ultimate meaning.

Trungpa Rinpoche expresses this emanationalism in the *Epic of Lha* where a deity of the absolute commands nine lha who create the preeminent features of the relative world: light, space, direction, mountains, bodies of water, and so on—things which in the view of standard Madhyamakan texts would not exist except as illusory appearance. The direct action of the absolute invests this world of mountains and valleys with nature spirits. The next step will be the creation of the tribes of men and the animals, and then finally the events of recorded history. It is as if Aristotle had explained how pans, satyrs, and naiads had come into being as elaborations of the primordial *nous*.

We must note how this view is at odds with traditional Buddhist cosmology. Ordinarily, all gods and spirits would be considered in no way different in substance from human beings and animals—all are illusory beings within the six realms of samsara. Outside the ever-turning wheel of the six realms is the indefinable limitless world beyond world of the buddhas. The gods are not part of that world or particularly connected with it. They are not really higher beings, and their form has no cosmic meaning. Brahma is not, except in poetic allegory, the spirit of creation. Shiva is not an essence of destruction. The god known as Yama is not truly lord of death. Local spirits do not express the nature of the places they occupy. None of them are quintessences of anything; they are all simply confused beings with very long lives and bodies invisible to us. For everything in relative truth is deceptive. As Trungpa Rinpoche put it once when describing the cosmology of abhidharma, "All the gods are simply glorified ghosts."

The emanational view of the gods is at odds with the above view. The animistic deities of Silk Route religion do express essences connected with places and self-existing qualities of the phenomenal world, for the phenomenal world in the precise details of its form elaborately expresses the nature of the absolute, the dharmakaya. The empty and luminous absolute contains qualities, as *The Peerless Continuum* says, "as numerous as grains of sand in the Ganges," and these qualities elaborate themselves through manifestation down to the smallest detail of the phenomenal world. They express themselves with what Chögyam Trungpa called precision. The absolute expresses itself in manifestation, as he put it, "even down to the shapes and colors inscribed on the backs of beetles."

It is interesting to note that when he expounded this philosophy in mythological form in his epic, Trungpa Rinpoche chose as his exemplary deities not the Indic gods of the Buddhist or Hindu pantheon, but the dralas, the war gods of native Tibetan religion. This is the strategy of Mipham's Gesar epic—an approach found in the writings of the other Eclectics, particularly Jamyang Khyentse Wangpo, who wrote his own cycle of Gesar rituals.

The oral literature of Eastern Tibet and Amdo, the Tibetan provinces on the northwestern border of China, shows the characteristics of this view. For example, there is the autobiography of Do Khyentse Yeshe Dorje, a Golok master who was a reincarnation of Jigme Lingpa, one of the greatest thinkers of the Nyingma lineage. The birth of his famous previous incarnation is described in the first chapter. It is actually written in the Golok language.

Do Khyentse's autobiography is typical of the miracle stories of the birth of famous lamas, except for the curious fact that the mother and child are surrounded not so much by Buddhist deities as by figures from the

Gesar epic. While the miraculous child is being born, war gods perform weapons rituals, and invisible bards sing the epic as they dance on smoke-offering shrines. Invisible mounted warriors ride in circles around the mother's tent. Mountain gods give their blessings along with the Indic deities of dzogchen.

Gesar and the Shambhala Teachings

Trungpa Rinpoche's first teachings in the West, given in Britain, did not focus on the native Tibetan symbol system. They were mainly concerned with the highest, most abstract practices of the Nyingma lineage. When he came to America, he changed the curriculum, focusing on the Kagyü teachings and the life stories of the Kagyü lineage holders: Tilopa, Naropa, Marpa, Milarepa, and Gampopa.

In 1978 Trungpa returned to the teachings and cosmology of the Gesar epic, which became the basis for a series of weekend public programs that he called Shambhala Training. Trungpa translated about twenty-five percent of Mipham's Gesar chants and introduced the practice of lhasang, or smoke purifications, to his Western students. Over the next few years he discovered and wrote down a series of revelational texts that featured as the principal deities Shiwa Ökar and his circle of drala, Gesar of Ling and the principal figures from his epic, and the kings of the mythical kingdom of Shambhala.

The first text in this series was titled *The Golden Sun of the Great East*. It read like a Buddhist tantra, presenting a mandala of deities who performed ritual practices and contemplations and who were themselves the objects visualized in contemplative exercises. The central deities of *The Golden Sun* were drawn from the introduction to the most complex of all Buddhist esoteric texts, the *Kalachakra Tantra*: they were the enlightened kings of Shambhala called *rigdens*, or holders of noble family.

The retinue of these kings in *The Golden Sun*, however, was drawn not from among the hundreds of deities of the mandala of Kalachakra, but rather from the heroes and war gods of the Gesar epic. In later texts in his Shambhala cycle of revelations, some deities from the *Epic of Lha* were added. Over the following years, more scriptures appeared from the fertile mind of Trungpa Rinpoche, all featuring the same characters.

The collection of Shambhala texts evidently constituted a single tantric cycle. Trungpa Rinpoche's oral commentary on these texts showed that although the new canon was relatively short, it was extremely pithy, containing an elaborate system of teachings and practices.

The Shambhala texts read strangely. Unlike translations from Indian tantras, they were written in a unique poetic idiom that combined the sound of bardic song with the brassy, bragging heroic tone of nativist warrior rituals. All in all, their voice is that of cocky Asian nomads—proud of their independence and resourcefulness, bold in every action, given to banditry and sudden violence, in love with their own eloquence and braggadocio. Trungpa Rinpoche's Shambhala lectures matched this sassy martial tone with a familiar contemplative principle—that the mystic practitioner was like a warrior in battle and the mystical religious path was the way of the warrior.

This message was not welcomed by his American disciples in the 1970s, when the pacifist movements of the Vietnam War era still held sway over the minds of American youth—especially those who had decided to follow Asian religion. This despite the fact that mahayana Buddhist rhetoric is totally penetrated by martial imagery. The word *bodhisattva*, for example, means in Tibetan "warrior of enlightenment." The gods of tantric mandalas are called *dakas* and *dakinis*, male and female warriors. But centuries of usuage had worn away the military sense of these Indic terms. The word *warrior* had a fresh sound in the Shambhala teachings, because it evoked Central Asian nomadic mounted guerrillas, not the elegant, settled aristocratic knights of the Indian epics, who like their Greek counterparts fought from chariots and charged their enemies in formation.

The Shambhala texts represented the spiritual path as a field of battle where nomadic warriors on horseback fought against the demon enemies of the four directions, who now represented four sorts of moral hypocrisy. The pitfalls on the spiritual path became the kind of threats Gesar's troops met in their epic contests: the poison of arrogance, the trap of doubt, the ambush of hope, the arrow of uncertainty. Each of these obstacles was elaborated into lists of moral failings, spiritual missteps, and movements tangential to the direction of the path. The lists were drawn from Buddhist scholastic manuals, but here they were clothed in the garments of epic discourse.

For example, whereas a Buddhist text would say that a practitioner should be "homeless" (Pali *anagarika*) in the heart, the Shambhalian text recommended that he or she follow the dictates of "tent culture." The nomadic pastoralist life of Northeastern Tibetans became a metaphor for the mental conduct of modernist Western disciples.

In the early days of Tibetan tantric lineages, the disciples lived with their gurus and there was a tradition that structured the family of the guru as if it were the mandala of a tantric tutelary deity (Tib. *yidam*). So, for example, the plantation of Marpa the Translator, the founder of the Kagyü lineage, was allegorized as the mandala of the wrathful buddha Hevajra. Marpa was considered to be Hevajra himself. His wife was the consort of Hevajra, Nairatmya. The son and principal disciples of Marpa were the retinue deities of the four gates, and so on. To study with Marpa meant that you joined his family and took up a position as one of the Hevajra deities. This practice has fallen out of fashion within the Kagyüpas, who today are mainly monastics. But it is continued in the Nyingma lineage.

Trungpa Rinpoche continued the tradition with his own disciples, except that instead of using a Buddhist mandala he used the hybrid Gesar/Kalachakra mandala of the Shambhala teachings. He called his home Kalapa Court, naming it after the capital of the Kingdom of Shambhala. He abandoned the customs of humility and the appearance of poverty cultivated by Buddhist lamas and took up the formal observances and honorifics of royalty. He allowed himself to be allegorized to the Rigden King of Shambhala, the central deity of the Shambhala mandala, and had his close disciples address him as Sakyong, or King. His wife was the queen. The mandala of the Shambhala cycle of revelations, just like the epic and the Gesar chants of Mipham, included ministers, generals, queens, ladies in waiting, and host of armored warriors.

The disciples at the court were allegorized to these roles despite the fact that it brought them infinite confusion, because they were not yet in contact with the Asian oral epics which were the true previous texts of this discourse world.

One of the central signifiers of Buddhist religion is the notion of a noble family (Skt. *kula*). The Buddha originally deployed this metaphor as an attack on the Indian caste system. Since all sentient beings possessed the buddha nature, all of them, no matter what their birth, were equally capable of gaining buddhahood. By taking Buddhist vows, one became a son or daughter of noble family. One transcended all castes, to become the caste of the Buddha.

In the context of the Gesar epic, however, the word *family* took on a different meaning; it was, in fact, replaced by *tribe* or *clan* (Tib. *ldong*). Gesar himself was a member of the Mukpo clan, one of the primordial tribes of Tibet. Trungpa Rinpoche was a member of the Mukpo clan and therefore mystically descended from Gesar. Receiving the Shambhala teachings and being given permission to read the Shambhala scriptures made his students in effect adopted members of the Mukpo clan.

This, actually, was in perfect keeping with nomadic tradition, for in the political world of nomadic confederations, *tribe* was an extremely elastic term. Political relations were expressed by kinship terms, so that people who entered into close alliances or relationships of loyalty often considered themselves cousin-brothers, sister-cousins, or uncle-fathers. So, for example, in the Gesar epic the emperor of China was addressed by Eastern tribes as "Uncle." People who bound in marriage alliance or any other sort of bond of loyalty were addressed as kin when they were not. Adoptive kinship was extended relatively easily.

This loose notion of tribal bonding changed the organic relationship between disciples and the deities of the mandala. In Buddhist tantra, a disciple received the right to visualize a certain metaphysical principle as a certain deity through an empowerment ceremony called an abhisheka or anointment. The energy of empowerment was passed down a lineage from guru to disciple in much the manner of Christian apostolic succession or the Islamic notion of descent of *barakah*. But the Shambhala deities, whose iconography was based on native Tibetan religion, were received not from Buddhist lineages, but from the Mukpo family, since the deities were, in effect, the lares and penates of the guru's blood family.

Thus, in Chögyam Trungpa's new dispensation of Shambhala teachings, the tribal metaphor of a Central of Inner Asian nomadic pastoralist world was scrupulously maintained. Bodhisattvas in training became shamanic warriors in the style of the oral epics. The guru's family mandala became the court of Shambhala kings. The abstract metaphysical deities of Indian tantric mythology became the earthy nature deities of Inner Asia. The wandering life of a monk as an allegory for a lifetime's spiritual journey became the everywhere-wandering tent culture of a pastoralist. And, significantly, disciples were considered as adoptive members of the Mukpo clan.

Finally, and most significantly, the pattern of energies within the body moved from the Indian system of yogic signifiers to the shamanic symbols of the Sino-Tibetan marches, wherein Taoist deities mixed with native Tibetan deities. That is to say, whereas ordinary tantric practitioners would talk of the movement of prana or wind through the nadis or channels of the body, Shambhala practitioners would talk about the auras of energy that shone in splendor from the warrior's body.

In the Gesar epic, the bodies of warriors are invested with invisible war gods who perch on their head and shoulders and within their torso as invisible defenders. In order to defeat an epic warrior in battle, one must first frighten away these native deities, who protect the person wearing them against assassination.

In the same way, confidence replaces faith in Shambhala discourse. Fear, the opposite of confidence, replaces lack of faith as the primary problem to be solved. Thus, in Trungpa Rinpoche's Shambhala path, defeat of fear was regarded as the greatest spiritual accomplishment. A disciple who is free from fear cultivates an elegant, impecable exterior, like a cavalry soldier jauntily accoutred for battle. This fear signifies religious faith in one's own buddha nature, which has been allegorized as the noble fury of a horseman in battle. When an epic hero has extinguished doubt and conquered his or her fears, the war gods descend on the body and fill it with light. The divine energy of battle bravery, known as windhorse, rises in the body, and a divine field of power envelops the warrior's form. The spiritual technology of this battle charisma is fully developed in Mipham's version of the Gesar epic. Trungpa Rinpoche's commentary gave this shamanic presentation a metaphysical and contemplative explanation and turned the epic's depiction of the exemplary behavior of warriors into practices for the spiritual path of students.

The system was already present in the encyclopedic writings of the Eclectics. There in the volumes of rituals, manuals, empowerments, and philosophical commentaries of Jamgön Kongtrül, Mipham, and Jamyang Khyentse Wangpo a system of spiritual culture and mystical metaphysics was worked out in detail. The system related the native shamanic religion with high Indian scholastic philosophy and the Indian tantric iconographical language with Sino-Tibetan spirituality. Although they did not invent the syncretic philosophy at work here, it was the Eclectics who crystalized it into a single system explicated in a single textual corpus.

At a flower show, Boulder, Colorado. Photograph by Robert Del Tredici.
Used with permission.

Trungpa Rinpoche
and Zen

Tensho David Schneider

The title of this article supposes that Trungpa Rinpoche is one thing, Zen another, and that the two can simply be placed in relationship to each other. But Trungpa Rinpoche was not one thing. If ever a person manifested an astonishing array of forms, and spoke wide-ranging, even contradictory truths to meet the needs of varying situations, Chögyam Trungpa Rinpoche was such a person. On the other side, the Zen meditation tradition cannot be crammed into any box of definition; it is as various as its practitioners. Zen masters of the past and present have looked different from one another, used radically different teaching methods, and proposed divergent, if complementary, understandings of truth. When pressed, no Zen teacher would even admit that there *was* such a thing as Zen. Yet all of them belong with pride to a lineage and to a style, even if it is as ungraspable as a cloud.

Having voiced these cautions, one might look at Trungpa Rinpoche's relation to Zen by looking at his connections to the active Zen teachers of his day in North America. Through these friendships, one can feel his respect for Zen tradition altogether, and how it led to his using certain

Zen forms for his public meditation hall and rituals. Equally, it will be clear why Rinpoche inherited many of the students migrating through the spiritual scene in the early 1970s, a significant number of these coming from Zen sanghas. Such practitioners had a definite effect on the emerging character of his "scene," and Rinpoche developed in return a humorous, teasing—sometimes mocking—approach in dealing with these people. As he began to define more clearly the path for his own followers, Trungpa Rinpoche started to teach about the distinctions between Zen and tantric Buddhism. In the first months of 1974 he delivered two seminars titled "Zen and Tantra."

In the spring of 1971, Trungpa Rinpoche paid a visit to the San Francisco Zen Center, to deliver an evening talk. The lecture was moved from the Buddha Hall, where such discourse usually took place, to the dining room, to accommodate the large audience expected. I was practicing as a guest student at the time, and we were told simply that the evening schedule would be replaced by a talk from "Trungpa."

This was thrilling news, because as far as I could see, there were two penetrating teachers of meditation available to a young seeker at the time: Suzuki Roshi and Trungpa Rinpoche. There were other teachers around, of course, but some didn't speak English, others didn't have books out yet, and still others were just beginning their careers. The day before Rinpoche's visit, in fact, a few of us bunking in the men's dorm had huddled around a cassette recorder, listening to a talk by him. I'd been surprised to hear the high pitch of his voice as he taught: "We shouldn't say, 'Things aren't as bad as they seem.' Things *are* as bad as they seem!"

Following afternoon zazen and dinner, we worked to arrange the dining room into a lecture hall. Seats for the teachers were placed in front—a wingback chair for Suzuki Roshi and a small sofa for Trungpa Rinpoche. Mats went down on the floor in front of these, for those who wanted to sit close and low. Rows of chairs filled the central part of the large, airy room, and dining tables lined the perimeter. Because I'd been called on to move furniture—that is what guest students did in addition to sitting: we worked—I secured a good seat down in front. By the time the talk started, sometime after eight p.m., every seat was filled, and people were sitting or even standing on the tables around the edges of the room.

A commotion arose near the door, and we turned to watch Trungpa

Rinpoche enter. He lurched forward, limping heavily and grinning broadly, followed by a group of his students. He took a seat on the sofa and surveyed the crowd. A drink of some sort was poured for him and set on a side table. An ashtray was set out. Suzuki Roshi seated himself in the wingback chair, folded his legs under him, arranged his robes, put his hands into the meditation mudra, and sat there in what looked like perfect zazen posture.

Someone began the chants traditionally done before a lecture; Suzuki Roshi and the Zen students all put their palms together and vertical (elbows out, middle fingers the height of their noses) and intoned vigorously. Trungpa Rinpoche sat with hands almost together, his body weaving in circular motions during the chant. He looked drunk. There was no other way to describe it. We had heard that Rinpoche sometimes, though not always, gave teachings after having consumed goodly quantities of alcohol.

He was, in fact, drunk this time. At least in the quiet room where speakers waited before giving their talks, he'd greeted Suzuki Roshi a few moments earlier, with the words "Hi, Roshi! I'm drunk!" The two teachers were close friends by this point, but this pre-talk meeting was apparently a short one, ending when Trungpa Rinpoche fairly dismissed Roshi, saying,"You can go now, Roshi. I'll be in in a moment."

Now Trungpa Rinpoche sat on the couch, looking at the audience, who, astonished, looked back at him. They also looked at Suzuki Roshi a few feet away from him. Trungpa Rinpoche sat there a long time. Finally he said, "Dopa way." At least this is what I heard, and I racked my brain for what it could mean. We were not long past the psychedelic era, and hippies galore were in the room; perhaps he was addressing them? No! It finally dawned on me: he'd said, "The open way." But in thinking this through, I'd missed his next several sentences.

In any case, the talk seemed short, and very different from the Zen talks I'd heard from Suzuki Roshi. Those talks struck me as crystal clear, even if the words didn't always track in grammatical English. Roshi's meaning, conveyed also with hand gestures and facial expressions, got through. But now I was having trouble understanding Trungpa Rinpoche's inflected English, which seemed halting, with pauses and new starts. At one point he crossed his legs, pulling a foot up onto his knee, but it slipped off again. His students whispered to one another.

The atmosphere in the room became increasingly electric. Something was happening, but no one—at least no one in the audience—was quite sure what. It was very provocative to see two enlightened masters—and there was little question for anyone present that both were enlightened— to be manifesting in such extremely different ways: Suzuki Roshi, still, proper, arranged, looking for all the world like a statue; and Trungpa Rinpoche, weaving, drinking, somewhat lounged on the sofa, and now lighting a cigarette! This performance distracted as well from the words of his talk. Shortly after, the talk stopped in any case, and he called for questions.

With the first question, an extraordinary transformation took place. Trungpa Rinpoche sat up, slightly forward, and energy seemed to flow into him. One had the feeling of seeing an image come from hazy into sharp, clear focus. I recall my impression that his body had become a sword or spear. He answered question after question brilliantly and with humor, often skewering the questioners with their own arrogance. One fellow called out from his perch on a table at the back of the room:

"Hey, it's said that you drink alcohol. You do, don't you?"

Rinpoche picked up his glass and drank, and looked at the fellow, and nodded yes.

"And you smoke cigarettes too, don't you?"

Rinpoche took a puff and said, "Sure," and smiled.

"Well, you know that it's no good for you, don't you? It's no good for your health."

Rinpoche said nothing but kept looking at the fellow, all the way across the room.

"Well, I do something that's good for *my* health."

"Mmmm hmmmm . . ."

"I do kundalini yoga!"

This last phrase came out with great pride, as if simply by associating himself with the practice, the young man had earned a credential.

Trungpa Rinpoche looked at him awhile, standing there on the table, and asked, slowly, with a smile, "You . . . do . . . kundalini . . . *yoga* . . . ?"

"I do."

Trungpa Rinpoche began to chuckle, first quietly to himself, and then with more and more energy, breaking at last into a real laugh. As his laughter built, the audience joined it, and soon the whole room was howling. The questioner looked around in bewilderment and finally sat down, visibly deflated. As the laughter calmed down, Rinpoche took another sip and looked out over the rim of his glass for the next questioner, the next challenger. I put up my hand. . . .

Of the many Zen teachers that Trungpa Rinpoche would meet during his seventeen years in North America, the first and most significant encounter was with Suzuki Roshi, founding abbot of the San Francisco Zen Center. By 1970, Suzuki Roshi had been practicing in North America for a dozen years, working intensively with the American students who'd joined his sitting practice and the community that had grown up around him. With the purchase in the late 1960s of Tassajara, a monastery deep in the mountains of Los Padres National Forest, and the publication of Suzuki's first book, *Zen Mind Beginner's Mind* in 1970, the population of Zen Center had begun to grow rapidly. Roshi often discussed the challenge of presenting traditional Zen Buddhist dharma in a cultural vacuum, to American students who fit no category that he, a Japanese teacher, was familiar with. He struggled with this, and his struggle gave rise to innovative, powerful teachings and a vigorous community.

Suzuki Roshi; his wife, Suzuki Sensei (mostly known simply as Okusan); and Trungpa Rinpoche and his wife, Diana Mukpo, were all introduced in May of 1970 by Rinpoche's publisher, Sam Bercholz. During a visit to Zen Center, an immediate affinity—what everyone who saw it called a "heart connection"—sprang up between the two teachers. Trungpa Rinpoche later confided to his wife that Suzuki Roshi was the first person he'd met in America who reminded him of his root guru in Tibet, Jamgön Kongtrül. He went on to say that in Roshi he'd found his first spiritual friend in the West.

According to biographer David Chadwick, Suzuki Roshi was familiar with Trungpa Rinpoche's work, as Roshi had read *Meditation in Action* and had heard praise from his own students who'd met the young Tibetan. Roshi had also startled his followers one evening by saying—apropos of nothing they could see—"Someone is coming. After he comes, maybe no one will be left here at Zen Center but me." He was referring to Trungpa Rinpoche.

Diana Mukpo recalled that on their first visit, Rinpoche was quite interested in how Suzuki Roshi taught his American students the technique of counting breaths during sitting meditation. Rinpoche also took careful note of the forms and atmosphere of Zen Center. Up to this point—in his first year in America—Trungpa Rinpoche had stressed sitting meditation for his students, in distinction from other practices in the Tibetan traditions, but had given little instruction in detailed form or technique.

During this visit and in subsequent joyful meetings and letters, the two teachers shared ideas for furthering buddhadharma in America, among them exchanging students and teachings, founding a Buddhist university, and creating a dharmically oriented therapeutic community. Trungpa Rinpoche did in short order send several of his senior students for training to Tassajara and, with Suzuki Roshi's blessing, used experienced Zen Center practitioners to lead extended sittings—day-long (nyinthün) and month-long (dathün) retreats—in his burgeoning scene in Vermont and the Rocky Mountains. Others of their shared visions took longer to come to fruition, but Trungpa Rinpoche always expressed his regard for Suzuki Roshi unequivocally in the meditation hall. One example of this is that during the first dathün in North America, Rinpoche allowed the rule of silence to be officially lifted only once each day, for a reading from Zen Mind Beginner's Mind. Rinpoche adopted the Zen-style sitting cushions known as zafu and the practice of alternating sitting and walking meditation throughout a practice session. Perhaps the most striking expression of veneration is that from their first meeting until his death in 1987, Trungpa Rinpoche had placed on every shrine wall, in every center associated with his work, a picture of Suzuki Roshi. The other few photos on these walls were Rinpoche's personal teachers and Buddhist ancestors; that Suzuki Roshi's Japanese face looked out from among Tibetan lineage holders was powerful poetry. It was also most fitting, for Suzuki Roshi referred to Trungpa Rinpoche as being "like my son."

If the two masters clicked on an inner level, it may have been that they recognized one another as lonely spiritual voyagers. In Allen Ginsberg's words they both had "burned their bridges. They gave all their energy to trying to enlighten America, rather than depending on their older companions and monasteries. They both gave themselves completely to American karma."[1]

The two teachers cut away at what Trungpa Rinpoche would later famously call spiritual materialism—using religious practice to bolster one's ego—and both saw sitting meditation as the primary path for American students. It is relatively difficult to manipulate *shamatha-vipashyana* for personal aggrandizement, or to make a trip out of *shikantaza*, as Roshi called the purest form of sitting. But both teachers ended up working patiently (if occasionally wrathfully) to keep their students on a goalless path. The America they found themselves in resembled a spiritual jungle: it was fertile, opulent, and rich; it was also overgrown, chaotic, and full of danger for the seeker. Suzuki Roshi and Trungpa Rinpoche shared between them the disappointments and loneliness they felt in walking through that jungle, and in leading others through it.

Perhaps because he could intuit what Rinpoche was going through, Roshi accepted his drinking—an acceptance that upset some of his own students. "He drinks because he's suffering," Roshi explained with some sharpness once. "When I saw Alan Watts, I couldn't accept his drinking, but when I met Trungpa Rinpoche"—Roshi threw up his hands, palms forward—"I gave up."

Later that year, Roshi, speaking after a serious operation, warned his students not to fix in any way only on what they could see. Discussing emptiness, he told them:

> The way you can struggle with this is to be supported by something, something you don't know. As we are human beings, there must be that kind of feeling. You must feel it in this city or building or community. So whatever community it may be, it is necessary for it to have this kind of spiritual support.
>
> That is why I respect Trungpa Rinpoche. He is supporting us. You may criticize him because he drinks alcohol like I drink water, but that is a minor problem. He trusts you completely. He knows that if he is always supporting you in a true sense you will not criticize him, whatever he does. And he doesn't mind whatever you say. That is not the point, you know. This kind of big spirit, without clinging to some special religion or form of practice, is necessary for human beings.[2]

Roshi and Rinpoche offered one another ceremonial honor at rites of passage. Descending from his apartment one May morning in a black mood to greet an unannounced visit from Trungpa Rinpoche, Roshi was softened and charmed to see the young lama holding his baby son in his arms and dancing strange circles with him in Zen Center's front hall. When Rinpoche explained that he'd come to ask for a blessing for the boy, Roshi returned to his upstairs apartment, donned extravagant pale green robes, came back down, and performed a blessing ritual in the Buddha Hall.

Soon, however, the performance of rituals was coming from the other direction, for as intense and loving as this relationship was, it was cut short by Suzuki Roshi's death in December of 1971. Roshi died after painful months in bed with stomach cancer. When Trungpa heard only the diagnosis, he wept so intensely that a blood vessel in his eye burst, and blood-reddened tears flowed down his cheeks. After the death, Rinpoche went to see Roshi in the funeral home where he lay. In the small chamber where Roshi's body was, Rinpoche meditated, chanted liturgies, and performed mudras.

Trungpa Rinpoche's presence at Suzuki Roshi's funeral was also dramatic. The event was enormous and lengthy, and when it came time for the dignitaries in attendance to contribute Rinpoche was invited to step forward. He stood for several moments before the coffin silently weeping and then tore the air with a passionate shout. At the same time, he threw open a long white silk scarf that arced down across the coffin.

As the ceremony wore on, Mrs. Suzuki took Rinpoche into a side room and gave him Suzuki Roshi's walking stick—something Roshi had requested. One would be hard-pressed to imagine a more appropriate gift for a teacher treading the path, especially with the hobbling gait Rinpoche had, the result of a car accident some years earlier. If there *were* a more symbolic gift, however, it might be the *oryoki* set (ritual eating bowls) that Rinpoche also inherited from Suzuki Roshi.

In the early days of Chinese Zen, transmission of the lineage was symbolized either by the gift of a text from master to student or the passing on of the master's robe and bowl. The walking stick, regarded as the legs of the Buddha, and the bowls, seen as Buddha's body, together with other ritual implements, have continued until the present to be instruments of transmission. This is not to say that Suzuki Roshi's lineage went to Trungpa Rinpoche alone, instead of to Richard Baker Roshi. Suzuki Roshi installed Baker as his successor at Zen Center with proper pomp and ceremony—and with great bravery as well, for Roshi was at death's door when he did the ceremony. But something did indeed flow from Suzuki Roshi to

Trungpa Rinpoche, something more than the gifts, the pictures, the hints, the smiles, the invitations, accommodation, and protection. Something even more than the many students who, with Suzuki Roshi's explicit permission, left Zen Center to study with Trunpa Rinpoche.

The next important Zen connection Trungpa Rinpoche made was with the soft-spoken but powerful master Kobun Chino Otogawa. When Rinpoche had asked Suzuki Roshi about calligraphy, Roshi directed him to Kobun (as he liked to be called), living at that time about an hour's drive south of San Francisco. Their actual meeting turned out to be almost accidental. Trungpa Rinpoche had come to Los Altos to consult with a group of psychologists who were busy transforming the humanistic psychology movement they'd founded into a new branch, later called transpersonal psychology. Abe Maslow, Anthony Sutich, and others, including Sonja Margulies, editor of the influential *Journal of Transpersonal Psychology*, wanted to meet Trungpa Rinpoche because of his startling presentation of psychology as fully integrated into spiritual life. Margulies happened to be studying Zen under Kobun, and when Rinpoche arrived, she made a point of introducing the two.

"They hit it off immediately," Margulies recalls. "They were both young men, Asians out of their cultures; both had married young Western girls—Kobun, a redhead, Trungpa, a blond—and both had young children. They had a lot in common." Beyond that, both men had admiring connections to Suzuki Roshi, were poets, would prove themselves master calligraphers, and had an intuitive ability to speak the dharma to Western students, though in very different styles. On this early visit they did calligraphy together. Kobun had a variety of fine Japanese brushes, including a very large one. Trungpa Rinpoche had never worked with a brush of such a scale and delighted in using it. They left Ms. Margulies an enormous calligraph: the words for "self-realization" written in both Tibetan and Japanese scripts.

On a subsequent visit, Rinpoche met Kobun at Margulies's house to do calligraphy. The two men asked after one another's families, but neither answered as large sheets of rice paper were laid on the floor. They began drinking (green tea as well as sake) and mixing ink. Kobun deferred to Rinpoche, who first wrote out Tibetan letters for the names of Kobun's two children. Delighted, Kobun returned the favor by writing the names of Rinpoche's children in Japanese and patiently explaining the characters. Rinpoche then took another, larger sheet and wrote in thick Tibetan letters, "Mindfulness is the way of all the buddhas."

Kobun responded by brushing "Great no mind" over his own large paper, to the delight of onlookers.

Kobun had come to the States in 1967 at Suzuki Roshi's invitation; having trained at Eiheiji Monastery as a ceremony master, he'd helped with many aspects of formal practice at Zen Center. Starting in the middle 1970s, as Trungpa Rinpoche gradually introduced more discipline and form to the Shambhala-Vajradhatu community, Kobun performed this same role again for Vajradhatu. He taught students the traditional approach to chanting, drumming, ritual procession, and, most invasively for the students, Zen-monastery-style eating, with oryoki bowls. Kobun introduced oryoki practice with care and a certain trepidation, for it is an intimate, inner practice of the Zen tradition. Trungpa Rinpoche prized this practice highly but struggled for its acceptance at his programs.

Another important stream of teachings flowed into Shambhala-Vajradhatu through connection to Kobun: the practice of the way of the bow, *kyudo*. In the mid-1970s Kobun introduced Trungpa Rinpoche to his own kyudo master and family friend, Kanjuro Shibata Sensei, twentieth in a familial succession of bowmakers to the throne of Japan. Trungpa Rinpoche invited Shibata Sensei to teach his martial art to the Shambhala sangha and to take up residence in Boulder. Over time, Shibata Sensei acceded to both requests and propagated a form of kyudo that he felt cleaved to its spiritual roots. Sensei scorned what he termed "sports kyudo"— purely trying to hit the target and win competitions. In Shambhala, Shibata Sensei was able to pass on the profound heart of his tradition.

When Trungpa Rinpoche created Naropa Institute in 1974 (fulfilling another part of the vision he'd shared with Suzuki Roshi), he asked Kobun to help with the place, and to look after it in the future. Kobun visited Naropa every year until his tragic death in the summer of 2001, guiding the school through his own elegant, understated presence and his serious practice. At the time of his death, Kobun held the Wisdom Chair at Naropa, and numerous of his artworks graced the campus.

The friendship between Kobun and Trungpa Rinpoche remained through the years as it had begun—gentle, loving, creative. "It was like family," observed publisher Sam Bercholz. "There was absolutely no one-upmanship; they connected in a way that was simply like sharing food and drink. Kobun was always just there." Indeed, early in their friendship, Kobun and Rinpoche pledged to be reborn as brothers throughout their lives.

Of the five roshis with whom Trungpa Rinpoche had significant relationships—Suzuki, Kobun, Eido, Maezumi, and Kwong—the next two were fruitful, but not without difficulty.[3]

In 1971, Eido Shimano Roshi hosted a visit from Trungpa Rinpoche. Eido Roshi—in the early days known as Tai-san—was a student of the great Soen Roshi, who'd sent him to the West. Tai-san had been eager to come and had learned a very good English; he'd first visited New York in 1963, serving as translator to Yasutani Roshi. During that visit, he stayed with disciples of D. T. Suzuki. Eido Roshi was by 1971 a dynamic, macho-tending Zen teacher of the old style: he favored things Japanese and strict. He could, on the other hand, create an electrifying atmosphere through the dramatic use of Zen forms and his intense personal presence. He was also a talented artist.

Eido Roshi and Trungpa Rinpoche sat together a number of times in his home in New York, at least once together with Soen Roshi himself. On this occasion, Eido Roshi warned Trungpa Rinpoche—who was famous for making his students wait hours for a talk—that if he were to come to meet Soen Roshi, he would have to be on time. Rinpoche arrived a very correct ten minutes early. The masters all did calligraphy together, and they were served sake by a devoted student who'd bizarrely kept the bottle against her body for three days because she'd been told that sake tasted best at "human body temperature." Conviviality aside, Eido Roshi remained in equal measure suspicious of and fascinated by Trungpa Rinpoche. "Who is this guy?" he asked a student who knew them both.

What Roshi seemed to want to know was how Trungpa Rinpoche could be an acknowledged lineage master and a scholar with a devoted following, and at the same time have habits like smoking cigarettes, drinking alcohol, and conducting extramarital affairs with his students. Every time Eido Roshi had ventured into these behaviors—and it appears he ventured fairly often—he suffered unpleasant consequences. It was explained to Roshi that Rinpoche hid neither his drinking nor his philandering. Deceit and shame played no role in his approach, and he genuinely seemed to love all his students, not only the female ones with whom he went to bed.

Eido Roshi, on the other hand, hadn't really been friends with his followers, nor had he ever relaxed with them until 1981 when, at the suggestion of Brother David Steindl-Rast, he was invited to participate in a Buddhist-Christian conference in Boulder. There he saw how Trungpa Rinpoche worked closely and daily with many students, something Eido Roshi apparently began doing as well from this time on.

Roshi also commented on how Rinpoche was served like a king by the sangha. This can only have reinforced his suspicions about Rinpoche; there are indeed powerful hierarchical distinctions drawn in the Zen world, but they tend to be more subtle and hidden than the British and Japanese forms for service that Rinpoche organized in his own home. Mixed feelings aside, the two teachers maintained a quiet, mutually respectful friendship during Rinpoche's latter years—a friendship that weathered the withdrawal of Eido's invitation to the Buddhist-Christian conferences, owing to rumor of scandal offensive to the Christians.

After Rinpoche's death in 1987, Eido Roshi came to Karmê Chöling, where Trungpa Rinpoche was to be cremated in a few days. Unable to stay for the ceremony because of prior commitments, Roshi meditated with Rinpoche's body, met with his wife and eldest son (the present Sakyong Mipham Rinpoche), and performed private rituals. He also left as a gift a box of priceless incense that was subsequently used at the cremation.

Roshi felt so touched at Karmê Chöling that he stayed until the last minute before his flight, soaking up the atmosphere of devotion, and of the mindful, cheerful, indefatigable preparation that had been going on for many weeks. He also took the opportunity to meet with arriving Tibetan lamas and dignitaries. As his car finally raced at illegal speeds toward the airport, he proclaimed to his attendant over and again that he'd at last seen the greatness of Trungpa Rinpoche; he'd seen Rinpoche's greatness in the environment of Karmê Chöling and in the comportment of his students.

Roshi went on to announce to his stressed driver that Trungpa Rinpoche was in fact *kami*. This nomination from Shinto tradition would have pleased Trungpa Rinpoche very much, as it refers to a larger-than-human energy usually associated with environments—rivers, valleys, mountains, springs, and so on; such energy could also be found associated with noble clans, nation-states, and genuine spiritual practice. *Drala* was the Tibetan term for much the same sort of thing. Invoking and manifesting drala had filled the last ten years of Trungpa Rinpoche's life and teaching.

In recent years, Eido Roshi has made a stream of visits to the Shambhala community, speaking at major practice centers, and guiding several Shambhala students through Zen retreats. Still fascinated with Trungpa Rinpoche's regalness, Eido Roshi commented in print that Trungpa Rinpoche had indeed been born to the manner of a king—that because of his utterly natural ease with it, Rinpoche made others happy in allowing them to serve him.

Finally returning to Naropa University in 2002, Eido Roshi gave the yearly Practice Day talk to the assembled community. He had conducted a wrenching funeral a few days before for Kobun Chino Roshi, and now, at the end of his talk he told Naropa students, "With large heartedness, sit, sit, sit—to experience our gratitude to Trungpa Rinpoche, the founder of Naropa University, or to express our gratitude to Kobun Chino Roshi, our long-time friend. The best way to express our gratitude is to practice, practice, practice and practice. And if you have extra time, practice more."

It was at the 1976 ceremony installing Eido Roshi as abbot of Dai Bosatsu Monastery in upstate New York that Trungpa Rinpoche met Maezumi Roshi. A week-long sesshin preceded the event, timed for July 4, and many important roshis and Zen teachers were there. During a pause in the ceremonies, a thunderstorm broke out. Milling and chatting monks scattered in the downpour, but many a fine robe was soaked through. Trungpa Rinpoche, not so mobile as the Zen brethren, had seated himself comfortably under an awning during the break and remained the lone dry VIP.

The lesson in holding one's seat was driven home more pointedly later in the day to Dennis Genpo Merzel Roshi, who at the time was acting as Maezumi Roshi's attendant. Genpo had been scurrying around between events, inviting people to come to Maezumi Roshi's rooms. Trungpa Rinpoche accepted the invitation and sat next to Genpo during the palaver. At one point Rinpoche leaned over and quietly asked, "Are you Roshi's attendant?"

Until this time, Genpo had only thought of himself as Maezumi Roshi's student, so he replied, "Sort of."

"Then you should never leave his side!" Rinpoche told him sharply.

Genpo felt this direct address as a wake-up call—for himself personally, and for the entire Zen Center of Los Angeles community—on how to attend their teacher.

After the installation Trungpa Rinpoche invited Maezumi Roshi to fly back to Boulder with him, which he did, together with students Tetsugen Bernie Glassman and Genpo. In Denver, they retired to a good Chinese restaurant, where, following Japanese decorum, Roshi kept pouring sake for Rinpoche during the meal. Rinpoche did not, however, pour sake back for Roshi, a seeming violation of etiquette. Later Genpo, incensed about this, asked Roshi, "Why are you serving that guy all the time?"

Roshi replied, "He's royalty and I'm a servant."

Roshi went on to say, though, to his startled disciple, "It's like in martial arts: the higher your stance, the easier it is to be knocked down."

In 1977, Trungpa Rinpoche took his first extended retreat since arriving in North America. He asked Maezumi Roshi to come to Naropa Institute, there to serve as spiritual leader. In effect, he asked Roshi to be the spiritual reference point for the entire Boulder community, which numbered many hundreds of students. When Roshi arrived, Rinpoche took him for a drive through the gorgeous foothills surrounding the town, and they ended up at a lookout point over Boulder. "This is my town," Rinpoche pointed out, "and now I'm going to share it with you." In a symbolic and probably necessary act, they pissed, mixing their streams as they did so.

During the subsequent five weeks, Roshi and two students—Genpo and Daishin Buksbazen—taught many things to the Boulder group: they led meditation, gave further instructions in oryoki and shrine-hall etiquette, and helped decipher an ancient text by Dogen Zenji, founder of Suzuki Roshi's lineage in Japan.

The friendship between Rinpoche and Maezumi blossomed: they exchanged visits; Rinpoche extended invitations; Roshi gave gifts, among them a beautiful brocade *rakusu* (Buddhist chasuble) and another fine oryoki set; Rinpoche taught about the brilliant sun of inherent human goodness; Roshi responded by playfully titling his own first book *The Hazy Moon of Enlightenment* and inviting Trungpa Rinpoche to write the introduction. In the piece, Rinpoche praised Zen as the "vanguard of buddhadharma" in the United States, noting that it "remains genuine and powerful. Its simplicity and uncompromising style have caused Western minds to shed their complexities and confused ideology." He concluded:

The Venerable Taizan Maezumi Roshi's teaching has caused true Zen to penetrate into people's minds and has cut through the trappings of their ego-oriented intentions. I have strong conviction that through his wisdom, buddhadharma will shine into the world, dispelling the darkness of samsaric confusion and bringing the gentle rain of compassion.

Riding the horse of mirage
Watching the sea of stars
Blossoming great eastern sun.

From his side, Roshi told his students that one reason Trungpa Rinpoche was so powerful and successful was that he was not afraid to fully embrace opposites, chaos, and negativity.

But their own relationship was not without difficulties. Deep into the evening at a dinner party one night in 1979 at his house, Roshi suddenly challenged Rinpoche to answer a famous Zen koan: "What is mu?"

"Mu"—meaning something like "no" or "not"—was how the great Chinese master Joshu responded to a question about a dog's buddha nature. The ancient encounter, indeed the syllable itself, became Zen's most famous turning point. Disciples in the Rinzai lineage, which Roshi also held, were usually given the koan as their first spiritual hurdle. But this breach of collegiality seemed to irritate Trungpa Rinpoche, and he refused to play along—or perhaps in stonewalling the question, he was, in a very Zen style, mirroring "mu" back to Roshi. In any case, the dinner party drew to a rapid close.

Though there was little contact between the two in the early 1980s, Roshi came to see Rinpoche during his last visit to Los Angeles, in 1985. The atmosphere during their meeting was warm and affectionate, and two years later, upon news of Trungpa Rinpoche's death, Maezumi Roshi immediately went to the Shambhala center in London, where he was teaching, and gave a glowing appreciation of Rinpoche's life and work. A few days later he visited the Paris Shambhala Center and gave an equally poignant, if very different eulogy. Maezumi Roshi's first Western disciple, Tetsugen Bernie Glassman, continued through the years to play an advisory role to the Shambhala community, through teaching and serving on the board at Naropa University.

Though Trungpa Rinpoche emphasized regular sitting practice for his Buddhist students and for those following the path of Shambhala Training, it was not exactly the same method Zen people used. Particularly in the early 1970s, students noticed that Rinpoche did not emphasize absorption techniques, nor concentration, and certainly not concentration on specific parts of the body, such as the *hara*—an area roughly between the navel and the genitals. This body region plays a role in Zen meditation teachings, and more widely in Japanese culture. It is often taught that one should breathe from there, chant from there, or simply put strength there.

Instead of focusing inward on the meditator himself, the technique Rinpoche settled on taught practitioners to "go out" with their breath, and dissolve. Alternatively, he told many early students that they could simply, directly "open." In other words, his technique did not point inward, nor toward, a center, but rather outward, eschewing any central reference point at all. "Radiation without a radiator" was one way he described this.

In the ocean of Buddhist meditation techniques, a minor difference in how to follow one's breath may seem insignificant, but this subtle shift played out in broader consequences. If one meditates with awareness joined to one's environment, then it follows that the arena or theater of meditation is more open, loose, and inclusive. Going further, Trungpa Rinpoche instructed his students not to make sharp distinctions in their approach to formal sitting periods and to postmeditation. He taught (and demonstrated) that with mindfulness and awareness, secular life could equally be seen as spiritual life. This view reached its fullest development in the Shambhala vision. Here, every aspect of existence—from the manner in which one sat in the meditation hall or in an airplane, to how one ate, drank tea or liquor, ironed or stored or wore one's clothes, adorned oneself with jewelry or perfume or not, shopped, cooked, conducted business affairs, family affairs, or romantic affairs—all these were suitable fields for practice. One could rouse precision, elegance, cheerfulness, humor, and insight, regardless of the situation. Having done so, Rinpoche taught, a person would be able to experience sacred world, no different from the very world one was already in—but seen with eyes cleared of pettiness through meditation and mindfulness.

When Trungpa Rinpoche leveled criticism at Zen students, which he did at various times, it was either for being attached to Zen or Japanese forms, or for having too strong a dichotomy between their formal practices—in robes, in the zendo—and their deportment in daily life, which he described as often "full of hanky-panky, very *un-Zen-like* hanky-panky."

And when, in the early to mid-1980s a series of scandals hit American Zen communities, it was not so much the sex, alcohol, or misuses of power and finance that brought teachers down, though these were certainly unwelcome surprises for many students. Under the rage that burned in many Zen communities smoldered deception, and apparent hypocrisy. What went on with the teachers and leaders behind the scenes, it was discovered, was not concordant with what went on out front, before the community's gaze, or the public's.

When Trungpa Rinpoche took criticism, on the other hand, which he did in no small measure from moral authorities outside his community—including a number of Zen teachers—he took it for what he'd openly done, not for what he'd hidden. If one went to practice in the scene around Trungpa Rinpoche, one found out quickly what the score was, if one hadn't known already. Because he'd simply been who he was all along—naked, so to speak, before his students—Rinpoche spared the community and himself the exhausting degradation of a schism.

One might wonder why Trungpa Rinpoche had so much contact with Zen people altogether; what was behind this association, which few other Tibetan teachers have pursued? Partly it seems to have been circumstance: when he began teaching in North America, the other active practicing lineages were chiefly Zen. Partly Rinpoche's connection to Zen was rooted in his wide-ranging intellectual and spiritual appetite, his ecumenical approach. He'd read Alan Watts's books on Zen while he was studying at Oxford and had admired them immensely. (After Bercholz introduced them in 1972, Trungpa Rinpoche and Watts enjoyed one another's friendship. Interestingly, in November of 1973, Rinpoche and Watts spent a very pleasant afternoon and evening together—the last of Watts's life. He passed away peacefully in his sleep that night. Later, Rinpoche worried that Watts was stuck in an intermediate state—a ghost. He went with several students to Watts's library, which was then housed in a shed in Marin County, California. There in a field outside the building, Rinpoche had students chant several liturgies from the Kagyü Buddhist tradition, while he performed an exorcism.)

Through Naropa, Trungpa Rinpoche hosted teachers of many traditions. In addition to the roshis mentioned so far, many others also visited, among them Joshu Sasaki Roshi, Katagiri Roshi, Vietnamese Zen masters

Thich Man Giac and Thich Nhat Hanh, Korean master Seung Sahn, and American teachers Tenshin Reb Anderson and Lou Nordstrom. One student laughed as she recalled her exasperation at a tea for Rinpoche and Thich Nhat Hanh—an appointment she'd worked hard for weeks to set up: "It was awful. They were both terrible. They were so completely polite and formal. Neither one of them would say a word!"

Perhaps a deeper reason behind Rinpoche's truck with Zen lay in his quest to plant Buddhism in the West, fully and properly. Early on he saw that for the dharma to take root, it would need a sympathetic cultural container. This he found notably lacking in North America, plagued as it had been with centuries of big-scale, industrial materialism, physical and spiritual. Trungpa Rinpoche thus began to draw on his own upbringing as a secular ruler of a large area of Tibet (as well as a spiritual ruler), and to give teachings on creating an enlightened society. Specifically, he taught how one might work on oneself and one's surroundings to establish an uplifted, dignified culture featuring a daily life founded in and supportive of human goodness and beauty. These teachings—Shambhala vision—looked as well to other cultures for inspiration and example, including specific periods and leaders of India, China, Japan, and England.

It would be fair to say that in working with Japanese teachers and forms—this includes the Zen-influenced ways of archery, tea, flower arranging, poetry, and calligraphy, all of which played significant roles in the Shambhala community—Rinpoche was seeking to enrich the atmosphere for the practice of genuine spirituality.

The distinction between importing teachers, teachings, and forms for the purposes of enrichment, on the one hand, and borrowing things from other traditions from a sense of impoverishment, on the other, is critical. To those who knew him, it was quite clear that Trungpa Rinpoche had no need to borrow anything. Drawing from the profound well of his own education and enlightenment, he had more than enough spiritual wealth to share with students. Despite his reputation as an outrageous *siddha*, he was equally the most exacting of teachers, taking no short-cuts on the meditative path, and offering none to his students. He loved the traditions he'd inherited and worked tirelessly to propagate their authentic transmission. In early 1974, he felt it sufficiently pressing to draw some distinctions: he held two seminars on the theme of Zen and tantra—one at Karmê Chöling in Vermont and one in Boston.

While Rinpoche spent a good deal of time comparing and contrasting the two lineages in these talks, he also seemed to be conducting an experiment in how and how much to present tantric teachings altogether in a public context. The tradition of these teachings has been handed down in fiercely guarded, secret, oral transmissions. Trungpa Rinpoche began exploring how to talk about these things publicly late in 1973; he continued with the two "Zen and Tantra" programs and finally, in the summer of 1974, gave a series of fifteen talks on tantra to a public audience numbering more than one thousand at Naropa Institute. These talks were later collected into the book *Journey without Goal*.

"Zen is wild; tantra is crazy."[4]

In the "Zen and Tantra" programs, Rinpoche examined aims, methods, aesthetics, and artworks of the two paths, stressing to his audience that both were based in traditional Buddhist meditation and that both had elements of a gradual path, as well as the famous sudden awakening. He said that sudden enlightenment was actually impossible. At the risk of reducing to a few simple themes what took Trungpa Rinpoche seven insightful talks to elaborate, some points might be sketched out.

Trungpa Rinpoche located Zen at the fruition phase of the mahayana (Great Path) tradition. He praised Zen as an "extraordinary development of precision"; he called it fantastic, he pointed out exactly how Zen, with its sharp black-and-white distinctions and its exhausting monastic schedule, led to a full realization of *prajna* (wisdom). Then he went on to say that tantra, or vajrayana, was a further step.

Where Zen stands as the fruition of mahayana, Rinpoche said, tantric teachings reach the fruition of vajrayana, the third great aspect of the Buddhist path. Where Zen leads to a clear, open, lofty mind, tantra points to ordinary mind, the lowest of the low. Whereas the Zen aesthetic, based in the Yogacharin tradition of "mind-only," leads to statements of refined simplicity and elegance, tantra needs no statement at all, opting instead for the naked bluntness of "things as they are." Rinpoche pictured such differences for his hirsute audiences as being like a beautiful tea cup (Zen) compared with a skull cup (tantra); as like a beautifully dressed nobleperson (Zen) compared with an unemployed, unshaven samurai. That the tantric aesthetic was rougher stemmed not from its lack of sophistication or practice. The difference came from the notion that refinement or self-conscious artistic statement was no longer necessary for the tantric yogi. Such yogis conducted themselves in a direct, immediate manner, beyond dualistic distinction.

It's startling that Trungpa Rinpoche could posit tantra as an evolution of Zen, a step beyond it, and yet convey absolutely no sense of belittlement to the Zen tradition. But that is exactly what he manages in the seminars, through sympathetic insight and admiration. The matter of their relative status for him is not clear-cut. In other talks on Zen, Rinpoche acknowledged that it would definitely be possible for Zen practitioners to attain tantric realization, and he mentions Suzuki Roshi as an example. He further allowed, in a stunning commentary on the Zen Ox-Herding Pictures, that the latter illustrations portray tantric understanding. He wrote that "the final realization of Zen leads to the wisdom of maha ati" (the highest level of tantra). But according to Rinpoche's commentary, this is portrayed in the seventh drawing of the sequence. The eighth, ninth, and tenth pictures—all further steps on the Zen path—show aspects of tantric enlightenment. Thus it seems that, on the one hand, Zen leads to tantra, but on the other hand, the path of Zen, seen through its art, accurately describes tantric fruition. How could this be? Perhaps Zen and tantra are not what one imagines?

More practically, it is clear from the way Trungpa Rinpoche discusses Zen that he has an insider's view of the training. When he describes the philosophical basis of Zen, or the koans, or what life in a Zen monastery feels like, it is as though he has been through it. Perhaps, having been a monastic for many years himself, he had in a sense done so. Such sensibility gave him an unnerving grip on the Zen students who came to his sangha after studying with Suzuki Roshi—a great many of these after Roshi's death—or from other Zen teachers. Rinpoche lauded their good sitting records, but seemed to know precisely how any Zen person might have corrupted or gotten tricky in their practice, and what problems this tendency could pose in the tantrayana.

. . . The laughter died down, and Rinpoche took another sip, looking out over the rim of his glass for the next questioner, the next challenger. I put up my hand. He nodded at me, and suddenly it felt like being in the paralyzing gaze of a lion.

"Don't we have to try to take care of ourselves?" I blurted.

"What do you mean?"

"I mean, if we want to see, don't we have to protect our eyes?"

He smoked his cigarette and took his time answering. I busied myself with thinking what I could say to his possible responses.

"There's nothing to protect."

I hadn't thought of that. I looked up at Suzuki Roshi, who glanced at me with raised eyebrows. Rinpoche repeated, "There's nothing to protect."

That left only one thing to say.

I bowed and said it:

"Thank you."

Notes

Many people generously gave time and energy to this project, sitting still for interviews, answering questions, providing materials, allowing materials to be used, tracking down details. Among them are Richard Arthure, John Bailes, Hathaway Barry, Sam Bercholz, Stephen Bodian, Cheryl Campbell, David Chadwick, Sarah Coleman, Carol Gallup, Carolyn Gimian, Robert Mipham Halpern, Moh Hardin, Lynele Jones, Judy Lief, Sonja Margulies, Genpo Dennis Merzel, Fabrice Midal, Bonnie Miller, Martin Mosko, Diana J. Mukpo, Henry Schaeffer, Paul Shippee, Judith Simmer-Brown, Michael Wenger. I thank all of these kind people, as well as anyone I've stupidly neglected to mention. Despite all this help, there may be errors in the piece; responsibility for these lies with me.

This article exposes some interesting fields for further research and study. It can't do much more than that, I'm afraid, since the topic of Trungpa Rinpoche and Zen is potentially quite vast. It is risky to write an article like this one in any case: the author can get things wrong, leave things out, offend people. I've only undertaken it because if people don't take such risks, a rich vein of teachings may be lost to the future. May this foolishness inspire others.

1. "Interview with Allen Ginsberg" by David Chadwick at www.cuke.com.

2. David Chadwick, *Crooked Cucumber: The Life and Zen Teachings of Shunryu Suzuki* (New York: Broadway Books, 1999), p. 375.

3. An excerpt from Kwong Roshi's own reminiscence appears in the last chapter of this volume, "Testimony and Reminiscence."

4. Chögyam Trungpa, "Zen and Tantra" seminar, Karmê Chöling, Barnet, Vermont, 1974.

Leaving Karmê Chöling for retreat, February 1977.
Photograph © 2004 by Mary Lang. Used with permission.

The Body of Reality

John Daido Loori

A monk asked Yunmen, "What is the body of reality?" Yunmen answered, "Six do not take it in."

THE BODY OF reality—dharmakaya—is one of the three bodies of the Buddha. It is referred to as the true body of all that exists and is the most essential and inclusive aspect of the buddha nature. In some schools of Buddhism, it is said to comprise two aspects, knowledge and principle. In most schools, it is seen as the manifestation of the primordial buddha, Vairochana.

The other two bodies of the Buddha are sambhogakaya, the bliss or enjoyment body, and nirmanakaya, the earthly body or body of transformation, the form in which the buddhas appear to people in order to fulfill their vows to alleviate suffering and to lead all beings to liberation.

In Zen lore, these three bodies are depicted in the last three stages of the classic Ox-Herding Pictures, a well-known graphic and poetic representation of Zen spiritual training of the mind. Dharmakaya, the eighth stage, is symbolized by an *enso*, a spontaneous circle, frequently drawn not fully closed. The gap invites the viewer to actively participate in the completion of the painting. At this point on the path, there is no effort, no separation, and no reference point. This is the realm of no eye, ear, nose, tongue, body, and mind—the perfection of primordial emptiness.

Sambhogakaya, the body of bliss, is depicted by a bamboo grove swaying in the wind, or plum blossoms scattering their petals. There is a sense of intrinsic relaxation and enjoyment pervading the whole space, of natural and inexhaustible energy. This is the treasury of compassionate activity.

The tenth Ox-Herding Picture, depicting nirmanakaya, shows a buddha in the form of an old man emerging from the mountains. He is "ragged of clothes," covered with dust, carrying a jug of wine under his arm and a bundle on his back. His eyes gleam and engage you. His captivating smile disarms you. There is no air of enlightenment about him. You are not sure whether you are looking at a sage or a fool. This is the manifestation of the multiple forms of the Buddha appearing in infinite ways, each appropriate to the circumstances. At this stage, the buddha has no concern for his own life but seeks only to fulfill the boundless vows of compassion and to save all sentient beings.

I first became aware of Trungpa Rinpoche in 1971. I used to frequent the Vanguard Café in Greenwich Village in New York City, where Allen Ginsberg, Gary Snyder, and other poets offered regular readings. During those days Allen also hosted an eclectic television show in the metropolitan area that provided a forum for avant-garde artists, spiritual teachers, prophets, notable hippies, and New Age experts. Allen cultivated the counterculture look, with a full, scraggy beard, colorful Indian clothing, and strands of beads and malas. His guests matched that style and attitude. So I was very surprised one day when, in contrast to this status quo, his featured guest appeared in front of the camera in a stylish, elegant three-piece suit and tie. This was Trungpa. He was utterly comfortable in his Western attire, completely present, jovial, and clear. My seasoned, scientific skepticism melted away as I listened to his straightforward teachings on the dharma, his accurate assessment of American culture and pointed warnings against dilettantism, spiritual shopping, and spiritual materialism.

Soon after this introduction, I had an opportunity to see Trungpa in person. He was doing a series of public talks in New York City; and, intrigued by his television appearance and message, I went to hear him. The auditorium was packed with a hodgepodge crowd of some thousand expectant people. Trungpa was late, but when he finally arrived, he immediately galvanized the attention of the audience with an overview of fundamental teachings of Buddhism and the importance of sitting meditation. After the lecture was over, Trungpa invited the participants to bring forth questions so that he could clarify any difficult points. Many of the queries were academic and theoretical. Then a young woman stood up and started to make her way toward the middle aisle, where the microphone was set up. As she struggled to pass in front of the others, I could see that she was agitated, her darkened face twisted in a grimace. Speaking in a broken voice and with a bit of sarcasm, she told Trungpa her sad and angry story, ending by saying that she was on the brink of killing herself. Throughout the woman's tale, Trungpa's eyes were glued on her without shifting away. When she stopped talking, he quickly responded that he would not recommend suicide. When the anxious wave of laughter from the audience subsided, he remained silent for a long while, holding the woman in his attention; then he proceeded to ask her questions, gently at first, then walking deeper into her life with her. His contact with her was total, lifting her from the crowd. There were only two people in the universe, an eye-to-eye, heart-to-heart connection being forged or recognized, and honored. Yet we were also there, witnessing something unusual and utterly plain. Trungpa was not selling anything—no clarifying understanding, no concrete recommendations, no solutions or hopes. But with his awareness and caring, he was allowing this woman to regain her self-respect and trust, her basic humanity. Everybody was learning something in the process, becoming a little more alive and real.

Each of the Ox-Herding Pictures has a poem attached to it. The one accompanying the tenth stage says:

> Entering the marketplace,
> barefoot and unadorned,
> Blissfully smiling,
> though covered with dust and ragged of clothes.
> Using no miraculous powers,
> you bring the withered trees spontaneously into bloom.

In Buddhism, there are various ways of appreciating miraculous powers, also at times called supernatural or mystical powers. On the rudimentary, technical level, they are linked to disciplining the mind through the development of penetrating concentration in seated meditation. From this perspective, the traditional texts list six miraculous powers: supernatural sight, supernatural hearing, mind reading, recollection of past lives, omniscience, and perfect freedom. But there are also the superior powers of the Buddha that are transmitted mind to mind, and the powers intrinsic to one-body reality.

One day, when the great master Dongshan served as an attendant to Yunyan, Yunyan asked him, "What are your miraculous powers and marvelous activities?" Dongshan folded his hands on his chest and stood in front of his teacher. Yunyan probed further and again asked, "What are your miraculous powers and marvelous activities?" Dongshan replied, "Please take care of yourself." Saying that, he left.

In 1975, one year after Trungpa established the Naropa Institute in Boulder, Colorado, I joined the summer staff to teach a course in mindful photography and to establish the curriculum for the master's degree in contemplative photography. During my two-month stay at Naropa I met with Trungpa many times, attending private meetings, lectures, and impromptu parties. In all circumstances, I witnessed his tireless commitment to his students and to maintaining the integrity of the teachings while searching for viable ways of transmitting the dharma. His signature instinct to see into people's games and posturing, and his focused power to cut through their neurotic patterns were already remarkable, and getting more refined.

On one occasion, on a Saturday morning, I was outside my apartment washing my car when two of Trungpa's bodyguards arrived in a black sedan, announcing that Trungpa wanted to see me immediately. I told them that I would be happy to go when I finished my work. When they then pressured me to come, I countered by explaining to them that he was not my teacher and that they could pick me up later. They stayed. When the car was washed and waxed, they asked me to bring my large-format camera; Trungpa wanted me take some formal portraits of him. I packed my Hasselblad and film plates and got into their car.

When I arrived at Trungpa's residence, the place was abuzz. Trungpa was sitting behind a desk in the outer office, immaculately dressed and groomed. Around him circled a small crowd of his students, wielding all sorts of cameras, shooting pictures, searching for unusual angles. Trungpa remained immobile within this mayhem, a slight smile on his lips. Apparently, word had gotten out that an "outsider" was getting a chance to photograph Trungpa, so some of his students, miffed by this, also showed up. I was clearly being seen as an unwelcome invader of the inner sanctum. I stood back and watched. After a while, Trungpa turned to me and asked, "So, what are you going to do?" I motioned toward the crowd and said that I was ready to shoot the portraits only when everybody left. I wanted to take the pictures one-on-one. Trungpa indicated that we should go into his personal office. He got up, followed by his guards. I objected and Trungpa told them to remain behind. Only David Rome, his personal assistant, trailed behind, helping him. When Trungpa was settled in the new space, sitting in front of a huge Bengali tiger pelt—a gift from his community that hung ceremoniously on the wall—I asked David to leave. He was surprised by this request, but Trungpa again nodded in agreement. Finally, we were alone.

As I started to set up my equipment, I explained to Trungpa that during the session, he would choose when to make the exposures. I asked him to hold in his right hand a book of matches. When I was ready, having completed all the meter readings and adjustments, I would indicate that; and then, when he was satisfied with the feeling he was projecting, he would drop the matches. At that instant, I would release the shutter. The first shot was completed without a glitch. Trungpa dropped the matches; I pressed the shutter. I reloaded the camera, ready to take the next picture. I got under the cloth and started to clear my mind, using the chant NAMU DAI BOSSA—"Being one with the Great Buddha"—something that my first teacher, Soen Nakagawa Roshi, taught me many years before. I would use that silent invocation whenever I needed to center myself. As I was repeating the words in my mind, looking at the smiling, upside-down image of Trungpa in the viewfinder, I heard a distinct, high-pitched version of NAMU DAI BOSSA coming from somewhere in the room. I popped out from under the tent, to find Trungpa gleefully smiling, fixing me with his gaze. He put down the matches and said, "We won't need them this time." I got back under the cloth, adjusted a few settings, and took hold of the shutter cable. I looked at Trungpa and kept my thumb on the button. We stayed poised like that for a few moments. Then, suddenly, the shutter released by itself. I heard Trungpa say, "I think we got the shot." I agreed, "I think we got the shot."

A monk asked Yunmen, "What is the body of reality?" Yunmen answered, "Six do not take it in."

The "six" can be the six miraculous powers. It can be the six perfections of giving, morality, exertion, patience, concentration, and wisdom. It can also be the six senses—seeing, hearing, tasting, smelling, touching, and thinking. It can be the six sense objects or the six consciousnesses. That "six" really means infinite or boundless. It means, "no matter how you slice it." And Yunmen emphatically states that whatever your apprehension, it does not take in the body of reality. Your calculating mind will never grasp it.

Once, a seasoned lecturer of Buddhism presented a discourse on the dharmakaya. He expounded that it reaches vertically through the three times and horizontally over the ten directions, which is definitely true. There was a Zen traveler in the audience, a master on a pilgrimage, who on hearing that assertion, let out an involuntary laugh. The lecturer stopped the talk, came down from his seat, and inquired, "What was my shortcoming just now? Please explain so I can see." The listener said, "You only lecture on that which pertains to the extent of the body of the reality. You don't see the body of reality." The lecturer asked, "After all, what would be right?" The traveler advised, "You should temporarily stop lecturing and sit in a quiet room. You have to see it for yourself." Basically, shut up and sit. The lecturer followed this advice. He sat in zazen all night. At dawn, he heard someone hitting the bell outside for the morning meditation. On hearing the sound, he was greatly enlightened.

Our understanding cannot absorb the body of reality. In getting to the truth of the matter, intellectual interpretations are irrelevant. If you want to see it, there is no room for rationalizations. The truth of the body of reality is not something that calculating thought and discriminating consciousness can appreciate. That is why there is practice.

In Zen training, the process starts with recognition of your dissatisfaction—its breadth and depth. It begins with making a personal discovery of the first noble truth—the truth of suffering—and with wanting to go beyond it. You generate and focus your intent. You make a vow to put an end to all suffering. Through concentration, you collect your scattered energy and discipline your life. Gradually, as you study the mind in zazen, seeing your thoughts and letting them go, you make yourself empty.

When you have established the groundwork of stillness, you take up the first koan—Mu, the sound of one hand clapping, the original face. You plumb the questions: What is truth? What is life and death? Who am I? What is the body of reality? To work on a koan is to become intimate with these questions. To see into a koan, you have to forget the self. You have to abandon the idea of a separate and distinct reference point. That first glimpse into the true nature of reality is transformative. Once you verify it for yourself, you can never live your life in the old way. The itch becomes unbearable. You have seen enough to know that there is more to who you are than this bag of skin. But you don't really appreciate the implications of that, just how far it reaches, how far beyond the "six" it really takes you.

To abandon the notion of self and other is to glimpse the dharmakaya. This is called kensho. Within the matrix of the ten Ox-Herding Pictures, this bit of clarity shining through our lifetime of delusions marks the third stage. You get a quick view of the ox. This usually happens around the time of passing through the first koan. And it gets clarified through working with one hundred miscellaneous koans, most dedicated to deepening our appreciation of the dharmakaya. You are getting familiar with the dharmakaya, its all-pervasiveness and ungraspability. But you still have not seen its nature clearly. That happens much later, in the eighth stage of training. It takes much more development. This process takes quite a while because your conditioning runs very deep. Even though you develop some insights by breaking through the barrier of self-centeredness, you immediately fall back into your habit patterns, as everything in the world reinforces those patterns. "Beyond the six" means beyond any traces of the conditioned habit patterns, beyond any way of formulating and delineating reality.

The body of reality is nothing but the self. The body of bliss is nothing but the self. The transformation body is nothing but the self. You have been carrying it with you all your life. You were born with it; you will die with it. And you will never attain it. Trungpa has not attained it. Buddha has not attained it. How do you expect to attain it? It can't be attained. It can't be given; it can't be received. It's been right here from the very beginning. Even though you pile up all kinds of baggage and debris to hide it from yourself, it is here; and the amazing thing is that every single practitioner, on some level, knows that. Deep in our marrow, we feel that clarity and perfection. If we did not know that there was something more to our lives than the daily vagaries, pain, meaninglessness, and confusion we encounter, we could not seriously engage in any spiritual work. We would not have the dedication and the power to do it. Once the bodhi mind, the mind of enlightenment, is raised, practice, enlightenment, and nirvana are immediately complete. The rest is just the illusion of time.

Soon after arriving in America, during his early visits to the West Coast, Trungpa made a strong connection with Suzuki Roshi at San Francisco Zen Center, and later with Maezumi Roshi at Zen Center of Los Angeles. He was moved by the spiritual power and integrity of these teachers, and impressed by the discipline in training he encountered at their centers, especially the basic dedication of students to seated meditation, zazen.

Trungpa's early exposures to the genuine practice of Zen in America were perceived by him as incontrovertible evidence that authentic Buddhism could be established here and encouraged him in fulfilling his own vision and mission. His fondness for Zen continued throughout his life. He visited Zen Center of Los Angeles many times during my training there with Maezumi Roshi. He helped us with fund-raising by offering public talks and invited us to lead sesshins, meditative intensives, at Karmê Chöling and in Boulder. He incorporated into his training matrix some of the elements integral to Zen—the liturgical meal of oryoki, the Zen arts of flower arranging, calligraphy, and archery.

In 1977, when we were ready to publish *The Hazy Moon of Enlightenment*, the third volume in a series of books on Zen training, we asked Trungpa to contribute a foreword. In Zen lore, the "hazy moon" symbolizes mature clarity, edgeless and filling the whole sky with a soft glow. Trungpa wrote his introduction and soon after visited us in Los Angeles to do a public talk. The topic of his talk, announced with huge posters plastered all over the city, was "The Bright Sun of Enlightenment." Trungpa did not hesitate to engage us in a delightful dharma dance, both helping and pushing the envelope.

His foreword began: "It is a privilege to write this foreword, which seems to mark a joining of the clarity of the Zen tradition with the vividness of the Tibetan tradition. In the United States, Zen has been the vanguard of buddhadharma, and it remains genuine and powerful. Its simplicity and uncompromising style have caused Western minds to shed their complexities and confused ideology. It has been remarkable to see Western students of Zen giving up their territory of ego purely by sitting, which is the genuine style of Shakyamuni Buddha. On the other hand, some people tend to glamorize their ego by appreciating Zen as a coffee table object, or by dabbling in Zen rhetoric. Another problem has been fascination with cultural beauty, causing a failure to appreciate the austerity of the true practice tradition."

After discussing the sudden and gradual paths leading to realization of the buddha nature, and the relationship of samadhi and prajna, concentration and wisdom, he warned: "However, if there is no exertion and wakefulness, we are not even finger painting, but deceiving ourselves in the name of the dharma. I feel that the existence of the practice tradition is the only hope. It alone can wage war against the ego. It alone is the way that we can comprehend the dharma."

He ended the introduction with a poem:

Riding the horse of mirage
Watching the sea of stars
Blossoming great eastern sun.

When Trungpa died in 1986, his cremation ceremony took place at Karmê Chöling, Tail of the Tiger Meditation Center, in Vermont. I went there with two of my students to pay respects and offer a memorial poem. The evening before the ceremony, we were shown a video from the cremation of the sixteenth Karmapa, during which several auspicious signs appeared. In the video, just before one of the lamas was about to start the fire, the narrator announced, "Right before the fire was lit, a rainbow appeared in the sky." With that, the camera shifted to the sky, revealing a beautiful rainbow. The next morning, thousands of people gathered around the cremation site, covering the hillsides. Trungpa had a huge following. There were many dignitaries and representatives from various schools of Buddhism, including some of my dharma brothers and sisters from Maezumi Roshi's lineage. Most of the teachers were seated in an open tent, very close to the cremation pyre. As soon as the fire started, electricity filled the tent as everybody started looking for the rainbow. Many were peering beyond the enclosure. Some got up and started walking outside. To the disappointment of many, there was no rainbow. The reason they were looking in the first place is that they did not know that the appearance of a rainbow is nothing extraordinary, and yet, it is certainly a miraculous event.

After we left, on our way back to the monastery, some forty miles south of Karmê Chöling, a rainbow appeared. The sky was pure blue with a single, fluffy cumulus cloud drifting across its expanse. The rainbow looked like it was riding the cloud. One of the students had fallen asleep across the back seat. Silently, I pointed out the rainbow to the other, who was riding next to me. We proceeded further on our journey, maybe another twenty miles, and I asked, "When I pointed out that rainbow to you, did you see it?" He said, "Yes, I saw it." I explained, "The reason I ask is that I was wearing sunglasses, and sometimes, when you look through them, sunglasses are known to produce miraculous things. Sometimes, simply wearing sunglasses is a miraculous event." But he said, "No. I saw it." And he wasn't wearing sunglasses.

The poem I offered for Trungpa, at his cremation ceremony, went like this:

Bright sun, rising in the East, setting in the West.
Trackless journey from which countless generations appear.
I ask, "Where are the master's relics to be found?"
The bones are here, but where is the master?

The body of reality is never one-sided. It is about deeply appreciating that you and I are the same thing, but I am not you and you are not me. It is about seeing how these two realities work seamlessly together. Not to realize that is to perpetuate a religion that does not function in the world, a religion that is completely irrelevant to the reality of this life. That is not what Zen is. Zen is about living one's life and using one's mind, and doing that with other people, with all beings. And the wonderful thing about it is that there are no spiritual manuals on how to do that. You will not find it in a book. You will have to plumb the depths of your being and discover it deep within yourself. That is what Trungpa did in bringing the teachings to these shores and finding a way to communicate them within a strange, unruly culture. Buddhism offers skillful means with which to study the self, practice and train the mind, and realize and actualize our lives. Ultimately, this is the task for each one of us. We should wake up and realize it.

Chögyam Trungpa

Father of Tibetan Buddhism in the United States

GEHLEK RIMPOCHE

You and Trungpa Rinpoche lived together with Sister Palmo in New Delhi, and you became very close friends with him. What are your memories of this period? What was Trungpa Rinpoche like at that time?

SISTER PALMO, THEN known as Mrs. Freda Bedi, who was an officer in information and broadcast ministry in the government of Prime Minister Nehru, took a keen interest in Tibetan refugees when they first came to India in 1959. She made several visits to the first Tibetan refugee camp in a place called Musamari in Assam State. She especially took interest in children and young adults. She also visited and took a keen interest in young incarnate lamas (*tülkus*) in a place called Buxas in Assam. There she chose me and Trungpa Rinpoche as her "favorite" young lamas. She invited us to come to New Delhi. Meanwhile, I was selected by the Dalai Lama to complete my education in Tibetan Buddhism to be able to present to it to a non-Tibetan-speaking population interested in Tibetan Buddhism and culture, Under a grant from the John D. Rockefeller III Fund. So I went to Dharamasala, and Trungpa Rinpoche went to Delhi.

Interview by Fabrice Midal with the participation of Kathleen Ivanoff.

I was invited very often by Mrs. Bedi to come to her home in Delhi so that I could learn English. I still remember the address: A-3D/II Moti Bug Diplomatic Enclave. So we spent time on and off, two to three years in this way. That was long before they established the Young Lamas Home School in Delhi. Trungpa Rinpoche worked as a leader in the Young Lamas school; I did not join the school at all.

Trungpa Rinpoche was a very strict monk. He not only wore monk's robes, but also insisted on carrying the ceremonial yellow robes on his shoulder. He also did not eat anything after noon. Yet he was very open, friendly, and funny. He carried very strongly the tradition of his own lineage, yet he was absolutely open to the other sects of Tibetan traditions. Not only that, but also he was quite open to the Judeo-Christian religion as well.

He was very enthusiastic about learning English, and spent a lot of time reading and writing English. I was just the opposite. My excuse for not learning to read and write English was that I was a visitor in Mrs. Bedi's house, and I was not living there. We both had a strong monk's superiority complex, but we learned to respect women and others with the help of Mrs. Bedi (whom we called Mommy Bedi) and her friends, in general, and particularly a Hungarian artist named Elizabeth Brunner (who, like Mrs. Bedi, was also a guest of Nehru). Mommy Bedi's official quarters were not that big—two bedrooms and a living room. There was also an enclosed verandah. In that verandah, she had a long stretched bamboo bed that looked like a big shelf. Four or five of us all had to sleep on that. Even any extra guest, like a young Tibetan girl, had to sleep there. In the beginning we all hated that, and later we all liked it. At first we fought over who would sleep next to the girl, like it was degrading, but later we fought over who would sleep next to the girl for the opposite reasons!

Then Mrs. Bedi was arranging with the universities in England, who would take in the young lamas to get an education. Of course I was dying to go. She offered the opportunity for Trungpa and me to go together, but I did not get permission from the Religious Affairs of His Holiness.

Do you have any idea why Sister Palmo picked you and Trungpa as her favorite young lamas?

She probably thought we were the most open, adaptable, maybe the most intelligent (if not brilliant).

When you and Trungpa Rinpoche were trained in India, what was your course of study and who were your teachers?

We did not really have a common Tibetan study, though we did try to learn English together. On the other hand, Mrs. Bedi tried to give us a little training in presenting the dharma in English, by sharing how Western people think and explaining to us the difference between Tibetan culture and Western culture. In the audience were Mrs. Bedi and her son, Kabir Bedi, a well-known Indian film star; and her daughter, Gulima; and Gulima's husband, who was both a political leader (in the Communist party) and a Hindu spiritual leader in India. He had a lot of spiritual followers as well, who watched and corrected us. However, we did Tibetan practice together.

Do you have any memories of the kind of advice that Mrs. Bedi gave to both of you?

Yes, a lot. She constantly told us how open Western society is and how they don't have Tibetan habits like hiding their mistakes and exaggerating any simple nice quality. Western society is very contrary to that—it is very open.

Did you ever talk with Trungpa Rinpoche about how to teach the dharma to Westerners in connection with the difference between the Tibetan and Western cultures?

Later, in Colorado, yes. I very much enjoyed and the important advice that Trungpa gave me, and I kept it in mind. He said that in the East, it is not only what you know that is important, but you must demonstrate some scholarship. In the West, no one is interested in your scholarship. They like simple straightforwardness, not circling around. We are not producing scholars, but sincere practitioners.

Besides the fact that you both were learning English, what did you have in common that made you become friends? Did you share some common views?

We were both young and open-minded, had revolutionary ideas, and appreciated the old culture, but very strongly saw that it needed to change. We both had a great deal of interest in Western people, culture, history, and politics.

Did Trungpa Rinpoche talk to you about his wish to teach in the West? Did he mention his interest in Shambhala?

Yes, he did. I did not see Trungpa Rinpoche for a long time after he left India for England, and I did not meet with him again until he revisited India in the mid-1970s. He was staying with the Canadian High Commissioner in Delhi, and I spent some time with him there. We had a long conversation about what he was planning to do in America.

Later, I met him in Boulder. He invited me to stay in Boulder in the White House. He had given me a very lavish reception. It was probably in the early 1980s, and at that time he said he was moving to Nova Scotia. He was complaining about the American news, how biased it was, how little coverage there was, how poor the English language was. He talked to me about Deleks [groups of people organized into small neighborhoods] and Dekyongs [Delek leaders] in Shambhala. He wanted me to join forces with him and give training to all the Dekyongs, and I told him I didn't know what to teach. He replied, "You know old Tibetan government functioning much better than I do," and that's what he wanted me to teach the students.

Shambhala was his secular program, a vehicle for teaching and serving a large number of people and preparing them for the spiritual path. He was hoping that it would be helpful to the people like "sunshine from the East."

Then he told me that if I didn't want to join forces with him, I should not go back to India but stay in America and teach. He also told me, "Don't let your students handle your finances. If necessary, hire someone to handle it, even if you have to pay sixty thousand dollars to do it."

He was sick for a while and then got better, and was telling me about that. He also spent a lot of time talking to me about his gold cigarette lighter that came from King Hussein of Jordan. He liked it very much. He also talked a lot about his new car, a Mercedes or some German import that the federal government was not releasing. He spoke of buying a helicopter to be able to travel from Boulder to the Rocky Mountain Dharma Center. And he shared with me his personal experience in the Tagtsang caves in Bhutan, which was very profound, as well as his mirror readings.

Why did Trungpa Rinpoche advise you not to go back to India?

He said, "The West needs you, and you need the West."

What did Trungpa Rinpoche tell you about his retreat in Tagtsang?

He told me about his visions, fears, and joys.

Was this friendship between two Tibetans from different schools—Geluk for you and Kagyü/Nyingma for Trungpa—unusual at this time?

Not unusual at all. Although Trungpa Rinpoche was quite a staunch Kagyüpa and I was quite a conservative Gelukpa at that time, we got along very well.

Did you discuss your differents lineages?

We made jokes. I would say mine was superior, and he would say his was superior. We didn't mean anything by it.

Did Trungpa display any interest or curiosity to know more about the Geluk lineage?

I think he had more knowledge about Gelukpa traditions than he showed.

Did Trungpa Rinpoche explain to you his decision about the way he presented the Buddhadharma in the West?

He told me that Shambhala was his main vehicle for presenting the dharma in the West. He also told me that it is more important to give teachings that are clear and accessible within the cultural context than to give very profound teachings. He also talked to me about the Karmapa's visit and its advantages and disadvantages.

Who was Trungpa Rinpoche for you? Is there is any aspect of his teaching that is particularly significant for you?

He was a great Tibetan yogi, a friend, and a master. The more I deal with Western Dharma students, the more I appreciate how he presented the dharma and the activities that he taught. Whenever I meet with difficulties, I begin to understand—sometimes before solving the problem, sometimes afterward—why Trungpa Rinpoche did some unconventional things. I do consider him to be the father of Tibetan Buddhism in the United States. In my opinion, he left very early—too early. His death was a great loss. Everything he did is significant.

Tendrel

A Meeting of Minds

ANNE WALDMAN

Chögyam is merely a stray dog
He wanders around the world,
Ocean or snow-peaked mountain pass.
Chögyam will tread along as a stray dog
Without even thinking of his next meal.
He will seek friendship with birds and jackals
And any wild animals.

—Chögyam Trungpa[1]

ONE OF THE most seminal and perhaps fortuitous occasions in the world of contemporary poetics and the world of Tibetan Buddhist psychology and meditation was the arrival of Chögyam Trungpa into a very particular environment in the United States, which included what is referred to historically as the "New American Poetry." His primary contacts were with poets and writers associated with the Beat literary movement, a branch of the New American tree—principal among them Allen Ginsberg, Diane di Prima, William Burroughs, Gregory Corso, Philip Whalen, Joanne Kyger, and myself. This unprecedented conjunction fostered the Jack Kerouac School of Disembodied Poetics, which was a wing of the larger Naropa Institute (now Naropa University). Founded in 1974 in Boulder, Colorado, by Trungpa and his closest students, Naropa expanded to include, in addition to poets, a range of American Buddhist scholars, artists, playwrights, dancers, political and cultural activists, filmmakers, translators, psychologists, as well as guests from other cultures and traditions—primarily Zen Buddhists, Native Americans, and Christian and Jewish mystics.

Trungpa, a reincarnated tülku, meditation teacher, and rinpoche (literally "precious one") in the Buddhist and Shambhala traditions, had been writing traditional formal poetry in Tibetan for some time and had also composed masterful sadhanas (practice liturgies) that emerged from profound meditative states or mind-transmissions (texts known in Tibetan as *terma*). He was a master calligrapher as well, and a catalyst for a prodigious range of projects that evolved meditation centers, the Maitri programs, retreat sites, seminaries, a body of orally transmitted teachings, and the development of strong sanghas, or spiritual communities, in the United States and Nova Scotia, Canada.

Trungpa taught what is referred to as Dharma Art on many occasions at Naropa. As poet Reed Bye has written in an essay on these specific teachings: "Dharma means something like form or 'is-ness' and refers to the experience of things as they are, free from projections. 'Art' comes from an Indo-European verb root meaning 'to fit together.' Dharma Art, then, refers to anything perceived and put together from the unbiased openness of original mind. Meditation is the practice of gaining direct familiarity with this openness."[2]

Trungpa was an indefatigable activity demon and a beloved spiritual leader until his untimely death in 1987. Allen Ginsberg's playful thumbnail sketch of Trungpa reads:

> a reincarnated lama trained from age 2 in various ancient practices aimed at concentrating attention, focusing perception, minding thought-forms to transparency, profounding awareness, vasting consciousness, annihilating ego, & immolating ego-mind in phenomena: a wizard in control of day-dream, conscious visualization & thought projection, vocal sound vibration, outward application of insight, practice of natural virtues, and a very admiral of oceanic scholarship thereof.[3]

The Jack Kerouac School of Disembodied Poetics, founded by Ginsberg and myself, has had a singular rich history of its own, preserved in part by a significant literary audio archive and several key anthologies, in addition to transcribed and written documents. The Audio Archive contains readings, lectures, and seminars from a constellation of poets and writers (from 1974 to the present). The overall mission of these writers, who have been core participants and guests at Naropa over the years, has been to restore the poet's ancient role, both scholarly and shamanic, as keeper of the culture, as well as "performer," teacher, and social commentator. The Archive is proof of these important trajectories and in part a legacy of the important conjunction of Trungpa with the poets and the viability of the vision of the Kerouac School.

The philosopher and critical theorist Jacques Derrida has mulled over the subject of "archive," referring specifically to Sigmund Freud's legacy in his book *Archive Fever: A Freudian Impression*, conjuring the sense of "permanence," of motive from the psychological sense, of a power move to establish canon, and so on. It is ironical that a school based on the Buddhist tenet of "impermanence" should preserve its legacy—which some might say the world needs—so that creative and spiritually minded people of the future (should any remain) will comprehend that not everyone in our historical time frame was caught up in a maelstrom of greed, violence, and war psychosis. Trungpa spoke often of the dangers of the "three lords of materialism": the Lord of Form, the Lord of Speech, and the Lord of Mind. Each is an aspect of a psychological reality that can be distorted in a dark time.

There is also the very intriguing subject of the "institutionalization" of a poetics program inspired, in part, by Buddhist theory and practice. Trungpa, whose dharma teachings have also been archived for posterity, had hoped to establish a "comprehensive library" in Nova Scotia, which would preserve spiritual traditions that he and others perceived as endangered in the coming dark age, which we now experience upon us.

Many constitutional civil liberties are threatened in America, the quality of education wanes, corporate media control information, a narrow Christian fundamentalist theocracy holds sway in the U.S. government, and there seems to be less and less tolerance for "difference" and the creative imagination. Religious conflict—or, one might say, power struggles masked as competition among religious ideologies—is pandemic in our world. The planet itself is threatened by criminal stewardship. Walt

Whitman warned in *Democratic Vistas* that unless American materialism was tempered by a spiritual influence, the United States would turn into "the fabled damned of nations." His antidote was "adhesiveness" among citizens and "candor" of "poets and orators to come." Trungpa has commented that in Whitman's poem "Crossing Brooklyn Ferry," the image of universal transitoriness was equivalent in perception to Buddhist sutras.

I do not mean to shift the tone to one of doom and apocalypse, but rather to make the point that key to the far-sighted activities of Trungpa was a sense of urgency ("Don't tarry, don't tarry" is a refrain from a Buddhist chant) and that his friendship and collegiality with a number of poets in this country was in fact an occasion of what the Tibetans call *tendrel*—"auspicious coincidence," which has empowered the life and work of many individuals, not least of which are the numerous students who continue to flock to the Kerouac School and maintain a continuity of adhesiveness.

The encounter of these two worlds—that of Chögyam Trungpa (who carried an ancient wisdom tradition that included classical Sanskrit-based poetics, and who narrowly escaped the communist invasion of Tibet) and the world of the "New American Poetry" (a lineage that contained and honored the larger "canons" of world literature and prosody: Homer, Sappho, Dante, Shakespeare, Rimbaud, Yeats)—also proposed radical shifts of attention for literature after the Modernist period.

Modernist poet William Carlos Williams's "no ideas but in things" and attention to the "minute particulars" resonates with Buddhist attention to "ordinary mind." Ezra Pound's useful triad *melopoeia* (sound), *logopoeia* (the dance of the intellect), and *phanopoeia* (the image cast on the mind) resembles the Buddhist triad of "body, speech, and mind." And Gertrude Stein's attention to tracking the grammar of her own thinking was akin to Buddhist mindfulness and discriminating-awareness wisdom.

Allen Ginsberg writes of Trungpa's progression as a poet:

> . . . consider the progression of style, from early poems adapted out of Tibetan formal-classic modes, to the free wheeling Personism [a term coined by poet Frank O'Hara] improvisations . . . and the Guru mind's wily means of adapting techniques of Imagism, post-surrealist humor, modernist slang, subjective frankness & egoism,

hip "fingerpainting," and tenderhearted spontaneities as adornments of tantric statement. We see respect & appreciation given to the "projective field" of modern Western poetry . . .4

Chögyam Trungpa had been schooled in Tibetan poetics, which was part of one's training as a reincarnated Buddhist lama. The term for poetry in Tibetan—*nyen-ngak* (Skt. *kavya*)—means "ornamental language." This writing is characterized by the use of rhetorical and phonetic ornament, and may be written in prose or verse. There is little deliberate use of rhyme. In the use of quatrains, the lines are five to fifteen syllables. The shorter lines are characteristic of archaic and folk poetry. The Sanskrit models are usually more than seven syllables (often eleven). Tropes include various sorts of simile and metaphor, and the use of stylized literary synonyms. The Buddhist yogins created a distinctive family of verse forms collectively known as *gur*, or spiritual songs, as manifested in *The Hundred Thousand Songs of Milarepa*, which are "devotional songs" written to lineage gurus and deities in the Buddhist tradition. One finds many of these characteristics in Trungpa's "Sacred Songs," a section of his book *Timely Rain*, including the song entitled "Supplications."

> The corpse, bloated with the eight worldly concerns,
> Is cut into pieces by the knife of detachment
> And served up as the feast of the great bliss.
> Is not this your doing, O Karma Pakshi?
> Although I live in the slime and muck of the dark age,
> I still aspire to see your face.
> Although I stumble in the thick, black fog of materialism,
> I still aspire to see your face.5

Trungpa also invoked the notion of "crazy wisdom" as a quality that poets have, a sublime compliment and at times a misunderstood one. It echoed what the poet John Keats deemed "negative capability," which was the ability to hold contradictory thoughts in the mind "without any irritable reach after fact or reason." It was more like surrealism and engaged *ulatbamsi*, or upside-down language and behavior, as in lines from Trungpa's poem "Samsara and Nirvana":

A crow is black
Because the lotus is white.
Ants run fast
Because the elephant is slow.[6]

A later poem of Trungpa's, "Glorious Bhagavad Ghetto," has a very different form and tone, much more in the American "ordinary mind" vein of Williams:

Glory be to the rain
That brought down
Concentrated pollution
On the roof of my car
In the parking lot.[7]

The New American Poetry—coming on the heels of World War II—specifically refers to various communities and associated "schools" of writers who at that time thrived outside the literary mainstream and outside the controlling literary mafias of New York publishing and literary journalism. These individuals and communities fostered small presses, engaged in major literary correspondences and debates with one another, and benefited (some might disagree because there were also differences and rifts between some of these communities) from the famous reading on October 6, 1955, at the Six Gallery in San Francisco, where Allen Ginsberg launched his poem "Howl." A range of poets from these different loci convened on several historic occasions (Vancouver, 1963, and Berkeley, 1965), and a full number were represented in Donald Allen's now-classic defining anthology *The New American Poetry*, published by Grove Press in 1964, a book of major import to young writers of my generation at the time.

The schools thus named were the New York School (in the work of John Ashbery, Barbara Guest, Frank O'Hara, James Schuyler, Kenneth Koch, Kenward Elmslie), Black Mountain (in the work of Charles Olson, Robert Creeley, Robert Duncan, Denise Levertov, John Wieners), San Francisco Renaissance (in the work of Robin Blaser, Jack Spicer, Robert Duncan [again], Joanne Kyger), and the Beat Literary Movement (Allen Ginsberg, William Burroughs, Gregory Corso, Peter Orlovsky, Lawrence Ferlinghetti, Michael McClure, Diane di Prima, Gary Snyder, Lew Welch, and others). Over the years, the Jack Kerouac School has hosted many of the writers associated with these communities and their inheritors. In addition to its palpable presence within the Audio Archive, the work of these authors has been present in the Kerouac School curriculum, and many of their books are in the holdings of the Allen Ginsberg Library at Naropa. Writer-composer John Cage was also an early guest at Naropa, along with Jackson MacLow, Robert Kelly, and Jerome Rothenberg. MacLow has a range of Buddhist-inspired poems. Robert Kelly is a Tibetan Buddhist practitioner and has studied the Tibetan language extensively. Jerome Rothenberg, a major anthologist as well as a poet, has been attentive to oral and spiritual poetries for decades and has done his own translations of texts by Milarepa and Marpa. Before he founded Naropa University, Trungpa Rinpoche had known the poets Robert Bly and W. S. Merwin, the latter having briefly taken Trungpa as a spiritual teacher in 1975.

The scope and influence of the New American Poetry and its offshoots and cross-fertilizations with other writers of the expansive poetry world is an Indra's Net of interrelatedness and is thus difficult to codify. Confluences that took place coast to coast continue to be analyzed and commented upon, and are somewhat outside the scope of this piece.

Suffice it to say that some of the writers most closely associated with the Beat movement were already very cognizant of and extremely well read in Buddhist philosophy and psychology. Gary Snyder had majored in anthropology as an undergraduate at Reed College and then did graduate work at the University of California at Berkeley, where he studied classical Chinese and pursued his Zen Buddhist practice. He received a scholarship from the first Zen Institute, which led to nearly fifteen years in Japan. He and the poet Joanne Kyger, who were married at that time, traveled with Allen Ginsberg and Peter Orlovsky to India, where they met the fourteenth Dalai Lama. Jack Kerouac befriended Gary Snyder, who provoked in him an interest in Buddhism. Kerouac's novel *The Dharma Bums* adopts a veiled Snyder as its central character, and triggered the "rucksack revolution," which set young people "on the road" with a resolute spirituality more at home with Buddhist and Taoist thought than with any Western philosophy. "Meditation is the art of deliberately staying open so that myriad things can experience themselves," Gary Snyder has written.

Kerouac also authored *Some of the Dharma* (musings from his extensive readings in Buddhism) and *Wake Up*, a biography of the Buddha.[8] Philip

Whalen discovered the writings of D. T. Suzuki while rooming with Gary Snyder at Reed College, lived in Kyoto in 1967 and then from 1969 to 1971, when he wrote *Scenes of Life at the Capital*. Once back in the States, he moved into the San Francisco Zen Center in 1972 and became an unsui, a Zen Buddhist apprentice monk. In 1975 he served as head monk of the Tassajara Zen Center. In 1991 he was installed as abbot of the Hartford Street Zen Center in San Francisco, where after retirement he lived until his death in 2002. Diane di Prima had encountered the Zen teacher Suzuki Roshi in 1962 and has stated: "I sat because he sat. To know his mind. It was the first time in my twenty-eight years that I had encountered another human being and felt trust. It blew my tough, sophisticated young artist's mind."9

Allen Ginsberg had first turned toward Eastern wisdom through the instigations of Gary Snyder and Jack Kerouac, and while in India had spent time seeking out Hindu and Buddhist teachers, and meditating in charnel grounds. Although thoroughly saturated in the sophistications and subtleties of Buddhist thinking by the time he met Trungpa, Allen immediately took on Trungpa's dharma teaching for his own writing mind. He had immense curiosity about the machinations of his own mental discourse—his hang-ups—and was assiduously attentive to the particulars of his prolific creative practice. His meeting with Trungpa led to an immediate vision of a dharma poetics. Allen enthusiastically proclaimed his spiritual insights to the world, and his own writing and teaching after this time was permeated with references to his guru.

Allen speaks from an interview in 1976 at Naropa conducted by Paul Portugues:

A.G.: The Tibetan monks I've talked to all report that Trungpa's experienced—seems to know all the angles. His teaching of meditation is excellent; acute, practical. From his own experience, he's gone to the center and is able to teach it well. He said some amazing things to me, like I was hung up on where does my breath begin and end. I went through it very early, and he gave me the image of the breath continuing, sort of, from one breath to another like an opening up of a telescope. Beautiful. I mean one breath leading to another, like the unfolding or opening up of a telescope. Very beautiful, precise image; and once I thought of it in those terms, it seemed to resolve a psychological, mental thing I had, or self-consciousness I had in proceeding from one breath to the other.

P.P.: But you've always been concerned with breath, much longer than you've been studying in the Tibetan tradition.

A.G.: That's true; it was implicit in the long-line poems like "Howl."

P.P.: Has it changed, the poetics of breath, since you've been practicing *shamatha*, etc.?

A.G.: No, because poetry, poetic practice, is sort of like an independent carpentry that goes on by itself. I think, probably, the meditation experience just made me more and more aware of the humor of the fact that breath is the basis of poetry and song—it's so important in it as a measure. Song is carried on the vehicle of the breath, words are carried out through the breath, which seems like a nice "poetic justice" *(laughs)*—that the breath should be so important in meditation as well as in poetics. I think that must be historically the reason for the fact that all meditation teachers are conscious of their spoken breath, as poets are. That's the tradition, the Kagyü tradition, that the teachers should be poets. That's the reason for the Naropa Kerouac School of Disembodied Poetics; originally, Trungpa asked me to take part in the school because he wanted the meditators to be inspired to poetry, because they can't teach unless they're poets—they can't communicate.[10]

Allen taught meditation practice regularly as part of his writing workshops, and he sought a resonance to dharma with the poetry of William Blake. He and Trungpa came up with the slogan "first thought, best thought." Allen turned Trungpa on to Jack Kerouac and writes in a piece entitled "To America: Kerouac's *Pomes All Sizes*":

My own poetry's always been modeled on Kerouac's practice of tracing his mind's thoughts and sounds directly on the page. Poetry can be "writing the mind," the Venerable Chögyam Trungpa phrased it, corollary to his slogan "first thought, best thought," itself parallel to Kerouac's formulation "Mind is shapely, Art is shapely." Reading *Mexico City Blues* to that great Buddhist teacher from the front car seat on a long drive from Karmê Chöling Retreat Center (1972 called Tail of The Tiger) [Vermont] to New York, Trungpa laughed all the way. "Anger doesn't like to be reminded of fits . . . The wheel

of the quivering meat conception . . . The doll-like way she stands /
bowlegged in my dreams waiting to serve me. . . . Don't ignore other
parts of the mind. . . ." As we got out of the car he stood on the
pavement and said, *It's a perfect exposition of mind.*

The next day, he continued, "I kept hearing Kerouac's voice all
night, or yours and Anne Waldman's." He said it'd given him a new
idea of American poetry, for his own poetry.[11]

Trungpa's "International Affairs of 1979," subtitled "Uneventful but
Energy-Consuming," clearly echoes some of Allen's political concerns
with his own particular sense of irony:

Where is the spirit of Communism?
Marx, Engels, Lenin—
If they returned and saw what a mess they made in the
    universe they would be horrified.
We find nobody practicing true communism.
The Chinese declaration of religious freedom in Tibet
    is humorous:
You are free not to practice religion!
And the Panchen Lama beckons the Dalai Lama.
Opening the door of Sino-Tibetan tourism fooled the
    sharpest and most professional journalist;
they lost their critical intelligence.[12]

There was a very particular flavor—lively, probing—to these poetic
exchanges that took place between Trungpa and the Beat writers. At a
"Poets' Colloquium" held in Boulder in 1975, William Burroughs begins
the conversation, challenging Trungpa's reluctance on the issue of "psychic practices" such as astral projection and telepathy and their relevance
to spiritual practice. Trungpa replies:

Well, I wouldn't say "reluctant," actually, but the question seems to
be that these phenomena we experience are made up in our psychic
level, which we can't actually share with somebody. They're not as
real as a dollar bill. So that seems to be the problem, always. And,
also, there's a tendency to get into a new world, a new dimension

that nobody can share, that people in the street can't share, can't experience. And further, how much are we making these things up, or are they actually happening? That's the kind of question. No doubt a lot of experience occurred. They do function on an individual level, but do they in terms of public phenomena? Someone might see a TWA jet flying overhead, which is everybody's common knowledge. These other things are not actually common knowledge. It may be common knowledge to a certain particular circle. That seems to be the problematic point. Are we going to encourage people to pursue something that is purely in their minds or to pursue something they can actually share? And half the world, or even more than that actually, 99 percent of the world, haven't realized who they are to begin with, so it's quite a burden.[13]

At the same colloquium, Burroughs and Trungpa discuss and disagree about the propriety of taking a typewriter on retreat. Later Burroughs comments on this exchange after he's written *The Retreat Diaries*. This excerpt of Burroughs is from *The Burroughs File* (1976):

Last summer in Boulder I was talking to Chögyam Trungpa Rinpoche about doing a retreat at his Vermont center. I asked about taking along a typewriter. He objected that this would defeat the whole purpose of a retreat, like a carpenter takes along his tools— and I see we have a very different purpose in mind. That he could make the carpenter comparison shows where the difference lies: the difference being, with all due respect for the trade of Jesus Christ, that a carpenter can always carpenter, while a writer has to take it when it comes and a glimpse once lost may never come again, like Coleridge's *Kubla Khan*. Writers don't write, they read and transcribe. They are only allowed to access the books at certain arbitrary times. They have to make the most of these occasions. Furthermore I am more concerned with writing than I am with any sort of enlightenment, which is often an ever-retreating mirage like the fully analyzed or fully liberated person. I use meditation to get material for writing. I am not concerned with some abstract nirvana. It is exactly the visions and fireworks that are useful for me, exactly what all the masters tell us we should pay as little attention to as possible. Telepathy, journeys out of the body—these manifestations, according to Trungpa, are mere distractions. Exactly. Distraction: fun, like hang-gliding or surf-boarding or skin diving. So why not have fun. I sense an underlying dogma here to which I am not willing to submit. The purposes of a Boddhisattva and an artist are different and perhaps not reconcilable. *Show me a good Buddhist novelist.* When Huxley got Buddhism, he stopped writing novels and wrote Buddhist tracts. Meditation, astral travel, telepathy, are all means to an end for the novelist. I even got copy out of scientology. It's a question of emphasis. Any writer who does not consider his writing the most important thing he does, who does not consider writing his only salvation, I—"I trust him little in the commerce of the soul." As the French say: *pas serieux.*[14]

It was interesting—in hindsight—to gauge the response here, to feel a demarcation in the spiritual path of Burroughs, whose writing had in fact "rescued" him from a life of addiction and despair. Because Burroughs had been responsible for the death of his wife in a notorious accident involving a William Tell–like game, I once brought up in conversation the story of Padmasambhava, the powerful magician-avatar who brought Buddhism to Tibet, and who had been responsible for many deaths before becoming a highly realized tantric teacher. There was a sense that persons involved with death or crime were more apt or ripe for dharma. I remember William taking it all in with fascination. His disposition seemed, finally, more existential, or Sufi perhaps, the sense of predestined fate—"It is written"—weighed on him. He was interested, however, in very specific advanced Buddhist practices: dream yoga; *tummo* (Skt. *chandali*, heat yoga), practiced in Tibet's cold winters; and any kind of mind travel. William was not about to sign on to anything, join a sangha, give up a sense of himself as a professional writer—a respectful identity earned under duress. He was an *éminence grise, un homme invisible,* a consummate hipster. As with John Cage, Trungpa's attitude was: these were beings of considerable accomplishment and siddhi (yogic power), and we should not try to seduce them into the Buddhist scene but just let them be.

The relationship with Allen was much more complex. Allen had taken Rinpoche as his root guru, his fiery vajra master. Trungpa pointedly wanted to puncture Allen's cherished role as self-appointed spokesman for the Beat literary generation. It was his job to do this. And to pop as well Allen's political and cultural activist manifestation, a formidable—and world-renowned—presence. Allen was a major "culture hero." Trungpa challenged and teased Allen about his "aggression." There had been earlier encounters, one in which Allen shaved off his beard at Trungpa's instigation. Trunga had been goading him about his identity. Trungpa had also demanded at one point that Allen compose on the spot publicly, at which point Allen burst out singing the poems of William Blake. Their repartee resembled the classical dialogues between gurus and disciples, with the guru pushing on the student's ego. Here is a brief exchange from the "Poets' Colloquium":

Rinpoche: Why do you write poetry?

Ginsberg: I took a vow when I was fourteen years old that if I were admitted to Columbia University I would work hard on the salvation of mankind.

Rinpoche: Did you think you were going to be famous?

Ginsberg: That was not the original intention.

Rinpoche: But the second one?

Ginsberg: You know, I don't think I'm going to be famous. I'm already famous, so the future isn't necessarily fame.[15]

And later:

Rinpoche: If you criticize the government or if you talk about homosexuality or whatever, it would be a real statement on your part, something you take pride in.

Ginsberg: What takes pride in mirroring what went past?

Rinpoche: Well, that still somehow has the residue of the coming out.

Ginsberg: Well, I'm confused. Do you feel that this coming out is just pure ego with no value, or do you think it's a useful work that we do?

Rinpoche: Please don't panic.

Ginberg: I'm not panicking, now will you please stop that! I was examining very closely what you were saying. I'm an expert in this area. I know my own moves.

Rinpoche: Well, I'm trying to study the sociological or psychological set-up of poets, and how they are aware of the audience. A lot of people begin to deny this completely but it is not quite true. You would like to make a proclamation. People write me a poem sometimes. They say, "Please destroy this after you have seen it." But they didn't really want it to be destroyed.[16]

Trungpa also parodies or spins off Allen's opening line from "Howl" (among the most famous words in contemporary poetry) with these lines from "Burdensome":

The best minds of my generation are idiots,
They have such idiot compassion.[17]

Diane di Prima, a key presence in the early years and development of the Jack Kerouac School, had became closer to Trungpa Rinpoche after the death of her own teacher, Suzuki Roshi, and worked on her *ngöndro* (preliminary practice involving one hundred thousand prostrations, mantras, and mandala offerings) under the auspices and guidance of the Vajradhatu mandala. "Trajectory," a poem from those early years, carries a sense of poignant irony that suffering is the greatest blessing: "So this / 1970 must be an excellent time / when even the telephone poles scream in agony. . . ."[18]

Joanne Kyger, who had an early affiliation with Zen practice, frequently honors and refers to the teachings of Trungpa in her poetry. She also has a long poem on the life of Naropa, pandit and onetime abbot of Nalanda University, who was both a wild yogin and a university administrator. From her "Continuing Adventures in the Life of Naropa":

burnt out   nobody's home
nothing doing   okay
keep that vivid vivid experience alive[19]

My own seminal poem "Makeup on Empty Space," written in the 1980s, was inspired by a talk Trungpa gave on the feminine principle:

I am putting makeup on empty space
all patinas convening on empty space
rouge blushing on empty space
I am putting makeup on empty space pasting eyelashes on empty space

painting the eyebrows of empty space
piling creams on empty space
painting the phenomenal world
I am hanging ornaments on empty space—gold clips, lacquer combs,
plastic hairpins on empty space
I am sticking wire pins into empty space
I pour words over empty space,
enthrall the empty space
packing stuffing jamming empty space
spinning necklaces around empty space
Fancy this, imagine this:
painting the phenomenal world
bangles on wrists, pendants hung on empty space
I am putting makeup on empty space
undressing you
hanging the wrinkled coat on a nail
hanging the green coat on a nail
look what thoughts will do, look what words will do
dancing in the evening—it ended with dancing in the evening
I am still thinking about putting makeup on empty space
I want to scare you the hanging night the drifting night, the
moaning night, daughter of troubled sleep
I am binding my debts, I magnetize the phone bill
bind the root of my pointed tongue
I cup my hands in water, splash water on empty space
Look what thoughts will do Look what words will do
from nothing to the face
from nothing to the root of the tongue
from nothing to speaking of empty space
I bind the ash tree
I bind the yew
I bind the willow
I bind uranium
I bind the uneconomical renewable energy of uranium
dash uranium to empty space
I bind the color red and seduce the color red to empty space
I put the sunset in empty space

I take the blue of his eyes and make an offering to empty space
renewable blue
I take the green of everything coming to life, it grows &
climbs into empty space
I put the white of snow at the foot of empty space
I clasp the yellow of the cat's eyes sitting in the
black space I clasp them to my heart, empty space
Take the floor apart to find the brown,
bind it up again under spell of empty space
the thin dry weed crumbles, the milkweed is blown into empty space
I bind the stars reflected in your eye
from nothing to these typing fingers
from nothing to the legs of the elk
from nothing to the neck of the deer
from nothing to porcelain teeth
from nothing to the fine stand of pine in the forest
I keep it going when I put the water on
when I let the water run
sweeping together in empty space
There is a better way to say empty space
Turn yourself inside out and you might disappear
you have a new definition in empty space
What I like about impermanence is the clash
of my big body with empty space[20]

Another oral poem of mine, "Skin Meat Bones," in which the three words become notes that are sung in varying registers, resonates with the mantra OM AH HUM. A poem entitled "Pratitya Samutpada" (Sanskrit for "conditioned coemergence") has tathagata (meaning "the 'thus-gone' one," one of the names of the Buddha) embedded in its refrain. A trip to Vietnam inspired the long piece "DARK ARCANA / Afterimage or Glow," which is a series of dharmic questions on the nature of war and colonialism. The book-length poem *Structure of the World Compared to a Bubble* takes the stupa at Borobudur in Java as a paradigm for Buddhist exploration, laying out the path of the boddhisatva in a kind of walking meditation. Many of my writings over the years have attempted to actualize dharma insight and inspiration.

Thus the conversations, readings, performances, collaborations, panel discussions, poems, and the like, occurring with many of the poets who passed through the Naropa gates, particularly those I've cited as Beats (this is a historical and handy term, but does not convey the full complexity of the individual writers or their work) constitute what I perceive to be an as yet unacknowledged body of uniquely articulated and salutary "dharma-poetics," which derives from Buddhist psychology and philosophy around such issues as spontaneous mind, the is-ness of language, the sense of "right view," of coemergent wisdom (similar to Keats's "negative capability"), "intentionality," "first thought, best thought," "Things are symbols of themselves," which is a teaching of mahamudra. My own personal poetics has evolved with insights through Buddhist study and practice. It is always interesting to observe where the meditator's mind and the poet's might resonate, and to be able to describe the processes of mind (which Buddhism does to such discriminating degrees) as an artist.

For a writer, the bottom line was considering the very nature of thinking, of the watcher, and the notion of being willing to give up that "shadow," your twenty-four-hour-a-day commentator who follows you constantly. What does that mean to a writer? Is it the watcher who gathers up sense perceptions and writes them down at the end of the day? What is the ego of your art? Is it necessary? *Dzinpa* means fixation or "holding." Do you need fixation to survive? Are you genuine? Are you appropriating and in what way? Are you writing in a way that's simply in fashion? What is the ultimate goal? Are you motivated by greed? . . . and so on.

These were basic questions for any sentient being, let alone the ambitious artist. Do artists require special pleading? Do you need the discursive mind, which always comments on *how you are doing*? Do you need passion, ignorance, and aggression to be an artist? Isn't Burroughs too extreme in his suspicion that the work can't be legitimate unless the art is the only salvation for the artist? Isn't this, in fact, a time of grieving where, as human beings, we are being called upon to transcend Art or use it as *upaya* (skillful means) on the boddhisattva path? Theodor Adorno asks in his famous question, *Kann man nach Auschwitz noch Gedichte schreiben?* ("Can one write poems after Auschwitz"). Or to paraphrase, can there be beauty, can there be art, after Auschwitz? The dharmic answer would be *There must be*. To ease the pain of living. To wake people up. To create alternative realities–cultural interventions—in the samsaric world of passion, aggression, ignorance. To propagate sanity.

Trungpa clearly stated from the beginning of the visionary Naropa project that he hoped the poets could make the Buddhists more articulate through original speech and mind, and that the poets might benefit by sitting meditation, which would provide a greater grounding to their lives, and that this would benefit others. And he further hoped that there would be no conflict between poetry and religion. Allen Ginsberg and I declared in our "mission statement" in 1974:

> Though not all the poetry teachers are Buddhist, nor is it required of the teachers and students in this secular school to follow any specific meditative path, it is the happy accident of this century's poetic history—especially since Gertrude Stein—that the quality of mind and mindfulness is probed by Buddhist practice. There being no party line but mindfulness of thought and language itself, no conflict need arise between religion and poetry, and the marriage of these two disciplines at Naropa is expected to flourish during the next hundred years.

Allen also wrote in 1978: "Whatever the fate of the Jack Kerouac School of Disembodied Poetics, some climactic event has taken place in American poetry which will leave its imprint of frankness and wisdom on future American lyric thought."[21]

Clearly this continues to be evident, as generations of writers and meditators have had the benefit of dharma teaching and the auspicious occasion, site, and example of the Kerouac School. The poetics program, with its unique pedagogy and its attention to poetic and spiritual lineage—written, spoken, performed—is a cultural intervention of enormous perspicacity and magnitude, and as such is a reminder of the initial spark of crazy wisdom East meeting maverick outrider West.

NOTES

1. Chögyam Trungpa, "Stray Dog," in *Timely Rain* (Boston & London: Shambhala Publications, 1998), p. 10. © 1972, 1983, 1998 by Diana J. Mukpo. Reprinted by permission of Diana J. Mukpo.

2. Reed Bye, "No One Spoke: Chögyam Trungpa's Teaching of Dharma Art," in *Civil Disobediences*, ed. Anne Waldman and Lisa Birman (Minneapolis: Coffee House Press, 2004).

3. Allen Ginsberg, Naropa Archives.

4. Allen Ginsberg, *Deliberate Prose: Selected Essays*, ed. Bill Morgan (New York: Harper Collins, 2000).

5. *Timely Rain*, pp. 170–171.

6. Ibid., p. 46.

7. "Glorious Bhagavad Ghetto," in *Timely Rain*, p. 58.

8. Serialized in *Tricycle: The Buddhist Review*, issues 8–15, in 1993.

9. Diane di Prima, in *Beneath a Single Moon: Buddhism in Contemporary American Poetry* (Boston: Shambhala Publications, 1991).

10. David Carter, ed., *Spontaneous Mind: Selected Interviews with Allen Ginsberg, 1958–1996* (New York: Harper Collins, 2001).

11. Ginsberg, *Deliberate Prose*.

12. *Timely Rain*, pp. 96–99.

13. "Poets' Colloquium," in *Loka II: A Journal from Naropa Institute* (Garden City, N.Y.: Anchor/Doubleday, 1976).

14. William S. Burroughs, *The Burroughs File* (San Francisco: City Lights Books, 1984).

15. "Poets' Colloquium."

16. Ibid.

17. *Timely Rain*, p. 62.

18. Diane di Prima, *Selected Poems, 1956–1976* (Plainfield, Vt.: North Atlantic Books, 1977).

19. Joanne Kyger, *Just Space* (Santa Rosa, Calif.: Black Sparrow Press, 1991).

20. Anne Waldman, *Makeup on Empty Space* (West Branch, Iowa: Toothpaste Press, 1984).

21. Allen Ginsberg, Naropa Archives.

Arranging fronds with an assistant, Boulder, August 1980.
Photograph by Rachel Homer. Used with permission.

Embodying Elegance

Displaying the Everyday and Living the Display

Alexandra Midal

IN THE TWENTIETH CENTURY, domesticity broke into the world of art, philosophy, architecture, and design. It cracked open a new world of creation while absorbing everything that a home can represent in terms of a private, inhabited space. Though historically associated with architectural work, its focus shifted to fields being explored by avant-garde artists who were working in the realm of total art,[1] before later becoming associated and intertwined with design. Design is often seen as the production of manufactured objects, but it really signifies the space in which these objects are to be found. Design started to convey a new meaning at the end of the 1960s and the beginning of the 1970s. For the first time in its short history, it had to face up to industrialized production and mass distribution. Finally, an idea that had been there right from the start reemerged: design could provide the largest possible number of people with useful and cheap consumer goods that would make them happy. Faced with the chance to make their dream come true, designers also weighed up the resulting limitations and alienation in terms of the development and freedom of the individual.

Translated from the French by Ian Monk.

Displaying Everyday Life

Because of these reasons, some designers refused to produce consumer products and instead sought to devise housing on a human scale, made for human beings and by human beings. Such a methodology implies a conception of habitat based on the needs of the individual. Such redefinition of design is a political step because it aims at showing people that they can choose to lead their lives according to their own nature, not based on principles of industrial rationalization. To give shape to this revolution, designers organized exhibitions to display in tangible terms the social project they wanted to instigate. The presentation of objects on plinths or under glass was against their aims. This point had preoccupied museums for some time, as is reflected in this striking remark from a curator of the Museum of Modern Art in New York: "The public is apathetic towards an exhibition of photographs of architecture. A scale model increases their interest, but it is obvious that proportion and enclosed space cannot be shown except at full size."[2] For this reason, the curators at the museum came up with the project "House in the Garden,"[3] where three different architects were invited to design fully furnished and equipped homes.

In 1980, Chögyam Trungpa displayed a series of exhibits along similar lines. At the invitation of the Institute of Contemporary Art in Los Angeles, he organized an exhibit entitled "Discovering Elegance." Instead of hanging up Tibetan works of art, as might have been expected from an exiled Tibetan monk, Trungpa arranged a series of rooms as if they were a real apartment. Nor was this a re-creation of a traditional home; for example, it contained Japanese ikebana, furniture from various traditions (modern, Oriental, Western), and a variety of other objects. Each item was chosen for its specific qualities, and each was self-contained and worthy of admiration. All of the selected items were linked together, making up a domestic landscape in which the highs and lows were prearranged and whose dynamic was based on the multiplication of the relationships between them: "The exhibit will comprise a series of about six rooms, each furnished in a combination of Oriental and modern decor and each featuring a flower arrangement appropriate to the activity of the particular room. The first room will be a kitchen, followed by living and dining rooms, a bedroom, a study, a meditation room, a warrior's shrine room, and a chamber in which a large drum will be installed."[4]

Each room had a precise function, as in an ideal apartment. Each of them united ephemera (such as flower arrangements) and permanence (such as furniture), or else history (a warrior's armor). The exhibit married styles and periods but made no historical or stylistic statement. What is decisive is not so much the intrinsic quality of the objects or their various characteristics, but their position in a given space and their ability to create a harmonious dwelling. The well-known American architects and designers Charles and Ray Eames are a precedent to Trungpa in this respect. In 1949, the couple presented their own home in Pacific Palisades, California, as *Case Study House #8*, sponsored by *Art and Architecture* magazine. The Eameses chose and assembled numerous objects from around the world, such as souvenirs, canvases—including one hung on the ceiling—animal sculptures, kites, and plants. Everything was arranged with the greatest care, giving their house a sophisticated coziness. The most striking reaction to their project can be seen in the film *House: After Five Years of Living*:

> Rather than a step-by-step record of each room, the film is a visual tone poem that leaves the viewer with a feeling for the qualities and atmosphere of the house. The close-up shot, a technique that rapidly became an Eames trademark, is used here to "experience" the house by concentrating on its parts and details—objects, folded textiles, shells, a flower against a window pane, rain on the windows, leaves on the path, architectural details—the way a person might see the house, changing focus from close to far with each glimpse.[5]

Their project was based on a careful selection of objects, whose arrangement then created an intimate space. The film was a manifesto for a manifesto house: *Case Study #8* enabled the Eameses to proclaim a way of life based on a poetics of the everyday. Quite likely for the same reasons, Trungpa accompanied his exhibit with a film, also titled *Discovering Elegance*. He conceived his exhibit as an arrangement of objects that would create a new space, one that was not a museum exhibit but a home. He reproduced the process that all of us have experienced when moving into a new dwelling. For this to be successful, we all know that we must evaluate the space and consider how best to place our possessions with precision and taste. The problem is not so much that only one position is viable for a given object, but rather that there is a need to choose just one among the myriad possibilities on offer. This arrangement is a precise orchestration of the space where we want to lead our everyday lives.

After the success of "Discovering Elegance," with around four thousand visitors, Trungpa organized several other similar exhibits, in Fort Mason Auditorium in San Francisco, and also "Winter Beauty" in the Boulder Center for the Visual Arts in the fall of 1981. All of these projects were based on the same invitation to walk around freely. The visitor experienced the space in a physical and dynamic way. Museums are often seen as dead spaces where objects and works are suspended in time. But by adopting this approach, Trungpa encouraged a mobile perception and freed the visitor from passivity. Environmental exhibits draw our bodies into the exhibition space and provide a shifting experience of it. In addition to introducing movement into a display space, which is generally static, Trungpa used it as if it were a three-dimensional canvas and assimilated a field of experimentation in which the colors of the palette have been replaced by objects.

When displayed in this way, everyday life is no longer viewed by the spectators in normal terms; it escapes from the purely material restrictions to which it is subjected, while at the same time explicitly referring to these restrictions. An atmosphere is created that juxtaposes reality and presentation. Even though the ordinary life being exhibited is no longer the same as the one we experience every day, its nature has not in fact changed but has simply been shifted to a context that is different from its familiar one. This transfer casts fresh light on it. What comes into play in the process is our very relationship with our daily environment. When we no longer see design as necessarily producing consumer goods, it acquires the capacity to establish a space, which is also a revolutionary idea. The designer's role is no longer limited to the creation of objects but now includes the establishment of a living space.

During the 1960s, architecture attributed little importance to domestic life, as can be seen in the dismissive expression "interior design." But the renowned Milanese designer Joe Colombo upset the world of design by no longer producing furnishings, no matter how much they were appreciated. He considered that, no matter how well such objects are conceived, they still remain above all an indicator of social class.

Furthermore, he criticized the exploitation of the workers who not only produce the furniture in factories but also dream of possessing such items. These reasons incited Colombo to abandon those architectural principles that are based on a notion of content, on the definition of each room's functions, and on the delimitation of spaces through the construction of walls and by the installation of water pipes and electric cables. Instead, he proposed a concept that would be invented by the inhabitant. Colombo wanted all people to be able to reappropriate their living spaces according to their desires, demands, and needs. He invented a domestic project in which objects and the separations between rooms vanished, to be replaced by one or more mobile multipurpose units that offered a variety of different functions, with specific answers to each person's needs, desires, and habits. Colombo inverted conventional methodology; from now on, individuals would have no need to acquire and install appliances and furnishings, which could be seen as being suitable to a home because of their size, style, qualities, and so forth, or to adapt them to the specific function of each room. Instead, the container would be adapted to the content. With Antidesign (as Colombo called his project), the home was based on the person. This idea renewed design by giving it a global mission for the conception of products and structures associated with domestic life. Antidesign raised questions about the living space and suggested what Colombo defined as "a totality embracing architecture, town-planning, production, the means of communication,"[6] with the objective of transforming society.

Familiar Space

Trungpa's exhibits draw visitors into a physical experience of their relationship with space while walking between flower arrangements and furniture. The environment is made up of objects that are exhibited in a certain volume and bathed in a certain light, to which are added the scents of the flowers and branches. This approach broke with typical design exhibitions. It adopted the Antidesign logic and gave up any architectural practice. Colombo's ideas invited architects to completely rethink domestic life from the viewpoint of the individual, and thus of design. Colombo set up design as the appropriate model for all conceptions related to private spaces. In this way, he considered that design is the microcosm in which each individual lives and moves, and it thus becomes the starting point of everything. For Trungpa, on the other hand, who showed how to enter into contact with space and thus find a way to learn to live differently, everything is design. Exhibition curators who base their approach on the inhabitant become designers in turn. This term minimizes neither the designers' expertise nor their professionalism; on the contrary, it is an explicit declaration of their intent. In "Discovering Elegance," Trungpa recognized the home and confirmed its strategic role in social transformation, as can be seen in the references in many of his texts to an "enlightened society" that would result from each individual's practices and attitudes. Trungpa's exhibits initiate this perspective, because this sort of domesticity provokes a reflection that could be extended to cover all of society. Its power lies in its very capacity to effect a transition, thus showing how fundamental changes can arise from simple, ordinary shifts.

The rooms arranged in "Discovering Elegance" are based on an experience of the ordinary that we generally turn away from at once. By founding this approach on domesticity, while constantly reminding his students of the great importance that should be given to the non-events of daily life, Trungpa reaffirmed that the ordinary is the irreducible basis of all things: "domestic harmony is considered the foundation of all other activities." Daily life is the primordial ground from which the human essence, and in particular elegance and dignity, can grow. Domesticity is a point of entry into each person's existence. This is what Trungpa was implying when he used the expression "art in everyday life,"[7] which he described as follows: "We begin to appreciate our surroundings in life, whatever they may be—it doesn't necessarily have to be good, beautiful, and pleasurable at all. The definition of art, from this point of view, is to be able to see the uniqueness of everyday experience . . . a kind of intimacy takes place with the daily habits that you go through and the art involved in it. That's why it's called art in everyday life."[8]

It is not so much the generally held notion of an artist that should be understood here, but rather that of a designer: art scorns the microcosm because it is too prosaic, unless it is transfigured and so magnified into an artwork. But this lack of interest is the very stimulus behind the way Trungpa organized his exhibits, and it overturned the relationships of equivalence that lead us generally to see anything ordinary as being beneath contempt. He incited us to reconsider daily life.

Democratizing Excellence

Trungpa constantly defended a democratic approach, according to which "art is not an elitist and specialized activity distinct from everyday considerations. Instead, the arts should be seen as a precise and clear practice for the carrying out of the most ordinary and domestic tasks, just as much as for the most ceremonial ones."[9] As we have already seen, here the term "art" could once more be replaced by "design." As in the position adopted by the British artist William Morris, cofounder of the Arts and Crafts movement and a Pre-Raphaelite painter, this vision envisages design as a lifting up of daily life, with the aim of creating a better society: "You whose hands make those things that should be works of art, you must be all artists, and good artists too, before the public at large can take a real interest in such things . . . and what is an artist but a workman who is determined that, whatever else happens, his work shall be excellent? . . . I do not want art for a few, any more than education for a few, or freedom for a few."[10]

Morris's project was a political one, and for this reason it influenced the ideas of hygienists in France and Britain, and continues to have a lasting effect on the mission of design. For example, when the poet and physician Jean Lahor (pseudonym of Henri Cazalis) discovered Morris's writings at the beginning of the twentieth century, he then published a series of books about decoration. He encouraged his fellows to educate the poor so that they would leave aside decoration and ornament that often simply concealed dirt while worsening health conditions, and instead adopt simple ideas such as whitewashing walls, which would improve urban hygiene and reduce centers of contamination. In fact, over and above such hygienic considerations, Lahor was nurturing an artistic project: "What should be sought for is an approach to decoration and to art that can be applied just as much to the most modest of houses as the richest: this approach has now, I think, been found. . . . In these two houses, one modest the other rich, there is no difference of principles, or of decorative subjects, but only of materials, or of how the materials are exploited; it is just necessary to remember that the simplest lines, when of perfect proportions, are often the finest in both furnishings and architecture."[11]

At the same time, in his new approach to decoration, Lahor was promoting the rational aesthetics of the modern movement. Similarly, the "Discovering Elegance" exhibition imposed a nondecorative relationship with its objects, in a far more profound way than the decoratively functional attributes of standard design, which often reduce the activity to a mere service industry. Trungpa organized his exhibits in such a way that each of their elements was autonomous and remarkable, and contributed to the creation of a living atmosphere. This promoted a politicization of domestic space that would act as the starting point for a new, more human society because it would display the basic principles of a lay Buddhism and, using no other outside discourse, display how important it is for each of us to examine in a new way our private space and its furnishings, if we want to lead a life that is dignified.[12]

Living Everyday Life

When Daniel Defoe described the life of the hero of his book, *The Life and Strange Surprising Adventures of Robinson Crusoe*, he emphasized ritual. Despite being alone on his island, where no one can see him or judge him, Robinson bathes every week, dresses with care, and neatly lays the table before enjoying his dinner. Such ceremonies are vital because they sustain the humanity of someone who has lost all contact with civilization. Our conditions of life may be far less extreme than those experienced by Robinson, but we still have difficulties in identifying the importance of forms and their worth. In this respect, design once again plays a primordial role: the presence of a single object can sometimes transform everything around it. It is not only its individual position that helps to raise the quality of its surroundings but also its intrinsic qualities. If you look at chairs in a purely functional way, they are all the same. Why bother choosing one rather than another, or thinking about the question instead of just going to buy any article in a mass-market store whose extreme standardization allows the manufacturer to cut costs? Because some chairs have qualities that reach us, that have, as the French say, a *je ne sais quoi*. In exhibitions of designer furniture, visitors can sometimes admire displays containing dozens of chairs that have been selected for just this reason. Apart from the technical skills shown in some, or the historical interest of others, they all have their different and at the same time significant characteristics. It is because of the presence of such articles that space is invested. Most chairs produced with no particular intention have no qualities of their own. Trungpa emphasized the relationship we all have with the material world, the special quality that some objects possess intrinsically and our resulting appreciation of them. The aim of exhibiting everyday life provokes a double shift: after seeing "Discovering Elegance," walking through its rooms and imagining that they live there, visitors feel an impact on returning home. In their own ways, they are then free to manifest an interest in the qualities they have noticed by being equally attentive to their own environment.

The figure of Trungpa cannot be reduced to facile exoticism and even Tibetan Buddhism, because he profoundly redefined the nature of exchanges between the East and the West, between tradition and modernity, and between the various disciplines themselves. This is brought out in a letter dated August 17, 1975, that Trungpa received from F. Lanier Graham,[13] exhibition director at the Arts Museum of San Francisco. In it, he compared Trungpa's exhibition with the Bauhaus,[14] hailing him as the true heir of that famous German institution. Indeed, Trungpa's project can be placed in the tradition of avant-gardes which considered that thinking about forms transformed our relationship with the entire world— and that this change takes place through a collaboration between disciplines.

Just as important as the schemes conceived in the past by Gropius, Kandinsky, Moholy-Nagy, Klee, and many others, Trungpa's project for society was based on the home. This, too, was the ambition of the Bauhaus (literally, build + house) but here it was developed in quite a different way. Trungpa's exhibits celebrated the importance that should be given to everyday life—he often spoke of the importance of bringing problems down to a kitchen-sink level—whose dimension should be fixed by objects and above all by how they are arranged in space. Trungpa thus showed that living is a complex act that requires involvement with the real.

Design is applied to the environment in its entirety, as well as to all the means that can be used to fix it. Design is a concept that is far larger than the reductive notion of industrial production of functional objects. Instead, it is addressed at the private sphere and subsequently determines our surroundings. In the same way that Colombo claimed that everything is design, Trungpa declared that in certain circumstances everyone can act as a designer. He was himself an accomplished example of this: apart from his exhibits, where he constructed an ephemeral space, he also patented a large amount of furniture,[15] while the dimension he aimed at was even vaster. Because of its diversity and ability to constitute a habitat, design was Trungpa's favorite means of expression. He designed the interiors of meditation halls, and designed the banners on the walls and studied the position of the altars, as well as their decorative objects. Trungpa also designed a cushion for sitting meditation, which he adapted to the Western physique by making it wider and as high as the step of a staircase, thus creating a direct relationship between the body and the house. With discernment, he chose the extraordinary tents in which seminarians stayed on the sides of the Rocky Mountains for three months. His work spread in so many directions that it is difficult to cover them all. But his passion for graphic design cannot be left unmentioned: he worked long and hard on the page layouts of the brochures that announced the seminars he organized, as well as that of his periodicals—of which the five issues of *Garuda* are magnificent examples—and he illustrated his own books. He was also a designer in the way he focused on the clothes he was going to wear, or on those meant for his students, or even in the choice of his jewelry and watch. He was clearly a designer when he paid ever closer attention to protocol, a term that covers both ceremonies during great occasions and the gestures of everyday life. This attention to detail was constant and led him to borrow forms from other traditions: from Scottish bagpipes to British army uniforms, from the oryoki ceremony transmitted by Zen monks to the traditional Japanese tea ceremony, from calligraphy to English equitation. Design is everywhere, present even in the countless pins that Trungpa designed, wore, and gave to his students. Trungpa was still being a designer when, for similar reasons, he carefully chose the music to be played during certain ceremonies and when he composed songs and poems. By placing design and domesticity at the epicenter of existence, Trungpa found a way to express the fullness that he advocated in his characteristic desire for excellence.

NOTES

1. In 1849, Richard Wagner published *The Artwork of the Future*, in which he sought to reforge the fundamental alliance among the arts. Later, this synthesis became a subject of research for the avant-garde, which produced what were called "total works of art." The aim was to integrate the spectator so that its meaning would be fully invested, and life and art would merge.

2. "Interim Report: House in the Museum Garden," May 12, 1948, records of the Registrar Department, Marcel Breuer House in Museum Garden, Museum of Modern Art, quoted in Mary Anne Staniszewski, *The Power of Display: A History of Exhibition Installations at the Museum of Modern Art* (Cambridge: MIT Press, 1998), p. 200.

3. The first house, created by Marcel Breuer, opened to the public April 1949; the second, by Gregory Ain, the following year; and the third, by Junzo Yoshimura, in 1954. For images and a descriptive commentary concerning the project, see Mary Anne Staniszewski, *The Power of Display: A History of Exhibition Installations at the Museum of Modern Art* (Cambridge: MIT Press, 1998), pp. 198–204. The same idea for an exhibition can be found in many countries and especially in England with the Daily Home Exhibition (see Deborah S. Ryan, *The Ideal Home through the Twentieth Century* [London: Hazar, 1997]) and in France with the household arts show in Paris.

4. *Nalanda News*, October-November 1980.

5. Ray Eames, John Neuhart, and Marilyn Neuhart, *Eames Design: The Work of the Office of Charles and Ray Eames* (London: Thames & Hudson, 1989), p. 199.

6. Joe Colombo, in answer to the question "What is your definition of design?" in Joe C. Colombo, Charles Eames, Fritz Eichler, Verner Panton, and Roger Tallon, *What Is Design?* Exhibition catalogue for Pavillon de Marsan (Paris: C.C.I., 1969), unpaginated.

7. Chögyam Trungpa, *1973 Seminary Transcripts: Hinayana-Mahayana* (Boulder: Vajradhatu Publications), talk 11.

8. Chögyam Trungpa, *Dharma Art* (Boston: Shambhala Publications, 1996), p. 27.

9. Proposal for an exhibit dated January 18, 1982, addressed to the Fashion Institute of Technology, New York (Sara Kapp archives, Milan).

10. William Morris, "The Lesser Arts," in *William Morris: Centenary Edition: Stories in Prose, Stories in Verse, Shorter Poems, Lectures and Essays* (London: Nonesuch Press, 1946), pp. 502–514. This comes from the first of Morris's conferences, "The Decorative Arts: Their Relation to Modern Life and Progress," held at the Trade Guild of Learning, probably at Cooperative Hall, Castle Street, Oxford Street, London, April 12, 1877.

11. Jean Lahor, *Les habitations à bon marché et un art nouveau pour le peuple* (Paris: Librairie Larousse, 1905), p. 58.

12. This is a recurrent term in Trungpa's teachings and stands for the notion of greatness and nobility. Dignity emanates from our own profound nature and can be manifested at any time, so long as the conditions are correct. For this to happen, it is necessary to be attentive at all times to how we carry ourselves, to our surroundings (be they objects or furniture), and to cleanliness, while at the same time concentrating on the way we continuously relate with this environment. Trungpa wanted all of us to conduct ourselves like aristocrats and insisted that nothing should be left to chance or be neglected: education, rules of conduct, decorum, the way to address others in speech or by gestures, as well as one's living space. To achieve elegance, nothing should suffer from neglect; everything should express close attention.

13. "Perhaps you remember a major study of the Bauhaus that was published by the M.I.T. several years ago. It documented the opinion of many people that the Bauhaus was one of the most important schools that had developed in Western civilization since the original, medieval concept of 'University.' . . . my principal regret was that there seemed to be no signs of anything like the Bauhaus starting up again. Happily, that was just before you came to the United States, and began what I believe is the most significant." Correspondence from F. Lanier Graham, Shambhala Archives.

14. The Bauhaus proposed reforming the teaching of art based on a union between the arts so as to create a new form of society. Its first program, entitled "Bauhaus Program in the Weimar Republic, 1919" was written by its founder, the architect Walter Gropius, and is based on three objectives:

   - saving the arts from isolation by encouraging craftsmen, painters, and sculptors to conceive projects together that would combine their talents and so attain "the supreme objective of all creative activity, which is architecture"

   - raising the status of the crafts to that of the fine arts, because there are no important differences between artists and craftsmen

   - working with industry, to aim for financial independence from public funding, and selling the products it produced

   Accused of decadence and Bolshevism by the Berlin police, under orders from the Nazi government, the Bauhaus was closed down on April 11, 1933.

15. In the 1970s, Trungpa designed furniture, which he officially patented. The legal document specifies, as is customary, that the drawings and plates submitted "represent the product of [Trungpa's] own creative and expressive effort and design." Legal document deposed January 31, 1974, Shambhala Archives.

Fulfilling the
Aspirations of the
Vidyadhara

KHENCHEN THRANGU RINPOCHE

CHÖGYAM TRUNGPA RINPOCHE played a very important role in the establishment of the teachings of the dharma in the West. He transmitted the depth of the entire teaching of the buddhadharma to the West, and his activity of establishing and spreading the dharma was exceptional, not like any others. While I was still in Tibet, I heard about him, and I knew that Chögyam Trungpa Rinpoche was a very special lama, one with perfect meditation, view, and conduct. I had a dharma connection with him because we took our full monastic ordination together from the sixteenth Karmapa in Palpung, when the Karmapa was returning from China with the Dalai Lama, around 1956. I knew that Trungpa Rinpoche was someone to whom one should show reverence.

We both escaped to India, but we lived in different parts of the country. Although I continued to hear about his special qualities and his activity, I had no detailed knowledge of what he was doing. Then Trungpa Rinpoche moved to the West, where we had more contact. Trungpa Rinpoche invited me to visit and to teach in his community, which I did on several occasions. He also asked me to be the abbot of Gampo Abbey, the

Translated from the Tibetan by Peter Roberts. Edited by Carolyn Rose Gimian.

monastery that he started in Nova Scotia. So we had the opportunity to meet a number of times in North America.

After Chögyam Trungpa Rinpoche's death in 1987, being requested to do so, I composed a prayer, or a chant, about Trungpa Rinpoche and his qualities. There are some details from this chant that I'd like to explain. The fifth stanza says:

> In order to remain in nonwandering, the ground of dharma,
> Relying on the meditation practice of dathün,
> Completely free from the movement of discursive thought,
> May we give rise to the samadhi of one-pointed shamatha.

One of the very special methods that Trungpa Rinpoche introduced was the conduct of the dathün, a month-long period dedicated to the sitting practice of meditation. Trungpa Rinpoche understood that, in order to have a good practice of the dharma, one needs to practice shamatha meditation for stability. If one achieves the stability of the mind, then one will have a clear and stable practice of the dharma. If one doesn't have that stability, although the practice of the dharma will still be a positive thing to do, it won't produce the same degree of clarity and stability. Therefore, Trungpa Rinpoche recommended to all of his students that they undertake a month-long practice of sitting meditation, which he called a dathün. This shows how exceptional his methods were, because dathün was not something that was practiced in Tibet. But considering what would be beneficial for his students, Trungpa Rinpoche established this tradition of dathün. On the basis of the stability of mind that arises from this, people are able to progress and develop understanding and realization in their practice. So the practice of dathün is both very special and very important.

Some people who come to me for private meditation interviews tell me that they've been practicing for years but still are not getting anything out of their dharma practice. They feel they're not reaching the inner essence of the practice. Some students have very great expectations for what they can accomplish through meditation, and they find that their expectations are not fulfilled. They are not getting that result that they aspire to. What does one need in order to attain that result? It is further practice of shamatha meditation that is needed. All one needs to do is to apply oneself diligently to this practice of shamatha meditation. If one has the stability of mind that is gained through shamatha, then whatever dharma activity one undertakes, whether one is reading or meditating or doing any other practice, one is able to do it thoroughly and completely. For example, if one practices meditation for one hour, then with stability of mind, one will have the benefit of one hour of practice. If one doesn't have that stability of mind, one may practice for an hour, but one won't really have a complete hour's worth of practice, because the mind will often be distracted by something else. Therefore it is good to continue to develop shamatha meditation, so that one's practice will become profound and stable.

The next verse of this prayer of aspiration says:

Having trained the mind on the paths of the greater and lesser vehicles,
Through hearing the oral instructions of the view and meditation of the
    secret vajrayana
And through direct transmission,
May we give rise to completely pure conviction in our beings.

This verse refers to Chögyam Trungpa Rinpoche's establishment of the Vajradhatu Seminary as a vehicle for the advanced training of his students. At the seminaries, people made an in-depth study of the hinayana, the mahayana, and the vajrayana teachings. At Seminary, people learned about the view, meditation, and conduct of each of the three yanas. In addition to the study aspect of the Seminary, Trungpa Rinpoche also gave direct pointing-out instruction on the nature of the mind. It is very important to hear the teachings, to study them, and to contemplate the view, meditation, and conduct of the hinayana, mahayana, and vajrayana. Through inference and deduction, one gains an intellectual understanding of the teachings. However, there's also the need for direct experience. Knowing this, Chögyam Trungpa Rinpoche gave his students these direct instructions pointing out the nature of mind. They thus gained the certainty that comes from study and analysis as well as the certainty that comes from direct experience.

The next verse of the chant says:

Through the practice of the general and special preliminaries—
By purifying our beings, completing great accumulations of merit,

And by the power of the guru's blessing entering us—
May devotion, the root of dharma, be firmly planted.

Having been given these special practice instructions at Seminary, Trungpa Rinpoche's students then received the teachings on what are called the general and the special preliminaries, which refer to the contemplations and the practices done as part of one's entrance into the vajrayana path. This is a very important teaching. In fact, in the scriptures it is said that the preliminaries are more profound than the main practice that follows after them. In the main practices of the vajrayana one actually eliminates the obstacles that need to be eliminated and one attains what needs to be attained—the qualities of buddhadhood and so on. Nevertheless, whether the main practice goes well or not depends on the practice of the preliminaries.

Understanding their importance, Chögyam Trungpa Rinpoche gave his students extensive teachings on the preliminaries. The special preliminaries are the ngöndro practices, which include 108,000 repetitions of the refuge formula combined with 108,000 prostrations, 108,000 repetitions of the Vajrasattva mantra, and 108,000 mandala offerings, concluding with a guru yoga recitation. Through prostrations and the Vajrasattva mantra practice, one trains and one purifies oneself and one's being. Having purified one's being, through the practice of the mandala, one gathers the accumulation of merit. Then, having gathered the accumulation of merit, through the guru yoga practice, one receives the blessing of the guru.

Students need to develop and maintain strong motivation to practice. Sometimes students come to me and say, "I have faith in the dharma, and I have the aspiration to practice. I really want to practice, but I seem unable to do so, because there are obstacles or I don't have the motivation." This happens to people quite often. We are living in samsara, in the midst of confused existence. It's the characteristic of samsara that we will feel that way at times. So the advice I give to people at such times is to encourage them especially to practice the dharma through meditation on the four general preliminaries. These are contemplations on the nature of precious human existence, the inevitability of karma, the nature of impermanence and the constant suffering of samsara. Through the repeated study and contemplation of these four topics, one will gain encouragement to apply oneself with diligence to practicing the dharma.

In particular among the four general preliminaries, the contemplation of impermanence is important in order to develop the motivation to practice. Meditation on impermanence is a great encouragement at the beginning, when one is just entering into the practice of the dharma. The realization of impermanence will give one the faith to enter into the dharma practice. In the middle of the path, impermanence is like the stick that is shaken at us, which keeps us going in the practice of the dharma. When one's diligence lessens as one progresses on the path, contemplation of impermanence will make one's diligence grow again. In the end, impermanence becomes our constant companion; one appreciates impermanence as the helper that has enabled one to accomplish the result.

Some people tell me that although they have been practicing diligently for many years, their kleshas, or their emotional upheavals, seem to be just as strong as ever. To help diminish these kleshas, there is the practice of Vajrasattva, which is one of the special preliminaries. In general, for diminishing bad karma and the kleshas, one can do the practices of repentance and confession. Then, particularly in the vajrayana, one can follow the instructions for the Vajrasattva visualization. One visualizes the yidam or deity Vajrasattva as a youthful white prince sitting above one's head. In Vajrasattva's heart center, there is a hundred-syllable mantra, which is the essence of all the peaceful and wrathful deities of the bardo. When one supplicates Vajrasattva, amrita flows from this mantra circle and descends through Vajrasattva's body, entering into the practitioner through the crown of his or her head. The amrita fills one's body and washes away the stain of the kleshas, bad karma, and obscurations. While doing this practice, one may think, "My anger is causing me so much trouble. I really want to get rid of it." One supplicates Vajrasattva to please get rid of the anger, or whatever klesha is the problem. One imagines that this amrita is coming down and that all of that anger is being washed out and one is becoming completely cleaned of it. Or one might think, "I'm full of envy, and I need to get rid of this envy." So one prays to Vajrasattva for that purpose. One imagines that the obstacle is being washed away by the amrita. Doing this visualization again and again is a way of bringing a remedy to one's kleshas.

Sometimes, one may have problems with a lack of material wealth. Those kinds of difficulties may become obstacles to practicing the dharma. The mandala offering that one does as part of the ngöndro is a way to overcome that problem. Through making the mandala offering, one accumulates merit, and through that merit, one will have prosperity, enjoyment, and so on.

Deshung Rinpoche once told a story about his own teacher and what resulted from his practice of the mandala offering. His lama had been a very poor monk, with very little clothing, food, or other belongings. However, he did own a brass bowl. So he asked someone to take this bowl and make it into a plate that is used for making the mandala offering. Then he used the brass plate to make one hundred thousand mandala offerings. As a result of that, he became very prosperous and accumulated a great deal of merit. Deshung Rinpoche said that a rain of prosperity fell upon his teacher.

The Vidyadhara, Chögyam Trungpa Rinpoche, gave all of these teachings to his students, to prepare them for further vajrayana practice and also to help them overcome difficulties in their life.

The next verse of the chant says:

Prajna in the form of the mother Varahi,
Supreme upaya in the form of the father Chakrasamvara—
Through the practice of unified utpatti and sampannakrama
May we attain supreme siddhi in this life.

Trungpa Rinpoche also gave his students the teachings of Vajravarahi and Chakrasamvara, who are two important deities in the Kagyü lineage of Tibetan Buddhism. He gave his students many vajrayana teachings on these two yidams, and he instructed them in the visualization and mantra practice for Vajravarahi, as well as the visualization and mantra practice for Chakrasamvara. He gave instructions in both the formal aspect, or the utpattikrama practice, as well as the formless or sampannakrama practice that goes along with these deities. He taught his pupils that first one needs to do the utpattikrama practice, or the visualization of the deities, and having done the utpattikrama practice, then one does the sampannakrama practice. Since he gave these teachings to his pupils, we should continue to practice them. Through practicing them, we will gain the benefit of them.

Finally, I would like to say something about the next verse:

Through Ashe, the essence of Shambhala—
The place of the seven dharmarajas and twenty-five rigdens—
May confidence enter our hearts,
And through the power of that may drala and werma gather like clouds.

This refers to the very special teachings that Chögyam Trungpa Rinpoche gave, the teachings on Shambhala, which are taught in the *Kalachakra Tantra*. In the mantrayana, which is another name for the vajrayana, you have four orders of tantra: kriya tantra, acharya tantra, yoga tantra, and anuttara tantra. Within the uttarayoga tantra you have father tantra, whose teachings are principally about method; and you have the mother tantra, whose teachings are principally about wisdom. Then you have the nondual tantra, which is the union of method and wisdom. So method is emphasized in father tantra, wisdom in mother tantra, and the union of those in nondual. The nondual tantra is the Kalachakra. Then, within the Kalachakra, you have an outer Kalachakra and an inner Kalachakra and what is called the "other" Kalachakra. The palace of Kalachakra, the deities of the mandala of Kalachakra, the practice of the utpattikrama and the sanpannakrama of Kalachakra—all that is called the other Kalachakra.

You find the teachings on Shambhala in the Outer Kalachakra; it is a branch or section of the Outer Kalachakra. The Outer Kalachakra is also concerned with predicting what good things are going to happen and what bad things are going to happen through an examination of the planets, the lunar mansions, and so on. It includes a description of the physical nature of the world and how the world was formed, and also discusses how the dharma will prosper in the future.

So the connection between the Shambhala teachings and the vajrayana teachings is found in the Outer Kalachakra. There, the text describes how there were the seven dharmarajas, the dharma kings of Shambhala. Then there is a lineage of twenty-five Rigden kings.

Beyond that, the essence of all the Shambhala teachings is to develop primordial confidence and power. Chögyam Trungpa taught, not only how to develop relative or temporary confidence and power, but also how one can attain the ultimate result, in order to be able to benefit great numbers of beings. The practice of the Shambhala teachings, in addition to creating courage, confidence, and power, brings the protection of the drala and werma (deities). If we are able to practice these teachings that he gave, then we will gain that benefit from them.

That is a brief explanation of the meaning of some the verses of this chant. In general, a great deal has been accomplished through the kindness and the activity of Trungpa Rinpoche. Many good things have come about. In the future, because of Trungpa Rinpoche's kindness and his activity, the merit will increase and the power of the dharma will continue to spread, becoming greater and greater.

FULFILLING THE ASPIRATIONS OF THE VIDYADHARA, THE VENERABLE CHÖGYAM TRUNGPA RINPOCHE

NAMO GURU-KARMAKAYE

Through the power of practicing the holy dharma in general and the utpatti and sampannakrama of the anuttarayoga tantra of the secret mantra vajrayana in particular, may we, his disciples, in this life and through the entire succession of our lives, be endowed with the good fortune of practicing, by means of hearing, contemplating, and meditating, all the exceptional oral instructions of the great Vidyadhara Chökyi Gyatso.

As we practice and come to understand his profound oral instructions, may exceptional experience and realization arise in our beings. All the blessings without exception of the mind of the supreme vidyadhara having entered our beings, may we easily attain the supreme and ordinary siddhis. Having attained them, may we instruct and teach fortunate students, and may this spread throughout the entire expanse of Jambudvipa, completely fulfilling the wishes of this lord.

Accordingly, to provide a refuge from suffering, may the bravery, confidence, intelligence, exertion, gentleness, and so forth of the excellent tradition of Shambhala, which arose as his mind terma, spread and flourish. Based on the power of that, may the growing suffering of poverty and destitution due to the decline in prosperity, the affliction of various diseases previously unknown, the horrors of a war that could destroy the world and its inhabitants through poisons and other weapons, and other problems facing the world be completely quelled. May all beings without exception on this earth enjoy peace, happiness, and complete prosperity.

In particular, in this place on which this lord walked, which he blessed, and which he prophesied—the land of Kalapa and so forth—may drala and werma gather like clouds. Through completely increasing and expanding the teaching of Vajradhatu, the Dharmadhatus, and Shambhala, may we be able to fulfill effortlessly and spontaneously all the buddha activity and wishes of the great vajra-vidyadhara, the supreme Chökyi Gyatso. Please grant your blessings.

In order to remain in nonwandering, the ground of dharma,
Relying on the meditation practice of dathün,
Completely free from the movement of discursive thought,
May we give rise to the samadhi of one-pointed shamatha.

Having trained the mind on the paths of the greater and lesser vehicles,
Through hearing the oral instructions of the view and meditation of the
    secret vajrayana
And through direct transmission,
May we give rise to completely pure conviction in our beings.

Through the practice of the general and special preliminaries—
By purifying our beings, completing great accumulations of merit,
And by the power of the guru's blessing entering us—
May devotion, the root of dharma, be firmly planted.

Prajna in the form of the mother Varahi,
Supreme upaya in the form of the father Chakrasamvara—
Through the practice of unified utpatti and sampannakrama,
May we attain supreme siddhi in this life.

Through Ashe, the essence of Shambhala—
The place of the seven dharmarajas and twenty-five rigdens—
May confidence enter our hearts,
And through the power of that, may drala and werma gather like clouds.

Through relying on the blessings and the power of the truth
Of the genuine three jewels and three roots,
May all the excellent fruition of our aspirations
Be spontaneously accomplished, quickly and effortlessly.

—Translated by the Nālandā Translation Committee

At the request of the Sawang Ösel Rangdröl Mukpo, the great holder of the family and dharma lineages of this holy one, this was written by the one who holds the name Thrangu Tülku. Through its power, may it be a cause for the teachings to spread everywhere.

Testimony
and Reminiscence

Continuity

Khandro Rinpoche

If you look at the history and development of Buddhism in the West, so many teachers have contributed. But many would agree that two teachers in particular have played a pivotal role in making Buddhism accessible to westerners: namely, His Holiness the Dalai Lama and Chögyam Trungpa Rinpoche.

Trungpa Rinpoche's main contribution, I would then say, was his ability to provide continuity. This was done by planting dharma in a deeper way; by strengthening its roots and introducing dharma in a traditional way that was, nevertheless, easy for westerners to understand. This was achieved through a great deal of direct communication between teacher and student, and through the direct involvement of their minds and lives. In this way, people felt they were actually living the tradition; they were not just students of a tradition. They were not just adopting a new philosophy, but a way of living their lives. Trungpa Rinpoche presented this fullness of dharma so well.

Trungpa Rinpoche had learned very skillfully, upon coming to the

West, from the Zen tradition—especially, Suzuki Roshi. He then took what was workable and used this as a balancing factor with the Tibetan tradition. In this way, he created the basis of a mandala, which hadn't been there before. This was the first time a proper mandala was established. And because of this, Buddhism was able to shift from many small units to a whole, larger model—a model that others could emulate, to create larger organizations.

From the Western perspective, the understanding of dharma shifted from being just a philosophy to becoming a way of life, with a hierarchy of communication and application. It was at this point that Buddhism became an actual citizen—and not just a visitor—to the West.

Excerpt from an interview conducted by Helen Berliner.

New Upayas

BERNIE GLASSMAN

I was tremendously affected by Rinpoche's presentation of the five buddha families. In 1979, I worked with Maezumi Roshi on translating a Zen liturgy called the *Kan Ro Mon*. It was created by a Soto Zen master who made use of teachings from the Shingon tradition, the Japanese form of tantric Buddhism, and it is structured according to the mandala of the five buddha families. I was tremendously drawn to this liturgy—it is used in the important Japanese ceremony called Obon that is done once a year for ancestors, and also for any dead person who doesn't have anyone to do services for them, such as a soldier who has died far from home or a homeless person. It struck me powerfully as a practice for those aspects of society—and those aspects of oneself—that aren't getting taken care of. In this liturgy, called *The Gate of Sweet Nectar* in English, the energies of the five buddha families are invoked in order to feed and comfort those abandoned, suffering spirits.

Trungpa Rinpoche gave very lucid explanations of the five buddha families, and through studying his teachings and seeing how he made use of them, I was able to apply them in my own work. Rinpoche had developed a way of working with different states of mind and psychological problems based on the five families. Called the Maitri Program, it involved meditating in a set of five rooms, each differently shaped and colored, and with a different body posture for each room. My wife, Jishu, and I adapted this work, using the postures but replacing the rooms with colored goggles that made everything appear blue or red or green, and so on. We conducted sesshins, Zen retreats, from the standpoint of different families. So I played with what I got from Rinpoche.

Even more important to my thinking was seeing how Trungpa Rinpoche adapted the basic Tibetan Buddhist tradition to teaching dharma in America. Zen, as it came to this country, was very hierarchical and aimed purely at producing teachers. The temple system of Japanese Zen didn't come over, except among ethnic Japanese living here, and at that time there was almost no contact between them and non-Japanese Americans interested in Zen. The primary purpose of Zen Center of Los Angeles was to produce American Zen teachers. But Trungpa Rinpoche was talking about building a sane society.

That was of great interest to me. I wanted to bring what I was learning into the community. Here also I adapted Rinpoche's approach. Rather than focusing on building sane society within the growing sangha of Western Buddhist practitioners, I wanted to work with the whole society. I stayed in a Buddhist venue, as a Zen priest and teacher, but in my work I moved out into the general community.

I followed the shift in Rinpoche's own teaching during the late 1970s as he began presenting his Shambhala teachings, putting more and more emphasis on the creation of enlightened society. I think that Trungpa Rinpoche was open to expanding Buddhism itself to fit the needs of American culture, which was a very different attitude from the traditional Zen view of the way. In the end, I think Trungpa Rinpoche still expected that people would come around to Buddhism. Later on, the Dalai Lama took a further step of moving into an open space of common humanity, beyond being Buddhist or something else, which is the direction that I have moved in. But at the time Trungpa Rinpoche was opening the path in that direction and that influenced me. He was a role model.

So these were the three main ways I was influenced by Trungpa Rinpoche: his example of working with the larger society, his teaching on the five buddha families, and his way of pulling the rug out, of going beyond boundaries—which could be painful, but I loved it. Zen only has the first six paramitas, which don't include upaya—skillful means or method. Rinpoche was developing new upayas. That was very interesting to me, especially methods for getting people out of the structures they are used to working from and into a space of "not knowing." In my own teaching, I use "plunges," experiences such as living on city streets for five days with no money that get people completely out of their usual ways of thinking.

Excerpt from an interview by David I. Rome.

Fishing with Trungpa

JAKUSHO KWONG ROSHI

In 1974, before Naropa was accredited, Trungpa invited me to teach, and to bring my whole family, to Red Feather Lake, Colorado. On the way, I decided to follow the nearby rushing river to its source, where, to my surprise, we discovered a rock face gushing and rushing with tiny drops of water, the life-force of the river itself. After, when we pulled into the parking lot of what would become the Shambhala Mountain Dharma Center, a Seminary was in progress. We parked next to Trungpa's cabin, and the next morning, my oldest son, Ryokan, who liked to fish, invited Trungpa's son (now Sakyong Mipham Rinpoche), then twelve years old, to fish with us. Trungpa's attendants warned us that there were no rods, but we had our own, and Rinpoche was accommodating, so off we went to Poudre Canyon, where, on a warm, beautiful day, we uncannily caught more than many rainbow trout—at one point I even had three on one line! After a while, however, the Sakyong, who I noticed was holding a bent stick with no line, admitted that his father had told him not to fish, and afterward we found that Trungpa himself had handed the fishing poles over to the Girl Scout Camp next door. Tibetans eat only larger animals, thereby killing less and feeding more. That evening we cleaned, cooked, and ate our catch. We discovered years later when we dedicated Trungpa's stupa here at Sonoma Mountain that, without saying a word to each other, no one in our family had ever fished again.

Rinpoche and I talked often that week, our exchanges mostly brief and often delivered through example and demonstration. One evening, when I suddenly said during a conversation, "It must be the myth of freedom," I was startled to see Trungpa staring at me, eyes wide, glasses sliding down his nose—I had unknowingly pronounced the title of his next book. As we continued to converse that week and long after, such quick encounters between us happened from time to time.

Excerpt from a talk given on October 25, 2003, in Santa Rosa, California.

Teaching Kyudo

KANJURO SHIBATA SENSEI

Trungpa Rinpoche was attracted to Kyudo because it was not a sport. Rinpoche thought that for Americans just sitting was too tiresome a way to always do their meditation. Whereas in Kyudo there is change and movement, so he thought it might be a good method of meditation practice. Sometimes, when you are meditating or when you are doing Kyudo practice, you hit the true target, and naturally you show a sort of happiness on your face.

Other martial arts place a great importance on your rank, but this is not the case with how we do Kyudo. In some forms of Kyudo, you might determine rank by whether or not you hit the target with your arrow, and when you do, you move up another rank. How can that be a reason for being happy?

Man, lady, young, old—many many different people practice together. Hitting the target or increasing your rank is about the ego; it's not about this happiness. Getting enjoyment for your ego just makes a lot of trouble, a lot of problems. In Japan, we have a saying that if you get stuck on the idea of hitting the target, then you'll start going down the wicked path. So that's not the point.

What Trungpa Rinpoche felt was very important about the teaching of Kyudo is that it identifies that problem with ego. When your heart is clear, that makes for good Kyudo. When you achieve freedom from ego, that clearness makes for good practice. In other martial arts, of course, you have an opponent whom you cut or attack in some way. In Kyudo, you cut your own ego.

Excerpt from a talk given on October 3, 2003, at the Shambhala Meditation Center,
Silver Spring, Maryland. Translated by Michael Rich.

Our Little Secret

SAMUEL BERCHOLZ

I first came across Trungpa Rinpoche's work while I was a university student in 1967. Browsing through the library, I found his autobiography, *Born in Tibet*, which had just been published in the United States by Helen and Kurt Wolff. Reading it made me quite interested in learning more about Tibetan Buddhism, especially as I also happened to be reading *The Life and Teachings of Naropa*, a text of one of the Indian forefathers in Trungpa Rinpoche's Kagyü lineage.

In the spring of 1969 I traveled to Great Britain, hoping to meet Trungpa Rinpoche at Samye Ling Tibetan Meditation Centre in southern Scotland, but due to a rail strike, it wasn't possible to get there. Vincent Stuart, a publisher in London, gave me the short manuscript of Rinpoche's entitled *Meditation in Action*. That manuscript had an extraordinary effect. Its presentation of basic Buddhism was so immediately present; it spoke in a clear and natural language I'd never encountered before. It was as if the author were speaking straight to me. I'd been thinking of starting out as a publisher for a while now, and it seemed more than auspicious that this book would become the first title of Shambhala Publications.

Mr. Stuart printed one thousand copies by letterpress for a North American edition, published in the autumn of 1969 to coincide with his British edition. And over time, in the thirty-five years since its first appearance, many scores of thousands have found that Trungpa Rinpoche's iteration of Buddhism spoke to them in their language too.

Trungpa Rinpoche was surprised when he received the first copy of the North American edition of his book. He looked at the spine and saw:

Trungpa
Meditation in Action
Shambhala

He later told me that at first it looked like a hallucination to him, so he had to put it down and look again. By auspicious coincidence, the name that was chosen for the publishing company was the same as a tradition of which Rinpoche was a principal lineage holder. The Shambhala Teachings were revealed by the Buddha at the request of the king of the ancient kingdom of Shambhala, as documented in the *Kalachakra Tantra*.

During Trungpa Rinpoche's escape from the Chinese occupation of Tibet, he was writing a book, *The Annals of the Empire of Shambhala*, which was unfortunately lost during a river crossing just before he entered India. Occasionally, in later years, when Shambhala was mentioned, he would refer to it as "our little secret."

A Man Who Could See Two Worlds as One

ROBERT WILSON

Fabrice Midal: When did you first meet Chögyam Trungpa and what was your impression of him on that meeting?

I met him first with Allen Ginsberg in New York, and later with Jean-Claude van Italie in Colorado. I found him extremely open and free-minded, with a great sense of irony and humor: a man who could see two worlds as one. There was always this space behind what he was saying and doing. That fascinated me.

You were invited to attend the Mudra Conference in February 1973, in Boulder, along with the Open Theater, the Manhattan Project, the Magic Theater of Berkeley, and the Provisional Open Theater of Los Angeles. What recollections do you have of the conference?

Order and chaos.

Excerpt from an interview by Fabrice Midal.

The Dharma Art and Shambhala Teachings

MEREDITH MONK

Chögyam Trungpa pointed out that there is something to always keep in mind when you're creating: "Is the work you're making of benefit?" The Dharma Art teachings are very uplifting; they point out an awareness of the process itself and the relation between artmaking and practice. Artists develop a personal sense of discipline in the act of creating work, so in a sense the Dharma Art teachings verbalize and delineate something which is usually discovered instinctively. But the teachings are valuable for everyone to become aware of the elements that exist in every moment of perception. I always think of myself, particularly in my singing, as being a conduit of these fundamental energies. The teachings are a rich reminder of why I became an artist in the first place.

The Shambhala teachings made me slow down more in my daily life. In my working process I was always able to start from emptiness, but in terms of sitting on the subway, walking down the street, experiencing the basic aspects of everyday existence, I began seeing differently; appreciating the most ordinary kinds of events. When I first began working with these teachings and practice, I became aware that overlaying what Chögyam Trungpa calls basic goodness is the sense of terror that he speaks about, and so much of what we do is a reaction to that. Our aggression has to do with our fear. It was a revelation to discover that in myself.

Every time you make a piece, fear is always there and you're always working with it, playing with it, allowing the interest and curiosity of what you're making to become more compelling than the anxiety. Then you've actually walked through the fear, and there's a sense of discovery.

Excerpt from an interview conducted by Jozef Prélis, January 27, 2004.

An Epic Sensibility

DOUGLAS PENICK

The composer Peter Lieberson and I have been close friends for thirty years. We are both students of Trungpa Rinpoche and share many other interests. From a long time we had often talked about collaborating, and indeed I wrote two texts for him to set. The first was from a novella by Marguerite Yourcenar; she wrote expressing little enthusiasm for the project and urging me to look more into Oriental themes and models. The second was based on a life of Tilopa. Trungpa Rinpoche found exactly one line interesting, and in truth neither Peter nor I felt that we had found a proper meeting ground.

In 1990, Hans Werner Henze asked Peter to write an hour-long piece based on the Gesar epic for narrator and small ensemble for the 1992 Munich Biennale. Peter asked me for a text, but I found that it was necessary to make a new rendition of a large section of the Gesar epic before I could provide him with a coherent shorter text. Out of this collaboration, we decided that we would like to make musical-theater pieces about the lives of all four ancestral sovereigns [King Ashoka of India, second/third century B.C.; Gesar, legendary king of Ling; Yong Le, the third Ming Emperor, thirteenth/fourteenth century; and Prince Shotoku Taishi, sixth/seventh-century Regent of Japan]. So when Peter was approached by the Santa Fe Opera, we began work on a full-length operatic work based on Ashoka's life. Currently, we are working on a cantata for the New York Philharmonic, chorus and orchestra on Shotoku Taishi.

Our collaboration has been made possible by shared inspiration, passion, curiosity, and almost equally by the concrete circumstances that have been provided in the commissions. Out of all these factors, and regardless of the actual scale allowed for by the specific performing conditions, we have been drawn into exploring the possibilities of quasi-epic music-narrative. In this regard, the examples of Peter Brook and Ariane Mnouchkine have been especially important.

The stories and legends presented in the Shambhala tradition are not myths as such since we only refer to such material as "myth" when they no longer enjoy any believable function. Rather, the stories of the four ancestral sovereigns are closer to the epic tradition.

The focus of an epic may appear to be the hero and the struggles by which he becomes the exemplar of the society from which he has arisen. But the hero arises in a terrain which is also paradigmatic. Some epic cycles, such as the Homeric epics, clearly derive from the conflict between cultures; in others, such as the *Mahabharata* or *Ramayana*, the heroes arise from profound ethical and spiritual crises. Whatever the case, epic cycles have provided a vision of personal and social possibility as well as their obstacles. Performances, whether as recitation, dance, spiritual practice, or theater, have been a powerful factor in inspiring and binding together the cultures in which they flourish. One need only look at the many forms and elaborations throughout Southeast Asia which have derived from the two great Indian epics to see this possibility made real.

In our work together, Peter and I have wanted to explore the inner lives of these great cultural heroes and to make them accessible as direct experience to a contemporary way. We are not interested in presenting some kind of Shambhala propaganda or enact some kind of mythic revival.

Rather we have sought to present an inspiration and a gateway to an epic sensibility within the realities of contemporary living. Our main concern has been to present the living presence of real shared possibilities.

Inspiration and Devotion

PETER LIEBERSON

My sole inspiration in composing a cycle of works based on the four ancestral sovereigns of Shambhala has been a feeling of devotion and dedication to the Vidyadhara Chögyam Trungpa Rinpoche's teaching and example. I hoped that by creating these pieces, I would expand my understanding of these sovereigns and of their place in Trungpa Rinpoche's vision. And equally, I wanted to create musical/theatrical enactments which would bring a vision of enlightened society to others.

After I received the libretto for King Gesar from Douglas Penick, I had a dream that seemed to confirm our project. In the dream, Trungpa Rinpoche asked me if I wanted to see the original manuscript of *The Golden Sun of the Great East*, a major text of the Shambhala terma he discovered. I felt overwhelmed and said yes. He handed me the text. Each page of his manuscript had his text on one side and the story of Gesar of Ling on the other. In this way, I understood that the two were deeply related.

As far as any musical techniques were concerned, I began composing *King Gesar*, using the technique that had served me for twenty years. However, one morning as I was driving home, I saw and heard the music in my mind. I was halfway through composing *King Gesar* at that point. Afterward, my whole sense of technique collapsed. I had to trust my intuition and whatever techniques that had become part of me. I began to compose in a much freer way. Whether the music was better than before, I can't really say, but this is how I compose now.

Really Special

ATO RINPOCHE

Chögyam Trungpa Rinpoche was genuine. He was knowledgeable and had a lot of visions. While many teachers were not open about who they really were, Trungpa Rinpoche was completely open; he never hid anything. He drank a lot in front of everybody and had a lot of girlfriends! However, I always remind Trungpa Rinpoche's students and Buddhist teachers that they are not Trungpa and that they should not try to imitate his behavior. It will be better to follow his teachings.

After he moved to the United States, we seldom met, but we always remained good friends. Sometimes I come to teach in Trungpa Rinpoche's centers, and I ask his students what he taught them, what it is they need to polish. It's like the shoes you use every day: the dharma, too, you need to polish. But I don't need in this context to present my own ideas.

I do not present the Shambhala teachings either; I don't have the knowledge to do so. But his students should stick with them and continue the lineage. They have more knowledge about this than anyone else. That is the very special teaching of Trungpa Rinpoche. A lot of teachers say, "Oh, yes, I know Shambhala, I will teach it'," but my uncle, Dilgo Khyentse Rinpoche, said, "That is only Trungpa Rinpoche's vision." You understand why it is so important to preserve this tradition. Other teachers can present Vajrayogini and Chakrasamvara, mahamudra and maha ati, but only Trungpa Rinpoche presented the Shambhala teachings, according to his vision.

In general, all the teachings of Trungpa Rinpoche should be kept alive. In 1986 he gave a very famous talk in the middle of the night, saying, "Never forget hinayana." You can't say, "This is a high-level teaching" and decide to keep it, but "This is a low-level teaching that Trungpa Rinpoche gave us" and discard it. Lord Buddha said: "Nothing external, no enemy can destroy my teachings; but if you don't take care, my followers will gradually destroy them."

Fabrice Midal: In the way he presents Vajrayogini, did you see any particular aspects?

He presented it as a gateway to the mahamudra and maha ati teachings. For this reason, he presents it in a simplified way by uniting the outer, inner, and secret meanings. Also, it is very important to practice it, whether you like it or not. We should not get too excited; the most important thing is to keep our contact with the earth. The view of Trungpa Rinpoche is so profound, and at the same time he was able to keep the practice straightforward.

Nowadays people choose whatever kind of teachings seems the greatest, but this is too goal-oriented to be really meaningful for them. That is why Trungpa Rinpoche unified mahamudra and maha ati, and why before dying he insisted on never forgetting hinayana. This way he cut through sectarianism and *choosiness*. When a tree grows, first there is only one shoot and after that there are branches, and many leaves and fruit. To say that one branch is better than the other, that mahayana is better than hinayana, is nonsense.

After Trungpa Rinpoche died, his students followed Dilgo Khyentse Rinpoche; then he died too. But Lord Buddha died how many years ago? We are still following his teachings. We could also do the same with Trungpa Rinpoche. If you have faith and read his books, you could receive his blessings.

No other teacher who comes to the West is like Trungpa Rinpoche. His teachings have benefited Western people so much—particularly his view on mahamudra and maha ati. He was really special.

Excerpt from an interview with Ato Rinpoche by Fabrice Midal.

Books by Chögyam Trungpa

For earlier works, the first date of publication is given in parentheses following the title. Quotations in the text are generally from the current printings. Note that the Shambhala Classics editions are paginated differently from the earlier editions.

The Art of Calligraphy: Joining Heaven and Earth. Boston: Shambhala Publications, 1994.

Born in Tibet (George Allen & Unwin, 1966; Shambhala Publications, 1977). Fourth edition, Boston: Shambhala Publications, 2000.

The Collected Works of Chögyam Trungpa. Edited by Carolyn Rose Gimian. Vols. 1–4. Boston: Shambhala Publications, 2003.

The Collected Works of Chögyam Trungpa. Edited by Carolyn Rose Gimian. Vols. 5–8. Boston: Shambhala Publications, 2004.

Crazy Wisdom (1991). Boston: Shambhala Publications, 2001.

Cutting Through Spiritual Materialism (1973). Boston: Shambhala Publications (Shambhala Classics), 2002.

The Dawn of Tantra (1975), by Herbert V. Guenther and Chögyam Trungpa. Boston: Shambhala Publications (Shambhala Dragon Editions), 2001.

Dharma Art. Boston: Shambhala Publications, 1996.

The Essential Chögyam Trungpa. Edited by Carolyn Rose Gimian. Boston: Shambhala Publications, 1999.

First Thought Best Thought: 108 Poems. Boston: Shambhala Publications, 1983.

Glimpses of Abhidharma (1975). Boston: Shambhala Publications (Shambhala Dragon Editions), 2001.

Glimpses of Mahayana. Halifax: Vajradhatu Publications, 2001.

Glimpses of Shunyata. Halifax: Vajradhatu Publications, 1993.

Glimpses of Space: The Feminine Principle and Evam. Halifax: Vajradhatu Publications, 1999.

Great Eastern Sun: The Wisdom of Shambhala. Boston: Shambhala Publications, 1999.

The Heart of the Buddha. Boston: Shambhala Publications, 1991.

Illusion's Game: The Life and Teaching of Naropa. Boston: Shambhala Publications, 1994.

Journey without Goal: The Tantric Wisdom of the Buddha (1981). Boston: Shambhala Publications, 2000.

The Life of Marpa the Translator: Seeing Accomplishes All (1982), by Tsang Nyön Heruka. Translated by the Nālandā Translation Committee under the direction of Chögyam Trungpa. Boston: Shambhala Publications, 1995.

The Lion's Roar: An Introduction to Tantra. Boston: Shambhala Publications, 1992.

Meditation in Action (1969). Boston: Shambhala Publications, 1996.

Mudra (1972). Boston: Shambhala Publications, 2001.

The Myth of Freedom and the Way of Meditation (1976). Boston: Shambhala Publications (Shambhala Classics), 2002.

Orderly Chaos: The Mandala Principle. Boston: Shambhala Publications, 1991.

The Path Is the Goal: A Basic Handbook of Buddhist Meditation. Boston: Shambhala Publications, 1995.

The Rain of Wisdom: The Essence of the Ocean of True Meaning (1980). Translated by the Nālandā Translation Committee under the direction of Chögyam Trungpa. Boston: Shambhala Publications, 1999.

Secret Beyond Thought: The Five Chakras and the Four Karmas. Halifax: Vajradhatu Publications, 1991.

Shambhala: The Sacred Path of the Warrior (1984). Boston: Shambhala Publications (Shambhala Dragon Editions), 1997; Shambhala Library, 2003.

The Tibetan Book of the Dead: The Great Liberation through Hearing in the Bardo (1975), translated with commentary by Francesca Fremantle and Chögyam Trungpa. Boston: Shambhala Publications (Shambhala Classics), 2000; Shambhala Library, 2003.

Timely Rain: Selected Poetry of Chögyam Trungpa. Boston: Shambhala Publications, 1998.

Training the Mind and Cultivating Loving Kindness. Boston: Shambhala Publications, 1993. Shambhala Classics, 2003.

True Command: The Teachings of the Dorje Kasung. Vol. 1, *The Town Talks.* Edited by Carolyn Rose Gimian (Halifax: Trident Publications, 2004).

Transcending Madness: The Experience of the Six Bardos. Boston: Shambhala Publications, 1992.

About the Contributors

Venerable Ato Rinpoche is the eighth Tenzin Tülku of Nezang Monastery in Kham. He received a traditional education, including practice of the Six Yogas of Naropa, before leaving Tibet for India in 1959. In 1967 he married and settled in England, while continuing to teach, both in Tibet, where he is bringing to completion the rebuilding and reestablishment of his monastery, and in the West.

Samuel Bercholz, the chairman and editor-in-chief of Shambhala Publications, was a close student of Chögyam Trungpa Rinpoche. He is an acharya (senior teacher) in the lineage of Trungpa Rinpoche and the coeditor of *The Buddha and His Teachings*.

Françoise Bonardel teaches Philosophy of Religion at the University of Paris, Sorbonne. A disciple of Kalu Rinpoche, she has translated a volume of his teachings into French (*Instructions fondamentales*). Deeply interested in the connections between Buddhism and the alchemical and hermetic traditions in the West, she has published numerous books and articles, including a major study of Artaud, *Philosophie de l'alchimie* (Philosophy of Alchemy), *Philosopher par le feu* (Philosophizing by Fire), and *La Voie hermétique* (The Hermetic Way). She is currently preparing a work on Buddhism and philosophy. Professor Bonardel is also a member of the Université Bouddhique Européenne.

Reed Bye, Ph.D., is the author of several books of poems, including *Hearts Bestiary, Passing Freaks and Graces*, and a forthcoming volume of new and selected poems, *Join the Planets*. His CD of original songs, *Long Way Around*, was released in 2005. He teaches courses in creative writing, classic and contemporary literature, and dharma art at Naropa University.

Pema Chödrön became a novice nun in 1974 while studying with Lama Chime Rinpoche in London and received her ordination from His Holiness the sixteenth Karmapa. She studied with Chögyam Trungpa Rinpoche, her root guru, from 1974 until his death in 1987 and currently studies with Sakyong Mipham Rinpoche and Dzigar Kongtrul Rinpoche. Pema is the director of Gampo Abbey, Cape Breton, Nova Scotia, the first Tibetan monastery for Westerners. Her books include *The Wisdom of No Escape*, *Start Where You Are*, *When Things Fall Apart*, *The Places That Scare You*, and *Comfortable with Uncertainty*.

John Daido Loori is the founder and spiritual leader of the Mountains and Rivers Order of Zen Buddhism and abbot of Zen Mountain Monastery, as well as a lineage holder in both the Rinzai and Soto schools of Zen. Devoted to maintaining the authenticity of these traditions, Daido Roshi is known for his unique adaptation of traditional Buddhism into an American context, particularly with regard to the arts, the environment, social action, and the use of modern media as a vehicle of spiritual training and social change. His books include *The True Dharma Eye: Master Dogen's Three Hundred Koans*, *Sitting with Koans*, *The Zen of Creativity*, and *The Eight Gates of Zen*.

His Holiness the fourteenth Dalai Lama, Tenzin Gyatso, is the spiritual and temporal leader of the Tibetan people, who revere him as the living embodiment of the Bodhisattva of Compassion. Internationally recognized for his humanitarian efforts, he received the Nobel Peace Prize in 1989. Among his many books are *The Art of Happiness*, *How to Practice*, and *Healing Anger*. Chögyam Trungpa Rinpoche and his students helped host the Dalai Lama's first visit to America, in 1979.

Venerable Dzigar Kongtrül Rinpoche was recognized as an incarnation of the nineteenth-century Ri-me master Jamgön Kongtrül Lodrö Thaye. Kongtrül Rinpoche was trained extensively in the Nyingma tradition, particular the teachings of the Longchen Nyingthik, by his root guru, Dilgo Khyentse Rinpoche. He moved to the United States with his wife and son in 1989, soon thereafter establishing Mangala Shri Bhuti, a nonprofit organization dedicated to furthering the wisdom and practices of the Longchen Nyingthik lineage in the West. He is the author of *It's Up to You: The Practice of Self-Reflection on the Buddhist Path*.

Francesca Fremantle became a student of Trungpa Rinpoche in 1969 and collaborated with him on a translation of the *Tibetan Book of the Dead*, published in 1975. Her latest book, *Luminous Emptiness*, interprets the *Tibetan Book of the Dead* in the light of his teachings. She lives in London, where she translates Sanskrit and Tibetan texts and writes on Buddhism. She is a teacher with the Longchen Foundation, established by Trungpa Rinpoche and Dilgo Khyentse Rinpoche in the Nyingma tradition, and directed by Rigdzin Shikpo.

Gehlek Rimpoche is a member of the last generation of lamas to be born and fully educated in Tibet. He is the founder and president of Jewel Heart Tibetan Buddhist Learning and Cultural Center with chapters in New York, Chicago, Cleveland, Lincoln and Ann Arbor. He is the author of *Good Life, Good Death* and *The Tara Box: Rituals For Protection and Healing From the Female Buddha*. Now an American citizen, he is highly regarded for his understanding of contemporary society and his skill as a teacher of Buddhism to Western practitioners.

Carolyn Rose Gimian has been a teacher of the Shambhala path of warriorship for more than twenty-five years. She is the editor of many books by Chögyam Trungpa, including *Shambhala: The Sacred Path of the Warrior* and *Great Eastern Sun: The Wisdom of Shambhala,* and compiled and edited the eight-volume *Collected Works of Chögyam Trungpa.* She is currently at work on a book of memoirs with Diana J. Mukpo, Chögyam Trungpa's widow, as well as an anthology of Shambhala teachings by Chögyam Trungpa.

James Gimian is codirector of the Denma Translation Group, which produced *The Art of War: The Denma Translation,* a new edition of Sun Tzu's classic text with explanatory essays. He was a close student of and aide to Chögyam Trungpa Rinpoche and one of the chief architects of the Dorje Kasung. Gimian is currently publisher of the *Shambhala Sun* and *Buddhadharma: The Practitioner's Quarterly.* He also teaches seminars on the *Art of War* and is working on a book developing the themes introduced in the Denma Translation.

Bernard Glassman Roshi, Zen teacher and activist, founded the Zen Community of New York and the Greyston Mandala, a network of community development organizations. He is the author of *Instructions to the Cook: A Zen Master's Lessons in Living a Life That Matters.*

Pierre Jacerme was born in Algeria and taught philosophy at the University of New Caledonia in Noumea, France, from 1965 to 1970 and at the University of Paris, Sorbonne, from 1971 to 1998. His numerous published works in French include studies of Heidegger, Descartes, the filmmaker Jean-Luc Godard, and the eminent French poet Robert Marteau. Professor Jacerme has traveled extensively in India, Southeast Asia, Indonesia, and the South Pacific.

Venerable Khandro Rinpoche was recognized at the age of two by His Holiness the sixteenth Karmapa as the reincarnation of the Great Dakini of Tsurphu, Khandro Ugyen Tsomo, one of the most well known female masters of her time. Trained in both the Kagyü and Nyingma traditions of Tibetan Buddhism, Khandro Rinpoche has been teaching in Europe, North America, and Southeast Asia since 1987.

Sherab Chödzin Kohn is a close student of the venerable Chögyam Trungpa Rinpoche and was his personal representative in Europe. He is the author of *The Awakened One: A Life of the Buddha,* coeditor of *The Buddha and His Teachings,* and editor of several of Trungpa Rinpoche's books, including *Orderly Chaos, Crazy Wisdom, The Path Is the Goal, The Lion's Roar,* and *Illusion's Game.* In addition, he has translated numerous books, including Hesse's *Siddhartha* and Rilke's *Stories of God.* Sherab Chödzin Kohn has been teaching Buddhism and meditation worldwide since 1973.

Jack Kornfield trained as a Buddhist monk in the monasteries of Thailand, India, and Burma. One of the key teachers to introduce Theravada Buddhist practice to the West, he is a founding teacher of the Insight Meditation Society and Spirit Rock Center and has taught meditation internationally since 1974. He also holds a Ph.D. in clinical psychology, and is a husband and father. His books include *A Path with Heart; After the Ecstasy, the Laundry; The Art of Forgiveness, Lovingkindness, and Peace; Buddha's Little Instruction Book; Teachings of the Buddha; Living Dharma; A Still Forest Pool; Stories of the Spirit, Stories of the Heart;* and *Seeking the Heart of Wisdom* (with Joseph Goldstein).

Robin Kornman holds a doctorate in comparative literature from Princeton University, specializing in the history of narrative, the novel, and epics of the East and West. He became a disciple of Chögyam Trungpa Rinpoche in 1970 and has also studied with other Kagyü and Nyingma masters. He is a translator of Buddhist texts and a founding member of the Nālandā Translation Committee.

Jakusho Kwong Roshi, a successor in the lineage of Shunryu Suzuki, has been practicing and teaching Zen in the United States and Europe for more than forty years. He is the cofounder and abbot of the Sonoma Mountain Zen Center, Genjo-ji, in Santa Rosa, California. In 1995 he was given the title of Dendo Kyoshi, Zen Teacher, by the Soto school in Japan. He is one of nine Western Zen teachers to receive this acknowledgment. Jakusho Kwong's first book, *No Beginning, No End,* was published in 2003.

Peter Lieberson is an award-winning composer of numerous orchestral and operatic works who first met his teacher Chögyam Trungpa Rinpoche in 1974. His operas *King Gesar* (1991–1992; available on CD) and *Ashoka's Dream* (1997) are part of a tetralogy of works with librettos by Douglas Penick on the ancestral sovereigns of Shambhala. Other works, such as *Drala* (also available on CD), for orchestra, and *Red Garuda,* for piano and orchestra, also deal with specific Shambhala themes. Lieberson was the Gardner Cowles Associate Professor of Music at Harvard in the mid-1980s and then served as the International Director of Shambhala Training from 1989 to 1994. He now devotes his time to composition and lives in Santa Fe, New Mexico, with his wife, mezzo-soprano Lorraine Hunt Lieberson.

Judith L. Lief was a close student of the Venerable Chögyam Trungpa Rinpoche, who trained and empowered her as a teacher in the Buddhist and Shambhala traditions. Sakyong Mipham Rinpoche, his son and successor, recognized her as a senior teacher, or acharya. Ms. Lief worked with Trungpa Rinpoche as executive editor of Vajradhatu Publications and from 1980 to 1985 as the head of Naropa University, in Boulder. She is the editor of several of his books, including *The Heart of the Buddha, Transcending Madness,* and *Dharma Art.*

Larry Mermelstein was a close student of the Venerable Chögyam Trungpa Rinpoche and is empowered as a senior teacher, or acharya, by Sakyong Mipham Rinpoche. He is the Executive Director of the Nālandā Translation Committee, a member of Shambhala International's board of directors, and a long-time consulting editor for Shambhala Publications.

Alexandra Midal is a researcher in the history and theory of design and an independent curator, specializing in the relationships between art, architecture, and design. After having worked as Dan Graham's assistant and served as director for a public collection of contemporary art in France, she undertook doctoral studies at Princeton University, submitting a thesis titled "1969: Design année zéro." She recently published *Antidesign: Petite Histoire de la capsule d'habitation* (Antidesign: A Short History of the Habitation Capsule) and is currently preparing a design anthology.

Fabrice Midal holds a doctorate in philosophy from the University of Paris, Sorbonne. A practicing Buddhist in the tradition of Chögyam Trungpa, he teaches the dharma in France and elsewhere in Europe. He has published books on religious topics with major

French publishers, among them several titles on Tibetan Buddhism. His first English-language book was *Chögyam Trungpa: His Life and Vision.*

Meredith Monk is a composer, singer, director/choreographer, and creator of new opera, musical theater works, films, and installations. A pioneer in what is now called "extended vocal technique" and "interdisciplinary performance," Monk taught at Naropa Institute in the 1970s, '80s, and early '90s. She is a recipient of numerous awards, including a MacArthur Fellowship. In October 1999 Monk performed a Vocal Offering for His Holiness the Dalai Lama as part of the World Festival of Sacred Music in Los Angeles. She recently completed her first orchestral work, *Possible Sky,* and her first string quartet, commissioned by Kronos Quartet. Her latest music theater work, *The Impermanence Project,* premiered in London in July 2004. That same month marked the beginning of an eighteen-month celebration of Monk's fortieth year of performing and presenting work in New York.

Diana Judith Mukpo was married to Chögyam Trungpa Rinpoche for seventeen years, from 1970 until his death in 1987. Since then, she has continued to travel and teach in order to promote interest in and a wider appreciation of Chögyam Trungpa's life and teachings. Mrs. Mukpo also has pursued a distinguished career in dressage. She studied at the Spanish Riding School in Vienna in 1979 and is now the owner and director of Windhorse Dressage, a riding academy located near Providence, Rhode Island. She is currently working on a book of memoirs about her life with Chögyam Trungpa.

Douglas Penick is a librettist, a writer, and a teacher of Buddhism. He has written the librettos for several works composed by Peter Lieberson. *King Gesar* (1991–1992; available on CD) was the first in a projected series of four works entitled *The Cycle of the Ancestral Sovereigns,* dealing with enlightened society and enlightened rulership. Its libretto was drawn from Penick's book *The Warrior Song of King Gesar,* an updated version of an epic tale of the Tibetan warrior king, Gesar of Ling. The second opera was *Ashoka's Dream* (1997). Penick is currently at work on the third in the series.

The Dzogchen Ponlop Rinpoche is one of the foremost scholars and educators of his generation in the Nyingma and Kagyü schools of Tibetan Buddhism. An accomplished meditation master, calligrapher, visual artist, and poet, Rinpoche is also fluent in the English language and well versed in Western culture and technology. He is founder and president of Nalandabodhi and Nitartha International, head teacher of the Nitartha Institute, and publisher of *Bodhi* magazine, an internationally distributed Buddhist periodical. Nalanda West, located in Seattle, Washington, is the primary seat of his educational and spiritual activities in North America. His most recent book is *Wild Awakening: The Heart of Mahamudra and Dzogchen.*

Charles Prebish, Ph.D., is professor of religious studies at Pennsylvania State University, specializing in Indian and South Asian Buddhist history, Buddhist institutional and sectarian history, Western Buddhism, and the academic study of Buddhism. He is a founding coeditor of the *Journal of Buddhist Ethics* and the *Journal of Global Buddhism,* and a coeditor of the 'Critical Studies in Buddhism' series. His recent publications include *Luminous Passage: The Practice and Study of Buddhism in America, Westward Dharma: Buddhism Beyond Asia, A Survey of Vinaya Literature,* and *Buddhism in the Modern World: Adaptations of an Ancient Tradition.* He has been a Buddhist practitioner since 1965.

Reginald A. Ray is Professor of Buddhist Studies at Naropa University in Boulder, Colorado, and a member of the graduate faculty of the Religious Studies Department at the University of Colorado. He has written extensively on the history, philosophy, and practice of Indian and Tibetan Buddhism. His recent books include *Indestructible Truth, Secret of the Vajra World*, and two anthologies, *In the Presence of Masters* and *The Pocket Tibetan Buddhism Reader*.

Rigdzin Shikpo, a qualified master of the Nyingma tradition, has studied and practiced Buddhism for over fifty years. Before meeting his main teacher, Chögyam Trungpa Rinpoche, in 1965, he had trained in the Theravada tradition and in the Mahayana while working as a mathematician and physicist. Trungpa Rinpoche gave him extensive and detailed teaching in the preliminary and main practices of the Nyingma Dzogchen tradition, and before leaving for America Rinpoche made Rigdzin Shikpo a lineage holder of the mahamudra and maha ati, and told him to teach mahayana maha ati according to his instructions. He continues to teach students in the Longchen Foundation, founded in 1975 by Trungpa Rinpoche and Dilgo Kyentse Rinpoche, and entrusted to Rigdzin Shikpo to realize the vision. Taking further instruction from Khenpo Tsultrim Gyamtso Rinpoche, who gave him the title Rigdzin Shikpo, he is authorized to teach the whole of the Nyingma tradition.

Sakyong Mipham Rinpoche is the dharma heir of his father, Vidyadhara the Venerable Chögyam Trungpa Rinpoche, and head of the Shambhala Buddhist lineage, which descends through his family, the Mukpo clan. He is the author of *Turning the Mind into an Ally* and *Ruling Your World*.

Tensho David Schneider began Buddhist practice in 1970 and was ordained as a Zen priest in 1977. He lives in Cologne, Germany, where he served as director of Shambhala Europe for eight years. He an acharya (senior teacher) of the Shambhala International community and works for Vajradhatu Publications Europe. He is also the coeditor, with Kazuaki Tanahashi, of *Essential Zen* and the author of *Street Zen: The Life and Work of Issan Dorsey*.

Onyumishi Kanjuro Shibata Sensei is the twentieth in the Shibata line of masters of kyudo, the Japanese art of the bow, and a third-generation Bowmaker to the Emperor of Japan (now retired). He first came to the United States from Japan in 1980 to teach kyudo at the invitation of Chögyam Trungpa Rinpoche, with whom he founded Ryuko Kyudojo (Dragon-Tiger Kyudo Practice Hall) in Boulder, Colorado. Since then Shibata Sensei has traveled extensively and established kyudojos throughout North America and Europe. In 1985 he established permanent residence in Boulder.

Judith Simmer-Brown, Ph.D., is a professor of religious studies at Naropa University in Boulder, Colorado. She became a student of Chögyam Trungpa Rinpoche in 1974 and began to teach at Naropa in 1978. There she served as the director of the Buddhist-Christian dialogue conferences during the 1980s, as well as on the faculty of Buddhist Studies. In addition to her faculty responsibilities, she now serves as an acharya, or senior teacher, in his lineage. Dr. Simmer-Brown has been involved in Buddhist-Christian dialogue for over twenty years, serving on the Board of the Society of Buddhist-Christian Studies. She is the author of *Dakini's Warm Breath* and coauthor of *Benedict's Dharma: Buddhists Comment on the Rule of St. Benedict*.

Kidder Smith is codirector of the Denma Translation Group and a translator of *The Art of War: The Denma Translation*, a new edition of Sun Tzu's classic text with explanatory essays. He teaches Chinese history at Bowdoin College, where for many years he chaired the Asian Studies Program.

Venerable Khenchen Thrangu Rinpoche, the ninth Thrangu Tülku, is one of the foremost teachers of the Kagyü lineage of Tibetan Buddhism and the tutor of the seventeenth Karmapa. Thrangu Rinpoche is the former abbot of Rumtek Monastery in India and currently serves as abbot of Gampo Abbey in Nova Scotia, Canada. Among his books are *The Ornament of Clear Realization*, *Medicine Buddha Teachings*, and *An Ocean of the Ultimate Meaning: Teachings on Mahamudra*.

The ninth Traleg Kyabgon Rinpoche is president and spiritual director of Kagyu E-Vam Buddhist Institute, headquartered in Melbourne, Australia, with a major practice center in upstate New York and a practice community in New York City. Affiliated with the Kagyü tradition, he has been teaching, leading retreats, and lecturing in the United States, Canada, Australia, New Zealand, and Southeast Asia since 1980. Traleg Rinpoche is the author of *Mind at Ease* and *The Essence of Buddhism*.

Anne Waldman encountered the great Lama Geshe Wangyal in 1963, pursued Buddhist studies with Jadtral Sangye Dorge in Darjeeling and Nepal in 1973 and 1978, and later took Shambhala vows with Chögyam Trungpa. With Allen Ginsberg she cofounded the Jack Kerouac School of Poetics at Naropa University, where she is Chair and Curriculum Director of the Summer Writing Program. She is the coeditor of *Civil Disobediences: Poetics and Politics in Action*, a collection of essays from the Kerouac School, and the author of over thirty books of poetry, including *In the Room of Never Grieve: New and Selected Poems 1985–2003*, and *Structure of the World Compared to a Bubble*.

Robert Wilson is a stage director, designer, and artist who is internationally acclaimed as a major force in experimental theater.

Lee Worley was a founding member, actor, and director in Joseph Chaikin's Open Theater. At the request of Chögyam Trungpa Rinpoche, she moved to Boulder in 1976 to help found Naropa Institute. She was chair of the Theater Studies program for many years and created Naropa's pilot B.A. in Interdisciplinary Studies. She collaborated in the development of Naropa University's InterArts B.A. and is currently core faculty in the Contemplative Education M.A. She teaches Mudra Space Awareness in Europe and the United States.